Blood
Fire
Death

Ika Johannesson
Jon Jefferson Klingberg

Blood
Fire
Death

The Swedish Metal Story

Table of Contents

DESECRATOR
WAKE THE DEAD

DEATHMETAL

Nihilist

INGE MOSH!

Lör. 27:E MAJ
ORMINGE Folkets hus
SALTSJÖBANAN EL. NACKABUSSARNA
PSYKISKT FÖRVRIDEN

EVIL MOWE - 89

BRAWLING IN VOMITS
NYE DEMO UTE SNART!

Treblinka

POSER FRUIT

Nihilist

BJÖRKSÄTRASKOLAN
BREDÄNG
FRE 24/3 RUNT KL 20
CA 20:-

Entombed

TUNG JÄRV-BLUES MED:

Monkey Pus 50 BUCK

(FRÅN KAZAKSTAN)
FATBUREN 17:e April

"STÄNG UTE ME
HETTAN - STICK FRÅN
RÖKET!"

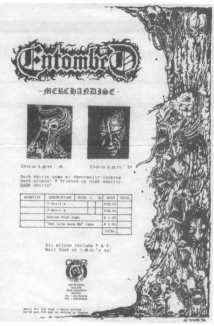

Entombed

-MERCHANDISE-

Design A   Design B

Both shirts come w/ Abnormally-looking
back prints! * Printed on high quality
DARK shirts!

QUANTITY	DESCRIPTION	SIZE	L	XL	EACH	TOTAL
	T-Shirt A				$13.50	
	T-Shirt B				$13.00	
	Button w/ logo				$ 1.00	
	"But Life Goes On" tape				$ 5.00	
					TOTAL	

All prices include P & P.
Mail Cash or I.M.O.'s to:

Sorry for the high t-shirt prices-
we've got 40% tax on a shirts in Sweden.

BLOOD RUNS FROM THE ALTAR

BLOOD RUNS FROM THE ALTAR
UNHOLY RITE OF SACRIFICE
THE WRATH OF THE LORD
INVOKED BY THE BLASPHEMOUS

C: BLOOD RUNS FROM THE ALTAR
IA LUCIFERICON

BLOOD RUNS FROM THE ALTAR
THE MASSES STARTS TO SING
THE WORDS OF THE BIBLE
INVERTED FOR THEIR KING

IA LUCIFERICON

BLOOD RUNS FROM THE ALTAR
UPON THE ALTAR LIES
A VIRGIN WHICH BLOOD
IS SPILLED FOR THE ONE BELOW

BLOOD RUNS FROM THE ALTAR
C: IA LUCIFERICON

BRIDGE: IA......
BLOOD....
BLOOD RUNS FROM THE ALTAR
THE PRIEST IS NOW IN TRANCE
A GLIMPSE IN HIS EYE!
HE RAISES THE DAGGER AGAIN...

IA LUCIFERICON

BLOOD RUNS FROM THE ALTAR
UPON THE ALTAR LIES
A VIRGIN WHICH BLOOD
IS SPILLED FOR THE ONE BELOW

C: BLOOD RUNS FROM THE ALTAR
IA LUCIFERICON

BRIDGE II: IA LUCIFERICON, HEAR MY SONG.....
I WANT YOU TO...GRASP OUT YOUR HAND
REACH FOR ME, I SELL MY SOUL
I.......IA !!!

Prologue

"GOOD EVENING, TEMPLARS OF GERMANY!" vocalist Joacim Cans calls out across the packed venue. "We are HammerFall from Gothenburg, Sweden! Ten years ago, our journey began in this country—and Cologne was one of the cities we played!" The crowd lets loose a unified roar, fists raised, surging forward as the band rips into their anthemic "The Metal Age."

The year is 2007, and HammerFall are in Germany promoting their just-released greatest hits collection, *Steel Meets Steel – Ten Years of Glory,* as well as to mark the band's 10-year anniversary. The Gloria-Theater in Cologne has a mere 1,000-person capacity, and the concert has been set up as an intimate, sweaty evening dedicated to the die-hard adherents. The set list tonight is fan-sourced from the HammerFall website, and after the show, devotees will be able to mingle with the band, seeking autographs and scoring merch. Tickets are completely sold out.

A few hours earlier, a diverse throng queues in the bright afternoon light outside the club: 18-year-olds sporting the obligatory black trench coats and Dr. Martens boots, rubbing shoulders with gray-headed men in motorcycle jackets—as well as thirty-something women, dressed as if they just got off work in a bank. In an adjacent alley, one guy wraps up his private pre-show party, downing a bottle of beer. His long, scraggly locks contribute to the impression that he's just been roused from a 30-year hibernation, commenced in the golden age of heavy metal. The man's worn jean jacket sports band names such as Accept and Anvil, and it might very well be a relic dating back to those halcyon days.

Inside the theatre, the evening's warm-up ritual has begun. A variety of football match-style chants resound from the front rows. The most frequent entails someone shouting, "LET THE HAMMER ..." and the rest of the crowd cheering, "FALL!" Though the band has yet to make their presence known, kinetic energy charges the air as if the show has already begun.

Sporting a thinning mullet, mustache, eyeglasses, and a denim vest, 36-year-old Jörg from Göttingen looks like a caricature of a German metalhead. He rattles off previous HammerFall experiences through a thick Teutonic accent: Dynamo Open Air festival in Eindhoven, 1998. The Rock Hard Festival in the spring of 2007. Et cetera. "The worst thing about Cologne is their shitty beer!" announces Jörg. He then excuses himself—even though he deeply despises the taste of Kölsch, he really needs another bottle.

Elisabeth from Mississippi is attending the show with her German boyfriend, Jens. She's never seen HammerFall before but professes her love for their look: the leather, the metal plating. "They're like gods," she says reverently. Her boyfriend is more of a black metal fan and is clearly less enthusiastic about the Swedes, despite having introduced his girlfriend to the band. Elisabeth says that Germans, with their limited command of English, can't fully understand HammerFall. She's almost ecstatic. "I'm excited! Let the hammer fall!"

As the house lights are killed, the collective roar is so intense that the hall itself seems to shudder.

———

From its genesis as a youth phenomenon, metal has evolved into one of the world's biggest music genres. Alongside the seminal bands of the '70s, many of which still record and tour, younger generations continue to reinvigorate and advance the genre. Much of metal's vanguard hails from Scandinavia—Sweden in particular.

It makes perfect sense for HammerFall to celebrate their anniversary abroad. Swedish bands such as Opeth, Ghost, Meshuggah, and Enforcer play to sold-out crowds in Europe as well as North and South America. And the interest keeps growing. Metal is bigger than ever. Each year, several hundred thousand tickets are sold to Swedish concerts and festivals geared toward metal. What was once an underground phenomenon has become, like so many niche movements, a gigantic industry.

Instead of writing a definitive history of Swedish metal, we've mainly focused on bands, individuals, and phenomena that to various extents have propelled the scene forward. The evolution has not only been musical but at times aesthetic or even ideological. It's primarily taken place within the more extreme and aggressive metal genres—such as death and black metal—where Swedish bands have been spearheading the movement from the very start.

We followed this development from two different parts of the country.

Jon Jefferson Klingberg, born in 1968, first encountered metal during high school in a tiny industrial town called Stugun, found in the rural northern Swedish province of Jämtland. A close friend's family would take in problematic teenagers from the comparatively massive urban jungle of Stockholm, one of whom showed up with an armload of Kerrang! magazines—the seminal British metal publication.

Jon inhaled this material, wide-eyed, absorbing everything about bands like Mercyful Fate and Angel Witch. Soon he would do pretty much anything for cash to get ahold of metal albums.

Ika Johannesson, born in 1974, spent her teenage years in the playgrounds of the southern suburbs of Gothenburg, drinking beer and cranking metal demos through boomboxes. Friends from her social circle would go on to form bands such as At the Gates, Dark Tranquillity, and In Flames—all of them pioneering acts within the melodic branch of death metal now known internationally as "The Gothenburg Sound."

Everything happened so fast. You'd be blasting an Entombed demo from your tape deck, and seemingly the next day, those Stockholm boys were one of the biggest death metal bands on earth. The primordial power in both the music and the movement itself was magnetic and intoxicating: for the first time, here was a scene blowing up before our very eyes—and these were kids our own age, and from our country.

The emergence of death metal was itself a profound remodeling of the metal genre. It also swept away all preconceptions of metal as something wimpy and soft, after a decade of keyboards, hairspray, and ruffled blouses. Death metal combined the brutality and DIY spirit of punk with musical innovation and technical skill, and it would soon reap unlikely commercial success. Just as immediately, the scene was stricken by serious growing pains, with an increasing number of bands adopting an identical sound and choking the market.

The counterreaction came in the form of black metal—an even more extreme subgenre, with Norway as its epicenter, dominated by acts like Mayhem, Darkthrone, and the infamous Burzum.

Black metal bands sounded harsher, rawer, and darker—and there was no irony in their claims to worship death and true evil. Soon, a series of highly publicized church burnings swept both Norway and Sweden, and suddenly, the Satanic element was clearly more than a pose or a stage prop. It was literal and deadly serious.

Not long thereafter, the first murder directly connected to black metal was committed in Sweden.

———

One premise of this book has been to try to establish why Sweden became a hotbed for such aggressive cultural expressions. In the course of our work, we discovered how the scene had reached extremes we could never have contemplated.

Many of the questions we've tried to answer here have puzzled us for a long time.

How did a teenager from the Stockholm suburb of Vällingby come to lay the cornerstone for a phenomenon like black metal? Were the members of Heavy Load nationalists? And who were the mystery pair behind the fabled self-torturing duo Abruptum?

The first edition of this book was released in the fall of 2011. Since then the Swedish metal scene has continued to expand in many directions. We've updated chapters in need of revision, like the one on Entombed, today split into two separate bands. In other instances, we've added footnotes with relevant information.

The individuals we meet in this book come from varying backgrounds and personal situations, but they are united—as are we—in a strong passion for metal. The source or spark of this fervor is, of course, subjective and naturally varies from person to person. Sometimes, it's ignited by the intro to a Deep Purple track, by the shock and awe of the pyrotechnics, or by the sheer power expressed by a wall of Marshall stacks. In other cases, it's about the aesthetics of spidery, sinister band logos, unreadable and arcane. And sometimes, the attraction is to actual Satanic worship and a quest to find the most evil band in the world.

Often, it can be traced back to a common love of three elements vital to metal: blood, fire, and death.

I.

Fuck Off!

We broke into a meat container at a slaughterhouse. We had the full spines of several cows and all kinds of things. Maggots were raining all over us during the whole gig.

—TYRANT, NIFELHEIM

THE BASEMENT WALLS of the Best Western Hotel Carlia in Uddevalla are covered with boulders constructed of gray-painted Styrofoam. It's almost 8 p.m., and the two bars in the venue are gradually filling up with rangy metalheads of the more unsavory, crusty variety, mixed with gawking, curious locals—men in smart casual wear and women with generous make-up and short skirts.

The stage is set with various props belonging to the black metal act Nifelheim. A big silver-painted plate with the band's bat-shaped logo and a candelabra with black candles have been placed before flanking Marshall stacks.

In the tiny backstage area to the left of the stage, the band members are getting ready, donning their spikes and leather outfits.

"It usually takes about an hour to put everything on," says vocalist Pelle "Hellbutcher" Gustafsson, biting down on a cord to secure the studded wristband around his left forearm.

Soon, spikes cover both of his underarms. The rusty nails are six inches long and look dangerously sharp.

"You can hurt yourself pretty badly if you're not careful, but I usually don't feel a thing until after the gig. I end up looking like a junkie, because of these big bruises I get, but I'd rather strap these on too tight than have them fall off in the middle of the concert," he says.

Chrille Eskilsson of the black metal duo Pest acts as stage manager for Nifelheim tonight. He shoulders his way into the room, balancing a big hunk of vacuum-packed beef chuck and about 10 pig's tongues. Chrille wonders aloud what to do with all the meat.

"Put it in the coffin," says Pelle's twin brother, Erik "Tyrant" Gustafsson, as he applies black makeup to his eyes.

Chrille tears the beef into smaller chunks and dumps the pig's tongues into the wooden children's casket that Nifelheim always have on stage. The silk interior is more brown than white by now and gives off a stale odor, though not quite as bad as one might expect, considering the amount of raw and rotting meat the coffin has seen over the years.

"Remember, you're not allowed to throw it around," Chrille says, glaring at the twins.

Black metal has seen plenty of cadaverous stage props over the years, but when Norwegian band Mayhem decorated their stage with close to a thousand pounds of pig's heads and meat at the Gates of Metal festival in the rural town of Hultsfred in the summer of 2006, the Swedish Board of Agriculture threatened charges, claiming severe violations of the animal by-products regulation. Following the outbreak of mad cow disease in Europe in the '90s, it became illegal to handle meat on stage without a special permit. Erik thinks they should just ignore the protocol, muttering something about judicial abuse of power. Pelle, on the other hand, is a friend of the owner and remains skeptical.

"I wouldn't want him losing his license to serve food here."

Erik rolls his eyes.

"All right, then, I'll just have to rub it on myself," he hisses, patting his slim, pale torso.

Drummer Peter "Insulter of Jesus Christ!" Stjärnvind, previously in bands such as Entombed and Merciless, helps Pelle strap on his leather hauberk. Hundreds of studs form an inverted crucifix and a star on his chest, while leather and even more studs decorate his black spandex pants. Pelle then secures a studded codpiece and a big leather girdle with a studded pentagram and adds a couple more studded belts and armbands with inverted crosses. Finally, he smears black makeup around his eyes and fastens two big, studded leather shin guards around his legs.

The end result is somewhere between Pinhead from *Hellraiser* and a psychotic biker risen from the depths of hell.

Before a mirror in the corner, Erik completes his makeup and struggles with his massive spiked leather shin guards.

"You must suffer for metal. It demands it," he says, contorting in an attempt to better see his calves. "Where's the fun in watching some useless guy performing in a white T-shirt on stage? I've always been into leather and spikes. Metal should remain metal, never change or evolve. It should be like the greaser culture, staying in its decade—for metal, the '80s, of course.

"Look at this! I suffer for metal every day!" he says, tying a black headscarf over his developing bald spot. His remaining hair is dyed black, the thin strands barely reaching his shoulders.

A guy with a thick southwestern Swedish accent shows up with a package for Pelle, containing rare and highly coveted metal belt buckles with the Nifelheim logo. Only about 10 have been produced, which were issued to a lucky select few. This evening, Erik wears one around his neck. Pelle has one attached to his belt.

All of the gear they use is homemade. Every single spike and stud has been fastened by the brothers themselves. Homemade equals authentic, and authenticity is of utmost importance to Nifelheim. Everything should be as evil, bleak, and rotten as possible. The brothers' prime influences are old metal bands from the Eastern Bloc. The deeper the misery, the better—ideally, the musicians should have procured their instruments on the black market, trading their younger sisters for them.

The fact that, by day, guitar player Sebastian "Vengeance from Beyond" Ramstedt is a popular preschool supervisor in Stockholm is something the brothers aren't too keen to mention. After all, this is the band who claims to have fired a member just for standing outside of a disco.

The supporting act, local black metal quartet Vornth, have just vacated the stage, and it's almost show time. Peter is busy writing set lists. He manages two of them: one for himself, and one for Pelle. The rest of the guys will have to follow their lead.

Peter wears the least amount of spikes in the band. The leather is too hot and heavy to play drums in, not to mention the very real danger of executing blast beats while wearing spikes. He appears quietly relieved not having to don the full attire of his bandmates.

Erik tries to turn around for one final stage gear inspection in the mirror, but in the cramped space, his six-inch leg spikes get snagged on a bag. He lets out a deep sigh.

The venue is filling up, with attendees as well as the liquid intoxicants they have inside of them. At the merchandise table in a corner, commerce is in full swing. Approximately 400 tickets have been sold, and there are rumors of people traveling from both Germany and Mexico for the concert. In the crowd, Watain vocalist Erik Danielsson can be seen, along with several journalists from Stockholm. From Gothenburg, we find legendary punk rocker Onkel and Jonas Björler from metal bands At the Gates and The Haunted. He became friends with the Nifelheim brothers in the early '90s—and maintains that even if the band's live shows are spectacular, their true strength lies in the songwriting.

"Many black metal bands just stack a bunch of riffs on top of each other. Pelle and Erik give much more consideration to the actual arrangements. Their songs are hits, really. Add to this the fact that they've been for real this entire time—completely authentic. They've stood their ground since the first album, both image-wise and musically."

Abruptly, the venue lights dim and there's a minor stampede for the stage. To the sound of a thunderous intro, the band members assume their places. They stand wide-legged and bold, making threatening faces. Finally, Pelle materializes. With a maniacal scream, the band unleashes the track "Unholy Death" from their very first demo.

The brothers' intense devotion to metal has made Nifelheim one of black metal's most renowned bands, as well as one of the least productive. Formed in 1990, they've released a scant four albums and played fewer than 100 shows.

In the early days, Nifelheim had no interest in performing live at all, instead focusing on becoming better musicians. Then followed 10 years of constant difficulties in retaining a consistent line-up, due to extremely stringent ideals and demands. It wasn't until 2001 that a full and functional performing band was assembled. The brothers' exacting attitude means that when Nifelheim finally do something—be it a concert or an album—it's always done with the greatest dedication and care possible.

Their first-ever concert was at the 2Heavy4You Festival outside the Swedish town of Falkenberg in 2001. Nifelheim would only agree to take to the stage on a bill that, they insisted, included Russian band Korrozia Metalla. The Russians cancelled, unfortunately, but were replaced with Root from the Czech Republic, which the brothers were equally satisfied with. Since they'd put off playing live for so long, they prepared an elaborate show with pyrotechnics, carefully painted backdrops, and plenty of animal cadavers.

"We broke into a meat container at a slaughterhouse. One of our roadies had a few connections and set the whole thing up. We had the full spines of several cows and all kinds of things," Erik says. "Maggots were raining all over us during the whole gig."

Pelle recalls the event as somewhat stressful.

"We'd spoken to the promoter beforehand and he told us it was a big stage, so we'd loaded up with tons of stuff—pyro here and coffins there. When we arrived, we found a tiny outdoor stage, primarily used for dance orchestras, with a huge pillar in the middle. We were forced to change our plans somewhat, to put it mildly."

After the first song, Erik smashed his bass. The plan was to break something during each song. His spare bass had a rusty barbed wire for a strap. The wire had been procured from a nearby grazing pen using a bolt cutter. The brothers also brought homemade explosives.

"Once we had connected all the bombs, some drunk fucker tripped over the cables attached to the ignition controls," says Pelle. "So, when we tried firing them during the show, not a single one went off! So, that was hundreds of dollars of fireworks for nothing. They're still packed away at home somewhere."

As the band began hurling slaughterhouse waste from the stage, the show took a more dramatic turn than initially anticipated. The rotting spine of a cow caught an audience member right in the face, splitting open his forehead and leaving him with a gushing wound. Erik mentions this was Jon "Necromancer" Woodring from American death metal band Usurper, who had traveled to Sweden specifically to see the gig.

"He was fucking stoked! We also threw out lots of meat. Some of the crowd barbecued and ate it later. The whole thing was hilarious. We were egging them on quite a bit; we always do. When we toured Finland recently, someone broke his leg on the first night. And then at the second show, someone had a heart attack."

Tonight in Uddevalla, no meat leaves the stage. The pig's tongues are left in the casket where Chrille put them. The audience is instead treated to a master class in old-school black metal. The band goes wild to the extent that they almost lose track of the songs. Pelle grimaces and glares menacingly while screaming the lyrics full force. His goal is to shred his vocal chords, so his voice breaks entirely.

His ambitions are fairly successful tonight.

After the concert, Pelle is in good spirits. The audience really got into it, and since he lives in Uddevalla, this is his home turf.

"We might not be the biggest band in the world. But our fans are committed. I once met a German with the covers of our EP and first three albums tattooed all over his back.

When we played in England, there were people from Chile and Australia who'd flown over just to see our show."

The backstage area is filling up with friends who have traveled to attend the gig, and both Erik and Pelle look rather pleased.

"Feel this!"

The tall, blond guitar player, Johan "Apocalyptic Desolator" Bergebäck, drops a Samsonite Cabin bag to the floor with a thump. It's extremely heavy.

"Fifty pounds of spikes and leather," he says with a satisfied grin.

Besides Peter, Johan is the Nifelheim member wearing the least amount of gear on stage. This gives an idea of the sheer weight of the attire the rest of the members strap on before a show.

"I don't need any more studs because I'm so fucking good-looking," he says, rolling his luggage to the after-party in his room. In day-to-day life, Johan is a car mechanic.

A few young fans loiter outside the restrooms, mesmerized by the unruly and by now quite intoxicated crowd of metalheads stumbling past them. They pay extra attention to the twins, whispering and pointing.

In the fall of 1998, Erik and Pelle Gustafsson became known as the "Hard Rock Brothers" to the Swedish general public. They were featured on a television show for teenagers called *Propaganda* in a segment called "Get a Haircut and Get a Real Job," a seven-minute-long display of their boundless passion for Iron Maiden and their ritualistic preparations before following the band on tour.

In the opening sequence, the brothers and their friend Jonas sit at a kitchen table discussing proper conduct for the upcoming Maiden concerts, such as the need to push through the crowd all the way up to the stage "to be able to call yourself a front-row banger!" They also mention the importance of using proper earplugs. "You can't damage your hearing; that has to be kept in perfect condition."

They pack toothbrushes in a plastic bag, pluck their passports from a glass jar in the kitchen, and debate whether to bring spare studs, all the while glancing nervously at the camera. Speaking over the phone, Pelle attempts to convince a friend that the new Maiden record is amazing.

"Have you heard the new album? Oh, oh! You have to hear it—it's the best thing ever recorded!"

The brothers are the biggest Iron Maiden swag collectors in Sweden, and literally hundreds of posters, patches, T-shirts, albums, and scarves filled the modest apartment they shared at the time.

Erik points to a poster on the wall, trying to put words to his feelings for the cover art of the *Live after Death* album.

"That one, for example, is one of the most beautiful things I have ever laid eyes upon in my entire life. It's just so damn gorgeous. It's so fucking metal, it's almost oozing from it."

His voice is nearly trembling with reverence.

"I pretty much don't give a shit about anything besides metal. That's more than enough to deal with. I do whatever interests me and just ignore the rest."

The guys then head out to pick up their heavy metal automobile: a souped-up 1970 Pontiac Firebird, jet black with flames. The trio takes off through the rural roads outside Gothenburg, lamenting the number of horses roaming around and swaying left and right to avoid driving over manure.

When the TV team catches up with the three friends in a dressing room of the Stockholm Globe Arena a few days later, they're tapping their knees in nervous antici-pation. Sveriges Television has set up a private meet-and-greet with Iron Maiden them-selves. Then-vocalist Blaze Bayley is the first to appear, followed by bass player Steve Harris. Genuine and profound joy radiates from the brothers' faces. They are given T-shirts and hugs, and they pose for photos with their idols. Erik and Pelle make evil black metal faces while Steve Harris smiles jovially.

It's difficult to say if it's the brothers' earnest and unconditional love for Iron Maiden, their thin mustaches, their nervous behavior in front of the camera, or their amusing rural-accented commentary that makes this segment so compelling.

Being of the pre-YouTube era, this episode was circulated on VHS tapes and achieved instant cult status. The clip was often played at pre-parties, just like the American mini-documentary *Heavy Metal Parking Lot*—shot in the parking lot of a 1986 Judas Priest concert—was 10 years earlier. The video has maintained its popularity to this day, perhaps touching on something fundamental in the soul of Sweden's past. In every classroom back in the day, you could find at least one person proudly sporting a denim jacket, a studded wristband, and a metal band T-shirt. We all grew up with the Hard Rock Brothers.

The producer, Marcos Hellberg, recalls that the *Propaganda* episode in question was intended to have a "general lifestyle" theme. He initially wanted to portray an over-the-hill metalhead in his or her natural habitat. He called Dolores, a label and record store in Gothenburg, which immediately referred him to the Gustafsson brothers instead. But when he reached them, they wanted no part of it.

"They had an incredible amount of integrity and didn't want the attention. I bought them a coffee and told them it would be great promotion for Nifelheim, but they refused. My final argument, after half an hour of trying to convince them, was: 'I'll shoot a 10-minute-long feature about you and your love for Iron Maiden, whose music will be heavily featured. This in turn means broadcast royalties for them.' That changed their minds," Hellberg says.

The premise for the episode was initially a depiction of people who clung to their chosen style, regardless of trends. The program also included interviews with a girl who was a full-time Salvation Army soldier and an older punk rocker.

"But the brothers somehow stole the show," says Hellberg. "When speaking about Iron Maiden, they're never putting on an act—they are always being completely true to themselves. There is a continuity with Iron Maiden that they appreciate. The band never abandoned their ideals, their clothes, or their studs, regardless of which way the wind was blowing in the music industry. They practiced what they preach."

Erik and Pelle say it was a conscious decision to not mention Nifelheim in the program. The band and their veneration of Iron Maiden are two entirely different things. Also, they had no idea it was going to generate any noticeable reaction. They'd already been interviewed about their collection in both radio and newspapers without anyone paying much attention. Suddenly, they couldn't leave their apartment without being reminded about the television spot.

"I just assumed people didn't watch a lot of TV anymore," says Erik. "Turns out they did. It was as if I had become Michael Jackson; we couldn't go anywhere without being approached. I was completely shocked by the hysteria it generated. And I still am."

Pelle was equally surprised.

"I'd hop on the tram and everybody would suddenly shout, 'Woooarrrghhh.' And that's not an exaggeration, unfortunately. It was utterly insane."

Erik thinks they weren't portrayed accurately. He blames their youth and naïveté.

"We're a lot more extreme than that. While filming, they'd ask us to do certain things, like 'sit and headbang to a record.' That might be something you do when you're drunk, but it certainly wouldn't look like it did on TV. That's why everything is so fucking contrived and unnatural. It was stripped of all irony. They turned us into caricatures."

"People think that we're all perky and entertaining," says Pelle. "Or incapable of doing much at all, being a bit slow in the head. Then again, that's precisely the impression you would get from watching the program."

The brothers feel the segment was edited in a dishonest fashion and claim the photographer often said the camera was turned off when it wasn't. Pelle says the questions they were asked were often difficult to answer.

"They would ask, 'Why are you a metalhead?' and things like that. I replied, 'Because I like metal.' Short answer! But that wasn't enough, so they filmed for an additional two hours. So, we just began rambling, trying hard to answer these questions. And then they edited select parts of it, much to everyone's amusement. Except ours."

Marcos Hellberg has no recollection of the brothers voicing any displeasure upon being shown the final cut before the broadcast.

One person who saw and loved the program was Johan van der Schoot, a copywriter at an advertising agency.

"Everyone at the office was taken by that documentary. There was a lot of talk about it afterwards, at least in the circles I move in."

Two years later, when Swedish insurance company Trygg-Hansa needed a new promotional campaign for their specialty insurances, Johan was part of the team that suggested purchasing material from the segment for a TV commercial.

The agency also made new interviews with the brothers for radio commercials.

"Trygg-Hansa deal with property insurance, and these guys loved their metal memorabilia. They loved the music too, of course, but also their shirts, the albums, that metal car, and so forth. In the advertising world, you are always supposed to be politically correct and focus on care and love for people, so it was refreshing how these guys fetishized their collection instead. And it was such an unequivocal love," van der Schoot remembers.

The theme of the campaign was "Take care of the things you love, by insuring them with Trygg-Hansa."

"They called us and asked if they could use a few clips for a marketing campaign," says Erik. "I told them no. Then they began baiting us with money. I think they first offered us 20,000 Swedish kronor, but I just laughed at them. We ended up getting significantly more than that. It was enough for two or three Iron Maiden tours," he says smugly.

The five commercials and radio spots catapulted the original program, along with the brothers, into even higher cult status. The radio commercial got so much attention that it received the most prestigious advertisement industry award in the country.

To this day, the brothers can't go to a bar without being commented upon—it really does happen every time they go out, Erik wearily observes.

"I recently discovered the term geliophobia. It's the paranoia that people are constantly laughing at you. I've developed something similar. Every time I pass by someone having a good time, I feel as if they're laughing at me, even if they're not. The film had a few benefits, however, in regards to Iron Maiden–related business. We'd met them several times before the documentary but have gotten to know them better since then."

Pelle agrees.

"Also, quite a few people with awesome Maiden rarities at home have seen it and thought, 'The Hard Rock Brothers should have this'—and then we get the thing for free, instead of having to pay billions for it on eBay."

Erik Gustafsson lives, proper black metal-style, in an old military fort somewhere in the middle of Sweden. He very carefully instructs us not to specify exactly where, since the Swedish Armed Forces are unaware of his residency. As such, we're also not allowed to describe his home more than that his stone-walled room is windowless and damp. It contains a bed and his share of the Maiden collection. Together, the brothers own some 2,000 records, and their band shirts are somewhere in the thousands. The children's casket that Nifelheim use as a stage prop stands in the middle of a dark chamber nearby, as if it were a ceremonial relic.

Erik gives us a guided tour of the citadel. Just outside his bedroom, there's a long corridor with small, cell-like spaces. The concrete floor is filthy and the adjacent alcoves full of clutter. He indicates a deep indentation in the ground, caked in mud.

"I had planned to throw a mattress on the floor here—trick you into thinking this is where I sleep," he says and laughs fiendishly.

When we ask why he didn't, he grins and shrugs.

"Bah, I didn't have the time," he says and saunters off down a murky tunnel.

We follow, and the hallway terminates at an impossibly long and steep stairway, heading straight up into the mountain. It's difficult to see where it leads, so Erik pulls a heavy lever on the wall, and the staircase is suddenly illuminated by light bulbs. It ends in a vast mountain cavern including a myriad of smaller rooms with portholes facing the water. A huge steel trident made out of rebar rests in a corner.

"Fitting, no? It was there already when I moved in." Erik shows us a heavy iron door with a small barred window.

"There's an old dungeon in there and it's haunted, for real. Sometimes, I'll come here at night to get in the mood, but I'm never going in there again. You can sense something really strange in there."

He refuses to go near the door, and we're not especially compelled to either.

Parts of the abandoned mountain facility can be seen in the music video "Blinded by Light, Enlightened by Darkness" by death metal band Necrophobic, which was shot here. Erik says that he often hosts parties inside the mountain. It's bitterly cold and desolate in wintertime, but it's perfect for barbecues during summer.

More than anything, it's the most metal domicile imaginable.

"The true dedication to metal has to be something innate," Erik muses. "I must have been three or four years old when I first heard metal. I remember my parents hating how I wanted to listen to it all the time."

The identical twins Erik and Pelle Gustafsson were born in Dals Långed, a small village in the province of Dalsland with a population of 1,700—mostly known for the art school Steneby and Sweden's only horseshoe nail factory. Erik came into this world six minutes before his brother, a fact he brings up every chance he gets.

Their father was an antiques dealer and their mother a teacher. There was little interest in music at home and no record stores in the area. Their first album was bought at an auction when the brothers were still in preschool. Artists like Steppenwolf, Alice Cooper, and Jimi Hendrix were the first that stuck.

"I was obsessed with Kiss and AC/DC for a while," says Erik. "After this, we got down to serious business. The first time I heard Iron Maiden was like opening a new chapter, so to speak. It must have been *Piece of Mind*. It was like finding the way home."

Besides Iron Maiden, the brothers soon discovered increasingly harder music. Their family often traveled around Sweden. Each time they arrived in a new town, the brothers immediately sought out the local record store and went looking for the albums with the rawest cover artwork. That's how they discovered *Show No Mercy* by Slayer and Sodom's *Obsessed by Cruelty*.

Around the same time, the twins took up playing music themselves. Erik insists that he began before his brother.

"I started playing bass. I'm assuming everyone realizes why."

He rolls his eyes.

"Because of Steve Harris, of course!"

At age 15, keen to leave Dals Långed, the brothers moved to the city of Uddevalla to attend a high school program with an advertising angle. This was just prior to the computer revolution, at a time when Letraset letter transfer sheets were still in use. The class spent 16 hours a week painstakingly lettering by hand.

The brothers met other metalheads at school and started attending parties in nearby villages. They began getting ahold of fanzines and were soon in touch with metal fans all over Sweden.

In 1990, their own band, Nifelheim, was founded and initially consisted of Erik and Pelle as well as a guitarist calling himself "Demon."

In Norse mythology, Nifelheim is the dark and unpleasant kingdom of winter—the name literally means "Mist Home." The twins decided on the name with the help of a classmate, after all previous suggestions turned out to have been taken already.

"We were heavily inspired by Treblinka, who had just released an EP, and I wanted something that sounded disturbing. Nifelheim had a cool ring to it. We really were quite far ahead of all other bands using Old Norse names. I'm proud of this. We were pretty pissed off when later about a billion new bands with similar names showed up," says Erik.

Treblinka's *Severe Abominations* was one of the first Swedish black/death metal releases on vinyl. Most people in the underground scene got hold of it through trading. Not the twins, however.

"I found it at a countryside auction around the time it was released. It was in a vinyl box among a bunch of tractor tires. It was completely random; I had no idea what it was. I bought it because it looked heavy and cool. Fate has intervened many times."

Inspired by Treblinka and Morbid, another Stockholm band, Erik sketched out the Nifelheim logo with the same type of bat shape and pointy letters.

In their rehearsal place, the brothers built a makeshift studio and dubbed it Moondark—a nod to Sunlight Studio in Stockholm, the primary death metal recording facility in Sweden at the time. The brothers considered the music recorded at Sunlight—Entombed and Dismember, for example—much too soft for their tastes.

Although Sunlight was by no means an exclusive studio, Moondark was even less fancy than its Stockholm counterpart. Instead of spending money on microphone stands, the brothers rigged up mics on tree branches tied to kitchen chairs. Since the portable studio only had four channels, "Demon" welded together the connections of three microphones in an eyeglass case with one outbound cord. Nifelheim started recording demos.

From the very beginning, the brothers made rules for the band. For example, to always wear spikes and corpse paint and to never make slow songs or sing about inane things—meaning anything that isn't satanic.

Back home in Dals Långed, they started socializing with Lennart "Phantom" Larsson, one of the few metalheads they were aware of and had access to. He was the editor of two publications called *Heavy Metal Massacre* and *Backstage* and a contributor to the influential Norwegian metal fanzine *Slayer Mag*.

Larsson remembers being shocked when he read a review of Nifelheim's first demo in a magazine called *Metal Zone*.

"It said they were also from Dals Långed, and I just couldn't believe it. Soon, they were at my place borrowing records. The two of them are quite amusing together. They do have a tendency to embellish, so to speak."

Lennart supplied the brothers with records and demos and—most significantly—recommendations for other bands.

"He had Volcano from Brazil, among other stuff," Pelle reminisces. "We'd heard of them, but he owned the actual albums. This was before eBay, so it required a bit more than pressing a button. You had to know your stuff. It's quite funny how many people from that insignificant little village have contributed so much to the metal world."

After graduating from high school, the brothers began working in a Volvo factory. Erik produced the strap with which one would pull out the backseat armrest. Pelle spent his days making headrests in a noisy room with no windows. Lunch was the only interruption during workdays.

"It was incredibly monotonous, I turned into a robot. One day, I thought: 'Fucking hell, I'm tired. I suppose I'd better go get some more material and get started.' Then I glanced up and noticed a pile of finished headrests next to me. I had been there for three hours assembling headrests without even noticing. That's when I thought, 'Enough of this, I quit,' which I then did."

Before leaving, he drew Iron Maiden's monster Eddie on the foam rubber in one of the headrests. Somewhere in Sweden, there is a Volvo with this secret piece of art under the cloth.

Erik also resigned. Now unemployed, the two moved to Tanum, a small coastal town known for its many Bronze Age rock carvings.

"There were lots of really entertaining metalheads living there back then," Pelle recalls. "Perra in Satanized was one of them. No celebrities or anything, just really cool people. Greaser metal dudes. I far prefer that above these plastic metalheads whose primary interest in the music is prancing around in the right outfit. In Tanum, moonshine and Saxon was the name of the game. I liked that, you know? And hot rod cars. It's an excellent style."

When many of the metalheads from the area relocated to Gothenburg, so did the brothers. They got an apartment in the suburbs together and started hanging out with members of At the Gates, Dissection, Swordmaster, and other local bands. They also recorded their first album. It was still the early '90s and Scandinavian black metal had hit the underground music scene full force. Some of the people in their social circles began experimenting with satanism. Despite the brothers' unswerving allegiance to the essence of black metal, they've never been outspoken satanists.

"I have some kind of attraction to the dark side," says Erik. "It's the same with metal itself; I can't put it into words. It's something I feel. But if you're going to get involved with that stuff, you have to control it very carefully."

Nifelheim's self-titled album was released in 1994, with Jon Nödtveidt and John Zwetsloot of Dissection on guitars, and rapidly sold 30,000 copies. Upon the 1997 release of their second album, *Devil's Force*, the brothers were contacted by American film director Harmony Korine, who asked to include a special version of their song "Hellish Blasphemy" on the soundtrack of his art-house white-trash epic *Gummo*. Nifelheim's audience widened significantly from this unexpected exposure, and with the third album, *Servants of Darkness*, in 2000, the band's reputation was established even further. The album is an exceptional celebration of melodic black metal, beautifully reflecting the ideals of the genre's first wave in the '80s.

Erik shows us pictures from parties of the era. They feature a variety of Gothenburg legends such as Tompa Lindberg and the Björler twins (of At the Gates fame). Another common participant was Patrik "Onkel" Andersson, known in Sweden as "The Shit Man." This unflattering nickname was a result of Patrik's deep fascination for urine and feces. "Onkel" was known for, among other things, climbing down into portable toilets at music festivals. Erik says they used to attend the now-defunct Hultsfred Festival, wreaking plenty of havoc together.

"One year, we had something really big brewing. A metalhead friend had hit a deer on the way to the festival and then put it in the trunk of his car. The plan was to stalk a group of sensitive-looking teenage girls. Once we had located their tent, we were going to shove the deer cadaver, which looked pretty fucking macabre, into one of their sleeping bags and then just wait for the screams. But when we went to fetch the carcass, it was gone. Apparently, police or security had seized it. It was such an anti-climax because we'd been scouting it out and had gotten really excited. But it was a damn solid plan."

The brothers lived together and worked the same jobs until 2001, when Erik moved to Stockholm. Pelle moved in with his girlfriend in Uddevalla.

"Everything calmed down once they finally moved apart," says Peter Stjärnvind. A twin himself, he is well aware of the constant bickering between close siblings.

"They still argue a lot, about virtually anything. About taking the other guy's stud belt before a show or refusing to help each other. Or just that one of them might be standing in the other one's way. Disagreements about the children's coffin, if it will fit on stage or not."

Despite metal having existed as a music genre for over 50 years, a lot of people still think it is something you eventually grow out of, pegging the genre as immature. There is, of course, a delicate balance, where extreme metal can become laughable. For black metal fans, Nifelheim are tiptoeing right on that edge—and the twins are well aware of this. At the Sweden Rock Festival in 2004, Pelle took the stage and shouted, "Are you having a good time?" to the audience, which collectively replied, "Yeaaaah!"

Pelle hollered back, "WELL, THAT ENDS NOW!"

"We've always wanted to be an obtrusive finger up the rectum of pretty much everything. On the other hand, I have to say there's always been a certain gravity behind it. I certainly don't think metal is all just good fun—I really do think it's awesome, for real."

Longtime friend of the band Jenny Walroth recalls how she and Erik once left a liquor store in Stockholm. They came across a really decrepit junkie with a horribly swollen face standing in the street outside, and upon catching sight of Erik, he hissed, "Into the morbid black!" That's one of the song titles from the *Servants of Darkness* album.

"Erik was ecstatic and said that's PRECISELY the kind of fan he wants. I don't think I've ever seen him in such a good mood over something not involving Iron Maiden."

The brothers have continued to follow Iron Maiden tours through Europe. It's been 10 years since the last full-length album, *Envoy of Lucifer*, but there's no immediate rush to record new material. Nifelheim have never had a major commercial breakthrough, but with their hardline metal attitude, they have become a group that many others look to for inspiration.

Erik tells us he's just come up with a new catchphrase for the band.

"Like a chainsaw to the roots of Yggdrasil," he hisses with a certain amount of satisfaction. "It came to me this morning!"

He says that as soon as the band had formed, a decision was made.

"In the early '90s, everyone started pretending to be things they were not. Our idea was to do the opposite. We tried simplifying everything by using the most primitive wording we could come up with. Instead of saying something darkly poetic or complicated, we said, "Fuck off!""

It's difficult to accurately convey the brothers' biting sarcasm in writing, and as a result, after a long period of skepticism toward journalists, the band finally stopped agreeing to interviews entirely.

"I understand them," says Peter Stjärnvind. "They're always ridiculed. No one mocks Watain, despite the fact that they burn just as fiercely for what they do. But with Nifelheim, it's easy to poke fun at them. I suppose it's more entertaining to make fun of the hillbillies. Any fool can pick up on that."

What's fascinating about Nifelheim and the Gustafsson twins is that their sincere love for black metal, along with the desire to create something as filthy and evil as possible, collides with their general personalities. The reason they end up in situations where they get interviewed, despite their discomfort, is that they're naturally accommodating and polite. Peter Stjärnvind sees no conflict in this paradox.

"Being the way they are, they don't come across as anything but good people. But this is, in my opinion, for the best. They are like two little old men. If they're having coffee, it has to be from these tiny grandmother cups. On a tray, preferably. And then some cookies with that, of course. When you have them over, you'd better get your porcelain out. It's charming and at the same time hilarious."

In January 2011—ironically enough, on the Gustafsson brothers' 35th birthday— Swedish tabloid *Aftonbladet* revealed that renowned director Ulf Malmros was working on a movie about two adult metal brothers from some backwoods village in Sweden. Malmros stated in the interview that he was inspired by the documentary about Canadian metal band Anvil and the classic old *Propaganda* segment from Swedish television. He insisted the film will not be about the Gustafsson brothers and that he's been fascinated by this kind of heartfelt dedication for a long time. The title of the movie is *The Hard Rock Brothers*.

Erik sounds exhausted when we reach him on the phone.

"In my world, this is just the icing on a cake made from nothing. Having once dodged horse shit on the road, who would have thought it would haunt me for the rest of my days? It's unreal. Time for another trashing, so some punter can have a laugh. And I'll be made a living advertisement for the movie every time I go out to buy a loaf of bread. I'm sure you can imagine how this feels."

He mentions that the brothers have sought legal counsel to see what can be done to distance themselves from the film project.

"You mock and taunt everyone in the entire world but ultimately end up the brunt of the biggest joke yourself. It's a pretty fucking ironic fate."

In addition to Erik and Pelle, Nifelheim today includes Felipe "Savage Aggressor" Plaza Kutzbach and Tamás "Satamás" Buday. They still haven't released a new studio album.

The feature film by Ulf Malmros was renamed Mammas pojkar (Momma's Boys) and premiered on Christmas Day 2012 to tepid reviews.

II.

Too Much Fucking Guck!

*No one really needs six
Marshall cabinets and four amps.
But I wanted it that way.
It was my thing.*

— RAGNE WAHLQUIST, HEAVY LOAD

THE JARLA THEATRE SITS RIGHT on the border between the swanky inner Stockholm districts of Östermalm and Vasastan. It's a school and theatre complex built in the early '30s that's been declared a culturally significant building by the Swedish state. During the second half of the '70s, it was the venue for some of the most memorable concerts of the era. The Ramones played here when they visited Stockholm for the first time in May 1977, and the four first rows of benches were ripped from the floor by the revved up audience.

Another incident two years later would leave the interior with damages of a different kind.

The band on stage called themselves Heavy Load, spearheaded by the two Wahlquist brothers, Ragne and Styrbjörn. A teenager by the name of Anders Tengner, who would go on to become Sweden's most important metal journalist years later, hid just outside the reach of the stage light.

Anders was fidgeting with a homemade detonation device. The bombs on stage were built by pyrotechnician Gunnar Ousbäck, whose resume included film productions by universally acclaimed director Ingmar Bergman.

"Ousbäck was stark raving mad, smoking cigarettes in his office full of dynamite, gunpowder, and all kinds of shit," Tengner recalls. "We called him before the shows and let him know what we needed. We referred to the explosives as *guck*."

One of Tengner's assignments as the band's all-around handyman was to "fire up the *guck*."

Unbeknownst to everyone else on the night in question, the veteran pyrotechnician had made a slight error when mixing the explosives.

"When I pressed the button, the blast was so powerful, plaster came crashing down from the ceiling," he says. "The bombs had too much fucking *guck*! At first, I thought we might have wiped out the entire crowd. People were coughing, their faces white with all the dust."

Someone in the front row was hurled backward and hit his head on the bench rows behind him. Heavy Load's vocalist and guitar player, Ragne Wahlquist, remembers how the blast wave lifted him off the floor and burned a good portion of the hair off his head.

"The cable was ripped straight out of my guitar. Everything went dead silent. The container containing the *guck* was completely gone—there was only a mounting board left on the floor."

The remaining three band members didn't stop playing until drummer Styrbjörn Wahlquist realized he had another bomb sitting only a few feet from his head.

"I thought, 'What do we really know about Anders? Maybe he'll set off the next bomb as well!' So, I had to stop, and it was just dead air. People just stood there staring, in complete shock."

"Funnily enough, no one freaked out on us or pointed out that our setup had been potentially life-threatening," says Ragne. "The people I spoke to afterwards thought it had been unbelievably cool."

The band's bass player at the time was a large Finnish guy named Eero Koivisto. He dismisses the story about the collapsing ceiling as something of an urban legend.

"It wasn't quite as dramatic as people try to make it out to be. On the other hand, I always thought our explosives were too powerful."

When Leif Edling, bass player in doom metal act Candlemass, is asked who the first real Swedish heavy metal band was, there is no doubt in his mind.

"Heavy Load. They were the first band that I'd ever seen with an entire wall of Marshall stacks on stage."

Edling grew up in Upplands Väsby, a suburb on the northern outskirts of Stockholm, and came across the fledgling Swedish heavy metal scene at an early stage. He remembers seeing huge Heavy Load posters with brutal Viking imagery all over Stockholm in the early '80s.

"We wondered how the hell they could afford it. But from what I heard later, one of the band members actually worked at a printing facility."

The question of where you draw the line between hard rock and heavy metal is a difficult one to answer and has been the subject of much debate. One rule of thumb is that artists with bluesy and melodic elements often belong to the hard rock category, whereas metal bands often combine harder, less groove-based, decidedly non-blue-based musical compositions with violent or diabolical themes.

En ny tid är här (A New Age Is Here), the debut album of Stockholm band November, was released in 1970 and is generally considered Sweden's first-ever hard rock album. November came out of the Stockholm suburb of Vällingby in 1969 and initially played blues-based rock influenced by Cream, Mountain, and Led Zeppelin.

Lyrics in their native tongue helped them blend in with the Swedish music scene of the early '70s. *En ny tid är här* reached #2 on the Swedish album charts. Simon & Garfunkel's *Bridge over Troubled Water* had the top slot.

Only two years later, the band members went their separate ways, burnt out after three albums coupled with intensive touring. However, their album title could not have been more relevant. Swedish music was in for one hell of a ride.

In the '60s, Swedish youth culture had been dominated by chart-oriented radio shows and clean-cut pop magazines. The only choice for Swedish bands with any inkling of ambition was to imitate international pop artists.

But far beyond the charts and plush major record label offices, an insurgency was brewing. The beginning of the music revolution was heralded by two illegal Stockholm music festivals in 1970. On stage were alternative acts like Träd, Gräs och Stenar, Arbete och Fritid, and Det Europeiska Missnöjets Grunder.

The following years saw the rise of several independent labels and music groups, heavily influenced by the prevailing leftist politics of the time. They were uniformly referred to as Musikrörelsen ("The Music Movement") and would drastically change the face of the industry. Despite a grassroots mentality and aspirations of breaking conservative norms, Musikrörelsen would serve as more of a hindrance than an asset to the first wave of Swedish hard rock bands. It would also effectively drain Sweden of rock groups without an overt political focus during the early '70s.

The problematic relationship between Swedish hard rock and Musikrörelsen is clearly illustrated by a review in the movement's mouthpiece, *Musikens Makt* (The Power of Music) magazine, of *A Dream of Glory and Pride*, the 1974 debut album by Stockholm band Neon Rose.

Critic Tomas Tengby summed up his impressions of the album with the words: "A cash-in product. By corporate swindlers." Indeed, he goes so far as to point to a different album entirely, something that met his criteria for quality rock: Gothenburg-based Nynningen's *För full hals* (At The Top of Your Lungs), on which the band set poems by Russian poet Vladimir Mayakovsky to music.

"Music back in those days was supposed to be recorded in the forest with two clogs serving as a tape recorder. We were so not a part of that scene," says Neon Rose vocalist Roger Holegård.

Neon Rose had lyrics in English and were the first Swedish hard rock band to adopt the look of their international counterparts. They would wear leather jackets with no shirts and occasionally performed live in white suits—even at minor shows at local youth centers. To add insult to injury, their album was released on a foreign label.

"There were even accusations that our record company was a producer of weapons and war materials. That's how far-fetched the discussions were. I somehow doubt Vertigo were arms dealers. Either way, did we investigate that before signing the contract? No, of course we didn't," Roger adds.

During his upbringing in Upplands Väsby, Leif Edling could clearly see the effects of Musikrörelsen's dominant position.

"Whenever there was a music festival where I grew up, it would always be a bunch of old guys with long beards playing political folk rock."

The Beatles and The Rolling Stones were the artists of choice on the Wahlquist family's portable gramophone in the late '60s—assuming father Ingemar wasn't at the piano playing Schubert or German romances.

While visiting their grandmother in Norway in the summer of 1972, the brothers first heard the Deep Purple album *Machine Head*. Nothing was ever quite the same again.

"Ragne just lost it completely," Styrbjörn recalls. "As did I, the first time I heard *Highway Star*. It was a completely new world. We were used to The Beatles and The Stones, basically vocals with a backing band. This was infinitely more powerful and catchy. So much was expressed through the drum kit. But what really got to me was how long the song went on before the vocals came in."

After returning to Stockholm, *Machine Head* was spinning pretty much nonstop on the family record player for a full year.

"By then, we could afford to buy another Deep Purple album. I got *Made in Japan*, and then we spent the following year listening to that," says Styrbjörn.

The brothers started rehearsing in the basement of their childhood home on Karlavägen, in Stockholm's Östermalm neighborhood, but the neighbors started complaining. After Ragne completed his mandatory military service, the fledgling band relocated to a youth center. A bass player was recruited and the trio took on the moniker Heavy Load, seeing as their backline was already quite massive.

"You can compare it to other things," says Ragne. "Like if we're going to a party—sure, we could show up naked. But we want to dress up. No one really needs six Marshall cabinets and four amps. But I wanted to. It was my thing. Either way, it was a major pain in the ass to haul everything back and forth."

When the band played their first gig in December of 1976, they had to rent a truck to transport all the equipment, including a gigantic drum riser built from pine wood as well as their own lighting rig.

"I don't think we even got paid," says Styrbjörn.

Heavy Load started scouting for a recording contract but were told by labels that there was little point, as no journalist would ever want to write about them anyway. Music columnist Mats Olsson of the tabloid *Expressen* was a powerful force in the industry back then, and he hated all kinds of hard rock and metal. So, the band decided to finance the album themselves, with help from the record shop Heavy Sound on Regeringsgatan in Stockholm. That store played a key role in the development of Swedish metal over the years.

In 1978, *Full Speed at High Level* was released. Several other Swedish rock bands were influenced by Deep Purple and Led Zeppelin, but Heavy Load took their music one step further away from the traditional blues influences. Instead, they honed in on the dramatic sound we today associate with the term heavy metal. The lyrics touched on classic themes in metal: the pursuit of personal freedom and the love of rock 'n' roll. The cover artwork—cliffs in a crimson sunset and an arched, stylized logo—greatly resembled the nature-oriented romanticism prevalent in contemporary progressive folk rock. Still, no one wanted to review the album.

That same year, 17-year-old Anders Tengner published his first articles in the music magazine *Poster*. He had previously started the Swedish fan club for The Runaways and was a major fan of Judas Priest and Kiss. After hearing of a new Swedish band with international aspirations, he was immediately intrigued. However, the young rock journalist's first meeting with Heavy Load was a bit surprising.

"The first thing that struck me was how upscale their home was. Their father, Ingemar, was a super-rich lawyer. A celebrity lawyer if you will, handling high-profile cases."

The Wahlquist brothers were equally taken aback. They were expecting a reporter in a suit and tie, but instead, they found a teenager in a Kiss jacket standing in the hallway. Regardless, Tengner soon befriended the brothers and would go on to become something of a silent member of Heavy Load for the rest of the band's career.

Despite a complete lack of media coverage, rumors of the new Swedish heavy metal band spread, and *Full Speed at High Level* finally reached an audience. Tengner became Heavy Load's greatest advocate and marketed them whenever possible. Above all, the band focused on playing live.

In need of a new bass player, the band hired Eero Koivisto, a wild rocker who would go on to cofound the internationally renowned design firm Claesson Koivisto Rune.

"It's funny—even back then, he would sit at home building miniature models of the Heavy Load stage-show, complete with drum riser, lighting rigs, and spotlight holders, all made out of cardboard," Tengner recalls. "Later on, he studied furniture design in Tokyo."

When Koivisto left to focus on the band Red Baron, Heavy Load made what Anders Tengner, in hindsight, describes as a disastrous mistake.

"They brought in their cousin, Torbjörn Ragnesjö, from Uppsala. Torbjörn was a nice guy but cheesy as hell. He was completely immobile on stage, looked like a geek, and moved like a nerd. We tried dressing him in sexier stage clothes, but he couldn't pull them off. It was impossible to make Torbjörn Ragnesjö look cool. He was a hopeless case."

The band also found a second guitar player in Eddy Malm of the band High Brow, and with this, the lineup was complete.

Styrbjörn's and Ragne's interest in history and Vikings was evident already in the debut album song "Sons of the Northern Light." Preparing for the mini-LP *Metal Conquest*, the band further developed the Viking theme into their band image. The cover artwork depicts a Viking sword battle in a mountain valley.

The historical Vikings that Styrbjörn and his classmates were introduced to in school had been a far cry from that of a sword-wielding adventurer.

"Vikings were portrayed as peasants in leather caps, plowing fields. At the time, there was an intentional suppression of the mythical, glamorized Viking."

He finds it only natural that Heavy Load modeled their concept after the fierce Viking warrior, as metal is a musical genre based on epic gestures and dark romanticism.

"All dramatic art, from ancient Greek plays and forward, is based on violence or a threat thereof. Metal is violent music. The Vikings, as we saw them in Heavy Load, were violent. Just like the Crusaders and everyone else that tried to build something grand. Sure, we've used an embellished and partly amoral image. But if you really want to emphasize the uniqueness or origin of a nation, I assume you would look to your history and try your best to ignore how everything has turned into McDonald's."

The Viking framework did little to change Heavy Load's predicament—quite the opposite. Despite the fact that they were now enjoying both some press coverage and a growing fan base, labels were still not interested. Heavy Load were forced to take matters into their own hands once again. The brothers founded Thunderload Records, to release and distribute their own albums all the way to Japan. They booked their own tours and even handled ticket sales. In their spare time, they made plans for new visual experiments. In the end, the band operated on their own for so long that when offers finally were made, the brothers immediately grew suspicious.

The album recordings were financed by the band. You'll hear different stories as to exactly where the money came from, depending on who you ask.

"We took out a bank loan," says Ragne. "I was working in a music store. And I was perhaps 36 when I finally got my driver's license."

"It wouldn't surprise me one bit if their father helped them out," says Anders Tengner. "But they also had very few other expenses; they still lived at home. Ragne eventually met a girl and took off. But Styrbjörn stayed and lived there with his retired mother until she passed away a few years ago."

Before long, the Heavy Load stage show was far bigger than any other Swedish rock band of the era. When starting out, the band had made a decision only to play large stages on principle, in order to better match their music with grand aesthetics. When Heavy Load released their second album, *Death or Glory*, in 1982, the only Swedish act with an equally impressive stage production was ABBA. The rig included a ramp that made it possible to stand on top of the Marshall stacks. The pyrotechnics were a chapter in and of themselves. The band wanted every song in the set to have explosions and smoke.

During a concert in the north of Sweden, 24 explosives were detonated in the final song alone.

"There was so much smoke that I couldn't find my way off the stage," says Styrbjörn. "I couldn't see a thing, so I didn't dare to move at all. I thought, 'This is fucking ridiculous.' We were supposed to walk off and then be cheered in for an encore. I had to just stand there until the smoke cleared."

He remembers the audience's response as somewhat mixed.

"The drum kit was too big. The riser was too big. I recall two older girls, perhaps around 25, telling us after a concert, 'You can't do it like this. The drum kit is way too big.' And sometimes it was difficult just to fit everything on stage."

Back in those days, there were virtually no Swedish rock festivals, but local community parks across the country were still in use, which had stages that were perfect for the band's grandiose vision. There was also a growing interest in metal, as well as a gaping hole in the Swedish music business. That was about to change.

———

Spearheaded by bands such as Iron Maiden, Saxon, and Def Leppard, the emerging "New Wave of British Heavy Metal" compelled many a youth to pick up an instrument. While Rågsved in the south of Stockholm became the stronghold of punk rock in the late '70s, metal dominated the northern suburbs. In 1981, Leif Edling and his friends founded a local music association, creating events in Upplands Väsby that would form the hub of Sweden's first metal scene. Among many other attractions, this was where their friend Yngwie Malmsteen played three of his scant 10 Swedish shows, before leaving for the United States and fame abroad.

Edling mentions that some concertgoers later appeared in early death metal bands such as Dismember. Leif himself went on to form Nemesis, a precursor to Candlemass.

"We did the same thing Candlemass did years later. Double bass drums and heavy riffs. Everyone in Väsby hated us. Väsby was always very melodic."

Another young band in Upplands Väsby at the time called themselves Force, later changing to the name that would be heard around the world: Europe. Leif recalls noticing a bunch of guys having lunch together in the school cafeteria several days in a row, thinking, "There is a band in the making right there."

"One day, we sat at a table close to theirs. Someone had written 'Joey Tempest' on the wall. I guess they were testing new names."

In 1982, Europe won the televised rock band competition Rock-SM, with a record deal as the grand prize, and the band's debut album immediately entered the Swedish top 10 music chart. Suddenly, Swedish rock bands were courted by labels that had previously shown no interest.

According to music journalist Jörgen Holmstedt, the impact Europe had on the Swedish hard rock and metal scene really can't be overstated.

"CBS signed 220 Volt. Axewitch got a record deal. Silver Mountain and Torch as well. Lazy were signed. A whole bunch of Swedish bands released their debut albums in 1983, and that was in great part thanks to Europe. Heavy Load were, however, the first to adopt the Viking image. That's one thing no one can take from them."

Holmstedt says he'll never forget an August night in 1983 when he was fortunate enough to be present as Thin Lizzy frontman Phil Lynott visited Heavy Load in the studio. He was in Sweden on a solo tour and had a day off in Stockholm.

"Anders Tengner would often tag along when I did interviews for the Thin Lizzy fanzine. He nagged Phil repeatedly, 'Please come down to the studio and play some bass for an album my friends are recording.' Finally, Phil agreed—he was incredibly kind and found it difficult to say no."

"Phil Lynott and Jimmy Bain came to the studio with cocaine and other stuff," Tengner remembers. "They were snorting like hell. We'd never seen cocaine before and thought, 'What the fuck are they doing? Could this be that thing we've been reading about?' We were so innocent back then. They were high as kites but very cordial. And they stayed around until the song was finished."

The song in question, "Free," is featured on Heavy Load's third album, *Stronger Than Evil*, from 1983. Despite using the track as their first single, there was no real breakthrough this time around either.

The band was eventually modernized and a vast part of the Viking image was scrapped.

A few years later, Ragne and Styrbjörn built the recording facility Thunderload Studios in an underground room connected to the Solna subway station. It was at this time that the band released the single *Monsters of the Night* through Warner Music. For the first time in their career, they had a record deal.

"But by then, it was too late," Tengner recalls. "That ship had already sailed, and then Eddy left the band."

"I wanted us to be more professional," says Eddy Malm. "Record with a producer, someone who could have molded us into something appealing to the masses. Perhaps that's a form of musical prostitution, I don't know. But that's how I felt at least. Everything around us changed. Europe just raced by us. Still, Ragne and Styrbjörn didn't want to change a thing. So, that's the way it went."

Even if Heavy Load never grew to be as big as the Wahlquist brothers had hoped, they laid the foundations of Viking metal, along with Bathory a few years later. Today, the Viking heritage is carried on by bands such as Unleashed and Amon Amarth and is still appreciated as something exotic outside of Scandinavia. When the American band Manowar visited Sweden in the '80s, they got in touch with Styrbjörn Wahlquist.

"I brought Ross the Boss, their guitar player, to the Nordic Museum. I remember him admiring the model of a Viking ship for quite a while. Then he turned to me and asked, 'Did they sleep in those things as well?'"

By the late '80s, the dust from Heavy Load's pyrotechnics had settled for the last time. The popularity of heavy metal was dwindling, and Swedish hard rock was commonly associated with the hairspray and synthesizers of Europe's pop-metal and the excesses of Yngwie Malmsteen—who, despite having risen to stardom as one of the top guitar players in the world, was still often ridiculed back home.

In the wake of the first Metallica LP, *Kill 'Em All*, in 1983, many younger musicians abandoned classic hard rock and instead adopted thrash metal: a more aggressive form of heavy metal characterized by fast tempos, double bass drums, searing riffs and shouted vocals. Some even came from a punk rock background. One of them was guitar player Pelle Ström, who spent a few intense years playing in punk bands such as Aggressiv and Svart Snö, crossover band Krixhjälters, and thrash metal outfit Agony. He recalls metal and punk as belonging to two separate worlds until this point.

"Metalheads lived with their folks in suburban houses, rode mopeds, used snuff tobacco, and played hockey—whereas the punks and their counterculture parents lived in central Stockholm. However, nothing exciting at all was going on in punk rock in 1986, so the only option for a somewhat dignified existence in alternative rock music was to switch to metal."

Agony was vocalist Pete Lundström's project. The lineup also included guitar player Magnus Sjölin, a real metalhead, unlike Pelle. This resulted in a clash of cultures but was a rewarding musical merger nonetheless.

"Magnus had an air of mopeds and Average Joe about him, with a dash of hockey," says Pelle. "I was a pompous inner-city wannabe from a leftist background, marching in the syndicalist parade on International Workers' Day. So, he became a great source of annoyance to me. But he could do what most metalheads can: play properly. And after busting my ass rehearsing his riffs for a full year, I had changed as a musician."

Their union resulted in songs like "Deadly Legacy" and "Execution of Mankind," both of which were released on a demo cassette in 1986. The tape soon attracted attention among youngsters looking for something more aggressive and nihilistic than ordinary heavy metal, as an angrier alternative.

The same year saw the release of the *General Alert* demo by Gothenburg band Ice Age. The quartet had formed a few years earlier, as a pure old-school heavy metal band.

"Then I heard Metallica and that was it," says Sabrina Kihlstrand, guitar player and vocalist. "I got hooked on the aggression."

Maninnya Blade, from the far north town of Boden, released their EP *The Barbarian/ Ripper Attack* as early as 1984, and together with acts such as Midas Touch and Damien from Uppsala, Mefisto from Stockholm, Kazjurol from Fagersta, God B.C. from Helsingborg, and Nyköping's Mezzrow, they formed a small, emerging Swedish thrash scene in the late '80s.

Adopting the DIY methods of punk rock, thrash demo tapes were sold in local record stores and through ads in underground fanzines published both in Sweden and abroad.

Having sent as many demos to fanzines as they could possibly afford, Ice Age soon received praise for *General Alert*. Significantly, their music was featured on the highly influential Swedish radio show *Rockbox*, and suddenly, the band was inundated with sacks of letters from listeners, who wanted to hear and know more.

"We divided the letters between us, piles of them, and answered as best we could. All in all, I think we sold a total of 5,000 copies of our three demos," Sabrina says.

Ice Age was interviewed by the major metal mag *Kerrang!*, with nothing but a demo tape to their name. This in turn caught the eye of notorious American rock manager Kim Fowley, of The Runaways fame. He travelled to Sweden in an attempt to talk the band into a collaboration, but Ice Age were not interested in being packaged as a girl thrash band—it was already enough that every article and review made sure to fall back on this easy classification. So, they declined the offer.

Ice Age instead opted to work with another manager. That collaboration proved poisonous, as he began sowing discord within their ranks. The group split up, sadly without having released an album.

Prior to this, Ice Age was on the road as part of the only notable Swedish metal tour of the late '80s, together with Candlemass and Hexenhaus. The few bands on the scene tended to keep in touch and made a concerted effort to travel around the country to catch each other's gigs. The Rockborgen venue in Fagersta was a common rendezvous point and served as the site of many excellent shows, with both Swedish and international acts.

Agony was one of the few Swedish thrash bands to be offered a record deal, and they released *The First Defiance* in 1988. A few years earlier, they had toured the United Kingdom with Gothenburg hardcore punk band Anti Cimex and British grindcore act Napalm Death. Napalm Death members have described the tour as the most extreme thing they've ever participated in. Pelle Ström can't really understand why.

"A few of the gigs were canceled, and we weren't paid. Before we'd even gotten off the ferry, [Tomas] Jonsson in Anti Cimex had pissed his leather pants—the only pair he'd brought along. The Napalm Death guys were just kids, and their drummer started crying all the time became he was so young and freaked out. They told us how they would charge the batteries for their distortion pedals by the light of an open fireplace. They reckoned it was a great, safe method," says Pelle.

Patrik Wirén, vocalist of Midas Touch, says Uppsala had a small but devoted scene supporting the local bands. Thrashers would hang out at local record store, Expert, where they would meet up to check out the latest releases. When Midas Touch's one and only album, *Presage of Disaster*, was released in 1989, it sold so well, it entered the top 40 chart in Sweden.

"I'm guessing quite a large chunk of those sales were in Uppsala. We would play the big rock club in town and pull a decent crowd. This was not always the case in the rest of the country," Patrik explains.

In the mid-'80s, American thrash bands such as Metallica, Exodus, Anthrax, Slayer, and Testament all proved themselves commercially viable. In Sweden, however, the domestic thrash scene never really took off. This was something that 18-year-old thrash enthusiast Robban Becirovic experienced firsthand in 1988, at a Damien show at the Crescendo jazz club in Norrköping.

Only 10 people showed up.

"I was expecting something like the video for the Anthrax song 'Gung-Ho.' It was filmed in Germany during a tour they did with Agent Steel and Overkill. The room was so crowded that people stage-diving never even risked landing on the floor."

Despite the turnout fiasco, Robban had his heart set on promoting a thrash show of his own. A few months later, he organized a gig with his friends Erik Sandberg and Devo Andersson. Agony, who had just released their debut album, was on the bill. And this time, the outcome was even more catastrophic.

"We didn't sell any tickets. The week before the show, we realized that everything was going straight to hell, and Erik jumped ship. We had booked a real dive bar on a small islet in the town canal. This meant we had to enforce an age limit … despite the fact that barely anyone who was into thrash had turned 18."

When the house audio system turned out to be completely broken, they rented a new PA system, despite being thoroughly broke themselves. The sound gear was transported to the venue in shopping carts stolen from the local grocery store. Outside the bar, a hoard of drunken youths had gathered, only to discover that they weren't going to be let in.

"It was total chaos! About 70 people had been hanging outside, drinking all day. The cops came and said, 'You have to let these kids in; it's going to be complete mayhem otherwise!' So, we had to close the bar, which cost us 5,000 kronor. Afterwards, the Yugoslavian owners demanded money from me—and closed off the bridge across the water so people couldn't leave. They brought me into a room where they kept baseball bats. I called my mom, who persuaded them to let me go in exchange for another 2000 kronor the next day. I should have learned from that fucking Damien disaster that the German scene was way bigger than what we had going on in Sweden. That Anthrax video is to blame for everything."

———

Thrash metal never really gained momentum, much less a solid foothold, in Sweden. One reason might have been Bathory, which had already paved the way for new levels of extremity by establishing a far more aggressive genre as early as 1984. Another reason could be that no single Swedish thrash band received enough attention for others to draw inspiration from.

"The Swedish labels, they were so fucking boring," Sabrina Kihlstrand says. "Back in those days, you needed a label in order to release an album. But they had no clue about this music."

An anonymous 1983 article in Swedish music magazine *OKEJ* asked why Swedish metal bands never seemed to break through. The answer given was that local bands simply emulated their international idols without adding something of their own; Heavy Load and Trash were mentioned as examples. The writer said, "Swedish bands find it difficult to create their own brand of metal. Sweden has no tradition in this area, which is why Swedish metal is never unique or original."

This logic is equally applicable to the first wave of Swedish thrash.

Candlemass were the exception to the rule. While thrash bands made a point of playing as fast as humanly possible, Leif Edling and his band did exactly the opposite. The Upplands Väsby group slowed the tempo way down to a menacing crawl and drop-tuned the guitars, and in the process helped to birth a brand-new style of metal that was extreme in its glacial, menacing atmosphere. Their debut album, *Epicus Doomicus Metallicus*, released in 1986, even gave the genre its name: doom metal. Thirty years and 11 albums later, the group's heavy sound has greatly influenced bands all over the world.

"I credit the success of Candlemass to the fact that we were so different," says Leif Edling. "I also think Nemesis were booed off stage in Upplands Väsby for much the same reason. We did the same thing with Candlemass one year later and pulled it off against all odds, and despite our debut album getting terrible reviews. If your sound is unique enough, you'll be noticed anyway. And those who like it really like it. After that, everything just exploded."

The heavy production on *Epicus Doomicus Metallicus* was courtesy of Ragne Wahlquist and Thunderload Studios. During the '80s and '90s, the brothers produced albums for several other bands in their studio. Not only did the facility house a respectable arsenal of instruments and recording equipment, it offered specially designed booths for recording percussion, electric guitar, vocals, and strings.

Over the years, an increasing number of people have discovered Heavy Load, and today, the band enjoys cult status among metal fans all over world.

In 1999, Gothenburg band HammerFall came to Thunderload to record a cover of the Heavy Load song "Run with the Devil" for a compilation album called *Power of the*

North. Many years had passed since his teenage years in Mora, but HammerFall vocalist Joacim Cans still felt he was in the company of his idols.

"We managed to get Ragne and Styrbjörn to provide some backing vocals. And we recorded the track using the old mixing desk they'd made in wood shop while they were still in school. Also, we were really hoping to get a listen to the unreleased Heavy Load album we'd been hearing rumors of for the past 10 years. That never happened, however. I still wonder if there ever was an album in the works or if it was just something they kept saying to keep the mythos alive. Otherwise, I imagine they probably would have finished the thing by now."

One morning in 2001, Ragne Wahlquist woke to a radio news report that sent chills down his spine.

"They said that there had been a problem with a water pipe in Solna. I started thinking that something might have happened to the studio."

He immediately headed down to the subway station and noticed already in the underpass that something was wrong. The walls were coated with silt and mud, but there was no water to be seen. Once he made his way into the studio, he understood why. "Since the facility was below ground level, all the water had poured straight in. Everything was in complete disarray."

"It was as if a giant had come in with a huge whisk and just whipped the place around," says Ragne. "The wooden floor had started swelling and buckling. One door had been lifted off its hinges. The bass guitar in the control room had floated out of its case and passed through two rooms. It turned out that the main water artery for the entire area had sprung a leak."

"Tapes and equipment, all gone," says Anders Tengner. "Everything destroyed, and their entire life's work vanished. This killed any remaining enthusiasm."

Despite this, Tengner doesn't entirely dismiss the notion that we might one day hear the album that's been in the works for so many years.

"I think they still have those tapes somewhere. I also believe there's been some talks about reuniting one day. They're probably keen to play Sweden Rock Festival or something like that. But you know, they all have kids and jobs now—how are they supposed to find the time for rehearsals? It would be really cool to see Heavy Load live again, though."

Heavy Load reunited in 2018 for three live gigs, one of which was at Sweden Rock Festival. The band also released remastered versions of their three albums and have confirmed that they are working to restore tracks from the fourth album. They are currently writing new material.

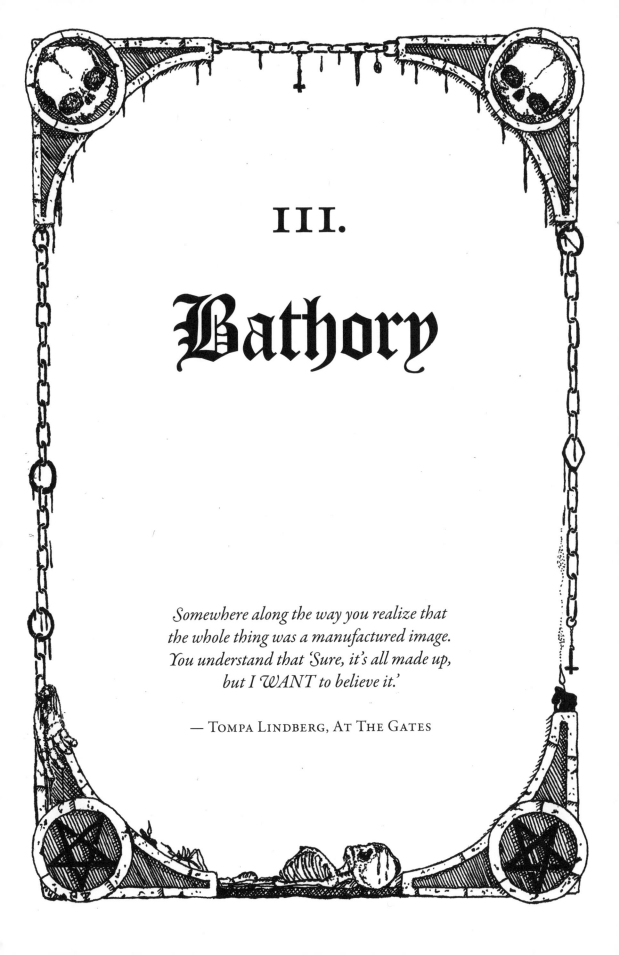

III.

Bathory

*Somewhere along the way you realize that
the whole thing was a manufactured image.
You understand that 'Sure, it's all made up,
but I WANT to believe it.'*

— Tompa Lindberg, At The Gates

THE YEAR IS 1984, and the Old English font has been established as the be-all and end-all of heavy metal typefaces. Among the thousands of kids reaching for a Letraset sheet of the gothic-styled letters is an 18-year old hailing from Stockholm. In true punk rock fashion, he is planning to paste his own record cover together. The songs on the debut album of his band Bathory touch on dark and occult themes, with titles like "Armageddon," "In Conspiracy with Satan," and "Sacrifice." By the fourth song on the track list, he has already run out of the letter C. Necessity is, however, the mother of linguistic modification, and the final C is replaced with an S. The standout song on the Bathory record is therefore known as "Necromansy."

When the self-titled album finally hits stores, a review in the all-important *Kerrang!* magazine declares that the fast and aggressive music is so horrible, it gives Satan a bad name.

However, with the support of an enthusiastic father who by day is a mainstream record producer, Bathory's frontman will eventually help set the foundation for the entire international death and black metal scene.

———

In the early '80s, the dawning hard rock movement is busy establishing itself in Upplands Väsby, to the north of Stockholm. Simultaneously, Swedish punk is gradually splitting into two factions. One adopts a more melodic and sophisticated style, incorporating pop and even reggae elements. The other is determined to push musical boundaries—the faster and more brutal, the better. This branch of the movement will come to be known as *hardcore*. While punk and metal are still musical oil and water, Swedish death metal will later emerge from this new and aggressive alternative punk scene.

Many Swedish metal bands at the time are in reality melodic hard rock bands, influenced by Whitesnake, UFO, and Michael Schenker Group. But the most ferocious bands in the country are Anti Cimex, Moderat Likvidation, and Mob 47, from Skaraborg, Malmö, and Täby respectively. The frenzy and DIY spirit of this emerging hardcore scene becomes the spark that ignites the next domestic musical revolution.

Ace Forsberg from Vällingby is one of these young punks. Born Thomas, he began calling himself Ace in his teens, out of a deep-set love for Kiss and especially their guitarist, Ace Frehley. After a stint with oi! punk band Stridskuk, Ace is seeking other methods of combining his interest in metal and dark subject matter. He searches for bandmates on notice boards at record fairs and music stores around Stockholm, naming GBH, Exploited, Motörhead, and Black Sabbath as primary influences.

Drummer Jonas Åkerlund and his cousin Frederick Melander respond to one of these ads. They've played together in several bands before but are still looking for the right people.

In mid-March of 1983, the three meet up at a music store in Sankt Eriksplan. "Ace showed up in pink-and-black–striped spandex pants and had chicken bones hanging from his jacket," Jonas says over the phone from Los Angeles, where he is now a renowned film and music video director.

"He was standing a little off to the side, and we wondered if it could really be him. And sure enough, it was. We walked the short distance to our rehearsal place, in the basement of a huge apartment building on Sigtunagatan. Ace pulled out his guitar—and to begin with, he could play better than anyone else we'd ever jammed with. He'd also written a bunch of songs. There was an instant connection between the three of us."

Jonas remembers being into heavy music in the vein of Black Sabbath, and that Frederick listened to more psychedelic bands such as Hawkwind and Uriah Heep.

"And the punk thing was draped over everything you did back in those days. Frederick and I had never played very fast, so when Ace picked up the guitar, we had some trouble keeping up, you know?"

Frederick remembers his excitement upon meeting Ace, as well as how different the cousins found him.

"We came from Bromma, a protected suburban bubble, and to speak frankly, we were both born with silver spoons in our mouths. We didn't have the balls to act or look like that. He'd dropped out of school and was very rebellious; we looked up to him."

The band rehearse up to four times per week—first on Sigtunagatan, then out in an industrial area, and finally on an island in the Stockholm archipelago. During practice sessions, they often play Kiss and Saxon covers, then go out for pizza. Following long discussions and multiple lists of names, they settle on Bathory.

The Hungarian countess Elizabeth Báthory is quite possibly the most notorious female serial killer in history. Naturally beautiful, she became obsessed with retaining her good looks. According to myth, one morning, a handmaiden was combing the countess's hair and accidentally scratched her. Elizabeth flew into a rage and had the maiden killed, whereupon she directed that the girl's corpse be drained of blood and then bathed in the still-warm liquid, believing it was a regenerative elixir. The countess then became obsessed with these blood baths and their purported effects. It wasn't until a young woman managed to escape from the castle that the countess's crimes were discovered. Legend maintains she had tortured, murdered, and drained dry over 600 virgins by the end of her career. She was imprisoned in the year 1610 and died four years later.

With the band name in place, Bathory set out to create the fastest and heaviest music ever.

"Ace was like a machine when it came to songwriting. In our previous bands, Frederick and I used to write the music, but we dropped that entirely now. We were pretty heavy in the beginning, but the music turned progressively faster. It was all Ace moving things further and further in that direction," says Jonas.

When he's not rehearsing with Bathory, Ace works as an all-rounder for the record label run by his father, Börje Forsberg.

Aside from more pop-oriented artists, Börje manages two metal bands: OZ from Finland and Trash from Stockholm. The bands have released a couple records that sell reasonably well. Börje acquires a good reputation in the business for seeking out new talent. Heavy metal is on the rise.

In 1983, Börje is contacted by RCA, who ask him to produce a compilation album showcasing Scandinavian metal and bands aimed at the European market. Börje records songs with Trash, OZ, Zero Nine, and another Finnish band called Spitfire. Ace then asks his father if his own band can be featured on the compilation, too.

"'What? You have a band?' I said. It was on that level," says Börje Forsberg. "I knew he'd head out to play with a few friends once in a while, but I hadn't heard anything about a band!"

Börje is in the process of recording the new OZ album *Fire in the Brain* at the time, and he asks Ace to bring his band to the studio for a test recording. At 11 p.m.—once OZ has left for the day—Bathory arrive and are allowed to use the already-miked-up gear to track their own stuff.

"Along came these three poodles; it was the funniest thing I've ever witnessed in a studio. They thought you had to look like Kiss when recording, so all three were dressed up in studded belts and leather jackets and began thrashing like maniacs," recalls Börje. "I thought, 'What the hell is this?' At the same time, it was genuinely endearing. And it was so fucking hard, I'd never heard anything like it. The Sex Pistols were like American Bandstand in comparison."

Börje records two Bathory songs, mixing them on the spot, with the band still in the studio. Yet when putting the compilation album together, now titled *Scandinavian Metal Attack*, Börje has second thoughts as to whether the two tracks should really be on the record. For one thing, Ace is his son, and for another, RCA are looking for more melodic hard rock, Börje reckons, with chart potential.

But there's just something about the Bathory material. Börje appreciates their honesty and energy—so in the end, he opts to include them. The record comes with a survey insert that listeners can fill out and send back to the record label, to let them know which bands they'd like to hear more of.

The album is pressed in large numbers and distributed all over Europe. Bathory's contribution sticks out dramatically, especially in the context of the more traditional tracks included. "Sacrifice" and "The Return of Darkness and Evil" have an entirely different soundscape and, measured by the standards of the time, the songs are light-ning-fast. Ace sings in a guttural voice about sacrificing virgins to Satan and raping the mother of Christ. It's filthy, dangerous, and completely without restraint.

In a few weeks, the surveys start pouring in.

"It was Bathory, Bathory, Bathory. On every single sheet," says Börje.

Like the businessman he is, Börje realizes he's on to something big.

"I said, 'Damn it, Ace, do you have more songs? You have to make an album now!' And he had lots of material. He went and got his little tape recorder and played me guitar riffs he'd written."

At this point, however, the trio is drifting apart. Jonas and Frederick are more inter-ested in heavy metal and punk, whereas Ace is fixated on increasingly darker and faster experimentations. Also, there was never any real social comradery within the group. As Frederick remembers it, he and Jonas consistently tried talking Ace into partying with them. Usually, nothing came of it.

"I don't think he really wanted to be friends with us. He was extremely headstrong, a really funny guy, but also very special. A one-man show. Generally speaking, I don't even know if he wanted a band at all. I think he only wanted to work out his songs. Ace was really hard to figure out, because he didn't talk all that much."

During the summer, while the cousins were on vacation in England, Ace seizes the opportunity to record an entire album with Börje, along with a drummer and a bass player who've never been identified. The session takes place in Studio Heavenshore in Huddinge. Heavenshore is in fact a garage belonging to one of Börje's co-workers, Peter Himmelstrand, an established composer and songwriter. ("Himmelstrand" is Swedish for "heaven shore.")

The identities of all the musicians who are actually playing on *Bathory* remain a mystery. Jonas Åkerlund remembers participating in recordings of the same songs but has no idea which versions are on the album. To Frederick Melander, it's obviously other musicians. It's long been speculated that Stridskuk member Rickard Bergman and Stefan Larsson from another punk band called OBS-klass were enlisted as the rhythm section. Börje presumably knows the truth but chooses to keep it to himself.

Ace confirmed the creative differences in the band's first lineup in an interview in *Close Up* magazine 10 years later: "The other guys in our first incarnation didn't believe in this kind of stuff—singing about Satan. They certainly weren't willing to dress up in leather, chains, and studs. (...) In Sweden, back in those days, you were supposed to look like Joey Tempest. You wouldn't get any gigs otherwise and definitely wouldn't pick up any chicks after the show. And I refused to stand for that."

Bathory is released in October of 1984. Ace doesn't provide any information about the band at all on the album's liner notes or packaging, immediately shrouding the group in mystery. All it says is that the record was produced by "Quorthon and The Boss." The name Quorthon is taken from a book about Satanic rituals. The only promotional material from the record label is a short, equally obtuse biography and some spectacular photos.

Today, oversized spikes, leather, skulls, and pig's blood are all aesthetic conventions for the genre. In 1984, however, Ace was the only one in Sweden (and one of the few in the world) to fully embrace such imagery. The few photos in circulation—showing Ace wearing inverted crosses and a pentagram necklace festooned with chicken bones—quickly build up the mystique.

Bathory is released on Black Mark Productions, a subsidiary of Börje Forsberg's company, Tyfon. Börje conservatively presses 1,000 copies.

"I had my office at Elektra Records in Kista. Every Friday, I had a meeting with the sales department to present the latest titles to them. You should've seen them when I brought *Bathory* up. Goddamn, they were gaping at each other. 'What the hell—has he lost his mind?' I told them it was going to sell like crazy, but no one believed me. Within a few months, we were into our second pressing."

The cover of *Bathory* is black, has the name printed in white gothic letters at the top and an image of a goat below. Ace wanted the goat to be in gold print for the first edition. But the printing plant screwed up, and instead, the album was delivered with a "piss yellow" goat, to quote Börje.

Today, the "Yellow Goat" version of the album fetches upwards of $1,000 USD.

A few years back, former Massgrav drummer Mattias "Indy" Pettersson paid just $600 USD for a copy in a newly opened record store in Stockholm.

"When I found out it was an archive copy that had never even been played, there was no doubt in my mind. Actually, my first reaction was 'How can it be that cheap?' so I suppose I'm somewhat damaged from years of buying obscure records. This particular copy was apparently found in the home of an old lady who used to work at the pressing plant Audiodisc, where the record was made in 1984. That's why it was never played. I went home and told myself, "It's a work of art, and in that sense, it's dead cheap—then I returned to the shop the next day and bought the album. All good."

It hasn't been properly established who drew the goat featured on the cover. Jonas remembers stealing it from a book, claiming to have Xeroxed the picture at home. Börje says he saw Ace draw it and that he has the original secreted away in a crate somewhere.

Regardless of who found the goat, the source is an original illustration by Joseph A. Smith for the book *Witches*, written in 1981 by American feminist icon Erica Jong. A Bathory fan happened upon the image by chance, noticing additionally that one of the poems in the book had been reworked into lyrics—"For All Those Who Died" on the 1988 Bathory album *Blood Fire Death*—further strengthening his conviction that the right goat had been located.

Elektra handles the distribution to record stores in Sweden, and Börje personally lugs boxes of the album to Heavy Sound in Stockholm, a hundred LPs at a time. Heavy Sound exports these records to metal stores abroad, and Börje is soon fielding international calls at the Black Mark office.

"A German rang me up one day and asked, 'Do you have Batlord?' He'd bought a few imported records and had noticed how quickly they sold. 'How many do you need?' I asked. 'I think I'll start with 5,000,' he said. 'Okaaay,' I answered. Needless to say, I didn't have 5,000 copies in stock, so I had to press more. I made him pay in advance."

The gentleman calling is Manfred Schütz from Booze Records, today known as SPV and one of the leading metal labels in the world. In total, he winds up purchasing 15,000 copies of *Bathory*.

Börje is also contacted by American label Relativity Records, hoping to negotiate a licensing deal for several Bathory albums.

Bathory's debut travels around the world, and the record is eagerly adopted by teens on the lookout for something harder and more dangerous than the current wave of thrash metal.

"It was an incredible feeling, finding an album that had exactly everything that you wanted," says Tompa Lindberg from Gothenburg, who would later form the bands Grotesque and At the Gates. He was 12 years old when *Bathory* was released.

"It was so dark. Everything was shrouded in secrecy. Who played on it—was it even a band to begin with? There was a myth and a legend surrounding it. I had the same feeling about Celtic Frost and Voivod, that these guys were a bunch of total maniacs. I mean, this can't possibly sell a single copy! They're doing whatever the fuck they want!'" Tompa recalls.

Bathory is praised in metal fanzines all over the world, but established rock magazines like *Kerrang!* butcher the newcomers.

"Many of the reviews were hilarious," Börje laughs. "*Kerrang!* wondered if someone was running water into a bathtub!"

Ace gives a few fanzine interviews but can't be bothered with details related to marketing and record sales. All he wants to do is write new music.

Letters start pouring in from fans in Poland, the United States, and Germany, who are dying to know more about their new favorite band.

"There were letters arriving every day for years. In the end, we had huge crates of mail under the kitchen table. Ace obviously didn't have the time to respond to all of them, but I'm pretty sure he read every single letter."

Ace begins referring to his fans as 'the Bathory Hordes.'

Börje Forsberg finds himself having less and less time for his other bands. A few tracks are recorded for a planned Bathory EP, but these are scrapped, and instead, father and son shift focus to a full-length sophomore release.

In early 1985, they book the exclusive Elektra studio and set about recording *The Return of Darkness and Evil*, with the help of Stefan Larsson and bassist Andreas Johansson. The album is named after one of the two songs featured on *Scandinavian Metal Attack*: Ace had simply forgotten to include it on the first record. Upon its release a few months later, fans greet the album with even higher praise than its precursor.

Just like on the debut, little information can be found on the cover and inner sleeve. And once again, "Quorthon and The Boss" are listed as producers.

Börje Forsberg meets us at the subway station in Vällingby. He's wearing a blue denim jacket, and his long gray hair is tied back in a ponytail.

"Hello. Welcome to the neighborhood!"

He mentions that the Forsberg family have lived either in Vällingby or the near vicinity more than 40 years. On our way to his daughter Jennie's place, he points out several streets relevant to their family history.

"That's where Limpan, my youngest son, lives. This way leads to Spånga, where our old house was. We snapped those promo shots for the first Bathory album in the basement."

He parks the Volvo at a row of wooden houses. For the past 10 years, he's been living in the small community of Bruzaholm in the province of Småland—he's visiting Stockholm for a health check-up and to see his grandchildren. We sit down in the sun on the terrace.

The family connection between Ace and Börje was kept secret until Ace unexpectedly passed away from a congenital heart disorder in 2004. There'd been rumors about The Boss' identity for years. As late as 2003, Ace shot down any speculation in posts on the Bathory website.

Only after the death of Ace has Börje agreed to be interviewed, to speak about his son. Convincing him to participate in this book took several years.

"When working with Black Mark and Bathory, we were The Boss and Quorthon. We learned to live like that. I never called him Ace when we were out promoting or working, only Quorthon."

In one way or another, Börje has been involved as a technician or producer on all of Bathory's records, as well as two solo albums in the '90s. Following *The Return*, he remained directly involved in the recordings.

"We wrote everything in the studio. He had lyrics and titles ready and usually no more than a tape with some guitars—there was no pre-production. Then we went in and created everything together."

A teenage black metal musician working so closely with his father must be quite a rare thing. But being part of the creative process came naturally to Börje.

"It's always been me and Ace. Always. We were friends. Of course, we were also father and son in a way; we lived together for many years and were big supporters of the soccer team AIK. And we worked together for a long time. We shared an even more profound passion for music."

Börje says Kiss was his son's first major musical crush. As early as primary school, Ace was enthralled with the band. When Kiss came to Sweden on their first European tour in 1976, he begged his father to let him attend the gig. Börje took Ace as well as his younger siblings, and from that moment on, music was the only thing Ace cared about.

One evening not long after the concert, Börje, coming home late from work, heard peculiar noises from the backyard. Ace was standing in the dark, pounding on an oil barrel. A former drummer himself, Börje immediately detected a sense of rhythm in his son.

A few days later, Börje pulled up in the driveway, having been grocery shopping.

"Ace would usually come out to help me carry things in, so I yelled at him, 'Can you help your old man out with the bags?' I had actually bought him a drum kit, and it was just sitting there in the open trunk. He came down to the car, spotted the drums, and was absolutely ecstatic. From then on, it was all about drums, drums, drums—there was an endless pounding."

The neighbors weren't nearly as delighted about the purchase. Having been forbidden to play indoors, Ace carried the drum kit to the nearby forest. When the sun set, he carried the kit back down again, piece by piece.

The family eventually moved to a bigger house, where they set up a music room in the basement. Ace put makeup on his three younger siblings and organized lip-synced Kiss concerts for their parents. Pyrotechnics being an important aspect of the Kiss experience, Ace taught himself to breathe fire. He experimented with both kerosene and gasoline but made the surprising discovery that chocolate milk powder has combustive qualities and works just as well.

"And goddamn, it didn't take long before he was able to play the whole drum solo from Kiss's *Alive!*— straight off. Everything he set his mind to was easy for him. It's the opposite for me. I can hear if something is good, but I'd have difficulty playing it myself. But it was so easy for him," Börje recalls.

Börje Forsberg's life in music began in the late '50s, and 1961 saw the release of the first Telstar single, a band he played drums for. He also played with Mike Doughan and the Ghost Riders, who released several albums on the classic Decca label.

"We were the wild and dangerous Stockholm band that mothers didn't want their daughters to come see."

As Börje's music career gained momentum, he was hired by a record label. Forsberg went to work alongside musician and label manager Hans Edler, a producer and sound technician for Marilla, a company focusing on '60s vocal groups and pop artists.

Ace was born in 1966, as Thomas Börje Forsberg.

"We were essentially two kids who had children," says Börje.

He and Ace's mother were only 20 and 16 respectively when Ace was born. The young couple had no family members in Stockholm to help them out, so they brought their son along everywhere. He spent most days with his father. When Börje worked as a sound technician, Ace slept in a corner of the studio. The young couple often had musicians visiting their house, and people got used to Ace being around.

In the '70s, Börje Forsberg founded the record label Tyfon, carving out a niche for himself as a dance band producer. "Dance band" is a peculiar—but to this day quite popular—musical genre in Sweden. Based on the simplistic early rock and roll of the 1950s, with a touch of American country music and polka, dance bands perform live at public parks and venues that are dedicated to couples dancing, singing saccharine lyrics devoted almost exclusively to the subject of love and heartbreak. Dance band concerts are a form of mating ritual—a place to find a partner for life, or perhaps just for the night. Some artists on Börje's roster achieved gold record status. He also developed a keen talent for spotting mainstream pop hits, and the EP *Det sa bara klick* (It Just Clicked) was released in conjunction with the Swedish royal wedding in 1976.

"It immediately entered the top slot in the charts. I think it sold about 40,000 copies, which was a lot, considering the size of Sweden. The cover was golden, with a photo of the royal couple. The photo was taken by the internationally acclaimed photographer, Lennart Nilsson. It cost me 10,000 Swedish kronor—but I got that back and more," Börje grins.

He also released several children's albums. Ace is present on some of these recordings. If you look closely, Ace can be seen sitting next to Swedish TV personality Ulf Elfving on the back cover of *Marillas Grammofonteater*.

As a kid, Ace was given an acoustic guitar by his uncle and soon taught himself to play it. His Kiss album collection was supplemented with Black Sabbath, Motörhead, and above all, a ton of punk rock.

In 1980, when Ace was 14 years old, his parents filed for divorce and the four siblings were separated. Ace moved into an apartment in Vällingby with Börje and his youngest brother, Anders. A few years later, their sister Jennie joined them.

Ace was now utterly consumed by music and dropped out of school in the 8th grade. Börje didn't worry though. He could spot a special talent in his son.

"I appreciated his enthusiasm, but I was so busy with my own things—I'd always be in the studio or running the label. Eventually, he started working for me part-time."

Ace worked in the studio, as well as on the tours Börje set up for his bands. He further displayed his artistic prowess by sketching out ideas for album covers and album packaging. For instance, the image of the hand holding a burning skull that makes up the cover of OZ's *Fire in the Brain* comes from Ace. He brought home all the leftover demo cassettes sent to Tyfon by hopeful artists. He then visited the Vällingby library, borrowing classical LPs and making cassette copies.

"He really loved classical music, especially Wagner. He had an entire shelf at home with all those tapes," says Börje.

Ace also dug deep into historical literature. With Börje working quite a lot as well as being a single parent with three children, Ace helped out at home and took care of his younger siblings.

Börje says the solidarity within their family remained strong, even after his divorce from the children's mother. All of the Forsberg children have been involved in Black Mark at one point or another.

The aura of mystique surrounding Bathory in the early years gave birth to wild myths and exaggerations. Through the years, Ace would hear increasingly bizarre stories about himself. That he would beat lambs to death and then devour them. How the albums had been recorded in a cave, with bats circling around his head. That he was a full-fledged Satanic madman.

On the other hand, Ace did little to disavow these rumors and distortions; in fact, he took to embellishing his own shifting narrative in interviews.

Journalists and fans doggedly strove to ascertain his real name, and Ace sought to further confuse matters. When speaking to foreign magazines, he'd occasionally introduce himself as Runka Snorkråka ("Wank Booger") or as Swedish ice hockey pros Mats Sundin and Peter Forsberg—names then enthusiastically unveiled by journalists, thinking they'd scored a scoop. In an early edition of the Norwegian-American book *Lords of Chaos: The Bloody Rise of the Satanic Metal Underground*, the authors claim Ace's real name is Pugh Rogefeldt—actually the name of a well-known Swedish pop singer.

The fact that Rogefeldt once made an album called *Hammarhjärta* (Hammerheart), which Bathory later named one of their albums as well, might have had something to do with it.

After the release of the first album, Bathory never played live, further propagating the image of Ace as an eccentric hermit, isolated from the outside world.

The 1983 lineup was said to have done a few live gigs, but no eyewitness testimonies have been confirmed. The booklet included in the 2006 Bathory CD compilation *In Memory of Quorthon* explicitly denies any live gigs ever taking place. However, Quorthon himself confirmed in several interviews having performed a half-dozen concerts. Frederick Melander says that, while he was never part of any proper concerts, they once played in someone's rehearsal space.

"A friend called Fredrik Östergren threw a party, and there we were—raising hell in a corner—but no one was particularly interested. So, I wouldn't say we ever really performed as a band."

Jonas Åkerlund has only vague memories.

"I maintain we played live three times. Only shitty little events—some dank party in a Stockholm basement, but at least in front of some kind of an audience. Most people on the scene hung out at a venue called Studion at Sankt Eriksplan, but we would've never gotten a gig there. We weren't nearly cool enough for that."

Jonas is also skeptical of certain details in the band's purported history. In interviews through the years, as well as on the Bathory website, Ace always claimed to have come up with the name Bathory after visiting the London Dungeon wax cabinet. Jonas remembers it being taken straight from the Venom song "Countess Bathory." Another tidbit repeated throughout the years is that Jonas used the name Vans McBurger during his stint in the band—because he liked Vans skate shoes and hamburgers. This is not true at all, he says.

"I have no idea where that came from. But it's true that Frederick used to be called Hanoi, because his hair was so big and he looked like a member of Hanoi Rocks."

In the *Close-Up* interview from 1993, Ace himself goes so far as to question whether Bathory would've found legendary status without the mystique surrounding them in those early years. "That's what we owe basically all of our success to. If that first lineup I used to play with had stayed together, the band wouldn't even have been known outside central Stockholm, because we were so ugly, played so badly and everything."

Even though Ace wasn't interested in talking about his music, Börje successfully convinced him to join in on a few promotional trips. Before the release of Bathory's third album, *Under the Sign of the Black Mark* in 1987, they traveled to the United States together.

Problems arose immediately: At the airport, a large ox bone that had Ace brought along for photo sessions was spotted poking out from his hand luggage. This item, added to his standard studs-and-leather outfit and signature chicken bone necklace, did not amuse United States customs agents.

"It took me half an hour to talk our way out of that one," says Börje. "They must've finally accepted our story, because we were allowed in, with bones and everything."

Ace and Börje both noticed the increasing popularity of Bathory in the U.S. Ace did a lot of press, and signing sessions were well attended.

One night in New York, they went to the Ritz to see Slayer play. A few fans recognized Ace, and in short order, he had a crowd around him. After the concert, Slayer members came up to say hello and take a picture with him.

As the years pass, the fairy tales and lies in circulation began to annoy Ace.

"Those first occult albums—to him, they were more of a story," says Börje. "When people completely misunderstood this and thought he was literally butchering lambs and eating them raw, it just became too much. He was extremely fond of animals; he wouldn't swat a fly. This was art to him—theatre. It was cool, avant-garde, and cocky. On the verge of being anarchistic."

Even if most fans were aware that Ace was never a genuine Satanist, they wanted him to be (at the very least) a genuine lunatic.

"Everyone knew Venom were fake," says Tompa Lindberg. "But I remember the interview with Quorthon on the *Rockbox* radio show, where he came off as really secretive and weird. We'd listen to it over and over again. We thought he was so fucking cool. Somewhere along the way, around the time of *Under the Sign of the Black Mark*, you realized that the whole thing was a manufactured image. You understood that 'Sure, it's all made up, but I WANT to believe it.' Same thing with the Bathory Hordes—on the first albums, he thanked Bathory Hordes from all over the world. It was such a complete myth, but one you wanted to swallow hook, line, and sinker."

With the exception of the American trip, Ace generally kept to himself—rarely went to gigs, didn't hang out with other musicians, and gave very few interviews. He was a legend to Sweden's young death and black metal musicians, and most have at least some memory of spotting him or trying to get in touch.

Erik Wallin from Merciless remembers the first time he saw Ace in real life.

"It was the first Kiss reunion tour in '96. I was sitting in the Globe Arena in Stockholm. Right behind me, over my left shoulder, was a guy who looked familiar. I froze when I realized who it was. 'Quorthon! Shit!' I'd managed to smuggle in a bottle of whiskey in my pants, and I'd read in an interview that Quorthon had whiskey for breakfast, that he was real badass. I was already pretty drunk, so I just had to turn around and say, 'Damn, you're Quorthon—right?' and he said, 'Yes, that's me.'

'Shit, I've been listening to you since 1984—will you please have some of my whiskey? I've read that you like it.'

He answered, 'I've actually given that up, but all right.' In hindsight, I think that was really fucking sweet of him."

Toward the end of the '80s, Frederick Melander moved to San Francisco to work as a graphic designer. It was only upon finding Bathory albums at Tower Records that he realized how far Ace had taken his vision and how strong the myth had grown.

"He was the nicest guy in the world. We had a rehearsal place at Jonas' father's house on the island of Värmdö. The bus on the way there was always full of children and old ladies, Ace would often pull out his guitar and sing songs for them and got everyone to sing along. The old ladies were so charmed by him sitting there with his chicken bones, playing. I'm happy and humbled to have been part of the two songs that allowed him to record the first album."

In the early years of Bathory, Ace auditioned several musicians before settling on any permanent lineup. Drummer Chris Witchhunter, of German thrashers Sodom, was one such musician. He was visiting Stockholm in 1986, when news of the Chernobyl nuclear accident reached Sweden. Radioactive clouds quickly traveled northwest, and rumor has it that Ace jokingly told Chris he needed to visit the German embassy to pick up medicine to counter the fallout. Witchhunter got scared and caught the first plane home. Cliff Lundberg, the bass player in Moderat Likvidation and later the guitarist in Anti Cimex, also came to Stockholm from Malmö. In a 2015 Bathory memorial article in *Sweden Rock Magazine*, he describes having offered his services to Ace when ordering a Bathory shirt. To his surprise, Ace called him up.

"It's still kind of a mystery to me. But I think he wanted somebody not part of the Stockholm music scene. Everything related to Bathory just had to be mysterious in some way."

He spent a weekend in Stockholm, learning some of the songs that would later turn up on *Under the Sign of the Black Mark*. Bathory kept getting offers to perform, and Cliff recalls Ace having big plans for a live show.

"The stage would be draped in animal hides and the drum riser would elevate. These were good and quite feasible ideas. I do think, however, he realized his audience grew with every new album. The fact that that he hadn't done any concerts from the start made it all the harder to live up to expectations as time went on."

Bathory's first four albums were crucial to the foundation of a death/black metal scene worldwide. Above all, the Satanic lyrics inspired black metal fans both in Sweden and Norway—a scene which by extension would lead to church burnings and murder.

Börje Forsberg emphasizes that Ace wanted nothing to do with what came to be called the second wave of black metal.

"He hated those bands and would feel ill when they mentioned Bathory. He wanted no part of that. And when those fucking bands started burning churches, he certainly didn't find it funny anymore. I think that's why he started getting into other stuff; he felt pretty much done with it."

In a 1990 interview with *Kerrang!*, Ace says, "People have this image of me as some sort of bloodsucking vampire living in a Satanic cave in Sweden. I don't spend six months of the year playing guitar, trying to write good lyrics, to then have to answer questions like 'When did you last kill a child?'"

Fed up with black metal, Ace begins composing more epic and dramatic music with lyrics inspired by history—primarily the Vikings of Scandinavia. This influence is first noticeable on the 1988 album *Blood Fire Death*, also the source of inspiration when naming this book. The 1990 *Hammerheart* album then becomes foundational in the development of Viking metal.

Börje mentions how *Hammerheart* was an immensely cumbersome project for only two people. These days, recording and producing music is primarily done with computers, and sampling is easy—but back then, every single sound and small choir phrase had to be created painstakingly in the studio and put to reel-to-reel tape. The album was a long time in the making, but it was an immediate success upon release, selling 200,000 copies in the first few months alone.

"When Ace and I worked together, we did everything in three dimensions. Writing the *Hammerheart* songs, we'd picture a movie before us—it wasn't just sound coming from the stereo. It was something visual and deep. When we'd finished mixing a song, we always turned the light off and tried sensing and seeing the music, so it would feel right. That's why I think it became so big; it grabs people in a way that perhaps not every record does."

During the '90s and '00s, Bathory released markedly diverse albums. They included everything from powerful Viking epics such as the *Nordland* albums to hard thrash records, as well as two rock albums under the Quorthon moniker.

Seven years have passed since Ace's death in the summer of 2004, but his father's pain is still excruciatingly evident. Börje has barely spoken to any outsiders about his grief and is still not comfortable discussing his son with journalists.

"I spoke with him on the Friday before it happened. We had a long conversation and I asked him how his ticker was holding up. He'd been to the Sankt Göran hospital back in November after experiencing chest pains, so I got him to visit a health clinic in Vällingby. After examining him, they sent him back to Sankt Göran for more tests. While being monitored on a stationary bike, his chest hurt so bad, he had to stop, and they sent him home again."

No one could reach Ace over the weekend, and the family kept calling each other. Börje wasn't too worried—Ace had spoken about attending a motorcycle meet over the weekend. But come Monday, he still wasn't answering his phone.

"I called Limpan, who was the manager of a car dealership in Vällingby at the time, and asked him to go to Ace's place. He went over with Jennie and they could hear his cell phone ringing in there. He never forgot his phone. So, I told them to call a damn locksmith."

An hour later, he got the call from Jennie.

"Limpan went in first, and Ace was just lying there looking as if he was asleep. He was lying peacefully on his side. But he was cold."

Börje's voice thickens.

"I almost died. I immediately jumped into a cab to Stockholm, and when I arrived at Sankt Göran, there he was, with his long hair on the pillow. It's fucking hell. There's nothing worse than losing your child, no matter how old they are."

Bathory's last albums were recorded in the Mimo Sound studio in Älvsjö, south of Stockholm.

Two dogs greet us at the door to the basement facility as we arrive in the fall of 2009. Micke "Mimo" Moberg has owned his studio since the '80s. He rinses out some coffee cups before setting them on the table and offering us some cinnamon rolls he just bought.

A big computer sits on a desk in the first room, but the two inner rooms are small and worn-down. There's a photo of Ace on a shelf, with a lit candle in front of it. The wall at the far end has another picture of him, signed by Ace with a personal dedication to Micke.

"Ace could have recorded anywhere, but he wanted to be here," he says, indicating a small, claustrophobic room behind the mixing desk.

"Go in there if you want to feel Ace's sweat!"

Micke Moberg engineered the last three Bathory albums. The four prior were done by Rex Gisslén, who sits on the couch wearing a *Requiem* long-sleeve. His long curly hair is tied up in a ponytail. His haircut was more extravagant back in the mid-'80s, as keyboard player for the glam pop group Shanghai. Gisslén is called Rex Luger on the Bathory albums, the name he used back in the early glam rock band Candy Roxx.

Rex first met Ace while doing some extra work as a technician at Montezuma Studio in Stockholm. Börje used to send his bands there, and Rex worked with OZ, among others. He remembers Ace hanging out in the studio—tall, silent, and dressed in black.

Börje called on Rex to help them out with the production of *Twilight of the Gods*. It would be the first time Bathory used a sound engineer other than Börje and Ace themselves.

"Working in a studio, you get used to a high tempo—you switch coworkers every two weeks, so it's very important to immediately establish some kind of chemistry. Some people are easy to work with, others slightly more difficult. It took some time with Ace; he was a bit introverted."

Ace relaxed over time and started socializing with Rex privately. Sometimes he'd hang out at a rock club that Rex managed. For the most part, however, Ace preferred to stay home, and he certainly didn't party a lot. In the end, Rex and Ace didn't really have all that much in common.

Once in 2002, they went to Gröna Lund, an amusement park in Stockholm, together to catch a Sahara Hotnights gig.

"He would call me up and ask if I wanted to go to a motorcycle show. He'd seen a Harley-Davidson Fatboy in *Terminator 2* and decided to get one of his own. So, we went to the Harley-Davidson dealer in Sollentuna, where he decided on a model. Two weeks later, he returned ... he had a plastic bag with 225,000 Swedish kronor in cash and said,

'I want that bike.' The guys in the store were petrified. Ace was the nicest guy ever, but it wasn't necessarily the impression he gave—6'7" and wearing a leather vest. 'This isn't how we do business,' they told him. 'Okay, so how do you usually do business?' Ace asked."

Rex and Micke gradually came to understand his particular creative process. Ace always had grand visions; everything was in his head.

"We always started with the guitars—then bass, drums, choirs, and sound effects. He often thought in terms of movie sequences rather than music. A fairly unique way of working," Rex recalls. "When it came to vocals, what was produced in the studio would perhaps not entirely match his vision. He'd lose his temper completely. He'd physically pull his vocal chords to achieve a vibrato …"

"He'd be throwing up blood when recording vocals!" Micke Moberg adds.

"Börje was also a super enthusiast, very exacting," says Rex. "That could be difficult in the studio. Quite a pair those two; they were extremely close and would speak their minds freely. They argued and carried on—Börje would suggest something, Ace would think it was crap and go home. Börje then said, 'Don't touch a thing! It sounds perfect! Just raise the snare a little—perfect,' always wielding a cigarette."

As Rex tells it, Ace never did anything halfheartedly. When he needed cover artwork for *Octagon,* he went to a quarry and bought a huge rock, weighing close to 100 pounds. He painted a pentagram in blood, lit candles, and then took the photo himself. Since Ace had no desire to keep the rock, Rex bought it and keeps it on display at home.

"If he bought a bike, he'd become a biker right away, with the right helmet and the right glasses. Everything was done with a strict sense of purpose."

He describes Ace as an individual with extreme integrity, often separating his life into different compartments. AIK soccer supporters knew him as "Snöret" ("The String"), not as an international metal icon. His girlfriend of several years saw him being interviewed on MTV, not having had a clue he was even a musician.

The extent of his secrecy only became apparent to Micke Moberg on the day Ace was found dead in his apartment. He went with Rex to a pub to have a beer and mourn their friend together.

"But what about Ace's father? How is he holding up?" Micke asked.

"Haven't you spoken to Börje?" Rex answered.

"I didn't have a clue Börje was Ace's father!" Micke admits. "And bear in mind that we'd been working together four or five years!"

In hindsight, Micke understands why Ace would smile when asked to have a serious talk about Börje.

"I wanted to make sure he knew what he was doing. I know what labels can be like. 'Just make sure the deal is good,' you know? 'You'll get ripped off,' I used to say. He kind of smirked at me when these subjects were raised, but I never made the connection.'"

Over the phone from Los Angeles, Jonas Åkerlund points out how Ace knew what he wanted to achieve with his music from his early teens.

"Everything he did came straight from the heart. Ace was very detached. His creativity came from within, while Frederick and I were anxious to keep track of what was going on in the world. That's something I've discovered in later years—how very few people possess this ability. He was probably one of the most insulated people, even compared to any of the big rock stars in music history. He was a genius."

The sun is setting over the terrace at Ace's sister Jennie's place. She brings out a few beers, and Börje mentions how there's still a lot of unreleased Bathory material packed away in Casa de Hammerheart—meaning his house in Bruzaholm. He's not quite sure what to do with it, since Ace isn't around to give his approval. The house has an entire room full of boxes with Ace's belongings. His motorcycle is there as well, and the family has decided never to sell it.

During the entire interview, Jennie has been sitting in silence. She doesn't want to comment on her big brother's passing at all. It's her way of processing it, she says. The siblings were working on an album together when Ace died but only got to recording the song "Silverwing." Jennie wrote the lyrics, and Ace wrote the music. After his death, she released it as an EP, along with a moving interpretation of "Song to Hall up High" from *Hammerheart*.

Börje takes a sip from his beer and asks what time it is.

"Almost four," Jennie says.

AIK are playing Elfsborg in an away game. Börje is planning to watch the match on TV and then play with his grandchildren. He watches the girls bounce up and down on the neighbor's trampoline, sighing heavily. Taking about his son's death hits him just as hard every time.

"It's really terrible. But I have all the CDs, so in a sense, I see and hear him every day."

Börje Forsberg passed away in September 2017.

IV.

Pelle Dead

*He's absolutely an icon, a sort of
Jim Morrison of black metal.
I believe everyone who's in the least bit
interested in black metal traces
the genre back to him.*

— Erik Wallin, Merciless

I T IS MONDAY, APRIL 8, 1991. Dark clouds loom over Kråkstad, a village a little more than 10 miles south of Oslo, where Norwegian black metal band Mayhem have set up their headquarters. The big red wooden house sits just on the edge of the forest, overlooking vast fields. The view is magnificent, even on a cold and gray spring day like this.

22-year-old vocalist Pelle Ohlin, better known as Dead, has spent the weekend alone in the house. The other band members are with their families.

They haven't rehearsed in a long time. Founder and guitarist Øystein "Euronymous" Aarseth dedicates most of his time to his newly founded record label, Deathlike Silence Productions, which he runs out of one of the bedrooms on the second floor of the house. He has grandiose plans for Mayhem, and he assures his bandmates, "We're almost there; we'll soon record the album." But nothing he says ever seems to happen. Pelle and Øystein have drifted apart lately, and the overall atmosphere in the house is tense. Bass player Jørn "Necrobutcher" Stubberud is rarely around, spending most of his time with his pregnant girlfriend. In an act of financial desperation, drummer Jan Axel "Hellhammer" Blomberg has sold the band's PA, forcing Pelle to sing through a guitar amp instead.

Recently, Pelle's father visited, yet again. The family back in Sweden are worried. During his stay, the two went through a brochure from a community art college. Maybe Pelle could apply for it, his dad suggested. He told his dad he would.

Now he's sitting in the basement, cutting himself with his new knife. He first tried to slice his wrists several times, in the forest behind the house, but the wounds just weren't deep enough. He's cut himself before, mostly on stage. Blood drips on the floor of the large recreation room and on the band's instruments.

He pens a suicide note. Over the weekend, he's written new lyrics for a song called "Life Eternal," and he includes them in the letter.

He's not bleeding as much as he'd expected. The blood issuing from his slender wrists coagulates too quickly. He tries to locate the main artery and cuts a deep gash in his neck. His white T-shirt with the print "I ♥ Transylvania" is now partially blackish-red. But it's taking too long.

Pelle moves to his bedroom on the second floor. He grabs Øystein's shotgun. The weapon has been in the house since they moved in.

The day before, Øystein had come to the house in Kråkstad. He knew Pelle was supposed to be there, but the door was locked, and he didn't have the key. He rang the doorbell but nobody responded, so he drove to a telephone booth to call Jørn.

"He asked if Pelle was at my place," says Jørn. "But he wasn't. I was supposed to drop by the house earlier in the day to check in on him but never got around to it. Øystein then told me Pelle was probably 'dangling' in his room. I thought that was a strange thing to say."

On Monday, Øystein heads back to the house and climbs in through a window. Entering Pelle's room, he finds the vocalist dead on his bed, with the shotgun and a knife next to him. The small room is covered with brain matter and blood.

Instead of calling an ambulance, Øystein runs to the car and drives to the nearest store to buy a disposable camera. He returns to the house and takes several detailed pictures of the body. Once he's done, he heads to the phone booth to first call the police and then Jan Axel at his parents' house.

"Øystein called me and said that Dead had gone home," Jan Axel explains. "'What the fuck, he went back to Sweden?' I said. 'No, he's gone home,' Øystein repeated. 'He's blown his head off.' Holy shit. I was completely stunned. Øystein was overly excited and told me, 'Don't worry, I've taken pictures!' It was definitely a very strange situation."

Later the same day, Jørn learns what has happened.

"Øystein called me to say that Pelle had done something really cool. 'Cool?' I asked. 'Yes, he's killed himself.' I didn't find it particularly cool at all, and I was shocked to the core. Then Øystein told me that he'd taken pictures of the corpse and that we could use them for Mayhem. I told him that this would never ever happen, and it escalated into an argument on the phone. The whole thing was a damn tragedy."

After Pelle's body had been retrieved by an ambulance, there was still plenty of blood and organic matter left in the tiny bedroom. For some reason, no proper cleanup is ever attempted. A few days later, when the stench becomes unbearable, Øystein enlists Jan Axel to tidy up, together with his friend Jon "Metalion" Kristiansen and a few others. They discover fragments of Pelle's skull scattered throughout the room. Øystein decides to collect as many as he can find. The largest pieces are bigger than a cigarette lighter, Metalion remembers.

Over the following months, Øystein sends skull fragments to people he considers worthy within the black metal scene. Among these are the Swedish musicians Morgan "Evil" Håkansson in Marduk, IT in Abruptum, Richard Cabeza of Dismember, members of the Swiss band Samael, and the drummer of Masacre from Colombia.

According to Metalion, others received skull fragments as well. Øystein also displays some in his new record store, Helvete, opened in Oslo later that summer, and makes jewelry for himself and Jan Axel from the remaining pieces.

It's been rumored that Øystein consumed some of Pelle's brain, to experience the sensation of cannibalism, but few in the inner circle believe this to be true.

A week after the suicide, Jørn and Øystein met up. Øystein had developed the photos and kept them in a white envelope.

"I immediately told him I didn't want to see them," says Jørn. "He again said they were going to be used for the new Mayhem album. 'I'll kill you if you do that,' I told him. And he could see I was serious. He was really disappointed; he thought it was a marvelous idea."

Ultimately, Jørn quit Mayhem in protest.

Seemingly unaffected by his friend's death, the skilled marketer Øystein began using Pelle's suicide to promote the band. In letters to Mayhem's international network of fans and fellow musicians, he thoroughly explained Pelle's actions as truly evil, saying that Mayhem was the only band practicing what they preach. Jørn was dismissed as a wimp who couldn't deal with the pressure of reality. But above all else, Øystein planted the idea that Pelle killed himself out of disillusionment with a diluted underground scene attracting people not dedicated or evil enough.

In the June 1992 issue of Sweden's *Close-Up Magazine*, he proclaimed: "Dead was a very evil man/goat. He hated every living being. The only thing preventing him from blowing his head off earlier was the black metal/death metal lifestyle, with evil bands worshipping death and wearing black clothes, studs, leather, bullet belts, and everything else associated with the true lifestyle. [...] We support his actions and respect his never-ending evil."

Øystein did nothing to quash the spreading rumors of his involvement in the suicide or the suggestion that he murdered Pelle. He's come to the conclusion that others' imaginations run amok generated far better stories than anything he could make up himself. He does, however, tell his friends that Pelle had asked him to stay away from the house over that fateful weekend, and that the two explicitly discussed suicide as a means to further promote the band on several occasions.

Soon, tales of the post-mortem photos emerge, and Øystein happily confirms them. Asked if taking these pictures was a sick thing to do, he tells the *Close-Up* reporter, "We're no fucking humanitarian joke band! When I say that we're into death metal, it means that we worship death. Nothing is too brutal, vile, or sick. People who can't understand that can just fuck off."

Øystein sends one of the pictures to Mauricio "Bull Metal" Montoya, drummer of the Colombian metal band Masacre.

The photo is sharp and detailed. Pelle's body is sprawled over the bed with the gun and knife next to him. Blood spatter creates patterns on the wooden wall panel, and next to his head lies what is left of his brain.

A few years later, Bull Metal releases the bootleg album *Dawn of the Black Hearts*, from a 1990 Mayhem concert in Sarpsborg. On the record cover is the photo of Pelle's dead body.

The year Pelle Ohlin committed suicide, the Swedish and Norwegian extreme metal scenes exploded. In Sweden, death metal continued to evolve, to subsequently spread all over the world. Norway became the epicenter of black metal. Soon, churches were set ablaze all over the country. Tabloid headlines spread macabre, breathless news of Satanists at work.

In light of the suicide and all the goings-on in Norway, the legend of Pelle "Dead" Ohlin grew, as more and more people took an interest in Mayhem. No one had ever decorated the stage with severed pig's heads before. Pelle cut his arms with broken bottles and fantasized about placing rotting meat in the ventilation systems of concert venues to enhance the atmosphere of death. He would collect dead animals and bury his stage clothes in the woods prior to gigs, in order to infuse them with the stench of decay. No one had ever seen anything like this before.

Even to this day, both old and new bands speak with reverence and awe of Pelle's morbid dedication.

"Dead was the one who brought the soul," explains songwriter and guitar player Morgan Håkansson of Marduk. He corresponded frequently with Pelle the year leading up to his passing.

"He took extreme metal to entirely new levels. Like inhaling the fumes of a rotting bird before recording vocals, in order to experience the vibrations of death. His commitment was a big inspiration to me."

The only Mayhem material that was recorded with Pelle are two studio songs on the 1990 compilation *Projections of a Stained Mind* and the *Live in Leipzig* album from the same year.

Even though it was recorded after his death, Pelle's fixations with cold and darkness are immortalized in the lyrics of Mayhem's second album, *De Mysteriis Dom Sathanas*, released in 1994. It is to this day considered one of the most important black metal albums of all time.

Erik Wallin, guitar player of Merciless, was a friend of Pelle's from his early teens and notes how Pelle has gone from obscurity to becoming a cult figure in the genre.

"He's absolutely an icon, a sort of Jim Morrison of black metal. I believe everyone who's in the least bit interested in black metal traces the genre back to him and Mayhem and what went down."

Instead of pilgrimages to the Paris cemetery of Père-Lachaise, Mayhem fans travel to Österhaninge cemetery outside Stockholm to chug beer at Pelle's tombstone.

Erik Danielsson, vocalist and frontman of Uppsala black metal band Watain, was 9 years old when Pelle Ohlin took his life.

"He is a huge inspiration to me. His aesthetics, and how his lyrics sum up the basis of my understanding of black metal," Danielsson says.

Many of Pelle's ideas live on through Watain, which is today considered Sweden's most extreme black metal band.

Erik Danielsson sees Pelle as a power source, defining what black metal is supposed to be.

"He was the one who made people understand that when this genre is carried to its natural conclusion, things get serious. If everyone thinks black metal is completely harmless, then it would be just that. Those who were motivated by him brought something that benefited black metal, and those who found it sick and repulsive vanished. Thus, the scene was efficiently purged of weaklings. He helped usher in a far more appropriate climate."

———

Jørn "Necrobutcher" Stubberud lives in a yellow remodeled summer cabin on the Nordby mountain by the E6 highway, some 20 miles south of Oslo. The living room is densely cluttered. He's recently had carpenters over to replace the windows and build a proper deck overlooking the big frost-covered fields surrounded by pine forest.

His adult daughter, Sabine, occupies a small room behind the kitchen. A fabric Mayhem poster and the classic Burzum poster of Varg Vikernes glaring at the camera are pinned to the wall. Mayhem's first backdrop hangs over the wardrobe. It was painted by Jørn and Øystein in Jørn's family home when they were still teenagers.

"We used my mom's skis to ensure the pentagram lines were straight," Jørn admits.

He serves tea in a white cup shaped like a female torso and tells us he's working on a book about all his friends who have died. There are quite a few of them—about 100, he claims. The idea came to him in 2002 while he was incarcerated for possession of drugs and weaponry.

"I've lived a hard life and been busted several times. That's what happens when you're a man—I like guns and girls! And hashish," he says with a smirk.

He's under surveillance by the Norwegian Police Security Service, and they've paid several unannounced visits in his cabin. Jørn pulls a worn photo album from the crowded bookshelf and frees up some space on the messy table.

"This is my latest project," he says and points at a document under a plastic-wrapped apple and a few records.

It's an invoice for his daughter's driving lessons.

"1,100 Norwegian kronor per lesson," he laments. "But she has to learn how to drive."

He opens the album. Every page is full of carefully arranged photos, taken at parties or of the band. It begins in 1984 with pubescent pictures of a teenage Øystein. Photos of Pelle soon appear, either joking around or glaring with painted eyes and stiff fingers. On one of the pictures, Øystein and Pelle are goofing around with fake blood, but Øystein has put too much in his mouth and starts drooling.

"Pelle notices and smiles just as the camera goes off. This is how I remember Pelle. That face. The happy face. He always had some sick pun ready—assuming you were alone with him. If there was someone he didn't know with you, he preferred not to speak at all."

Pelle's first contact with Mayhem was by mail. He sent a letter to the band's PO box—along with a crucified rotten mouse and the demo of his band, Morbid, a Stockholm underground band with high theatrical ambitions.

"I drove a pickup truck back in those days and opened the letter inside the cab," says Jørn. "I'd never received dead animals in the mail before, so I was quite surprised, it also reeked something fierce. I put the mouse and the letter on the flatbed of my truck, leaving the demo tape in the front seat. Unfortunately, everything flew off when I started driving, so I never got to read the letter, but the music was fucking great."

Mayhem formed in 1984 and soon made a name for themselves in the tiny, multinational extreme metal scene of the time. Their minimalistic band pictures, where they seldom showed their faces, quickly spread within metal circles, thanks to Øystein's networking talents. Mayhem was inspired both by early metal bands like Venom, Mercyful Fate, and Bathory and by more experimental and avant-garde music like Brian Eno and Diamanda Galás. They sought out the most extreme artists in all genres, caring less about musical classification.

Mayhem's 1987 debut, the mini-album *Deathcrush*, opens with "Silvester Anfang"—a piece written by renowned German experimental artist Conrad Schnitzler. He was an early member of Tangerine Dream and is considered one of the godfathers of krautrock. Øystein was a massive fan, and one warm summer day, he made the journey to Schnitzler's home in Germany and rang the doorbell. When Schnitzler didn't open the door, he slept on the porch stairs and was let in the following day. When Øystein later wrote a letter asking Schnitzler to write a piece for Mayhem, the German sent him a composition he'd just finished: "Silvester Anfang."

The combination of avant-garde innovation and extreme aggression gave Mayhem a menacing reputation that impressed and struck a chord with Pelle. In Morbid, he had cultivated the stage persona of Dead, modeled after his fascination for death and the beyond. Despite the fact that Morbid had only performed live a handful of times, their spectacular shows attracted attention within the budding Swedish death metal scene.

Jon "Metalion" Kristiansen was the editor of the *Slayer* fanzine—the first

Scandinavian publication for death and black metal. Øystein played him one of Morbid's rehearsal demos, and he immediately contacted Pelle.

"Back in those days, there weren't all that many good bands around. And along came this new Swedish act, sounding like Bathory! Damn, I knew that I had to get to know this guy."

Through their correspondence, Metalion and Pelle became good friends and begun having regular phone conversations.

"He could call me at 1 or 2 o'clock in the morning and then talk for four hours. He tried calling Mayhem as well, but Øystein had a pretty odd dialect, so Dead didn't really understand what he said."

Over the course of their many conversations, Metalion and Pelle touched on a great deal of subjects. The Stockholm scene, Bathory, and Pelle's increasing discontent with the situation in Morbid. The other members didn't share his uncompromising ideas, and he was frustrated. No band in Stockholm was hard enough.

"I spoke to Euronymous over the phone and he explained his idea for the most brutal stage show, and we discussed the problem with everybody wanting everything to be so normal, boring, and wimpy. We were in total agreement that I should come over and try out a few rehearsals, to find out if I fit in the band," Pelle said in an interview with *Slayer* that was published in 1994, three years after his death.

Metalion and Pelle also spoke about dying and the afterlife. Pelle shared a near-death experience from his childhood.

"He spoke of the light he'd seen. I think it affected him quite a lot," says Metalion.

In February 1988, 19-year-old Pelle landed at Fornebu Airport in Oslo. He'd barely spoken to anyone in Mayhem, and almost all communication had been via mail. Jørn and Øystein met Pelle at the airport, with no idea what to expect, as the decision to bring in the Swede was made in haste. When they spotted Pelle, they were relieved to see his long hair and metalhead wear. Their linguistic confusion persisted, however. Pelle barely understood a word the Norwegians were saying, so they switched to English.

Jørn remembers worrying about the possible effects the language issue might have. The most important aspect of a band is communication and maintaining an internal jargon. How was this supposed to work if they couldn't really understand each other?

On the way back from the airport, Jørn brought the Swede over to a friend's place. Pelle sat in a corner reading comics rather than engaging.

"Someone brought out hashish and the pipe was passed around. I think Pelle felt pressured to try it. Not a good idea. He went completely pale, and I understood never again to send the pipe in his direction unless he expressly asked for it. This was my first insight into who he was; he didn't like smoking pot or even cigarettes, for that matter. I barely ever saw him drink alcohol—perhaps twice in those three years."

Pelle spent a few days with Jørn at his parents' in Langhus, south of Oslo. After an additional few days in Øystein's home, he was housed in Mayhem's rehearsal space—an apartment in nearby Ski. Slowly but surely, the band members began to cross the language barrier and developed a gallows humor that ultimately brought them closer.

Pelle was soon settled in as Mayhem's new vocalist, and a bunch of new promo photos were sent out. In the pictures, Pelle wears white face paint with big black circles around his eyes, and black wisps trickle from his nostrils.

A few months after Pelle's arrival in Norway, Jan Axel "Hellhammer" Blomberg was brought in as the new drummer for Mayhem.

"The others told me he got on the plane just one day after the decision was made to bring him over. He had packed a bag with snus tobacco, plastic insects, a bunch of Dracula magazines, and books. He was a weird fucking guy but absolutely essential to us."

Even before Pelle stepped in as vocalist, Mayhem was a respected metal band. They were fast and heavy but still lacked the dark resonance and death-oriented ideology they'd later become known for. Up until this point, Jørn had been in charge of the lyrics, and he was primarily influenced by horror and splatter movies with a humorous undertone. As Mayhem began writing new material, Pelle focused on the lyrical content. The band's musical and ideological alignment shifted immediately. He described to Jørn a serious accident—an event that occurred when he was 10 years old—and of being pronounced clinically dead at the hospital.

"He was ice-skating and fell so badly, he ruptured his spleen." Jørn explains. "After that, he became obsessed with death and started collecting obituaries and pamphlets from funeral homes. When he started playing music later on, he simply called himself Dead. It was already a fully developed concept. As it was, I'd always felt the lyrics were our weakest link. But Pelle came up with stuff like 'Freezing Moon,' fantastic material about his own spiritual life. All the songs were about what happens after we die, and he strongly believed in an afterlife. That's how he conducted his life. Nothing was contrived," Jørn maintains.

Together with Øystein, the visionary leader of Mayhem, Pelle developed a framework for the band. Everything became harder, nastier, and more Satanic. Their plans for a new stage show involved severed pig's heads and blood.

"I want people to feel disgust when they see us live. I think of having rotting flesh in the air conditioner. Work out something more with cutting myself and have something more than only impaled pig heads, maybe an impaled cow or something," Pelle said in a 1990 interview with Swedish fanzine *Putrefaction*.

Pelle, who'd always been skinny, was eating less and less, with an aim to look as dead and pale as possible. His goal was to not have to use any makeup whatsoever. Jørn remembers Pelle's constant talk of death and of his near-death experience.

Pelle was back in Sweden during the summer of 1988 when the band's rehearsal place got burglarized. Guitar pedals were stolen, as well as Pelle's fake blood and comic books.

To compound the loss, the band was evicted as a result of the break-in.

Jørn often hung out in a nearby forest to shoot his rifle and had spotted an abandoned cabin. Pelle promptly moved in. The building had stood empty for 30 years, with no running water or electricity, but the summer was warm enough to make it habitable. In a gesture of solidarity, Jan Axel came to live there as well. The two spent the summer there, until a shotgun-wielding landowner showed up to forcibly evict the boys.

Like the other Mayhem members, Pelle survived on welfare support from the Norwegian state. Together, the band shifted their quarters to a camping village by the E6 highway, where social services housed some of their clients.

While searching for a new rehearsal place, the members spent most of their waking hours answering letters and sending demos to Mayhem fans all over the world. Expanding their distribution network and identifying owners of independent record stores in other countries was of the utmost importance.

Pelle connected with other musicians from the Scandinavian black metal scene. One of them was Tompa "Goatspell" Lindberg, vocalist of Gothenburg band Grotesque.

"We were corresponding for a long time and were pretty close. We had very similar views on things, both music and Satanism. He was fierce and quite romantic in his convictions," Lindberg says.

Tompa and Pelle met for the first time at Metalion's 1988 New Year's Eve party in Sarpsborg. Several musicians from Sweden and Norway attended this party.

"Pelle and Tompa together would result in complete chaos, especially back in those days," Metalion recalls. "They sat in my parents' bedroom cutting themselves. It looked terrible in there; we had to throw away everything with blood stains. Pelle went completely crazy that night—completely."

"Metalion's parents weren't home, so me and Dead sat on their bed drinking his mom's champagne," says Tompa Lindberg. "We were having intense discussions. 'We're going to Transylvania tonight, you and me, Tompa,' he said. Somewhere in that fog, I remember thinking, 'No, I don't think we'll be doing that this evening.' I remember it ended with me hiding in Metalion's room—not because Pelle was aggressive but because he was just totally fixed on the notion that we were undertaking this great journey together, since we were so close."

Pelle was running around with a knife and was so jacked-up that Metalion and Øystein had to wrestle him to the ground to contain him. René Jansen, of the Norwegian band Cadaver, brought out a pair of handcuffs and snapped them on Pelle in hopes of calming him down. The problem was that no one had keys for the cuffs, so they dragged Pelle to a nearby police station to get help removing them.

"But I remember then when we were going to sleep in the basement, we listened to *At War with Satan* by Venom," says Tompa. "Øystein and Dead slept in the same room, and all was well. It was a damn fine get-together."

Mayhem kept rehearsing and networking internationally, but progress was slow. Øystein established a record label, Deathlike Silence Productions, with the goal of releasing Mayhem's albums himself. The first title on DSP was the debut album by Sweden's Merciless. Pelle knew leading members Fredrik Karlén and Erik Wallin from metal parties in Stockholm. In June 1989, Merciless were holed up at Studio Tuna in Eskilstuna, recording *The Awakening*. Øystein, Pelle, and Jørn drove down from Oslo to visit, and Erik Wallin remembers noticing a change in Pelle.

"When we used to hang out at parties in Stockholm, he was more the kind of guy who liked to drink and have fun. He was never a dominant person; there were always others who were heard and seen more. But he was still different with the Norwegians— not as outgoing as before. In the studio, they mostly kept quiet, and we thought they were pretty weird. We were left wondering what happened to the old Pelle of Morbid. All three kept their distance."

Øystein was satisfied with what he heard in the studio, and the whole gang headed out for burgers once they wrapped up recording.

Pelle kept in touch with his Swedish friends, sometimes by phone but primarily by letters. There was a lot of correspondence with Jens Näsström from Morbid, who had carried on with a new vocalist since Pelle's departure. Gone was the death mysticism that characterized Morbid's earlier sound, and the band appeared to be lacking energy. Unbeknownst to the Mayhem members, Jens and Pelle planned a reunion with the old Morbid lineup. They even booked the Fryshuset venue in Stockholm for a concert on September 9, 1989, together with four of the most prominent Swedish metal acts of that era. Pelle sketched out a flyer, depicting a tombstone etched with the band's names and a moon with a bat suspended over it. In conjunction with the reunion show, the idea was to release an EP, with the working title *Ancient Morbidity*. The cover art depicted a monster with the wings of a bat. But in the end, the reunion was never realized, and the gig was canceled.

Things had at long last started moving in the Mayhem camp, however. The first live appearance with Pelle on vocals had been scheduled in Jessheim, just south of Oslo. The stage show was meticulously planned. For inspiration, they looked to a live video of Venom, featuring lots of explosives and fire.

Before the show, Mayhem procured several pigs' heads, which were to be impaled on stakes. Pelle buried his stage clothes in the forest, to imbue them with a stench of rot and decay. He's also kept a dead crow in a plastic bag and inhaled the fumes before the show, to evoke an authentic sensation of death. Onstage, Pelle got so immersed in his performance, he applied too much pressure while gouging his arm with a broken bottle.

"He slashed himself something fierce with that bottle, and blood was spurting on the audience," Jørn remembers. "The cut was way too deep. He had to leave the stage, and the local janitor patched him up with duct tape."

Yet Pelle took the stage again and made it through the final song before staggering off of the stage, close to fainting from blood loss. Jørn says Pelle never went to the hospital to get it properly taken care of. The scar was ugly and vicious.

"He used to cut himself quite frequently, but this was by far his worst scar. He only did it at concerts, I never saw him doing it privately. Øystein was very enthusiastic, but I didn't like it. I was always really nervous and tried slipping him dull knives. What he did was good enough; the audience didn't need to be more shocked than they already were."

Rumors of the spectacular Jessheim performance spread quickly, with stories not only of Pelle mauling himself but also of pigs' heads flying from the stage. When Metalion set up a *Slayer Mag* fundraising concert in Sarpsborg, near the Swedish border, Cadaver and Equinox played with Mayhem as the main attraction.

"It was in a venue called Furuheim," says Metalion. "People brought bagfuls of booze, but we were in charge of security ourselves, so all you had to do to be let in was to share the liquor. There was no trouble, though; everything went well. Mayhem had practically no stage lights that night, so the venue was really dark. The atmosphere was really something special."

Eager to keep pushing the boundaries with their live performances, Pelle wrote to Morgan Håkansson, suggesting a concert in Norrköping, Sweden, with Mayhem and Grotesque. He asked if he could come a few days in advance to suspend chunks of meat in the venue, in order to work up the sufficient stench.

"I even bought a butcher's saw for him to cut himself with on stage," says Morgan. "But everything turned out too complicated and the gig never happened."

Morgan was in frequent correspondence with Pelle and Øystein and noticed an increasing tension within Mayhem. For quite some time, the band had been looking for somewhere to live as well as rehearse. They finally wound up in a large house in Kråkstad, in the municipality of Ski. Jørn says he was quite shocked to find how nice the place was. The rooms boasted carved wooden details in the classic Norwegian style; in the basement was a fully equipped gym. There were multiple rooms for the band members to live in. The house was over 2,000 square feet, owned by the parents of an old classmate of Øystein's.

Despite the band now having a rehearsal place, the once-fruitful creative relationship between Øystein and Pelle had markedly soured. They bickered about the most trivial matters and hardly agreed on anything. Øystein poked fun at Pelle, wearing his patience thin. In turn, Pelle was gradually seeing through the constant assurances of studio recording sessions and upcoming tours: all stuff that never seemed to materialize. Jørn, a friend of Øystein's since childhood, was already used to the band leader's exaggerated plans.

"He'd always be fantasizing out loud, and Pelle started believing it. A lot of it was just insane bullshit. For example, Øystein had this idea to make tons of money by establishing a Deathlike Silence Productions office in Moscow as a front for selling computers to the authorities. He almost convinced me too. There were a lot of grand schemes."

Finally, one of the many plots actually led to something concrete. In November of 1990, Mayhem embarked on a European tour with shows in Germany, Greece, Turkey, and the Netherlands. The band traveled by train using Interrail passes. The first shows of the tour took place in the German cities of Zeitz, Leipzig, and Chemnitz. Afterward, the band members took the train back to Norway to pick up their welfare checks, then headed straight for a gig in the coastal Turkish city of İzmir. Jørn remembers Pelle having constant nose bleeds from malnutrition and general ill health.

In Turkey, nothing went according to plan. Electricity cut out several times during the gig, and the band was forced to bribe the promoters to turn it back on. After the concert, they didn't get paid.

"The equipment was shit and the people just hopeless," Jan Axel says. "There were no accommodations booked for us, and we got into an argument with Turkish customs. To top it all off, Pelle had his wallet stolen on the train. I've never been so miserable in my entire life."

The Ankara show was canceled due to the Gulf War. Also, while scheduling the tour back in Norway, Pelle misunderstood a letter, believing a Greek date to have been canceled as well, so the band headed straight to the Netherlands. Since they arrived three days early, the promoter—Bob Bagchus from Dutch band Asphyx—wasn't at home. The remaining tour was canceled, and Mayhem traveled back to Norway again.

Back on Norwegian soil, it was quite clear that the band once again found itself at a standstill.

"Pelle was stuck in the house," Jørn says. "The rest of us had families close by that we could visit for dinner or to get away for a few days. Pelle didn't. He had no way of escaping to the world outside the band, so his situation kept intensifying."

Come springtime, tensions in the house were escalating. Jan Axel recalls constant fights between Pelle, Øystein, and himself.

"Øystein told me Pelle had gone insane and was impossible to live with. Pelle said he wanted to go home. They almost started hating each other toward the end."

When conflicts in the house became unbearable, Pelle sometimes slept in the forest to get away from Øystein.

Back in Sweden, the family worried. Every time Pelle would visit, they'd notice his radical weight loss and his disaffection. They wanted desperately to help him. When his parents discovered all the money they'd wired to Norway for groceries had instead been used to ship Mayhem demos, they cut him off financially.

His father came to Norway a few times to talk and check up on him. The final trip was in March of 1991.

Jan Axel was one of the last people to speak to Pelle. They ran into each other at the Ski train station two days before Pelle's suicide. Pelle mentioned that he'd bought a new knife. This detail in itself was nothing out of the ordinary, but during the short conversation, he also describes its sharpness several times.

As far as Jørn knows, the last person to see Pelle alive was their neighbor, the only resident in the area they'd had any contact with.

"He later told us that for the first time in a long while, Pelle had seemed really happy."

Jørn Stubberud suggests a trip to the house in Kråkstad. He guides us through Ski, a small community with a remarkable number of roundabouts, pointing out different buildings with historical importance to Mayhem. His grandmother's house where he lived for several years, Øystein's childhood home on Bekkestien, and the grocery store that's a 5-minute walk from the Kråkstad house. There also used to be a post office here.

"That's where we sent all of our correspondence from."

As we approach the big red wooden house at the edge of the forest, we notice someone moving in the garage. Jørn tells us to keep driving without slowing down.

"It's not a good idea to show up here with Swedish plates. They've had quite a lot of black metal tourism here over the years. Just keep driving," he says, crouching in the back seat.

The house is still owned by the same family as in 1991. They've been quite understanding about the curiosity the place evokes. On one occasion, they even let a fan in and showed him the house. He had hidden a camcorder in a gym bag and the footage later surfaced in a Mayhem documentary.

"That's Pelle's bedroom."

Jørn nods toward a window facing the forest. Underneath is the brown garage on which Øystein climbed to peek into the room.

Jørn points to a church roof sticking up behind the trees in the distance, on the other side of the village.

"That's where the phone booth is, the one Øystein drove to when he called the cops. It's about three miles from here."

Despite the fact that more than 25 years have passed since Pelle Ohlin ended his life, he still evokes powerful emotions in his old friends. Many declined our request to interview them for this book. Pelle's Swedish friends were shocked by his suicide, and many are also still upset that Øystein exploited his death for personal gain. Every time *Dawn of the Black Hearts* shows up in a record store or the picture of Pelle's dead body is published online, they are reminded of what went down, and their anger is renewed. Old friends have demanded that record stores pull the bootleg album from their shelves.

When *Sweden Rock Magazine* used the album's cover image to illustrate a history-oriented article in 2006, editor Erik Thompson received a letter accusing him of being tasteless and disrespecting the dead.

Jens Näsström, bass player of Morbid and one of Pelle's closest friends, gets in touch with us six months after having first declined an interview. He's changed his mind. These days, he works as a psychologist in the town of Strängnäs, and he feels the myth of the Dead persona has grown to proportions too absurd to combat with silence.

"Psychologically speaking, something happens when people idealize and project themselves onto others, and it is very obvious in this case. The myth of Dead has become an egregore, a kind of psychic entity that's taken on a life of its own. It certainly draws details from the real Pelle but also exhibits traits he never had. For instance, he's often portrayed as lacking any humor and being antisocial."

Most of Pelle's Swedish friends are bewildered by the rumors and myths that have been twisted into pseudo-truths by documentaries, books, and articles on the internet. They don't recognize their old friend in these stories at all. Johnny Hedlund, vocalist and bass player of Unleashed, hung out regularly with Pelle in the years prior to his move to Norway. He remembers him as an easygoing guy who attended all the wild parties and would often spend the night, sleeping under Johnny's living room table.

"What we kept hearing and reading after he moved to Norway wasn't anything I or Fredrik Lindgren, who also knew him well, could relate to at all. You can't even comment on it," Johnny says.

Pelle's brother, Anders Ohlin, was also hesitant to speak to us at first, but we agreed to meet and test the waters. We soon discovered that the death of his older brother still affects him deeply. The night before the interview, he'd been at a party, drinking champagne. Despite the festivities, he woke up at 5 a.m. unable to go back to sleep. He describes feeling a knot in his stomach after we called, a sense of both curiosity and hesitation. He first consulted his mother, then his half-brother Daniel—both were skeptical.

Ultimately, he's not all that concerned with them—Anders says he wants to tell the story for his own sake.

"When I was studying to become an architect a few years ago, I'd walk past an exclusive art gallery in Stockholm. Suddenly, they had giant images of my brother and his band on display. There were a few photos of them drinking beer on the hood of a car, as well as a few live pictures."

Anders went inside and was told this was an exhibition by the Norwegian artist Bjarne Melgaard.

"Some woman explained to me that this Dead character was an unbelievably evil person and then proceeded to spout more absolute nonsense. 'What on earth is she babbling about?' I thought. Is this how he is to be remembered, as an evil and vicious person? That's not the full picture."

The mythification is problematic, since the entire foundation of what Pelle wanted to do is built on pushing boundaries further than anyone had before. Should the one-sided image of a merciless metalhead crucifying mice be left to thrive, or should some nuance be allowed in as well? After all, these fictions have interfered with the grieving process.

"It's incredibly frustrating, not being able to answer what's true and what's not. Because I don't know. In these circles, everything is about provocation. I've been really angry with him; he's not the one left suffering from everything that he helped build," Anders says, before turning silent for a moment.

"To be honest, I don't think I've properly processed his death yet. I was angry with him, and then I pushed it all aside. In hindsight, perhaps that wasn't the best approach. That's probably why that knot is still there in my gut, the one I feel when someone calls to ask if I am the brother of Dead."

Why did Pelle Ohlin, of all people, become such an icon of Scandinavian black metal? What made him the pioneer who would inspire the aesthetic frameworks for an entire genre?

Per Yngve Ohlin was born in Stockholm on January 16, 1969. He was the first child in a family that would eventually include a sister, a brother, and two half-brothers. He grew up in the suburb of Västerhaninge, half an hour south of Stockholm by train.

Early on, Pelle showed signs of being a bit different from his friends.

"He was quite eccentric," says Anders. "You could say that he was very pragmatic. He would always strive in one direction. For better or worse, he was unable to multitask. When engaging in something, he worked incredibly hard on it and always saw it to completion. But he had difficulty determining if the goal was feasible or even possible at all."

Pelle was unpredictable even as a child. One of the favorite family stories tells of a young Pelle, then a member of the Nature and Youth Sweden association, pointing at a lady wearing leopard fur on the train. He demanded to know if it was real or fake. The woman's face reddened, but she didn't answer. So Pelle asked again, this time raising his voice. "I said, is it real or fake?"

When his parents had guests, they would often worry that he'd say something inappropriate. Other parents considered him a bit odd, and he would often be blamed for mischief that other kids could just as likely have caused.

"My dad once told me that Pelle had been playing with one of his best friends but came home unusually early. Pelle then said his friend's mother had told him, 'All right, Pelle, you have to go home now because Fredrik is having his birthday party.' He wasn't invited. He didn't seem to care at all and just wanted to play with his Legos, but our dad took it hard," says Anders.

Pelle's interest in music grew gradually and exploded when metal became prominent in the early '80s. The brothers would read about bands like Kiss, Venom, and W.A.S.P. in the Swedish music magazine *OKEJ*. Like other kids hooked on metal, Pelle immersed himself in everything the genre offered.

Soon all forms of pleasant and soft music were out the window, and an arms race of sorts had begun—everything had to be increasingly hard and wild, from hard rock to heavy metal to thrash and speed. At the same time, Pelle developed a feverish passion for horror movies, the gorier the better. He'd always been fascinated by comic books and treasured his collection of *Chock*, a Swedish magazine reprinting the stories from American horror comics *Creepy* and *Eerie*. He was constantly drawing, primarily monsters and bomber planes.

As Pelle entered his teens, his parents divorced and the family broke up. Anders remembers the divorce as difficult and that Pelle took it hardest of the children. After having stayed with his father for two months, he refused to live with his mother. His parents had to drag him there, and he was furious. Then the same thing happened when he was supposed to go back to his dad.

"He came and went in the house like a cat. Everyone wanted to have him. He had taken the worst blow in the breakup, so I suppose having him in your home was some small victory for our parents. Everything became black and white. It wasn't until Pelle died that my parents started talking again; it was only then we found peace in the family."

At the same time, problems surfaced at school. In the fall of 1982, Pelle started 7th grade at Ribbyskolan in Västerhaninge. After having gone through middle school in a tight-knit class, he found himself in unfamiliar surroundings with entirely new factions, where neither he nor his many quirks were accepted.

"When junior high school started, he was bullied mercilessly," Anders says. "You were either into synth music or hard rock back in those days—everything was very categorical. But Pelle didn't fit in anywhere, so I suppose singling him out was easy. There was a whole gang of them, harassing and beating him up all the time. His old classmates from middle school didn't have the strength to back him up either."

Around this time, the famed near-death experience occurred, an event that would have tremendous impact on Pelle. But it was no skating accident as he would later tell Jørn, nor was it from eating poisonous mushrooms, as another friend was told. Anders has learned that Pelle came home earlier from school one day. He said that he'd thrown up and needed to get some rest.

"By sheer coincidence, our stepmother was home. Thinking he looked pale, she went to check on him and found him unconscious without a pulse. She's a nurse and immediately realized things were serious. She gave him CPR until the ambulance arrived."

First, Pelle said that he slipped on ice outside school and elbowed himself in the stomach. However, it was soon discovered he'd been assaulted by a gang from school. He'd been beaten so badly, his spleen was ruptured. He was hospitalized for several days.

Back in school, counselors tried to find the best solution for Pelle. The decision was made to transfer him to another school. He ended up in a good class and quickly made several friends who shared his interest in music. Before long, he declared to the family that he had formed a band. They were quite surprised, since he played no instruments.

Being that Pelle was the driving force in the band, someone suggested the name Ohlin Metal.

"He designed a really cool logo for the band, which he went around spraying all over Västerhaninge. Our dad noticed it at the train station, and since it said both *Ohlin* and *metal*, he immediately identified Pelle as the culprit. He'd been terribly embarrassed waiting for the train with his neighbors," Anders remembers.

Despite Pelle thriving in the new school and having found new friends, the beating affected him deeply. Anders recalls Pelle being very scared and afraid to go outside. He watched kung fu movies and even started taking aikido classes.

"But perhaps it was our father who persuaded him to do that."

Pelle's interest in music and horror movies took up an increasing amount of his time. When the rest of the family was on vacation, he covered his side of the room he shared with Anders in cobwebs bought at a costume shop.

"My mother said: 'Okay, and what's this supposed to be?' I was absolutely petrified of the dark and didn't want to sleep in there."

Pelle let his grades slip in school and grew his hair long, much to the distress of his parents. His fascination for the morbidity deepened further. One day, Anders searched through the pockets of his brother's denim jacket looking for candy. Instead, he found a dead frog.

His interest in war had been present since childhood, but mostly manifested itself in drawings of bomber planes. Now the fascination took on new proportions. Pelle applied for voluntary military training, hoping to learn how to shoot a submachine gun. Instead, the first day was spent orienteering in the woods. Pelle defected in anger.

"Officers shouting at him wasn't really something that suited Pelle. He was very passive and incredibly calm. You could probably perceive him being a bit slow," says Anders.

Pelle began heading into central Stockholm to hang out at the record shop Heavy Sound, by now a hub for the emerging thrash and death metal scene. He brought home new albums, always harder and faster. Most importantly, he discovered Bathory.

One day, he saw a note pinned to the wall in the store. A band from Åkersberga, outside Stockholm, were looking for a vocalist and bass player. They called themselves

Armageddon and mentioned Slayer as an influence. Pelle called the number and established first contact with guitar player John Hagström.

"We spoke over the phone, and he was excited we were also into heavier music. There weren't all that many bands back then," says John.

The first rehearsal took place in the music classroom of a school in Åkersberga. Pelle, John, and John's neighbor Sandro Cajander from Mefisto, one of the early thrash bands in Stockholm, were present. Things fell into place from the very start.

The band changed its name to Scapegoat. In the logo, the letter G had horns and a goatee. Pelle became known as Geten—the goat. Sandro left the band at an early stage. New members came and went, as Pelle's personal views and tastes set the agenda. From the very beginning, his outline for the band was strict and fully formed.

"There were no discussions about what to sing or how it should sound; he knew exactly," says John. "He led the band from the very first day and had strong convictions. He was a bit odd. Very gentle, but at the same time trying to give the impression that he was evil."

Pelle demanded a lot from his bandmates, especially the guitar players, and Scapegoat never really got off the ground. Instead, he formed a new band with John called Morbid. This time, the music was even heavier. Through another notice at Heavy Sound, Pelle found drummer Lars Göran "L-G" Petrov, who later became hugely successful as the vocalist of Entombed. During the summer of 1986, Pelle also encountered bass player Jens Näsström at a concert in the Kungsträdgården park in Stockholm. The original line-up of Morbid was now complete.

"It really pains me to say that it was a hairspray glam band called Treat playing in the park that night," says Jens. "But there was nothing else. We were too young to be let into the bars, and there were hardly any youth centers left. The punk rock place Ultra House was all there was. A free concert in central Stockholm—what else are you going to do on a Saturday afternoon? At least there'd be the chance of hanging out with other thrashers."

Despite being in their teens, neither Jens nor Pelle attended high school. Instead, they tended to hang out at Jens' place on Fridhemsplan. The two were brought closer by their theatrical ambitions for Morbid and their mutual interest in darker subjects. They took on alter egos for the band. Pelle adopted the Dead persona and started painting his face white with black circles around the eyes. He wore a T-shirt with cut-out obituaries stapled to it. Jens called himself Dr. Schitz and wore a doctor's coat and an IV at Morbid's first concert, at Ultra House in April of 1987.

Mutual friends Nils "Nisse" Gullbrandsson and Rikard "Rille" Synstad would often hang out with the band at rehearsals and remember the concert as chaotic. Morbid had rented a fog machine that no one knew how to work properly.

"Someone at this punk venue operated the machine, and he went full blast. He just kept pressing and pressing the button," says Rille. "Soon, you couldn't even see the stage, and we ended up headbanging with our backs facing the band."

"They got off to kind of a rocky start," Nisse continues. "Ultra House had the world's smallest stage. But Morbid achieved instant cult status."

The band rehearsed three times per week, with Pelle demanding greatness from the other members. They recruited technically skilled guitar player Uffe Cederlund, who would also go on to play with Entombed. John Hagström remembers Pelle getting extremely annoyed if someone made a mistake. If a riff wasn't tight enough, he might force the band to play the song 10 times in a row until he was satisfied.

During 1987, Morbid played several live shows. Pelle wrote the band's most popular song, "Disgusting Semla." A semla is a seasonal Scandinavian pastry: a sweet bun filled with cream and almond paste. While performing it, Jens threw semlas into the audience, sometimes filled with cream, sometimes with oatmeal if money was tight.

At a gig at the Birkagården youth center, the band decorated the stage with candles and a coffin borrowed from Sveriges Television, where Uffe Cederlund's father worked as scenographer. Pelle had created a tape with the audio from the crucifix masturbation scene in *The Exorcist* and crawled out of the casket with the fog machine on full blast.

Jens Näsström says that Pelle possessed an unusually strong ability to formulate himself artistically.

"It's very difficult to put into words, but I think that's one of the aspects people have picked up on. It was immediately evident that this was not contrived; nothing he did was to look cool. He was genuinely inspired, and with true connection like that comes a real sense of power. He could walk on stage and people were laughing for 15 seconds, and then they weren't laughing anymore. They realized, 'Wow, something's going on here.' This guy is wearing face paint, that coffin is turned over, there's 15 people in the audience, and you're in the middle of a living room. There is nowhere to hide."

Morbid becomes associated with these elaborate—at least for the time and place—stage performances. That, and the strange and terrifying impression Pelle left on people. He worked hard at staying quiet and peculiar, he never laughed out loud, and he wouldn't tell jokes if there was someone new nearby. Petrov describes Pelle as black metal in every aspect.

"Always the same clothes: denim jacket with patches, bullet belts, and studs. Bathory was the only band worth listening to. In that regard, he was uncompromising. It had to be the right music in the tape deck, always. When we were alone, we'd be laughing all the time, and then when heading out, the mask of evil came on again."

While several old friends speak of Pelle's fascination with horror and evil as being primarily an image, many remember him as having very peculiar thoughts and ideas.

"I remember once, on the way home in the middle of the night, he had walked into a cemetery," says Nisse. "Who the hell even does that? You just don't. He looked at all the graves and thought, 'Hmm, imagine if the graves had these huge eject buttons, and when you pressed them, the corpses would come flying out.' He would think about things like that. We would laugh at it intensely, but for him, it was a serious idea."

"He spoke a lot about death, even back in the Scapegoat days," says John Hagström. "But it never really occurred to me how serious it was. It was more that metal was something cool—at least I thought so. We never discussed his lyrics."

Anders Ohlin didn't give much thought to the content of his brother's lyrics either, but he remembers how Pelle would often speak about his near-death experience, even several years after it happened.

"He would talk about how he perceived it, that it was really weird and he couldn't figure it out. It was so unreal. Then he found out that he had actually been clinically dead. I don't think the fixation came back when it happened; he was more into bomber planes and metal back then. His obsession with death emerged later."

Pelle's primary idol was the one-man band, Bathory, the only really extreme Swedish metal band at the time. So, when Quorthon was scheduled for a signing session at Heavy Sound in 1987 to promote his third album, *Under the Sign of the Black Mark*, the members of Morbid all lined up at the store.

"The idolized image of Quorthon fell apart for a lot of people that day," says Nisse. "He came strolling in in sunglasses, wearing a leather jacket with metal trinkets hanging off it. He looked too much like a regular rock star. Someone took his picture and he gave the thumbs-up. What the hell is this? He wasn't evil enough!"

"He was like Yngwie Malmsteen," Rille adds.

"Pelle was incredibly disappointed," says Nisse. "He quickly diverted his attention to Norway and Mayhem. They became the new evil gods who replaced Bathory."

To express his disillusionment with Quorthon, Pelle wrote his former idol a letter.

"Once when we all were at Jens' place, we wondered where Pelle had gone off to," says Rille. "Turns out, he was down in the basement, about to vivisect a hamster. Jens was very upset."

"I was supposed to take pictures," says Nisse. "But once he started stabbing that poor hamster with his scalpel, I had to stop. I covered my ears; the squeaking screams were so awful. He was going to slice it up, nail it to a cross, and send it to Quorthon. That was the whole point. It was so fucking disgusting. And then he ended up not sending it. After a week, he left it in the reception at Bathory's record label. Given the putrid stench of that package, I imagine it probably went straight into the trash."

Back home, Pelle's family didn't hold a lot of sympathy for his intensifying interest in extreme music and horror. His parents believed metal music to be a harmful influence for his younger siblings, but above all, they worried that music took up all of his energy. Growing up in the socioeconomic reality of Sweden in the '50s, which valued a traditional education to fall back on, Pelle's grades were considered disastrous. He seemed completely uninterested in higher education and worked at a printing factory; all of his earnings were spent on microphones, stamps, records, and snus tobacco.

"They were provoked by how efficient and diligent he was when it came to music, while everything else fell apart—from grades to hygiene. While it was a source of grievance, they knew music wasn't something he could let go of; he would have nothing else left. It was the only thing in life that kept him going," Anders says.

"They were obviously proud of his achievements, though, like when Morbid released the demo and had their first gig at the Ultra House. My father filmed it without being asked to. I think he wanted to document it for the future. He probably thought this was something temporary—a funny old clip to show at Pelle's bachelor party."

In early December of 1987, Morbid entered the Heavy Load–owned studio Thunderload to record a demo. After two days of intense sessions, four songs were finished. The demo was aptly named *December Moon*. The cover was adorned with the bat-shaped Morbid logo and the words "*In Nomine Dei Nostri Satanas Luciferi Excelsi,*" an invocation used in Satanic rituals. Pelle and John copied tapes and headed to the post office in order to print booklets on a Xerox machine. John brought boxes of cassettes to Heavy Sound to sell at cost. Pelle, meanwhile, took care of the tape-trading scene, sending the demo abroad, to *Slayer Mag* and Mayhem, among many others.

"We dropped by Heavy Sound with new tapes once a week, about 15 or 20 every time," says John Hagström.

He estimates the demo sold a few hundred copies in total. Despite being pleased with the recording and enjoying playing with the band, John dropped out of Morbid in early 1988. He'd been offered a job in the telecom sector and no longer had time for rehearsals.

Pelle took the loss hard. To him, priorities outside of the band were unthinkable. Placing a job ahead of music wasn't in any way okay. Also, John wrote a lot of the material and was the musical anchor Pelle had played with from his very first day in a band. Disappointed, he began weighing his options.

Without anyone knowing about it, he'd been corresponding with the Norwegian members of Mayhem for some time. Only a few weeks after John's departure from Morbid, Pelle was on a flight to Oslo. Anders remembers his move happening so fast, the family barely realized what was going on.

"He told us that 'There's a really cool band in Norway. I have to head over to check them out—they're hard as hell.' We didn't understand anything. And then he was gone."

———

In late April 1991, Pelle Ohlin's funeral service was held in Österhaninge Church, a large old stone building from the 14th century. Even from a distance, you can tell that the steeple is a bit crooked, leaning back toward the nave. According to local folklore, the master builder was so devastated over the skewed result that he hanged himself in the tower.

Some friends misunderstood and went to the Skogskyrkogården cemetery on the day of the funeral, believing that the service was taking place there. However, Nisse and Rille, Lars Göran Petrov, Uffe Cederlund, Jens Näsström, John Hagström, and Fredrik Karlén from Merciless were present at Österhaninge, along with several others. The family had decided to omit psalms and instead play Rod Stewart's "I'm Sailing" and "Imagine" by John Lennon. After the funeral, coffee was served at Pelle's father's house in Vendelsö.

Jørn was the only member of Mayhem to fly in from Norway.

"I felt welcome, but when people started coming up to ask questions, I realized how little contact they must have had with Pelle over the past three years. That made me feel very uncomfortable. His uncle, for example, wanted to know how he had gotten hold of the gun. It wasn't a good experience."

If Pelle's friends were shocked by his suicide, few were actually surprised. After all, he called himself Dead and wrote lyrics exclusively about life after death. At the same time, he used to be happy and entertaining, even if his humor was always on the dark side.

The Norwegians were the least surprised.

"We'd spoken about him not feeling at home in this world," Metalion remembers. "I got the impression that there was plenty he didn't tell us. But he did give off certain signs, just little things, that contributed to my lack of surprise. In his letters, he'd often write that it was too cold in this world, and that probably had a lot to do with emotions. That people were cold."

Jørn was the only one of Pelle's Norwegian friends to stay in any form of contact with the family after his death. Metalion says that it was never an option for him to attend the funeral or speak to Pelle's friends and family.

"Back in those days, I wasn't really in touch with my emotions. You have to bear in mind that we were young men with aspirations of being tough. We didn't know how to behave when things like this happened. Most reacted by thinking it was ballsy and cool. It was difficult to process, because it was so new."

Few think that Pelle ended his life entirely by his own will. No one goes as far as claiming he was murdered, but almost everyone believes Øystein Aarseth drove Pelle to kill himself in different ways. Øystein would himself constantly feed the rumors of being involved in the suicide. Even close friends like Jan Axel and Jørn admit the possibility of Øystein having had a direct influence on Pelle's fate.

After the funeral, Swedish friends of Pelle's planned to avenge him by heading to Norway to beat the shit out of Øystein, but this never came to pass.

"That would have been difficult to live with," says Nisse. "But I think they exploited Pelle in every way they could. When they felt he was on his way back to Sweden, they drove him to end his life. Take things like the photos and everything afterwards—you have to be completely ice-cold to do something like that. I don't think that kind of an individual would have much difficulty in driving someone like Pelle over the edge. He was quite volatile already, as things were."

"Pelle always had the notion of becoming someone famous, and that it was only a matter of time until he'd get rewarded accordingly," says Anders. "He was obsessed with money, and I've been told that Øystein used this to manipulate him. 'Soon we'll have a record deal, and that will bring in the cash.' I think it was a heavy blow to Pelle that once things finally started happening, when they got good feedback from their concerts and a record deal, everything was too late and the band was falling apart. The only one who hadn't already realized it was Pelle himself. He must have felt so fucking disappointed— utterly devastated."

Metalion points out that it's important to separate Pelle as a person from the persona of Dead in Mayhem.

"Even if Pelle wanted things for Mayhem and had visions, he was also a human being. He couldn't be like Dead all of the time. I think that was the problem."

The Ski police remember the case clearly. A detective who's worked in the area for a long time mentions how it was never investigated as a murder, despite suspicions within law enforcement that it wasn't a regular suicide.

The police report has long since been archived and is no longer public.

The suicide letter is the only possession sent back from Norway to Pelle's family. Anders still keeps it in a plastic folder. The paper has yellowed and is stained with blood. The family never questioned his death as being anything other than a suicide, especially considering Pelle's emotional state at the time and the way the letter was written.

"A few days after Pelle killed himself, a package from him arrived for me in the mail containing *The Lord of the Rings*. He had borrowed the books from me, and I in turn had borrowed them from a friend. I'd been pestering him to return them. He included a note saying they were great, but he'd only had time to read one and a half. I thought I could sense a lot of Tolkien in that suicide note."

The shock of the suicide is still reverberating when the next tragedy strikes.

In the summer of 1993, roughly two years after Pelle's death, Øystein Aarseth is murdered in his Oslo apartment.

In May of 1994, Varg "Count Grishnackh" Vikernes, from one-man band Burzum and the temporary bass player of Mayhem, was sentenced to 21 years in prison for the murder. The motive was said to be an internal power struggle within the Norwegian black metal scene as well as a financial dispute between Øystein and Varg.

As if things weren't bad enough, two years later, the bootleg album *Dawn of the Black Hearts* surfaced, with Pelle's dead body on the cover.

Anders sees the photo for the first time in a record store. As per usual, he is browsing the Mayhem section and is initially happy to come across an album he hasn't seen. Then the horror hits him.

"I knew the photo existed but had purposely stayed away from it. Our family had never realized the photo was used on an album cover. I no longer browse the internet for anything related to Pelle, because that fucking picture is everywhere."

For many years, the family has been contacting websites that feature the image, asking them to remove it. Some have agreed; others have refused.

"Needless to say, I find it completely repulsive that Øystein photographed Pelle. But at the same time, I know how seriously they took all this. That's why I can somehow accept—no, not accept, but I can understand what drove them and what the idea was."

———

In early 2009, the old Morbid members had a few reunion get-togethers to which they invited Anders and his half-brother Daniel. They planned to gather all recorded material featuring Pelle for a compilation album. Anders also contacted Jørn, hoping to finally ask all the questions he's had about Pelle. He's wondered about a great many things but never felt ready to get the answers.

Later that same spring, Mayhem are playing Stockholm as part of their 25th anniversary tour, and Jørn and Anders meet for the first time since the funeral. Mayhem are staying at a shabby hotel, and Anders and Daniel sit with Jørn and Jan Axel for several hours. The following day, we catch up at the Mayhem concert at the Klubben venue.

Vocalist Attila Csihar took over after Pelle and sang his lyrics on the *De Mysteriis Dom Sathanas* album. He enters the smoke-filled stage wearing a priest's robe, swaying a chalice with incense burning in it, while chanting in a guttural voice. It's the first time that Anders has seen Mayhem live. Leaning against a wall, he calmly watches the stage. He's a bit tired after a long night in the hotel bar the evening before.

"I was nervous as all hell, but it felt good to meet them. It was almost like meeting a part of Pelle again—very strange. We talked way past midnight and drank horrible, cheap beer."

Since Øystein didn't have a will when he was murdered, all of his belongings went to his parents, as did legal rights for Mayhem. For a few months, Anders has been in touch with Øystein's father, Helge Aarseth, about transferring the rights to the picture of Pelle's corpse.

"Writing those letters was like stabbing myself in the arm. I was prepared for Helge freaking out completely, but he's been very cooperative. He's not too happy about that picture either. I know he burned the remaining photos he found."

His plan is to obtain the legal rights to the image and use this to combat the bootleg copies of *Dawn of the Black Hearts* that are still in circulation to this day. It's said to be one of the most bootlegged metal albums of all time.

After the gig, Jørn is in a terrible mood. His pupils are the size of dinner plates as he shouts, "No interviews!" so we sit down with Jan Axel in an adjacent room.

Mayhem will always be associated with the deaths in the band. Several documentaries have been made about the dramatic story, and interest in Pelle shows no signs of waning. The few short clips of him on YouTube are still very popular. Like the one with Quorthon signing Pelle's Bathory album or Pelle goofing around outside the cabin in the woods—and above all, the music video for the Candlemass song "Bewitched," where Pelle can be seen doing the doom dance with several other young members of the Stockholm metal scene. The video was made by Jonas Åkerlund.

In 2007, Morgan Håkansson sold his letters and drawings from Pelle and Øystein on eBay. Each document fetched several hundred dollars each. He's kept the skull fragments, though. Jan Axel has lost the one piece he wore in a leather strap across his neck.

"It disappeared during a Darkthrone party at Fenriz's place. I was banging my head when the necklace got stuck in a medieval axe mounted on the wall, and after that, it was nowhere to be found."

He shrugs his shoulders, his dark locks bobbing up and down, and adds that it was probably for the best.

"I thought the necklace was a nice gesture to honor a close friend. In our world, everything was different. What we thought was fully normal back then, regular people— including myself these days—would find completely insane."

When Mayhem were on a South American tour in 2008, Jørn tried contacting Bull Metal of the Colombian band Masacre, to, in his own words, have a serious talk about *Dawn of the Black Hearts*. But Bull Metal was dead. "From AIDS," says Jørn, who's now entered the room to check his email.

"Last night was something special, meeting Anders and Daniel. I had already gathered from our phone calls that they are calm people. It played out exactly as I had imagined," he says.

"They look a lot like Pelle," says Jan Axel.

Jørn admits that he'd been worrying about which anecdotes he would tell, and what the brothers might actually want to know.

"They asked to hear stories about him and had several very specific questions. It felt good. Remember, they're only now able to start really grieving, so many fucking years later. They've seriously had it rough."

Mayhem's tour manager sticks his head in and informs the band that they were supposed to have left the premises 10 minutes ago. Jørn sighs deeply. He's tired and just wants to go back to the hotel.

"I was devastated, so I can barely imagine how the family must have taken it. Keeping in touch is the least we can do for them."

The small graveyard surrounding the Österhaninge Church is beautiful. There is only room for a few graves, and most are from the 19th century. Swedish author and early feminist pioneer Fredrika Bremer rests behind a low iron fence.

Beyond the fields, further into the woods, lies the Österhaninge cemetery, a burial ground of several acres. In one of the many rows of graves stands a discreet, weather-worn rock in uneven red granite. It is adorned with a medieval Viking cross. This is the resting place of Pelle Dead, or "Pelle Ohlin," according to the engraving. In front of it, someone has placed a full tin of snus.

PELLE'S SUICIDE LETTER:

The famous line: Excuse the blood, but I have slit my wrists and throat. My intention was to die in the forest, so it would take a few days before I was eventually found. I belong in the forest, and I always have. My reasons for this will not be understood by anyone. To give some semblance of an explanation: I'm not human, this is just a dream and I will soon wake up. It was too cold and the blood kept coagulating, plus my new knife was too dull. If I can't die from the knife, I'll blow my head off. I don't really know. I left all my lyrics by "Let the good times roll"—plus the remaining money. Whoever finds it can have it. As my final greeting I hereby present Life Eternal. Do whatever you want with the damn thing.

/Pelle

This didn't come to me now, but seventeen years ago.

During the process of writing this book, Anders Ohlin got in touch with Jens Näsström, and together, they gathered old Morbid members and friends of Pelle. They soon received an offer concerning any unreleased material. In April 2011, the triple album Year of the Goat was released, compiled by former members of Morbid in collaboration with Anders and Daniel Ohlin. The proceeds from the album sales will go toward a scholarship fund.

To commemorate the release, a private party was held at Kafé 44 in Stockholm. The first recipient of the scholarship was Jon "Metalion" Kristiansen, for his work with Slayer Mag. The evening concluded with a performance by Morbid tribute band Mörbit including Erik Danielsson (Watain), Erik Wallin (Merciless), Erik Gustafsson (Nifelheim), David Blomqvist (Dismember), and Peter Stjärnvind (Nifelheim). Anders and Daniel Ohlin were in the audience, together with their older sister, Anna Ohlin.

In 2015 Jørn Stubberud published the book, The Death Archives.

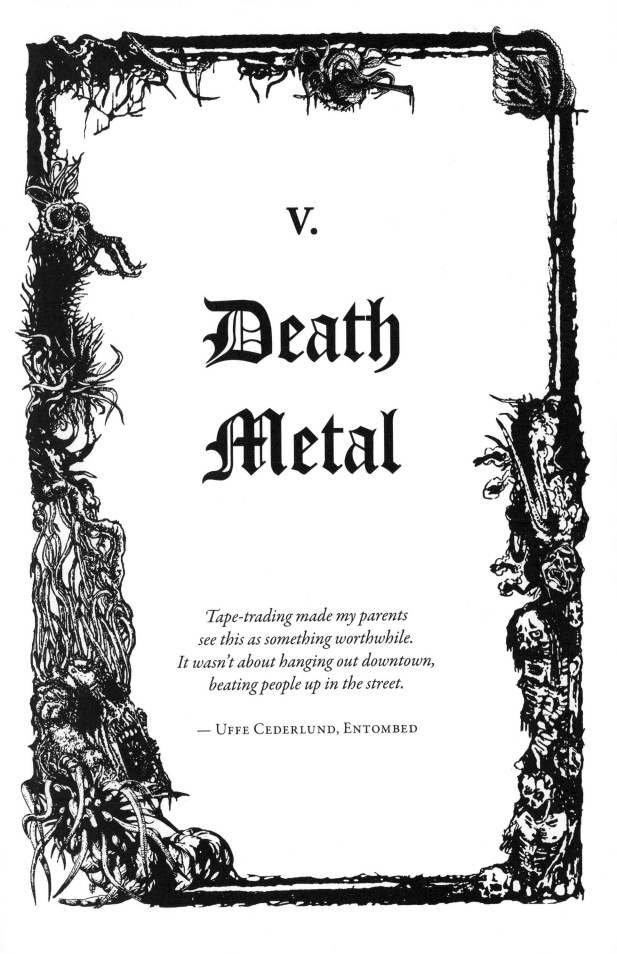

V.

Death
Metal

*Tape-trading made my parents
see this as something worthwhile.
It wasn't about hanging out downtown,
beating people up in the street.*

— UFFE CEDERLUND, ENTOMBED

T HE HISTORY OF ROCK is the tale of a rule book rewritten time and time again. The distorted guitar sound of British band The Kinks in the late '60s was one early milestone: achieved by lead guitarist Dave Davies slicing his speaker cone with a razor blade, the sound inspired a whole new generation of musicians to create harder music. Black Sabbath contributed another vitally important ingredient by opening their debut album in 1970 with the infamous dissonant tritone chord—often referred to as "the Devil's interval."

A different musical revolution came to life (or death) in the late '80s. Once thrash metal was no longer considered extreme enough, death metal was born from an amalgamation of hardcore punk and metal.

Music journalist Håkan Persson at Swedish Radio remembers the growth of death metal as a unique cultural phenomenon.

"When death metal emerged, it marked the first time Swedish musicians were spearheading a new music style. They were part of a worldwide movement, with demo cassettes being sent back and forth across the globe. Death metal wasn't just something you followed and imitated; it was molded as much in Sweden as in the United States, England, or South America."

———

Niklas "Nicke" Andersson was born in 1972 and grew up in the Stockholm suburbs of Alby and Vårberg. Like so many other kids of his generation, he was a huge Kiss fan. When Nicke and his best friend, Kenny Håkansson, found albums by The Damned and The Ramones in Kenny's father's record collection, the cartoonish American shock rockers found themselves facing fierce competition. The two friends decided to become punk rockers instead.

Every summer in the mid-'80s, Nicke was sent to a summer camp called Smedsbo in the province of Dalarna. Here, he befriended Alex Hellid and Leif Cuzner from Kista, on the opposite side of Stockholm. Nicke became the summer camp's punk evangelist, giving mohawks to the other campers. His interest in punk eventually morphed into a fascination with extreme bands with Satanic images, such as Bathory, Hellhammer from Switzerland, and the UK outfit Venom. His friends soon picked up on these groups as well.

The camp had instruments available, and the friends began playing together as Sons of Satan. During their last Smedsbo summer, in 1986, one of them stole a huge tube of contact cement, squirted a pentagram on the wall of a nearby barn, and set it on fire. The flames didn't spread, but the young city boys were caught in the act and forced to run through the woods, chased by an angry farmer. Today, Nicke Andersson laughs at the anecdote.

"We could have burned that old house down! You have to remember, we'd only just reached puberty, so I think it was okay. Not torching a barn, of course, but thinking burning pentagrams are cool."

Back in the city, Nicke soon found his way to the Heavy Sound record store and ventured into new musical territory, his prime selection criteria being "as fast as possible!" Heavy Sound listed new releases followed by a letter combination: HR meant hard rock, while SM stood for speed metal. The owners didn't really consider speed metal to be real music, but these were the records Nicke Andersson listened to first.

"If it wasn't fast enough, I'd turn it off right away."

His musical discoveries included American bands Cryptic Slaughter, D.R.I., and Wehrmacht. These were immediately followed by excited phone calls as Nicke informed his friends that he'd found the fastest bands in the world.

"It didn't matter if it was punk, hardcore, or metal—we loved any music that was fast enough to knock the wind out of you. I wish I'd recorded our conversations."

Many of the bands he found played a fusion of metal and hardcore, sometimes called crossover. Inspired by this music and its raw aesthetics, Nicke Andersson formed Brainwarp with his summer camp friends.

At Heavy Sound, Nicke also discovered underground fanzines containing demo pages with addresses for the featured bands.

"You could write to them yourself and order their demos, so we started ordering—a lot. During lunch breaks in school, I'd drop by home to look for the postman. If he passed my door without delivering anything, I'd think, 'NOOO, I was expecting a demo today! I've ordered fucking loads of them!'"

Once demos started turning up, the floodgates were open.

"Tapes were pouring in. We began coordinating our orders and then copying from each other. Suddenly, we had quite a collection."

Ulf "Uffe" Cederlund, one year older than Nicke, grew up a few subway stations further north, in Bredäng. When his friend Lars Göran "L-G" Petrov returned home from summer camp in 1983, he brought a musical discovery with him that turned Uffe's taste in music completely upside down.

"He said, 'You have to hear this—you're gonna shit your pants!' and then he played me Metallica's *Kill 'Em All*. That album changed my entire understanding of music."

Prior to this, Uffe and L-G primarily listened to heavy metal bands, such as Iron Maiden and Accept. The manner in which Metallica combined the down-to-earth and the extreme rejuvenated Uffe's interest in metal.

Inspired by Bathory and Metallica's first albums, the friends started several bands. They had their 1985 live debut in the Bredäng school auditorium in front of a horrified congregation of classmates and teachers.

Despite several people in the audience booing, Uffe remembers a sense of triumph.

"It was cool to have done it, but despite a population of 15,000 people, we were almost the only metalheads in Bredäng. Everyone else listened to Frankie Goes to Hollywood and Howard Jones."

Just as quickly as Uffe embraced Metallica, he disowned them when he discovered a ballad on their second album. He kept searching and found the compilation albums *Metal Massacre* and *Speed Kills*, with bands like the Canadians Razor and Exciter, as well as Slayer and Possessed from California.

When Uffe and L-G needed a bass player for their new band, Blasphemy, they put up a notice at Heavy Sound. With a voice that had yet to break, the first person who responded to their ad introduced himself as a guitarist. His name was Nicke Andersson.

Through Nicke, Uffe and L-G got to know other metalheads for the first time. Brainwarp had recorded a few rehearsal demos, and Nicke hung out with Kenny and Råttan ("The Rat"), whose real name is Fred Estby.

"L-G thought it was really cool to meet people who had long hair and looked even more metal than we did," Uffe recalls. "We were nerdy and didn't even have leather jackets. If someone wore a Kreator shirt back then, it would be a sensation."

In the mid-'80s, as quickly as it had opened new musical doors, thrash became uninteresting to many of the youngsters it targeted. These kids were always on the lookout for increasingly brutal expressions. All over the world, bands were ready to take metal one step further. Most of them were very young and had a distinct sound. Between 1986 and 1988, the musical development was lightning-fast. Uffe Cederlund thinks the primary reason was that everyone was writing letters to each other.

"Suddenly, you'd get cassettes with killer death metal bands like Master and Repulsion or Pentagram from Chile—even if no one was calling it death metal at the time. There were amazing bands everywhere."

The circulation of demo cassettes between fans was called tape-trading, and it became the group's primary interest. Nicke also recalls starting a fanzine called *Chickenshit*. While never even completing the first issue, it was a great way to get free demos from all over the world.

"That's how we were introduced to the whole death metal thing, because you'd never find this music on vinyl back then."

The term *death metal* has multiple origins. Tom G. Warrior of Switzerland's Hellhammer started a fanzine called *Death Metal* as early as 1983, and the band was included on a compilation album with the same name in 1984. Right before Christmas that year, the American band Death began calling their music style "corpse-grinding death metal." In 1985, Possessed named the final song on their incredibly influential debut, *Seven Churches*, "Death Metal." That album also led the way toward a significantly rawer sound than that of contemporary thrash metal records.

Death finally unleashed their debut album, *Scream Bloody Gore*, in 1987. It is often regarded as the first pure death metal album, alongside *Season of the Dead* by American band Necrophagia, released a few weeks earlier. Although the album was recorded in California, Death was primarily based in Florida, as were Morbid Angel, Obituary, Atheist, Massacre, and later Deicide and Cannibal Corpse. This made the Sunshine State one of the two focal points of the death metal world. The second was soon to become Sweden.

By 1988, these albums and the myriad cassette demos had made an immense impact on the fledgling Swedish underground scene. Among fans and musicians alike, terms like *thrash*, *speed*, or *death* were not really important yet. Many saw these diverse genres as simply different aspects of brutal metal. The album that ultimately changed everything was the 1989 debut by American band Morbid Angel. As much as *Altars of Madness* established the death metal genre even further, it also put the golden age of thrash to an end. By that time, the first albums by American acts Obituary and Autopsy had also found distribution in Sweden.

The music was characterized by heavily distorted and down-tuned instruments, a deep and atonal vocal style called growling, and fast tempos. Some of the bands used blast beats—an ultra-fast drum pattern.

The term *blast beat* is said to have been coined by England's Napalm Death somewhere around 1987. They were the primary advocates of grindcore—a super-fast form of hardcore punk, with blast beats as a rhythmical foundation. In his book *Swedish Death Metal*, author Daniel Ekeroth suggests that the earliest recording featuring blast beats might actually be the 1982 demo *How Could Hardcore Be Any Worse*, by Swedish band Asocial from Hedemora.

Tompa Lindberg, from the suburb of Billdal south of Gothenburg, was one of Nicke Andersson's tape-trading buddies in the '80s. When Lindberg came across the Brazilian band Sarcófago's demo *Black Vomit*, released in 1986, it was leaps and bounds cooler than anything he'd ever heard before.

"The music was so driven, simple, and primitive—it was like Bathory but bordering on grindcore. They wore spikes absolutely everywhere and posed on Brazilian graveyards with enormous monuments in the background. It looked so raw. We felt that we had to follow their lead."

Grotesque formed in 1988, with Sarcófago as the blueprint. Tompa and guitarist Kristian Wåhlin stole crucifixes from the gift shop of a church near their high school, hanging them upside down around their necks. An intense phase of amateur craftsmanship commenced in the backyard of Tompa's parents' house. Used car mats and nails were combined into spiked bracelets and pentagram-adorned breastplates. Tompa has vague memories of his father helping him construct the inverted crosses that Grotesque would later use as stage decor.

Kristian Wåhlin was in an arts program in school and an aspiring graffiti artist. He designed the Grotesque logo, drawing inspiration from both metal aesthetics and street art culture.

Later that year, a Grotesque gig at a junior high school dance in the southern suburbs of Gothenburg was shut down by representatives from the local parents' association. Nevertheless, the show made a deep impression on a few of the kids in the audience. Mikael Stanne, now the vocalist of Dark Tranquillity, clearly remembers the evening.

"When the adults stopped the show, Tompa started screaming about how the Devil would come after them. Then he scratched his face until he started bleeding. It was the coolest gig I'd ever been to."

Anders Fridén, the future vocalist of In Flames, was also in the audience. He recalls the stark contrast between the audience and the band on stage.

"The upscale suburban kids stood there in their brand-new designer jeans. Then this skinny, bearded guy with corpse paint burns a bible on stage. People totally freaked out."

Back in Stockholm, Nicke Andersson's crossover band Brainwarp had transformed into the death metal band Nihilist. Not even the band leader himself remembers all the members coming and going. In the early days of Swedish death metal, musicians would change bands more often than underwear. Sometimes they'd also switch instruments with each other, rendering accurate lineups even harder to remember decades later.

"There was so much going on before you'd finally make up your mind. For example, I was part of a hardcore band called Corrupt for a while. I believe Johan Edlund might have been too, before he started Treblinka," says Nicke, seemingly oblivious to the fact that, at one time, the drummer of Corrupt was none other than Uffe Cederlund.

Johan Edlund remembers having been in Nihilist for a short while.

"But I think Nicke finds it difficult to admit. When everything started revolving around death metal, I wasn't allowed to be part of it any longer. He didn't have the guts to fire me face to face, so he did it over the phone instead. But a bunch of us kept in touch and partied together. And all of us had bands."

Johan Edlund lived in the quiet suburb of Täby to the north of Stockholm, and he recalls that the guys liked to hang out there. One primary reason was the lesser likelihood of getting into fights. Parallel to the rise of death metal, another young subculture in

Stockholm was focusing on gangs, crime, martial arts, and street violence in particular.

"We'd head out into the forest and listen to music, drink beer, and hold vomiting contests. You'd simply shove your fingers down your throat and basically see who could puke the best."

In 1987, Nihilist played their first ever gig in a Kista youth center.

"The audience were all idiots," says Uffe. "Even the guy who worked there and videotaped the gig screamed into the camera microphone that we sounded like shit. Everyone was against us."

However, the countless parcels with cassettes inside that were flowing through the Cederlund family mailbox had an unexpected side effect.

"It helped my parents see this as something worthwhile. It wasn't about hanging out downtown, beating people up in the street. We also started drinking very late by Swedish standards. We were 17 or 18 when we started drinking *folköl* (a weaker kind of beer available in regular stores in Sweden). There were no girls either. We were so shy and so into what we were doing that it became like a fucking wall around us."

Death metal bands of the time drew inspiration from splatter movies and American horror author H.P. Lovecraft, to name a few sources. Many of the musicians wore inverted crosses and experimented with incantations from Simon's *Necronomicon*. However, Nicke Andersson describes the interest in real Satanism as rather low within death metal circles.

"I believe we found splatter movies far cooler than the Devil even back then. You could, of course, combine them, but our primary lyrical inspiration came from *The Evil Dead*. H.P. Lovecraft was cool, but I didn't read much of him. There were so many strange words, and he wasn't available in Swedish."

When Nicke Andersson and Uffe Cederlund graduated from junior high, neither had further studies in mind.

"Everyone I know went on to senior high," says Uffe. "But for me and Nicke, it was never an option. Fuck school!"

Instead, they started taking odd jobs. One of Cederlund's first was in a grocery store, where he injured his back carrying heavy sacks of potatoes. Nicke Andersson made a living cleaning hazardous substances off of printing plates.

"I like drawing and working with layout, so the job at a small family-owned company in Axelsberg sounded pretty cool when I saw the ad. Then on the first day, they said, 'Here is a gas mask and a protective suit—we're cleaning these screen frames.' It was really bad. And I never really bothered with the gas mask either, because it was so annoying to use. None of that really mattered though, because on the weekends, you got to go to Täby to party."

The job experience at least inspired one Nihilist song. Its title, "Severe Burns," is taken from a warning sign at the printers.

Because none of the guys had yet turned 18, going to bars was not an option. Instead, the huge Stockholm map that once adorned a wall at Stockholm Central Station's sub-level floor became a meeting point for Stockholm's young death metal circle. Johnny Hedlund often showed up at "the map." He was a former punk rocker turned death metal fan, distinguishing himself by being the first to get his own apartment.

"I was the grapevine," says Hedlund. "Everyone had my number, and I had everyone else's. I'd call perhaps eight guys, only to find 60 people waiting when I got there. There weren't very many of us in the beginning, but it grew all the time. We ended up partying in the Midsommarkransen subway station, because it had the least amount of security guards. We'd get off the subway there, 40 or 50 people with a boombox blasting Slayer on high volume. You couldn't drag everyone off to some party; we were simply too many."

Above all, Nicke Andersson remembers the overnight redundancy effect that death metal had on everything that could be classified as crossover.

"And thrash metal was the cheesiest thing you could listen to. 'What the hell, you like Testament? Still? Fucking poser!'"

It's worth mentioning how Nicke Andersson smiles each and every time he uses the *poser* term. He often refers to its fundamental function in his teenage years.

"A poser was someone who liked Metallica and commercial bands. Who didn't have enough demos at home or wore band shirts with readable logos. Who washed his hair a little too often or hung out with girls too much. The rules were very strict."

In 1989, Nihilist recorded their second demo, *Only Shreds Remain*. The lineup consisted of Nicke on drums, L-G Petrov on vocals, Johnny Hedlund on bass, and guitarists Alex Hellid and Leif Cuzner. This recording went down in history as the one where Leif Cuzner came up with the hallmark guitar sound of Swedish death metal. The gear in question was a guitar pedal called Boss Heavy Metal HM2—a black stomp box with orange buttons. It is quite useless for heavy metal, but its insane chainsaw buzz combined with midrange controls makes it perfect for extreme music.

The very moment Cuzner turned the knobs all the way up, Swedish death metal claimed its signature sound. When Cuzner eventually left Nihilist, moving with his family to Canada, Uffe Cederlund rejoined the band; the remaining members hoped to preserve Cuzner's sound. Cederlund first tried using Cuzner's guitar. Eventually, he realized that the secret doesn't lie in the instrument but in the black box.

Except for Morbid and Treblinka, producer Tomas Skogsberg of Sunlight Studio, which had only recently been founded, has recorded just a handful of funk bands. His collaboration with Nihilist makes him realize that he's onto something special. Instead of drawing inspiration from American death metal, Skogsberg decides to ignore previous concepts. This results in a brutal and intense production style, closely linked to Stockholm death metal.

The Swedish underground scene was growing rapidly. Fred Estby formed the first version of Dismember as early as May of 1988. Stockholm also has Therion and Treblinka—which released the *Severe Abominations* single, one of the scene's first releases on vinyl, before changing their name to the somewhat more politically correct Tiamat. Carbonized, out of Stockholm suburb Spånga, experienced continuous lineup problems after most of their members turn up in other bands such as Entombed, Dismember, and Therion.

Even if Stockholm and Gothenburg were the two hot spots of the Swedish scene, death metal was by no means an exclusively urban phenomenon. Filthy Christians were based in Falun, Nirvana 2002 in the tiny village of Edsbyn. Sandviken had Sorcery, while Eskilstuna's first contribution to the scene was called Macrodex. Off on the remote island of Gotland, there was Grave.

The competition of who really is "the rawest band in the land" was off to a great start.

As the scene develops, many of these groups introduce increasingly brutal elements in their music. One of the hardest and fastest bands, from a purely musical perspective, is Merciless, which formed in 1986 in Strängnäs with inspiration drawn from Kreator, Slayer, and early Metallica. Three years later, the band's debut album *The Awakening* is recorded in Eskilstuna, released by Norwegian label Deathlike Silence Productions. Guitarist Erik Wallin still remembers the band's instructions to the studio technician.

"We told him, 'It has to sound brutal! We want the vocals to have a parking garage feel to them,' and 'The bass drums have to sound big and brutal.' If you manage to pull it off under those circumstances, I'd say you have reason to be satisfied."

Thanks to an underground network of enthusiastic promoters and unlikely local venues, death metal bands began playing all over the country. Entrepreneurial band members and fans organized gigs, mostly at youth centers where you could get financial support to reimburse bands for travel costs.

In Strömstad, 14-year-old Jon Nödtveidt—who later would form Dissection—set up shows with bands from Stockholm, Gothenburg, and Norway together with his friends. Gothenburg bands attended gigs at Valvet, which also served as a meeting place for people who'd previously only communicated by mail or phone. People often seized these opportunities to party hard. They drank booze smuggled into the venues, engaged in intense band discussions, and went stage-diving.

Erik Wallin remembers a Merciless gig in a barn in Surahammar, together with Kazjurol and Tribulation. The promoters placed pillows in a corner close to the stage, for people to land safely in. It quickly became apparent that many in the audience had come specifically to stage-dive. All the jumping made the stage shake, and vocalist Rogga

Petterson hit his teeth on the microphone repeatedly as a result. Finally, he had enough, took the microphone into an adjacent room, and kept singing. When the song was finished and the young promoters realized the vocalist had left the room, they ran after him and immediately ordered him out of there.

"When asked why, they told him that two angry badgers lived under a hole in the floor," Wallin remembers. "It was like a youth center without any responsible adults around. You had to crawl over a footbridge through a window to even get in."

Toward the end of the decade, Fagersta resident Peter "Babs" Ahlqvist contributed immensely to the increase in live gigs through the local music association Tid Är Musik (Time Is Music). Babs was mainly into American hardcore. However, the crossover mentality allows metal and hardcore to coexist, and during the peak of death metal, Tid Är Musik became the leading promoter of extreme metal in Sweden. Babs was also responsible for the Bergslagsrocken festival, with bands such as Kreator, Morbid Angel, Pestilence, Carcass, and Napalm Death.

Fans travelled from all over the country to the shows. Robert "Robban" Becirovic from Norrköping began organizing bus trips.

"When Kreator and Death played, we drove up from Norrköping through Finspång, filling an entire articulated bus. But we had to keep switching bus companies every time, because people would be throwing up and wreaking general havoc.

There were significantly fewer important concerts in Stockholm at the time. The only hubs of Stockholm's alternative music scene were a youth center in Täby and an abandoned house in the suburb of Haninge called the Ultra House.

"A few bands playing there had tuned their instruments down to D or even C," Nicke Andersson recalls. "We still couldn't play properly. Generally speaking, I think the Gothenburg scene had a lot more skilled musicians than we did. I have no idea why. I suppose playing well made you a poser."

While Nicke has a hard time accounting for all his sojourns through early bands, he finds it easier to recall the pecking order of Stockholm's early underground scene.

"Dismember were okay, since they played exactly the same style as us. Merciless from Strängnäs were cool, despite not tuning down and therefore not being real death metal. Bands like Septic Broiler from Gothenburg were never okay, according to us. And Kazjurol was a hopelessly goofy 'baseball-cap-turned-sideways' band."

Despite this, Kazjurol were booked as a supporting act when Napalm Death came to Sweden in the fall of 1988. This caused serious indignation in the Nihilist camp.

"We didn't think they belonged anywhere near Napalm Death," Nicke remembers. "So, we nagged and nagged until they finally allowed us to play as well."

Along with Napalm Death came Digby "Dig" Pearson, founder of the UK label Earache in 1985. The venture was funded by a government project where young people could apply for grants to start their own companies.

"Dig was a lucky guy," says Uffe Cederlund. "He was friends with Shane Embury of Napalm Death, who would tell him exactly which bands to sign."

Shortly following the gig with Napalm Death, Pearson got in touch and wanted to sign Nihilist to the label. There was only one problem: Nihilist had already split up. Nicke had a hard time getting along with Johnny Hedlund, but he didn't dare to fire the bass player who was four years his senior. Instead, Nicke decided to break up the band— only to restart it as Entombed a few days later.

In the late winter of 1989, Entombed entered the studio to make their debut album *Left Hand Path*. Recording and mixing was completed in just a few days. Uffe Cederlund remembers it as a highly creative process.

"On Friday afternoon, we'd head down to the Sunlight studio and tweak the drum sound for about an hour. Then Nicke and I recorded all basic percussion in an evening, more or less. The following day, we'd spend maybe half an hour fine-tuning the guitar tone, and then record. It went fast, I really fucking miss those days."

In June 1990, *Left Hand Path* was released, incidentally on the same day Morbid Angel are in Sweden to perform at Bergslagsrocken. The record store House of Kicks in Stockholm organizes a Morbid Angel signing session. Store proprietor Calle von Schewen remembers the event as a turning point.

"That day changed my life as much as the first time I saw The Ramones. When I looked out through the window, the entire alley was filled with people—despite a stamp-sized ad in one of the tabloids being our only attempt at promotion. It was chaos. Suddenly, everything was for real."

The first few chords on *Left Hand Path* were enough to signal a new chapter in Swedish musical history, at least to those who were listening.

"That fucking hurricane grabbed you right away," says music journalist Håkan Persson at Sveriges Radio. "Finally, here was a power that earlier Swedish metal bands completely failed to capture when trying to imitate international bands. Hearing Entombed's music was totally crushing. You could tell this was for real."

Left Hand Path pushed everything else aside. The album inspired the formation of a plethora of new bands, and it made others change musical direction. This development soon transformed the entire Swedish metal scene. Tomas Skogsberg remembers established metal bands initially criticizing the down-tuned sonic assault of death metal.

"They said, 'There's no way you can tune the guitars down that much.' One year later, they'd done the exact same thing."

Within a year, Dismember and Unleashed had also released their first albums, followed by an even greater flood of demos from bands all over the country.

Meanwhile, in Gothenburg, Grotesque have split up. Tompa Lindberg forms At the Gates, quickly establishing it as the city's premiere death metal band—with Dark Tranquillity trailing just behind. In Flames also emerges in 1990. This more melodic and polished style of death metal will later be known internationally as "The Gothenburg Sound," while the Stockholm acts are characterized by a more brutal style.

This difference in sound and approach was tightly linked to the fact that most Gothenburg bands were heavily influenced by The New Wave of British Heavy Metal, whereas many originators of the Stockholm style had their roots in punk.

One possible explanation is that Nicke Andersson's influences indirectly shaped the orientation and preferences of Stockholm bands. However, the two scenes were separated by more factors than musical preferences. While many of the Stockholm musicians came from high-rise apartment buildings in distinctly working-class neighborhoods, the Gothenburg scene was dominated by kids from affluent residential areas in the city's southern suburbs.

Dark Tranquillity vocalist Mikael Stanne, At the Gates members Anders and Jonas Björler, Tompa Lindberg, and Kristian Wåhlin all grew up in single-family houses along the same bus route. Stanne describes it as an upper-middle-class environment and notes how none of them were ever left wanting.

"Instead, everything felt a bit too ordinary and common. When we discovered extreme music, we really wanted to stick out—to avoid becoming another average person who starts working at the same place your father's been at for 20 years."

The German albums *Endless Pain* by Kreator and *Walls of Jericho* by Helloween, both released in 1985, were his favorites. Prior to that, he'd only listened to classic heavy metal.

"I was completely shocked," Mikael said. "I had no idea that world was out there. Buying albums and immersing myself in this crazy world was absolutely amazing. It felt as if I was carrying a secret."

Thanks to his fascination with metal, he always had something to talk about—always something to drive him forward.

"I'd hang out with a bunch of friends every weekend, drink beer, and listen to American death metal demos. Later in the evening, we'd head out to a bar, and then do it all over again the next day."

Most people Mikael Stanne socialized with back then still play in bands to this day. He believes the reason for this is that all of them discovered the music at a susceptible age.

"It made a profound impression on us; the music and lifestyle that came with it molded everything that followed. Anything not involving demos and live tapes was completely pointless and uninteresting."

In Flames vocalist Anders Fridén started singing for Dark Tranquillity, but he eventually traded places with Mikael. He also feels metal offered him something different. In his case, it was an alternative to a lifestyle in which the most pressing matters revolved around wearing the right brand of clothes. Anders points out, however, that he was never particularly rebellious, and he can't really explain why he was drawn to extreme music. Rather than seeing it as an outlet, he found great appeal in the communal spirit, along with its general atmosphere and the fact that there never were any real fights.

"Everyone would just meet up to have a good time. But one thing led to another. It started with soft hard rock and got progressively heavier from there."

He remembers travelling with his friends to Bergslagsrocken in Fagersta in 1990, listening to Metallica's ... *And Justice for All*, and marveling at the production.

"We thought the drums were amazing, both Lars' performance and sound-wise. Today, it sounds like shit—like a cardboard box. I also remember Morbid Angel drummer Pete Sandoval asking if I could help him buy some weed. I was just a kid who didn't understand anything and replied, 'No, I can't help you—but ask the cool guys over there.' Afterward, I was euphoric over having spoken to him. And then when they were about to play and the intro started, we saw their guitar player, Trey, cutting himself and blood flowing from his arms. It was magical—absolutely massive."

He remembers Dismember coming to Gothenburg in the early '90s and finding out they were paid 7,000 Swedish kronor—750 U.S. dollars—to play.

"We were in complete shock. We had no idea you could get that much for a concert."

To the young Anders, catching Dismember and Entombed live was as big as seeing Iron Maiden today—with an added dash of rivalry.

"In your head, you thought, 'Wow, Entombed have been signed by Earache! And Dismember by Nuclear Blast. Damn, that's so cool!' So, we were probably trying to act a bit dismissive and perhaps even displayed a certain degree of envy."

During Anders' three years in Dark Tranquillity, they never played Stockholm.

"I imagine we were probably boycotted by the Stockholm crowd."

Neither At the Gates' nor Dark Tranquillity's lyrics or album covers are characterized by the blood and gore excesses that were otherwise prevalent in the genre. These themes are all the more prevalent among the Stockholm bands, with Dismember taking the concept farther than most.

For the promo shots taken in conjunction with their 1991 debut *Like an Everflowing Stream*, they decide to pose drenched in blood. But once in the photo studio, both guitarist David Blomqvist and vocalist Matti Kärki back out. Matti cites not having brought along a change of clothes as the reason. These days, he's not exactly sure how they came up with the idea in the first place.

"But I know our drummer, Fred, was a huge Kiss fan. So, it was partly a tribute to Kiss and Alice Cooper, even if we'd taken the concept to a more brutal level."

The cover artwork was painted by Kristian Wåhlin, under his Necrolord moniker. He would later shape the aesthetic framework of Swedish metal.

When the album was released, the band prepared for the bloody photos to cause an outrage. Instead, they barely drew any attention. Dismember also used blood for their stage show at a gig in Kolingsborg in Stockholm. Afterward, they agreed it was too messy and went back to performing the set as usual. Matti Kärki says the prevailing themes of gore within the Stockholm scene can in large parts be attributed to San Francisco death squad Autopsy—which was incidentally Nicke Andersson's favorite death metal band—being one of the strongest influences. Time constraints were another reason.

"We had to have something for lyrics, so we'd describe things we'd seen in movies such as *Hellraiser* and *Evil Dead* and didn't really give it much more thought than that."

The Dismember song "Skin Her Alive" had a different backdrop. The neighbor living underneath Matti Kärki's apartment in Tensta murdered his wife, and Matti's grandmother saw the corpse being carried out. Matti wrote the lyrics from the perpetrator's perspective, rather than that of the victim.

With the album finalized, a shipment of records was seized by British customs following a spot check. Despite the delivery also containing records with bands such as Pungent Stench from Austria and Britain's Benediction, Dismember's album and specifically the song "Skin Her Alive" drew the ire of British customs. Charges were pressed against the distributor. Matti Kärki remembers how they had to attend the trial in the UK, where their album was played in its entirety.

"Even if it's only half an hour long, it was pretty absurd. I then had to take the witness stand. Our lawyer's position was that the song was based on a true story, arguing that descriptions of real-life events couldn't be censored. Ultimately, the customs authorities lost."

The Victorian-era law specifically prohibiting the distribution of indecent and obscene material in Her Majesty's realm gave Dismember the title for the follow-up album: *Indecent and Obscene*. The case was covered by news agencies in Sweden, further promoting the band.

By now, death metal had become the most unlikely of successes, and the scene entered its most explosive phase.

The pioneers were joined by countless new bands, following the trend rather than having created it. Labels exploited the situation as best they could. Anders Fridén remembers his outrage when noticing the steady decline in standards.

"We went to Strömstad to play with Dissection and Cemetary. Cemetary were so fucking bad, but the next time we performed with them, they'd been signed to Black Mark and were featured on MTV's metal show *Headbanger's Ball*. We couldn't understand what was happening. These outsiders from Borås had a record deal, and we did not!"

Tomas Skogsberg, the increasingly popular resident producer at Sunlight Studio, also sensed a downside to this rapid growth.

"Many bands who wanted to record in my studio said, 'We absolutely don't want the Entombed sound!' But ultimately, that's the sound they ended up with. I think a lot of it had to do with bands being really envious of Entombed."

Tompa Lindberg suggests that many of these newcomers were actually thrash bands jumping on a bandwagon. They had no real insight into the nature of death metal.

"It wasn't only about brutality. You had to understand why Autopsy were gods, whereas Pestilence from Holland were just an okay thrash band."

When Entombed toured Europe for the first time, the band members were between 16 and 18 years old. Every night, several crates of free beer were waiting for them in the dressing room. This soon caused problems.

"We were completely clueless," Uffe Cederlund remembers. "Many shows were complete disasters because we were too drunk. Every time, we'd try to finish everything that happened to be on the rider. Quite a few years went by before we got that under control. It's a shame. I believe Entombed would have grown a lot bigger otherwise."

Shortly after the release of the first album, L-G Petrov was fired after having flirted with Nicke Andersson's girlfriend at a New Year's Eve party. Sweden's biggest death metal band was suddenly without a vocalist. At the same time, everyone was asking for new material. Entombed placed an anonymous ad for a new vocalist in a morning newspaper, stating that applicants have to like Motörhead, Black Sabbath, and Repulsion in order to be eligible. Over the course of several months, the band auditions several candidates. In the meantime, they recruit Orvar Säfström of Nirvana 2002, an old friend through the fanzine and tape-trading scenes. He sings on the 1991 *Crawl* EP.

"Uffe gave me a call a few days after New Year's Eve, asking me straight-out if I wanted to step in for an upcoming EP recording and European tour," Orvar says. "I was 16 years old at the time, and Entombed was the coolest band in Sweden—perhaps in the entire world. I didn't need many seconds to think about it. But it was always clear that they were looking for a permanent replacement. I was present several times when they tried out new vocalists—it was mostly about socializing, drinking, and checking if the person in question was cool to hang out with. It had way less to do with the actual vocal performance, which kind of explains what happened next."

Entombed ultimately recruited Johnny Dordevic from Carnage and began recording their second full-length album.

"When Johnny was supposed to record the vocals, it didn't sound very good," Uffe Cederlund remembers. "So, in order for us to finish the album quickly, Nicke sang instead—but since Johnny was meant to be our new vocalist, we credited him on the record. Nicke wanted everything to look professional and thought-through. That illusion soon shattered."

When the new lineup began playing live, a lot of people noticed that the vocals didn't sound even remotely like the album. For many years, Nicke Andersson denied the persistent—and true—rumors that the recorded voice actually belonged to him.

Despite having been kicked out, L-G refuses to be bitter.

"Instead, he'd always be in the front row singing along to every song he knew," recalls Uffe Cederlund. "Slowly, him and Nicke started talking—and suddenly he was part of the band again. Which left me in charge of firing Johnny."

Entombed's second album is titled *Clandestine*. Instead of living up to its title, it brings death metal into Swedish public perception, mostly thanks to Swedish media now taking an intense interest in the new movement.

Up until this point, the country's metal scene has been a marginalized subculture left to play at youth centers and punk clubs. In 1991, death metal suddenly became the highest fashion. The meeting of hip cultural spheres and extreme metal is manifested in full when Entombed records a music video with La Camilla from the Swedish pop group Army of Lovers.

In 1991, Metallica also release their self-titled black album, which becomes a worldwide sensation. Metallica, once sprung from the uncompromising thrash scene of the mid-'80s, are now able to reach an audience far beyond extreme metal.

Over the following years, Swedish musicians will constitute an increasingly large portion of the content of *Headbanger's Ball* on MTV. A new song by Hypocrisy from Ludvika might be aired next to American stadium rockers Poison or the Seattle grunge rock of Soundgarden. Besides Entombed, the leading ranks of the Swedish scene were Dismember, Therion, and Tiamat, as well as Grave, Unleashed, and At the Gates. All of them are by now signed by international labels. They've also been joined by new bands from all over the country, with names like Desultory, Crematory, Afflicted, and Edge of Sanity. With the massive influx of good bands rising from Swedish soil during this period, this is the first time Sweden could be said to have been the epicenter of a musical revolution.

By the time Morbid Angel come to play Fryshuset in Stockholm with Entombed and Unleashed, the capital's most trend-sensitive crowd has discovered death metal. The gig is sold out and Calle von Schewen, distributor of Earache albums in Sweden, remembers a giddy feeling of "tonight is the night" as the concert date approached.

"Leading music journalist Jan Gradvall had put Entombed on the cover of the *Nöjesguiden* magazine, and everyone who aspired to be someone in Stockholm was there."

Alas, on their way to Stockholm, the truck transporting Morbid Angel's equipment skids off the road, forcing the band to cancel their performance. Entombed and Unleashed decide to play anyway. Calle remembers the massive disappointment defusing much of the positive energy that had up until then been the trademark of the scene.

"I believe death metal would've kept growing in Sweden if Morbid Angel had played that show. But because Entombed and Unleashed played, it was still regarded as a completed concert and people weren't offered refunds. This had a lot of unpleasant repercussions."

In November 1992, a bomb went off at a Stockholm death metal gig with American band Deicide. No one was injured. The police stopped the show but finally allowed Deicide to perform a few songs—with the lights turned on. The evening was another setback for the scene. The culprits were never identified, but the week prior, Deicide frontman Glen Benton had provoked animal rights activists by promoting animal cruelty in an interview with Swedish tabloid *Aftonbladet*.

The Deicide bomb has been described as the Swedish death metal scene's equivalent of the flower power movement's Altamont. It definitely put an end to the golden era of death metal in Swedish musical history. Rather than animal rights activists, the genre's greatest threat had become its increasing standardization. Around 1993, the scene had grown so large that it started feeding upon itself. According to Dismember vocalist Matti Kärki, the sheer amount of death metal bands was the problem.

"In certain places, it felt as if we were only playing in front of a bunch of other bands. And the labels kept releasing so much shit. We couldn't understand what was going on—it wasn't even possible to keep up any longer. That's when I stopped following the scene."

In striving toward more primitive expressions, death metal had once again made metal a down-to-earth craft closer to punk clubs than to stadiums. On its way there, the movement sacrificed many of the aspects that made heavy metal entertaining. But perhaps death metal's greatest problem was that it no longer shocked or scared anyone. As opposed to the early days of heavy metal and later black metal, Swedish death metal would never become the focus of outraged parents or debates on live television. As soon as the moral crusaders dropped their guard, the movement lost its potency for young people in desperate search of social alienation.

A definite counter-reaction came in the form of the black metal wave sweeping over the mid-'90s Scandinavian scene—with bands such as Mayhem, Darkthrone, and Burzum. The soundscapes of these bands were even less listener-friendly than those of death metal. The black metal bands wore corpse paint and would soon make metal highly controversial again.

The stagnation within the death metal scene had not gone unnoticed among the members of Entombed. Uffe Cederlund says the scene lost most of its luster as early as 1992.

"By then, we'd already stopped listening to death metal and gotten into Helmet instead. And we laughed on our promo shots."

On their third album, *Wolverine Blues*, Entombed departed from the winning formula they'd created and instead drew influences from '70s hard rock and even grunge—though the down-tuned guitars and growling vocals remained. The result was an album earning them respect far beyond death metal circles, while their stocks within the extreme metal scene plummeted.

"An underground scene is always full of rules," notes Nicke Andersson. "And you can't abide by those for any longer stretch of time—at least we couldn't."

To this day, Uffe Cederlund says *Wolverine Blues* is his favorite Entombed album. The fact that it was dismissed by a vast part of the death metal community was a result of envy, he feels.

"That album is so damn good. That's where we showed how we weren't just 'Entombed—the death metal band,' but also the rock band Entombed. I'd like to think we were acknowledged not only for playing violent metal, but also for upholding a certain quality."

During the '90s, Nicke Andersson grew increasingly fed up with the musical limitations of the genre. In 1997, he left Entombed in order to focus on his rock band The Hellacopters, formed with childhood friend Kenny Håkansson in 1994.

"I thought we'd come as far as we could musically," Nicke says, adding that perhaps he wouldn't have reasoned the same way today.

During a Hellacopters tour in 2003, he spoke with Thunder Express guitarist Robert Pehrsson about their mutual love of Autopsy. They decide to do something in the same spirit and created Death Breath. Scott Carlson of legendary American band Repulsion sang on several tracks on the debut album, called *Stinking up the Night*, and later toured with the band.

Before the album was recorded, Nicke Andersson and Robert Pehrsson discussed how to best convey an homage to old-school death metal. They realized the best death metal recordings had taken place in studios where the sound engineers really had no idea what they were doing.

"We wanted something so old-school, it would feel entirely new. Before the recording, we played some old death metal to the studio guy and asked if he understood any of it. He didn't. 'Perfect,' we said. 'Let's do this!'"

With Merciless drummer Peter Stjärnvind as the permanent replacement for Nicke Andersson, Entombed remained one of the hardest-working bands of the '00s Swedish scene. Their career now encompasses 10 albums and over 2,000 shows. But contrary to bands such as In Flames, Sabaton, and Amon Amarth, Entombed would never become the main attraction in larger arenas.

Only after Nicke Andersson's departure did the Swedish metal scene complete its journey from underground culture to mainstream movement. Andersson seems well aware of the irony in this. He's surprised by the fact that many of the most established groups in the country today have their roots in the '90s death metal scene.

"I almost feel bad for giving up."

VI.

Metal and the Media

*What I can't wrap my head around
are these respected journalists
still spelling thrash metal as* trash
or Megadeth as Megadeath.
It makes me want to eat glass.

— CHRISTOFFER RÖSTLUND JONSSON

WHEN DISCUSSING THE STATISTICAL overabundance of internationally acclaimed metal bands out of Sweden, the country's long winters are often mentioned, as is the excruciating boredom of growing up in isolated rural communities. Occasionally, the nationwide system of local music schools, providing music lessons and instruments to children, also receives credit. Yet few mention a teen magazine that introduced an entire generation of youngsters to bands such AC/DC, Iron Maiden, Judas Priest, Accept, Venom and W.A.S.P. in the '80s.

In the '60s, German-born Hans Hatvig was working as a layout editor for the *Frankfurter Allgemeine* newspaper. After meeting a Swedish woman in 1967, he booked a one-way ticket to Stockholm, where he found work as a dishwasher in the canteen of a major publishing house.

Upon reading a job advertisement for a layout editor position at the less-respected publisher H-son Förlag, he applied immediately. As it turned out, H-son was Sweden's main producer of pornographic magazines, having been publishing pin-up magazines since the early '40s. Hatvig was highly ambitious and pioneered the use of photomontage in the publications. For example, a short story depicting a priest copulating with a country maid was illustrated with beautiful scenery and superimposed images of a porn actor dressed in a robe.

Hartvig's visual designs proved popular, and the publications became commercially successful. At H-son, Hatvig learned the tricks he would build his future career on.

"Curt H-son always maintained that every blank space has to be filled with something—a caption, a headline or a burst. Every page should be filled to the brim. Also, the cover should always include the word 'NEW!'" Hatvig says.

In 1973, Hatvig launches *Poster*. The name is a dead giveaway, as every sheet in the magazine has a poster on one side and articles on the other. Hot music acts like Kiss, Sweet, and The Runaways are paired with movie stars, hot rods, and popular television shows. His publication is an instant hit, and the visual focus of the magazine is admittedly an important contribution to the immense popularity of KISS in mid-'70s Sweden.

But after a few years, readers lost interest.

Hatvig was reassigned as chief editor of the porn magazine *Brud Special*, but he was reluctant to leave music and instead tried to sell the company another concept: a magazine designed like a porn mag, but with music and movie stars instead of sex. The publication was to focus heavily on images and gossip. He called it *OKEJ*. Management was not entirely convinced.

"They thought pop music and all that was over and done with. Finally, they agreed to let me have a go at it. I was given three issues to show them I could make a profit."

The first issue of *OKEJ* reached newsstands in 1980. The headline read, "Will Priscilla remarry the corpse of Elvis?" Another early *OKEJ* piece described German punk singer Nina Hagen masturbating on a TV show. Articles were heavily biased, and no topic was taboo. Elton John and the Village People were listed in an article called, "Artists that are homos."

Swedish news tabloid *Expressen* reacted immediately. With the headline, "Burn this shit!" they published a full-page photo of a burning copy of *OKEJ*. Swedish national television news warned of a new, tasteless youth magazine. Around 20 Swedish newspapers published outraged articles, condemning the newcomer.

Union representatives within the publishing house tried persuading Hatvig to discontinue *OKEJ*, as readers of moneymaking celebrity and gardening magazines threatened to cancel their subscriptions in protest.

After the allotted three test issues, OKEJ was put on hold for the media storm to die down.

"Sex, drugs, and rock' n' roll was the only way to go," says Hatvig. "I was very determined to create something profitable and felt the time was right for this idea. The commotion wasn't only about that Elvis thing but also a general consensus that *OKEJ* was the most reprehensible magazine ever made for kids."

Scandalous headlines aside, Hatvig had the full support of his younger colleagues, who realized the potential in the increasingly music-focused youth culture. After long discussions, *OKEJ* was turned into a monthly publication in 1982—in a larger format and with somewhat less sensationalistic content. The cover of the first issue depicted Hasse Carlsson, picture-perfect vocalist in Swedish teen idol band Noice. In its first three years, the magazine's monthly circulation increased from 18,000 to 148,000 copies.

OKEJ would ultimately grow into the publisher's number-one magazine. One factor that contributed to its success was Hatvig's sharp eye for scouting out new writing talent. He recruited Jörgen Holmstedt and Anders Tengner as well as photographer Micke Johansson. Full spreads with popular hard rock bands such as Mötley Crüe, W.A.S.P., and Twisted Sister mixed with features on domestic bands like Europe and Treat, always with just enough pop stars to appeal to mainstream readers.

OKEJ became an essential source of inspiration for a new generation of Swedish rock and metal musicians. Joacim Cans, today the vocalist of HammerFall, was one of the teenagers reading the magazine from cover to cover.

"*OKEJ* was hugely important. I covered my entire room with pictures from *OKEJ*. I became a W.A.S.P. fan thanks to this magazine, without even having heard them. When I got hold of their debut album, it was even better than I could have imagined. The last page was also important, because it always had an ad for new metal albums you could order by mail. I bought so many records through those ads," he says.

Heated debates raged in *OKEJ*'s letters section. Topics ranged from KISS's decision to drop their makeup and whether the band's name really was an acronym for Kids in Satan's Service (or possibly Knights in Satan's Service) to tips for aspiring groupies. One letter came from a young Jon Nödtveidt, Strömstad resident and later frontman of Dissection, who suggested a special issue featuring nothing but Venom.

Writer Jörgen Holmstedt points out that the publication was unique in the Swedish media landscape—it was the only outlet to take hard rock and metal seriously.

"Sweden had no commercial TV or radio back in those days, only state-run public service channels. As I grew up in the '70s, Swedish television showed a grand total of perhaps 30 seconds with KISS. A short excerpt from their "C'mon and Love Me" video was aired in some dreadful entertainment program. But the station had overdubbed the music with the sound of squealing pigs. I imagine that's what the producers thought the music really sounded like: pigs being tormented."

The reason *OKEJ* featured so much metal was more the result of Hans Hatvig's understanding of the target audience than it was that of any musical preference. He noticed the genre's popularity and realized there was a demand to be met. He freely admits he was never personally interested in music.

"When I made my pop magazines, the best course of action was to stay neutral, but I developed a nose for trends. I've always thought metal musicians are the nicest people. They had something I could sympathize with, having worked their way up from working class to becoming multimillionaires."

With a parental generation decidedly unimpressed both by W.A.S.P. posing with raw meat and commercial culture at large, the magazine remained a nuisance to the world outside of teenager's bedroom walls. When the *OKEJ* generation begin producing their own fanzines a few years later, the notion of them being nothing but passive media consumers in the hands of scrupulous entertainment companies was proven wrong. Dead wrong.

———

Fanzines have existed in Sweden ever since the punk movement of the '70s—early titles included *RIP*, *Heatwave*, and *Jörvars Gosskör*. As was the case with punk, metal and hard rock got little attention from mainstream media, prompting fans to produce their own publications.

The Hammer was the very first Swedish hard rock fanzine. It appeared in 1982, with Jörgen Holmstedt as a contributing writer. He remembers the zine being filled with the bizarre humor of chief editor Bengt Grönkvist.

"Bengt added lots of peculiar jokes throughout the magazine. It could be sick stuff like 'Don't say reggae is all bad; after all, Bob Marley is dead.' A lot of effort was also put into bashing popular pop singer Carola Häggkvist. More than anything, I wanted to produce a pure hard rock magazine, but Bengt always put the finishing touches on *The Hammer*, so we couldn't stop him."

A few years earlier, British music journalist Geoff Barton had coined the term The New Wave of British Heavy Metal, often shortened to NWOBHM. In an article series in *The Hammer* about Swedish bands such as Glory Bells Band, Six Feet Under, and Axewitch, the term Första Vågen av Svensk Heavy Metal (First Wave of Swedish Heavy Metal) was invented. Yet the FVASHM moniker never really caught on.

The Hammer's gossip column once mentioned a young Swedish guitarist being thrown into a swimming pool by Dio bassist Jimmy Bain at a party in Los Angeles, a punishment for spreading false rumors that he was the new axeman in Dio. This was the first time Yngwie Malmsteen was mentioned in print. In 1984, *The Hammer* ran a black metal special with Mercyful Fate, Venom, and—somewhat surprisingly—Canadian heavy metal band Anvil. In a series of articles named "From the diaries of a groupie," a young, blonde Swedish woman spoke candidly of her interactions with members of Saxon and Iron Maiden.

Whereas *The Hammer* primarily featured hard rock, a pure metal fanzine called *Heavy Metal Massacre* was started in Dals Långed by Lennart "Phantom" Larsson. A devout tape-trader, Larsson devoured everything he could get ahold of from the emerging thrash metal scene. In the first issue, released in the fall of 1983, he described Metallica's debut album as "a real killer, splitting your sanity in two, fangs and all," and dedicated an entire column to the lack of metal in Swedish public service radio.

That same year, Swedish public service premiered the first show dedicated to music videos on Swedish TV, called *Videobeat*. Hard rock and metal were rarely represented. On New Year's Eve, 1983, however, Swedish radio premiered the new show *Rockdepartementet* (Ministry of Rock). It was in no way a pure hard rock show, but every week, a few songs of the heavier kind were included. This was in all likelihood the first regular appearance of hard rock on Swedish radio, airing tracks by artists such as Van Halen, Motörhead, and Judas Priest.

March 2, 1984, will always be a night to remember for Swedish metalheads. That's when Swedish television and radio simultaneously aired the Heavy Metal Non-Stop gala taped in Dortmund, Germany, in December 1983. The edited show ran three hours and featured concerts with Iron Maiden, Judas Priest, Ozzy Osbourne, Def Leppard, and Krokus.

"It was aired late at night, and I wasn't really allowed to stay up. But I promised to clean my room for the next three years and got to watch the entire program. That's where everything started," says Anders Fridén of In Flames.

Anders Tengner hosted several televised rock shows in the mid-'80s. In a 1984 episode of *Norrsken*, he discussed Satanic bands and showed a brief glimpse of a Venom video before declaring it terrible and demonstratively turning it off. This led to a death threat by Mayhem on their first demo cassette.

"We'd never seen any moving images of Venom before *Norrsken* were supposed to play the video," says an agitated Jørn "Necrobutcher" Stubberud. "We were unbelievably excited. And then, after only a few seconds, he turns the video off and calls it shit. That was fucked up."

Anders Tengner, at the time also the chief editor of *Rocket* magazine, was often called upon to defend the extremes within hard rock and metal. In a classic television segment in the Swedish talk show *Svar Direkt*, the overtly Christian host Siewert Öholm took issue with the American band W.A.S.P. and vocalist Blackie Lawless wearing a saw-blade codpiece and eating raw meat on stage.

Visibly upset, Öholm suggested the magazine had a moral responsibility. An entire generation of metal fans cheered in unison when Tengner answered, "No—we give the readers what they want." The segment ending stepped into seriously bizarre territory when a young girl in the studio audience read an alternate version of a Christian prayer, reworded to denounce W.A.S.P. Years later, it was revealed that the girl was the daughter of one of the staff members and was just handed the piece of paper to read. She was, in fact, a metal fan and was naturally embarrassed that the clip has been viewed by hundreds of thousands over the years.

By 1986, increasingly harder genres like thrash metal competed with the radio-friendly hard rock bands. Metal fanatics all over the country waited in anticipation for Saturdays and the radio show *Rockbox*. The host, Pär Fontander, played Slayer, Anthrax, and Metal Church on Swedish radio for the very first time. He also interviewed many musicians, including Quorthon of Bathory.

In 1987, a local radio show called *Power Hour* premiered in the city of Norrköping. It could be argued that *Power Hour* almost equaled *Rockbox* in importance, despite only reaching a small region in Sweden. Hosts Robban Becirovic and Erik Sandberg surprisingly managed to fill their tiny show with high-quality content. According to Becirovic, this was largely due to the complete lack of interest from mainstream media.

"No one else cared when Metallica played Stockholm in 1986. We were able to get all the cool interviews with Metallica, Ozzy, Anthrax, Queensrÿche, and Testament. We were also sent tons of records from the labels, since they didn't really have anywhere else to send them. Those were great times."

Despite their limited broadcasting range, feedback was massive.

"At one point, we had a St. Lucia holiday wake and were on the air for 12 hours straight. People called in requesting songs all night. Mostly Norrköping residents, of course, but also listeners from nearby towns and even as far as the city of Linköping. I guess those guys had a really good radio antenna."

A new wave of fanzines flooded the scene as death metal took root in late-'80s Sweden. Some worth mentioning are Tiamat vocalist Johan Edlund's *Poserkill*, Patrik Cronberg's *To the Death*, *Hang 'Em High* courtesy of Orvar Säfström, and Tomas Nyqvist's *Putrefaction Magazine*.

To a certain extent, these fanzines were examples of how death metal adopted concepts from the punk scene, including networking and infrastructure. An overview of the content stemming from these publications also shows how punk and underground metal scenes were not separate entities. The third issue of *Kakafoni* included interviews with Entombed and Morbid Angel as well as punk bands Strebers and Headcleaners.

Overall, fanzine culture was vitally important to the development of the Swedish death metal scene. Fanzines spread the news about new bands and, most importantly, shared addresses for tape-traders both domestic and abroad.

"I got into fanzines specifically to know where to send demos," says Anders Jakobson, who went on to play drums in Örebro grindcore band Nasum.

One of these magazines was *Flotzilla*, edited by Niklas Pettersson in Skärplinge. Besides finding the addresses he was looking for, Jakobson also became a writer for the publication, and soon, he started his own fanzine, *Hymen*. The first issue was completed in 1990 and included an interview with Entombed, whose *But Life Goes On* demo had made them the most talked-about band in underground circles.

Anders describes the very inclusive approach of the amateur journalism, which contributed to the kinship cultivated within the death metal scene.

"Most newcomers were interviewed regardless if they were good or not. There was an appreciation just for having a band. That would qualify you for an interview."

Hymen soon acquired the reputation of a serious and quality publication. It was written in Swedish and maintained a more serious tone than competing fanzines. A total of seven issues were produced, from 1990 to 1994, in a circulation that varied between 350 and 500 copies.

"Ultimately, my growing ambitions got in the way. Toward the end, I published one issue per year, just like many other fanzines did. Yet material never became outdated, compared to today, when everything gets old in a week," Anders says. He still regularly covers music in a local newspaper.

The art direction of many of the zines from around this time testifies to the ways in which death metal liberated creative powers on more than just a musical level. The cover of the first and only issue of Johan Edlund's magazine *Poserkill* is an absolute masterpiece of the genre. The design is done with markers on a blood-red background, featuring a black silhouette of a desolate castle rising above an endless field of skulls.

The cover of the 1985 debut issue of *Slayer Mag*, the oldest and most respected of all fanzines from the Scandinavian extreme metal scene, was significantly more modest. The first cover drawing depicted a skull and a hand clutching a sword with a studded armband on the wrist. The illustration looks like something a bored 14-year-old would be drawing in secret in biology class and serves as a reminder of how many of the most important pioneers within the subgenres of metal have been teenagers—in essence, children.

The *Slayer Mag*'s publication history ran longer than anyone could have expected at the time and became something of a mouthpiece for the Norwegian black metal scene when it exploded in the early '90s. Editor Jon "Metalion" Kristiansen was at the epicenter of the scene, and his zine featured extensive interviews with bands such as Mayhem, Burzum, and Emperor—everything framed in aesthetics as suitably harsh as a windswept mountaintop.

With 20 issues in 26 years, *Slayer Mag* survived more paradigm shifts in the metal scene than most publications of its kind. Through the years, it retained its identity and managed to capture the essence of the subculture, even if the covers became increasingly striking.

Metalion mentions a few copies of *OKEJ* magazine finding their way to him across the Norwegian border in the mid-'80s. This opened him up to a style of music nowhere near as big in his own country at the time.

"Generally speaking, Sweden is far more interesting than Norway when it comes to metal. All the Swedes had been listening to Iron Maiden since they were 5 years old—that wasn't the case here. We had no natural metal background. A lot of Norwegians went straight to black metal."

Metalion completed the final issue of *Slayer Mag* in the spring of 2011, and later that same year, he collected all issues in a rather personal compendium called *Metalion: The Slayer Mag Diaries*. He confirms that the magazine is discontinued permanently, mostly because it's no fun making it anymore.

"Everything was better in the '80s to early '90s, before the internet came along."

Today, he finds it very difficult to find exclusive content.

"Add to that trying to explain to teenagers why they have to actually pay for the magazine."

Could it then be said that the internet killed *Slayer*?

"No, bad music killed *Slayer*, haha. There is still good black metal around, but not a lot of music excites me these days."

One of the few not stricken by fanzine nostalgia is Robban Becirovic, now the chief editor of *Close-Up Magazine*.

"At the *Power Hour* show, we found all fanzines completely worthless. They weren't even fit for wiping your ass with. Hardly anyone could write."

During his compulsory military service, Robban Becirovic was appointed driver of a bread truck. On his first day, he was sworn into a secret that's been passed down by young men for 30 years. The daily route to the garrison does not in fact take four hours, like their officers believe, but one and a half. The conscripts instead park in a forest clearing to get a few hours of rest.

During these breaks Becirovic formulates an idea that will make him a ubiquitous figure in Swedish metal. The articles that will make up the first edition of *Close-Up Magazine* are penned on a spiral-bound notepad right there in the clearing. Once he's written enough of them, Becirovic gathers friends and girlfriends at an advertising agency owned by someone's father. There, everyone helps type the handwritten articles on computers.

"Everyone sat at a computer, eating candy and potato chips, typing it out. We then printed the whole thing in four columns per page, cut out the single columns, and used them to glue a magazine together."

One of the people involved was Christian Carlquist, a schoolmate of Becirovic's with a huge interest in gore and splatter movies.

"Christian was somewhat of a nutcase. He would buy a huge chocolate bar and then watch strange autopsy videos he'd ordered from the U.S. He wasn't bullied or anything, but he kept to himself," Becirovic remembers.

The most challenging obstacle in the creation of the new magazine was coming up with a suitable name for it. Most pure metal fanzines back in those days were called something to do with metal: *Metal Invader*, *Metal Holocaust*, *Metal Command*. But Becirovic also wanted to include hardcore and punk. As he was browsing one of Carlquist's issues of the horror magazine *Fangoria*, he noticed an article about American sensationalist publications in the 1950s—and got an idea.

"One of them was called *The National Close-Up*. The cover story was 'Maniac eats his wife alive,' and it showed some guy who'd eaten a corpse or something like that. 'Fuck, that's cool!' we thought, and we stole the whole front page. It was a facsimile, so we just copied the entire thing. Gore and death metal was all the rage back then, so people really liked it. It provoked a reaction."

Once the time had come to put the publication on paper, the new publishers were so pleased with the result that they decided to have it professionally printed.

"They wanted 11,000 kr to print 1,000 copies. That meant 11 kronor per copy. We went ahead with the printing and then brought them along to Bergslagsrocken in Fagersta, where we sold them for 20 kr. That was certainly no rip-off."

The first issue of *Close-Up* was published in June 1991 and sold at festivals and through a handful of record stores in Gothenburg and Stockholm. After six months, all 1,000 copies were gone. For the second issue, they increased circulation to 1,500.

"The first issue had a really cocky editorial," recalls *Hymen* editor Anders Jakobson. "'There is not a single spelling mistake in this magazine,' they bragged, but there was. They came marching in and cornered the market. Then again, the magazine is still around to this day. They managed to maintain a regular publication rate that fanzines definitely couldn't match."

Instead of fading away, *Close-Up* established themselves as Sweden's biggest metal magazine in the '90s. Soon, the publication could be found in stores all over the country, next to car magazines and gossip tabloids. Becirovic has a paradoxical theory of how this happened.

"This was never our intention. Other magazines such as *Metal Zone*, *Heavy Mental*, and *Kool Kat News* started out with ambitions of becoming regular publications. They were meant to be commercially viable and provide income to the people involved. This was not the case with us. We made one issue but enjoyed it so much that we just kept going."

As pop culture was given increasingly extensive media attention during the '90s, more extreme forms of metal started attracting coverage in both newspapers and tabloids. In September of 1991, the influential monthly *Nöjesguiden* contained a long feature about the new death metal wave. Music journalist Jan Gradvall wrote about the record store House of Kicks and American death metal band Morbid Angel as well as Swedish bands Entombed and Dismember. Entombed even ended up on the cover. It's the first time that death metal is embraced and given attention by a respected journalist in Sweden.

"I remember the article contained a list of the best Swedish extreme metal albums, compiled by Johan Hargeby at House of Kicks and Fred Estby of Dismember. They put Bathory's debut album in third place," says Jan Gradvall. "Jonas Åkerlund called me and was really happy, because it was essentially the first time that Bathory were mentioned by a major Swedish magazine."

With death and black metal at its peak in the early '90s, mainstream magazines geared toward younger readers occasionally covered them. *Ultra* (no relation to the Ultra House) was a free publication provided to all high-school students. In one issue, Entombed were interviewed, and in another, Jon Nödtveidt and Ole Öhman from Dissection talked about dreams. They were pictured lying in a bed, pretending to be asleep. Leading tabloid *Expressen* interviewed At the Gates while they were doing laundry.

In 2001, *Close-Up* finally found a real competitor in *Sweden Rock Magazine*, run and financed by the organization behind the Sweden Rock Festival. Originally named *Bright Eyes Metal Magazine*, it was started as a fanzine in 1997 by Mark Frostenäs and Micke Svensson. Twelve issues later and with a steady circulation of a few hundred copies, Sweden Rock suggested a collaboration that would make their festival brand visible all year round.

Both magazines have covered most metal subgenres over the years, but there are factors clearly separating the two. *Sweden Rock Magazine* mainly focuses on classic, melodic rock, and heavy metal, while *Close-Up* features more extreme acts as well as punk bands. Whereas *Sweden Rock* has presented their readers with in-depth articles about rock history ranging from Queen to AC/DC, *Close-Up* has devoted countless columns to alternative art rock released by smaller independent labels. For most Swedish metalheads, the two magazines are easy to distinguish. Many fans buy both regularly.

These days, *Sweden Rock Magazine* is captained by Martin Carlsson, who once produced the fanzine *Megalomaniac* and worked with *Close-Up* for 20 years.

Becirovic talks about his competitors without sounding the slightest bit anxious.

"It's great if there's more than one magazine to read. If *Sweden Rock* does something really well, then we try to do something else much better."

As an editor, he could tell you in his sleep which bands and phenomena enjoy the most popularity with metal readers.

"Death metal has always been popular. And then artists with a hardcore following in Sweden—HIM, Thåström, Slipknot—stuff like that sells really well."

At times, he's been surprised by the conservative tastes of the metal audience.

"When we put The Donnas on the cover, the sales were so disastrous that our distributor called and wanted to discuss the matter. We thought it would be cool with girls on the cover, and they had a certain *Cosmopolitan* vibe to them. But the metalheads didn't want the girls. They'd rather not buy the magazine at all. If we put the ugly old guys from Iron Maiden on the cover, however, we sell like hotcakes."

Thirty-five years after the commercial breakthrough of metal, it remains one of the most popular music genres in Sweden. No one raises an eyebrow when nationwide mainstream media, like morning paper *Dagens Nyheter* or the cultural news on Sveriges Television, interview prominent bands like Opeth or Arch Enemy. In July of 2011, Sveriges Television aired "The Big 4" concert live from Gothenburg. Six hours of Metallica, Slayer, Megadeth, and Anthrax were broadcasted on the largest network in the country on a Friday night. Metal has truly become the music of the masses.

Yet there's been another development regarding more extreme outposts like death and black metal. While these subgenres are still covered by big media outlets, it's primarily in the form of reviews—not interviews or longer articles. At the same time, despite their aggressive and controversial nature, they tend to be treated with more cultural sophistication and respect than traditional metal.

Hipster culture magazine *Vice* began covering black metal in the mid-'00s, which lead to an increasing number of people discovering the style. This combined with Swedish black metal band Watain, which breathed new life into the genre's popularity and possessed serious media skills, resulted in the genre becoming surprisingly trendy—something to wear on your sleeve and use for positioning yourself as cool and hip. This has also been evident in newspaper culture sections.

When American photographer Peter Beste published his photo book *True Norwegian Black Metal* in 2008, it was received very well. Same with the artist Ragnar Persson, whose illustrations are strongly influenced by fanzine art and black metal motives. Yet mainstream media rarely interview the actual bands.

Journalist Christoffer Röstlund Jonsson has been writing about metal for 20 years, contributing to *Close-Up Magazine*, *Sweden Rock Magazine*, and leading tabloid *Aftonbladet*, to name a few. He says that even if metal is covered more now, the genre is still not handled in a serious manner outside of the metal magazines.

"It's still regarded as something childish. No one outside writes serious articles about metal artists—not like they would about Morrissey or other culturally accepted icons."

He points out that most major print media doesn't even have a dedicated metal critic.

"No one seems to care about knowing the subject matter when writing about metal. What I can't wrap my head around are these respected journalists still spelling thrash metal as *trash* or Megadeth as *Megadeath*. It makes me want to eat glass."

VII.

Black Metal

It wasn't enough to just have a Satanic image. You had to fully embody it in everything you did. It had to be a part of your life.

— It, Abruptum

I
T's 1992, ON A MILD SUMMER NIGHT in late July. 18-year-old Mara catches a commuter train to one of Stockholm's northern suburbs. In her bag is a record by Norwegian black metal band Burzum, a threatening letter, a knife, a container of flammable liquid, and matches. She gets off at the Upplands Väsby station, then walks the last stretch until finally reaching a yellow wooden house. Christofer Johnsson, vocalist and front man of Therion—one of Stockholm's best-known death metal bands—lives here with his parents.

It's almost midnight. Mara walks around the house surveying the surroundings. A terrace door is open. She hears sounds from a television but is unable to determine if Christofer is home. In the back of the house, she discovers a door situated out of view from the street. It will do just fine. She empties the container on the door, the excess liquid forming a small pool on the ground. She then unpacks the album and the letter. It reads "IT and The Count were here, and we will be back." On the record sleeve, "A greeting from The Count" is written with a black marker. The black-and-white cover artwork shows a shadowy figure on a windy plain, next to a tree with long serpentine branches. The back of the sleeve features a photo of The Count, also known as Varg Vikernes, in a black cape and corpse paint makeup.

She pins the record and the letter to the wall of the house using the knife. Then she strikes a match.

———

Parallel to the meteoric rise of Swedish death metal in the early '90s, a similar, albeit more sinister, subgenre was gestating in Norway. This offshoot would come to be known as *black metal*, a phrase originally coined in 1982 by British metal outfit Venom and their second album, *Black Metal*. However, the music being made in Norway had little in common with the bands that inspired it.

Apart from Venom, the so-called "first wave of black metal" consisted of bands like Bathory, Mercyful Fate, Sarcófago, and Hellhammer. They could arguably be defined as heavy or thrash metal outfits but differentiated themselves through explicitly dark themes. The vocals were rawer than most contemporaries, and the lyrics fixated on death, Satanism, and the occult rather than hot chicks, alcohol, and headbanging. Black metal bands were more extreme and often elaborately secretive.

The black metal wave of the '90s adopted similar lyrical themes but explored them much further. The sound was built on the same foundation of aggression as death metal but with a more primitive and barren soundscape. The riffs were infused with darkness and atmosphere, and vocals ranged from desperate shrieks to grunting snarls.

Mayhem by now sat in the epicenter of the Norwegian black metal scene. Having formed in 1984, they quickly made a name for themselves within the small underground scene of extreme metal. When Swedish singer Pelle "Dead" Ohlin stepped in as vocalist in 1988, the band cemented the stylistic approach that would later serve as the blueprint for the black metal movement at large. Pelle brought his fascination with death and darkness into the lyrics as well as the band's aesthetics. Band members began wearing corpse paint and posing with blood and animal parts in promo photos and on stage.

Spearheaded by guitarist and visionary leader Øystein "Euronymous" Aarseth, the band adopted an uncompromising approach to black metal. Their aim was to push boundaries as far as possible to render the music genuinely evil and repulsive.

When Pelle "Dead" Ohlin committed suicide in the spring of 1991, Mayhem drummer Jan Axel "Hellhammer" Blomberg observed increasingly idiosyncratic behavior in his bandmate Øystein.

"He became a lot worse then—far worse. I think he crossed a line when Pelle died. I remember him nurturing a bunch of weird ideas, like being able to control death."

About a month after the death of Pelle, Øystein opened the record store Helvete ("Hell") on Schweigaards Gate in central Oslo with financial help from his parents. The store immediately became the center of the emerging Norwegian black metal scene, with Øystein as its self-appointed leader. Helvete was strictly a store for extreme metal, selling records, fanzines, and other band-related merchandise.

The walls were painted black, and in a corner of the store, fragments of Pelle's skull were on display in a glass case. The basement of Helvete was converted into the label headquarters for Deathlike Silence Productions.

For the first time, the few active members of the scene had a gathering place to congregate. With everyone scattered across Norway, contact had been mainly been through letters and phone calls. From then on, the scene evolved rapidly.

Norwegian death metal band Darkthrone, whose debut album *Soulside Journey* was recorded in Stockholm's Sunlight Studio, realigned entirely and immersed themselves in black metal. Helvete was frequented by Emperor from Notodden, Immortal and Burzum from Bergen, and Thorns from Trondheim.

Swedish musician Jon Nödtveidt of Dissection took the weekend bus to Oslo to visit Helvete, together with other members of the small metal scene in the border town of Strömstad. They often stayed in the store overnight, partying with the Norwegian bands.

The Norwegians, on the other hand, traveled to Sweden to attend shows and hang out with friends from other bands.

The collective based around Helvete soon outlined a form of mutual agenda. They discussed ideological principles as well as the significance of Satanism and evil. A common thread is hatred for the world around them and undefined feelings of alienation that are fueled within the group. Conversations soon turn to discussions on taking real action.

Øystein forms a Satanic order called The Black Circle, a type of interest group for the evilest and most dedicated within the black metal scene. Others in the group include fellow Mayhem member Jan Axel "Hellhammer" Blomberg, Varg "Count Grishnackh" Vikernes from Burzum, Gylve "Fenriz" Nagell of Darkthrone, and fanzine editor Jon "Metalion" Kristiansen.

Whereas death metal at the time is more or less void of intellectual approach, black metal soon becomes synonymous with elitism, emphasis on the concept of the übermensch, and various other proto-fascist notions borrowed from German philosopher Friedrich Nietzsche.

The most central idea is to really practice what you preach—to be *true*.

"We took ourselves incredibly seriously and did not tolerate being questioned," says Jan Axel Blomberg.

Øystein was 23 at the time, a few years older than the others. With his background in Mayhem and his grandiose ideas, he quickly assumed a leading position in the group. 17-year-old Varg Vikernes also became a prominent figure. He was the sole member of Burzum as well as the new bass player in Mayhem.

———

In the small Swedish town of Finspång, IT of the black metal duo Abruptum began studying and experimenting with occultism early on, starting a metal band and labelling himself a Satanist by the age of 12. IT had founded his own organization, True Satanist Horde, back in 1989, parallel to the preparations for recording the band's first demo. The True Satanist Horde soon garnered a reputation in underground circles. The meetings in Finspång were attended by Jon Nödtveidt and Ole Öhman of Dissection, Morgan Håkansson of Marduk, and various other musicians with an interest in Satanism. According to IT, Øystein Aarseth and Varg Vikernes were initially members of the organization before deciding to found the Norwegian faction called The Black Circle.

"I'm not really sure if I should get into what we discussed in True Satanist Horde," IT explains. "It was largely about causing harm to people and how to affect humanity in negative ways. It could be through selling drugs, distributing underground pornography, burning churches, murdering priests, or whatever fucking thing we could come up with."

During get-togethers, the crew fantasized freely and made great plans. They drank cheap beer and dreamed of starting their own village in the wilderness, living completely outside of society. Terms like "prospect" and "hang-around" were appropriated from the infamous biker gang the Hells Angels, with the goal of creating a kind of brotherhood—a Satanic army at war with the world.

"We had a general hatred toward something larger that was hard to define," says Ole Öhman, then drummer of Dissection. "I was very cold."

Jan Axel Blomberg also finds it difficult to pinpoint the actual source of this hatred.

"It had nothing to do with society; this was no punk rock attitude. We spurred each other on, creating grand illusions about who we actually were and how we were supposed to behave, until we finally started believing it ourselves."

IT had perceived himself as different, almost inhuman, from very early on and was surprised to learn that neither Vikernes nor Øystein seemed to have had especially harsh or difficult childhoods.

"I found it very strange, because I had a very rough childhood with a lot of violence, alcohol, and drugs. The Count, on the other hand, seemed to have had a completely normal upbringing. He lived in a house with his mother in Bergen and had a nice and pleasant life up until then."

In the spring of 1992, two essential albums of the second wave of black metal were released.

Darkthrone's *A Blaze in the Northern Sky* opened with the track "Kathaarian Life Code." Desolate synthesizers and chanting voices set the atmosphere before the nearly 11-minute track really takes off. The overall sensation is one of cold aggression, more controlled than the hardcore punk-infused racket of early death metal.

In the same time period, Deathlike Silence Productions released Burzum's self-titled debut, which featured the desperate howling of Varg Vikernes over heavy melancholic riffs. The production was very raw and the fidelity quite thin. Both albums touched on themes of folkloric romanticism, both in the texture of the sound and in lyrical content— something that has continued to develop over the years until becoming practically synonymous with Norwegian black metal.

The Norwegian black metal contingent soon becomes more and more agitated with the increasing success of Swedish death metal bands. Their lyrics were seen as too socially topical and inappropriate, considering the brutality of the genre. There's also a growing disdain for the increasingly polished productions of major death metal bands. The release of Entombed's sophomore album, *Clandestine*, urged countless Swedish bands in a similar direction, which was met with fierce disapproval from the Norwegians.

Furthermore, death metal bands were now attracting mainstream attention from Swedish tabloids in a manner the black metal community perceived as farcical. Entombed's music video with model and vocalist La Camilla from tongue-in-cheek Eurodance group Army of Lovers was just too hard to digest.

During the summer of 1992, Varg Vikernes sent threats to several Swedish acts, including Therion and Entombed, accusing them of being too commercial and not *true* and of playing "life metal" instead of "death metal." Many bands received weird threatening phone calls.

"We were pretty pissed off, actually," says guitarist Uffe Cederlund of Entombed. "Suddenly, we were labeled a 'life metal' band just because we had fun playing. I hated that attitude. We had been friends with these people. It was like getting stabbed in the back."

His bandmate, drummer Nicke Andersson, says Darkthrone stayed at his place while recording their debut in Sunlight Studio and that they had been friends for a long time. One day, his phone rang, and on the other end, someone speaking Norwegian proclaimed they were on the death list.

"What death list? An anonymous death list? Fenriz was one of my first pen pals. Back in those days, he was a funny little glam rocker, strutting around in one of those Slash top hats and listening to L.A. Guns. He crashed at my place when they played Stockholm, and we had a great time. One year later, they didn't want to be friends anymore. We asked ourselves what we'd done wrong."

In the case of Therion, Vikernes simply dismissed their lyrics as pro-life and political. In his view, socially conscious or topical lyrics do not belong in death or black metal. There's one lyric he particularly detests about Coca-Cola destroying the rainforest.

Rumors of threats spread like wildfire through the Swedish underground scene. As The Black Circle and True Satanist Horde become increasingly notorious, the groups kept pushing the limits of how far they could go. Øystein prints shirts stating "*Drep de kristne*"—"Slay the Christians"—selling them in Helvete. Someone nails a dead badger to the door of the Hogdal church outside Strömstad.

"I remember IT being absolutely ecstatic about the *Estonia* disaster," says Andreas "Whiplasher" Bergh. The *Estonia* ferry capsized in 1994, resulting in the loss of 854 lives, and was the deadliest boat accident in non-wartime Europe.

"He walked around wearing a T-shirt that said, 'And kill those fucking whales.' We were anti-everything basically. A lot of it was about desensitizing yourself, and everyone's ambition was to be more evil than the next guy."

Today, Emil Nödtveidt and Andreas Bergh play in industrial band Deathstars, but they were part of the '90s Strömstad scene with the death metal project Swordmaster. They were well acquainted with many of the True Satanist Horde members.

"We weren't that involved with the things going on in Finspång. A lot of it was about being as extreme as possible. There was a lot of 'Evil night!' going on, or 'I wish you an evil Christmas.'"

Emil Nödtveidt, the younger brother of Jon Nödtveidt, continues:

"What the hell are you saying—the food tastes *good*? No, it tastes EVIL!"

Up until then, the struggle to become the evilest had mainly been a contest with words. Soon, however, petty mischief such as knocking over gravestones developed into far more sinister acts.

"Everything had become so fucking extreme," says Andreas Bergh, reminiscing about the time he sat on what they called the "beer mountain" in Grebbestad—a gathering point for local metalheads on the picturesque western coast of Sweden—wearing a King Diamond shirt.

"Perra, the vocalist of Satanized, who I'm good friends with today, was a real brawler back then. He approached me and shouted, 'Are you *true* or not? Are you *true?*' All from Abruptum beat up a cop that same night. I mean really smashed his face in. He then began walking the 20 miles back to Strömstad. After a few miles, he pounded on the door of some random house, screaming, 'Give me a fucking ride home!' He was covered in blood. They told him they were unable to drive him anywhere, but that he was welcome to stay the night."

During the summer, Varg Vikernes visited Strömstad to hang out with IT and Jon Nödtveidt. He walked around the coastal town with a 16-inch blade strapped to his thigh. They all partied together and sat around bickering.

IT remembers their discussions.

"According to The Count, there was no band more evil than Burzum. I remember arguing about it. I said, 'Abruptum is pure evil. It's not fucking music—it's the most evil sound you could ever listen to.' And he countered with 'No, Burzum is even *more* evil.'"

He mentions how it was first and foremost Øystein and Varg who nitpicked over which attitudes and opinions were deemed acceptable. They imposed strict rules, carving what qualified as black metal behavior in stone.

"All of that came from Norway. How you should dress, what music to listen to, which bands were *true*, and those who were not. It wasn't enough to just have a Satanic image. You had to fully embody it in everything you did. It had to be a part of your life."

On June 6, 1992, Norwegian media broadcast disturbing news: The Fantoft Stave Church outside Bergen had burned to the ground. The wooden church, a popular Norwegian historical monument built in 1150, was constructed with a special stave technique used in medieval times. The news caused outrage in the general public.

It's hard to determine when the term "true metal" was first coined. However, the band that undoubtedly worked the hardest to establish the concept was the American band Manowar. The word *true* remains a divisive moniker, especially within black metal.

Before even releasing their first album in the early '80s, Manowar accused other bands of playing "false metal." Acts like Twisted Sister became targets and were ridiculed for everything from haircuts to inadequate musicianship.

Manowar envisioned themselves living and dying for metal. Bass player Joey DeMaio had a history as bass tech and pyrotechnician for Black Sabbath, stating that things could hardly be more metal than that. When releasing their second album *Into Glory Ride* in 1983, Manowar signed the record contract in their own blood.

On the same record, Manowar coined their motto "Death to false metal." The album sold in excess of 100,000 copies, spreading the message across the metal world. In a music documentary from the early '80s, the young members of Metallica sit on a couch, proclaiming "death to false metal."

In hindsight, Manowar's zealous belief in their own authenticity and message was a brilliant marketing tactic. From this perspective, heavy metal also follows a tradition present in popular music since the dawn of the last century.

In the book *Faking It—The Quest for Authenticity in Popular Music*, authors Hugh Barker and Yuval Taylor tell the tale of Lead Belly, an African-American artist who performed American folk songs for an almost exclusively white audience. Born Huddie Ledbetter, he spent time in prison for both murder and attempted murder, and when released in 1934, folklorists Alan and John Lomax brought him out on tour. With his strong, immersive voice, he performed old folk songs he'd learned in prison and was immediately praised for being authentic and genuine.

To the white audience, Lead Belly came to embody notions of the primitive, untamed, and violent black man who performed emotional songs from the depths of his soul. When he had his commercial breakthrough in 1935, American newspapers seemingly competed in their attempts at exoticizing him. The *New York Herald Tribune* wrote an article with the headline: "LOMAX ARRIVES WITH LEAD BELLY, NEGRO MINSTREL: SWEET SINGER OF THE SWAMPLANDS HERE TO DO A FEW TUNES BETWEEN HOMICIDES." *Time* reviewed him as the "murderous minstrel," and the *Brooklyn Eagle* came up with "Virtuoso of knife and guitar."

But Lead Belly wasn't "genuine." Certainly, he'd killed a man and tried to murder another—but he was a puppet in the hands of "managers" John and Alan Lomax. They demanded he perform in prison clothes, instead of the finely tailored, well-pressed suits he preferred. They determined which songs he was to sing. It's telling that Lead Belly's audience was entirely white, whereas black youths listened to music that was truly theirs: blues, jazz, and the emerging R&B. This was music that underwent explosive developments and advancements throughout the two decades that Lead Belly was one of the main standard bearers for black music in the eyes of white America. Rather than highlighting this music, which was considered too sophisticated, John and Alan Lomax sought out "primitive" black artists: acts who better suited their prejudices about what black men were like.

Even though notions of authenticity can be considered marketing constructs, designed to sell more records, they remain important criteria within popular music to this day. We see this in rock music and to an even greater degree in rap and hip-hop, where an artist's legitimacy is an important promotional device.

The importance of being perceived as real can also be quite confrontational. When the dedication of Richey Edwards of Welsh band Manic Street Preachers was questioned in a 1991 interview with British music magazine *New Musical Express* (NME), he didn't respond directly but instead proceeded to carve the words "4 REAL" into his arm—so deeply that there was severe tissue damage. He had to be admitted to a hospital and received 18 stitches. Three years later, he disappeared, and he was pronounced dead in 2008.

According to his suicide note, Nirvana vocalist Kurt Cobain was so tormented by feelings of disingenuity that it was a contributing factor in his 1994 suicide. Grunge music, a genre founded on soul-searching and obtusely emotional lyrics, all but died out in the wake of Cobain's passing (save for pop faux-grunge acts like Nickelback, which bear as much similarity to hair metal and contemporary American country music as they do to grunge). Given the impossible standards Kurt felt he failed to meet, what could possibly be more *true* than suicide? In the note, which addresses the fans directly, Cobain writes, "The fact is, I can't fool you, any one of you. It simply isn't fair to you or me. The worst crime I can think of would be to rip people off by faking it and pretending as if I'm having 100% fun." One of his favorite artists was Lead Belly.

If Manowar kicked off the authenticity crusade in heavy metal, Øystein Aarseth dramatically raised the stakes. He took what was regarded as *true* within black metal to entirely new levels.

In a June 1992 interview for Sweden's *Close-Up Magazine*, he stated: "What they're doing is a mockery of all that death metal originally stood for, and it is an offense to us. Mayhem is the only remaining band from the early '80s not having wimped out. It's a travesty, seeing all these new idiots following whichever way the wind blows without having the faintest clue about what death metal really was. We're fairly sure that none of these trend bands have even heard Venom, to whom they owe their very existence. Regarding Therion, the worst of all Swedish bands, we have a message for them: If they dare set foot in Norway with the intention of playing their life metal, we shall kill them. The entire Norwegian black metal population will be there with knives. Knives that cut deep."

Word about the article spread rapidly, and soon, everyone in the underground had read the magazine. Mayhem had forged a reputation as an extreme band early on, but this brought things above and beyond. In the interview, Øystein also praises Pol Pot and promoted "War, sodomy, and dictatorship!"

"It was the first time anyone proclaimed death metal as wimpy," says Pelle "Hellbutcher" Gustafsson—vocalist of Nifelheim—who was 16 years old when he read the *Close-Up* article.

In the interview, however, Øystein envisioned a bright future: "Things have slowly gotten better since the death of the Goat—many bands who live according to the old, genuine lifestyle have emerged. Norway is a leading country—acts like Immortal, Burzum, Darkthrone, Thorns, Malfeitor, Incarnator, and so on are insanely good and incredibly evil."

———

The fire catches, but nowhere near as much as Mara had hoped. She'd have preferred to see the door fully engulfed in flames. Instead, it's merely smoldering a bit as she leaves, disappointed.

Christofer Johnsson is in Austria on tour with Therion and only finds out what has happened upon returning home. He's well aware of who Varg Vikernes is. While most recipients just throw their threatening letters away, Christofer Johnsson becomes so infuriated, he sends a letter in return, telling The Count to go fuck himself.

During the autumn of 1992, several more Norwegian churches burn to the ground: the 1887 Skjold Church in Vindafjord, a chapel from the turn of the century in Holmenkollen, the Åsane Church in Bergen that was built in 1795, and a Methodist church in Sarpsborg, where a fireman is killed trying to quench the flames. The police have no leads whatsoever.

On January 20, 1993, Varg Vikernes gives an anonymous interview to the daily newspaper *Bergens Tidende*. He has just recorded a new Burzum album and lures the journalists in with promises of "interesting information."

In the article, Finn Bjørn Tønder describes being invited to the home of the 20-year-old Vikernes for a midnight interview. The apartment is pitch-black, and the journalist has been warned that Vikernes is armed in the event that the newspaper has contacted the police. In the dark, Tønder can see a variety of weapons, Nazi memorabilia, and Satanic symbols. Vikernes sits in a corner and talks about burning churches. He says things like "Our intention is to spread terror and devilry. Fear of the powers of darkness, which is why we're revealing all this to *Bergens Tidende*. It started with the Fantoft Stave Church, and we're not stopping with the eight churches that have burned so far."

The journalist initially doubts the validity of Vikernes' sensational claims, but after double-checking with the police, it becomes evident how much of the detailed information could only have been known to the culprit. For example, the detail of a decapitated rabbit placed on the Fantoft Stave Church's stairs had been kept out of the media.

"We planned to ambush the first person to come walking through the woods, knowing how students often take that route. Unfortunately, no one came. It would have had more of an effect to sacrifice a dead student rather than a rabbit," Vikernes said in the interview.

The article ended with Vikernes claiming to know who set fire to the churches—and who committed an unsolved murder in the Lillehammer Olympic Park in August of 1992, which was an open case that had been stumping the cops.

Vikernes would later state how he thought the interview would result in a minor notice toward the end of the paper. Instead, he found himself on the front page under a headline that proclaimed, "We lit the fires" complete with the subtitle "Devil worshippers confess to eight church arsons."

The story launches the media portrayal of "The Count," along with a lurid presentation of the terrifying new youth phenomenon called "black metal." Later the same day, Vikernes is arrested on suspicion of multiple church burnings. Law enforcement already had an eye on him, because of a photo of the smoldering ruins of the Fantoft church that appeared on the cover of his latest Burzum EP, *Aske* (Ashes). The first 1,000 copies also came with a Zippo lighter.

Not long after, police knocked on the door to Mara's home in the Stockholm suburb of Nacka and arrested her on suspicion of arson and criminal threatening.

The article in *Bergens Tidende* garners significant attention both in Norway and the neighboring countries. Teenagers, metal music, and Satanism: It is irresistibly delicious, the perfect story. Tabloids in both Sweden and Norway follow the case closely, reporting on the "devil-worshipping sects." The British music magazine *Kerrang!* publishes a huge story on black metal with Varg Vikernes on the cover. Suddenly, the entire metal world knows what's going on in Norway.

Shortly thereafter, the police connect the attempted arson of Christofer Johnsson's home to the Norwegians.

A February 1993 article in Swedish tabloid *Aftonbladet* features a huge photo of The Count, posing with two knives and long black hair covering his face. Under the headline "He ordered the arson," the story speaks of The Count's girlfriend, "Maria," who acted under orders of her leader. In March of 1993, *Aftonbladet* write about "Maria" once again, this time with the headline "I'm guilty of arson." They publish excerpts from her diary and portray her as an ordinary, well-behaved teenager—except for fanatical devil worship and Satanic convictions.

The excerpts are written in typical teenage lingo but contain some unsettling information. "Oh, by the way ... this past Saturday I committed arson ... oops?" The diary also reads, "I love The Count. His imagination is the best! He's going to do it. I want a knife ... a nice knife. A sharp and evil one ... hehe."

On the photo, she poses with an inverted cross covering her face.

"Several journalists wanted to speak with me, but none of them seemed particularly interested in my story unless it was exactly what they wanted me to say—that I was a victim, how I was the little girl who ended up in bad company carrying out other people's orders. And I didn't find this picture of myself to be the slightest bit correct. I did things because I thought it'd be fun. This went completely over people's heads."

Mara has long blonde hair and eyes us suspiciously. Since that night in July of 1992, she's been interviewed quite a few times and not once does she consider herself accurately quoted. She doesn't want us to publish the name she went under during the '90s.

"This portrayal of me as the victim was quite shocking. I found an old issue of *Aftonbladet* with an article about me in it, written as if I'd actually spoken to the journalist. It described me as a typical girl next door who liked horses before I met 'the great rock star' at a gig. I suddenly and unexpectedly turned into a groupie who had gone to séances with him. Needless to say, I was furious."

Mara grew up in Nacka and describes her childhood as fairly normal—"no divorces, no weird stuff." She found metal through other kids living on the same block, and once she started high school, music had become her greatest obsession. Bands like Accept, Iron Maiden, and Judas Priest were soon traded for harder music. The urge turned into an addiction, as she would constantly seek out more and more extreme bands.

"The music is very suggestive. It was about manipulating my own state of mind. Listening to it made me feel good in some weird way. The reasons for it varied. The music was always there in the background."

Like most kids into death metal during the late '80s, she was also interested in macabre themes: horror movies, magic, and the spirit world. Mara studied *Necronomicon* and read Aleister Crowley. It wasn't enough that the music was good, the lyrics were equally important—otherwise, she felt cheated. She likens the feeling to buying a Stephen King book with a great horror title and cover artwork, only to find a sappy love story within—it just feels wrong. Not everyone felt this way, though.

"It was as if I'd been jogging along with people for a while, and then suddenly, there's a straight stretch, and I break into a flat-out sprint while everyone else keeps jogging. That's what it felt like. All of them were stuck in this strange phase. 'I like horror movies and all, but I'm against all forms of violence.' No, that didn't quite gel for me."

Why Mara herself didn't think violence was a bad thing is something she struggles to explain. She says it became an infatuation.

"I couldn't understand how someone could be so fascinated by something that they could watch hours of it on film, listen to songs about it, and constantly talk about it—but then not really believe in it. Either you're for or entirely against. I didn't understand the concept of gray areas back then. I hadn't really been subjected to actual violence either."

These days, she recognizes that attitude as both immature and a bit silly. At the same time, she points out how she was no oblivious teenager, but rather a pretty cynical one.

Mara believes feelings of empathy are developed quite late in life, and teenagers don't have very much of them. Especially not in extreme circles, which is why she found herself so drawn to them.

"I could finally be myself. No one was forcing me to adapt to their preconceived notions of how to behave. Some children have natural empathy, but not everybody. I imagine it's easier to push it aside during puberty if it hasn't developed fully. That's why I felt so at home in these crowds; I felt free."

Around this time, Mara ordered an Abruptum demo and received a response from IT, inviting her to join the newly formed group True Satanist Horde. Mara travelled to Finspång to hang out over a weekend and found a context where she felt she belonged.

IT and his girlfriend Alexandra Balogh lived in a small studio apartment that had become a gathering place for fans of the darkest forms of metal. Guests from all over the country came to party.

During the festivities, they'd play role-playing games and make plans for annihilating the human race.

"People were mostly just sitting around trying to outdo each other with evil ideas and various plans that never came to fruition, instead of actually getting up and doing something," says Mara.

By ordering an album by Burzum, Mara also got in touch with Varg Vikernes. They began exchanging letters and speaking over the phone, and plans were soon made for Mara to come visit him in Bergen.

On June 5, 1992, she caught an Oslo-bound train and spent the night at Helvete. The next day, she flew to Bergen, where she met an exhilarated Varg Vikernes. Fantoft Stave Church had burned to the ground the night before, and all the media headlines spoke of the fire. He brought her sightseeing, to witness the remaining embers.

"It was the first time something big happened," Mara says. "We spoke over the phone the night before I left; it was supposed to happen at 6 o'clock in the morning. The plan was for multiple churches to burn simultaneously, but everyone else chickened out. He'd taken lots of pictures. Wait a minute—I actually had the photos developed for him in Sweden. They were taken after the police sealed off the area, and there were also a few snaps of his brother on the same camera roll."

During her visit to Bergen, Mara and Varg Vikernes became a couple. She was attracted to his grand outlook and hateful attitude.

"Then it pretty quickly became obvious that he was just a big talker. According to him, he was the only one who was *true*—even though he constantly switched ideologies and then claimed to have had those opinions all along."

Later that summer, Vikernes travelled to Stockholm to visit Mara and other Swedish Satanists he'd been in touch with. One day, IT and Vikernes sat in Mara's room, raging about Therion.

They scribble out a greeting on a piece of paper and Vikernes also signs a Burzum album, which they ask Mara to deliver.

"IT said I had to prove myself *true* to become a real member of the Horde. Like a rite of passage," she says.

The scheme was for Mara to smash a window of Therion's rehearsal place and throw in the Burzum album with the accompanying letter, signed by both of them. However, Therion rehearsed in a basement, and Mara didn't know which window was theirs. They're not the only band in the building. She also thinks the task is kind of ridiculous for an initiation, and that's when she comes up with the idea of a home delivery.

In order for Christofer Johnsson to really notice the message, she wants to draw extra attention to it.

She stresses that the purpose was never to burn the house down.

"If so, there would have been little point in leaving a message behind."

Shortly after the attempted arson, Varg Vikernes sends Christofer Johnsson a letter in which he mentions having forgotten some matches and a signed record in Sweden—has Christofer seen them, by any chance? He writes that he will return, and perhaps Johnsson's parents will die an unnatural death before their son. "We Norwegians are mentally disturbed. I exist in medieval times ... as do my methods for death and torture." Then he asks if Johnsson has a sister, adding that he has a dildo with spikes.

Christofer Johnson brings the letter straight to the cops, demanding they take immediate action. Nothing happens. The media frenzy in Norway has yet to begin, and the police don't seem to be taking him very seriously.

In metal circles, there is plenty of talk about what actually happened that night. Despite The Count taking responsibility through his letter, everyone soon knows Mara was the one who did it. She's quite pleased with her achievement. She writes in her diary, "I'm now free to enter the Horde as a member ... but if I want I can join the Norwegian 'horde' instead ... it's called The Black Circle. If I must choose, I'll probably pick the Norwegian one, since I'm moving there either way ... in a year or so. It's also—in my eyes—more brutal than TSH. If someone gives me attitude, they'll come here and cut or slay the person in question."

Mara adds how she's considering asking her father for a crossbow with bolts, writing "That would be truly evil!"

The drunken tirades at True Satanist Horde meetings in Finspång ramp up, as more and more churches burn in Norway. Also, Bård "Faust" Eithun of Norwegian band Emperor has murdered a gay man in the Lillehammer Olympic Park during the late summer. The police don't know this yet, but news has reached quite a few in the inner black metal circles of Norway and Sweden. Bård works in the Helvete store and is close with Øystein.

Because there's loads of talk and very little action in both True Satanist Horde and The Black Circle, word spreads like wildfire when something tangible actually does go down.

"Euronymous called me one evening and said, 'The first murder has taken place,'" IT remembers. "It turned out that Faust has stabbed a gay man to death in the forest; they were infinitely proud of this. We had discussed murder and planned things like that, essentially daring and encouraging each other. Sort of like 'Let's see who does it first.' So, when he rang me, I imagine I answered along the line of 'It's probably time we act too,' or something like that."

Over the Halloween weekend, the True Satanist Horde gathered in Finspång for a meeting. Mara and Varg have broken up, and she's now seeing Jon Nödtveidt from Dissection. This weekend, the group is visited by 18-year-old prospect Johan Karlsson, who's been invited by IT. He has a solo black metal project and claims to be genuinely interested in Satanism. The meeting soon dissolves into a party.

"We got drunk, watched Monty Python movies, and did some role-playing. Him being there somehow made everything even more twisted. Like 'Okay, and who are you? Would you dare to kill someone?'" Then we went out to the pub, and Johan intended to prove to us that he truly had the guts," Mara recalls.

In the street, Karlsson approaches an elderly couple and asks for directions to the harbor. Finspång doesn't have a harbor, and as the man is about to respond, Karlsson stabs him in the throat with a utility knife. The older man almost bleeds to death, and Karlsson is later sentenced to four years in prison.

Mara recalls that no one reacted much; they thought it was more pathetic than cool.

"He didn't do it because he liked it—it was only to impress us. There's a difference," she says.

As the stabbing takes place, IT is in Norrköping to pick up Morgan Håkansson. They return to Finspång to find the group in complete disarray. He is annoyed by everyone's lack of resolve and drives Morgan back to Norrköping.

"The day after, we called the cops and told them it was Karlsson. We couldn't let anything jeopardize the inner circle, and we also really didn't like him," IT says.

In January of 1993, two policemen carrying a search warrant knock on the door of Mara's home. She can only watch as they descend upon the mess in her room, scooping up every paper they can find into big bags. They seize everything from casual notes to her employment certificate. They also find her diary.

Mara is arrested and transported to the Kronoberg detention center, where she's held under close watch. It's decided that Mara is to undergo a full mental health evaluation, and she's sent off to a psychiatric facility in Uppsala. After three months, she is diagnosed with borderline personality disorder.

"It's applicable to most people. Somebody has empathy disorders, sees things in black and white, has a foul temper—it's a standard diagnosis," she notes dryly.

While Mara is held in custody, additional incidents draw attention to the new Satanist wave. The Lundby New Church in Gothenburg is burned to the ground in February of 1993. Not until several years later are three teenagers convicted for the deed, claiming they were inspired by an article about The Count in the tabloid *iDag*.

An Entombed concert in Oslo is canceled by their record label after death threats from Norwegian Satanists.

Before her trial begins, Mara is contacted by Christian TV personality Siewert Öholm. He invites her to discuss the growing Satanist movement on his talk show, *Svar Direkt*. Since this is a live broadcast, a camera is rigged in the lunch room at the psychiatric clinic in Uppsala.

In the Gothenburg studio, Siewert Öholm welcomes Christofer Johnsson as the first guest. He has long blond hair and recounts matter-of-factly what happened the night of the arson. Öholm looks horrified. He introduces Mara through the livestream—black hair covering her face, she's wearing a black Mayhem shirt. Her arms show traces of fresh cuts. She slouches in the chair and gives sluggish responses to his questions. He wants to know if she's a Satanist. "Yes," she replies in a drawling fashion. He wants to know if this means that she worships the devil. "Yes," she answers again. Punk rockers in the audience snigger. She seems to struggle with words, seeming almost a bit stupid.

"I was pretty nervous sitting there, let me tell you. I doubt I made an especially good impression on anyone," says Mara.

Alexandra Balogh watched the show from her apartment in Finspång.

"I got angry when the audience laughed. She seemed drugged and had difficulties speaking."

IT decided to give an interview to *Aftonbladet*.

"I remember them asking me, 'Is murder OK?' to which I responded: 'Yes, if someone for example were to kill my mother,' and gave them my reasoning for it. The story's headline read 'Murder is right.' Suddenly, I had radio stations, TV, and papers calling me. It was pretty fucking rough there for a while."

Alexandra Balogh remembers being woken up one morning by TV talk show host Robert Aschberg ringing her doorbell, hollering about an interview through the letter box.

"It was given a disproportionate amount of attention. Adults like Siewert Öholm and Robert Aschberg sought to take advantage of the situation and blew it completely out of proportion. They didn't understand that we were all 17 to 21 years old and liked to exaggerate. Really, they should have been able to figure that one out for themselves."

The trial begins a few days after Mara's appearance on *Svar Direkt*, and in April of 1993, she is convicted and institutionalized with a special review required for discharge—essentially involuntary psychiatric treatment for an indefinite time. She's just turned 19 years old.

Mara herself hadn't quite grasped the scope of these events. She didn't consider her actions to be criminal and couldn't feel very upset over the situation she'd landed herself in. Today, she's unable to properly explain why she closed herself off so completely.

"It was something you worked on constantly. I learned to somehow disconnect from my emotions; that was the desired state. I imagine a lot of it is about fear. If nothing can hurt you, then no one can touch you. You can really shut yourself down. But why you would want to do that is a harder question to answer."

As the spotlight was turned on black metal, Varg Vikernes and Øystein Aarseth began to clash. Aarseth was angry that Vikernes snitched to *Bergens Tidende*. Vikernes, on the other hand, is annoyed that Aarseth has not properly capitalized on the situation Vikernes has created—how he's neglected to market black metal when the world media was watching. Instead, Aarseth closed Helvete down temporarily at the request of his parents. They also fight about money. Vikernes believes there to be discrepancies in Aarseth's sales reports.

On a night in August 1993, Vikernes drives from Bergen to Oslo with Snorre "Blackthorn" Ruch, the new guitarist in Mayhem. At 4 o'clock in the morning, Aarseth's doorbell rings. What then transpires has never been established completely. But when Vikernes leaves the apartment building, Aarseth is sprawled across the stairway, dead from more than 20 stab wounds.

Vikernes claims his ascent into a leadership position in their circle bothered Aarseth to the point that he was planning to torture and murder his rival. He also claims that Aarserth attacked him first and that he acted in self-defense.

The news quickly spreads to Sweden. The Strömstad crowd are just getting ready to board a train to the Hultsfred Festival when Jon Nödtveidt receives a phone call from Norway. Once on the train, they gather in their compartment, stand up, and raise their glasses in salute to Øystein Aarseth.

Jon Nödtveidt also calls IT to let him know what's happened.

"He told me the police suspected Satanists from Sweden," IT remembers. "At first, I simply sat there in complete shock before collecting my stuff and heading over to All's place."

Not sure whether someone is coming after Satanists who've been in contact with Aarseth, the two decide to take action. IT packs his Glock 17, and they hitchhike to Stockholm. They end up at a friend's party and get seriously drunk. Someone plays a cassette with Swedish dance band Vikingarna and IT flies into a rage, smashing the tape over his own forehead with such force that it draws blood. Later in the evening, he's arrested in front of the Royal Palace for trespassing.

"The guard kept poking my chest with his assault rifle, and by the time the police arrived, there were six of them with their fucking weapons aimed straight at me. The police said, "Why are you bleeding from your forehead? Why are you carrying razors? Did you cut yourself?" I just said, 'I'm a Satanist. Leave me alone!' The following day, I was interrogated for five hours by KRIPOS, the Norwegian National Criminal Investigation Service."

IT says Norwegian police had found old letters between him and Øystein Aarseth. Some were written in a hostile tone, and they suspected a grudge. However, in one of the last letters IT offered Øystein the help of True Satanist Horde in his conflict with Varg Vikernes, deeming The Black Circle unable to provide support. Accompanying the letter was the *Aftonbladet* article, which KRIPOS interpreted as IT claiming justification for committing murder.

"After giving them specific information that only I had access to at that point, I managed to convince them it was Vikernes who did it," IT says. "As it happens, it was later revealed how Vikernes had in turn called the police and tipped them off that I killed Øystein. When they found his 'death list,' my name was third on it. He couldn't reach me anymore, so he tried to frame me instead."

Approximately one week after Aarseth's murder, Vikernes was arrested and ultimately sentenced to 21 years in prison for homicide, three church burnings, one attempted act of arson, and the theft of explosives.

With their two leading figures out of the picture, The Black Circle dissolves.

"When The Count murdered Euronymous, everything that had to do with True Satanist Horde died. At least for me," says Ole Öhman. "Øystein was one of the great charismatic leaders. He was the one with the vision. Jon and I went out into the woods and lit a sacrificial fire of Burzum relics. Albums and shirts—we burned everything related to Burzum."

After eight months of incarceration, Mara is discharged from the Nacka youth facility for institutional care. She makes no effort to contact her old friends but keeps hanging out in black metal circles. Mara writes lyrics for black metal band Siebenbürgen, and on the cover artwork of their 1997 album *Loreia*, she sits within a circle of lit candles, holding a skull.

These days, Christofer Johnsson sees the event somewhat differently.

"Had the media not blown everything out of proportion, no one besides the involved parties would have cared. I saw the burn marks on the door, and that would never have turned into a proper fire. Needless to say, it was as unpleasant as it was inexcusable—but at the same time, it was portrayed as 'Satanists trying to burn babies alive.' These babies were in fact my teenage brothers."

Even if Johnsson was provoked by Vikernes's attacks, he regards Mara's deeds as teenage mischief.

"I mean, she was 18 years old. Some become skinheads or hooligans at that age, and then in their 30s, they're great family men and normal, taxpaying citizens. One shouldn't pass too harsh a judgment. By the way, I think Afflicted threatened *her* later on—but that was probably more of a prank. That's what people didn't seem to comprehend, that it was a bunch of teenagers being stupid."

Jon "Metalion" Kristiansen believes many of the people involved in these circles were in fact very lonely. He says the goal was to push all emotions aside. This combined with their young age became a recipe for disaster.

"I believe many of us longed for something that we couldn't really define. Since we had no opportunity to act out our emotions, we grew introverted instead. There really wasn't anything else. In order to express your feelings, there must be someone on the receiving end, and many didn't have that."

After Bård Eithun had committed the Olympic Park murder, Metalion visited him and Øystein in Helvete.

"Øystein asked, 'Do you know what Bård did?' Then they told me, laughing. That's how it was. We knew so much before the police did back in those days. It rips you apart inside, carrying that many secrets."

"A lot of the people who were into this music back then were teens struggling with identity crisis, searching for someone to follow," says Jan Axel "Hellhammer" Blomberg. "Then they meet someone like Øystein or Varg, and this natural urge to follow takes over. That's something that that is latent in everyone. For the weak-minded, this can really end in disaster. It has happened, and will no doubt keep happening within this music genre."

The church burnings, the murders, and the frenetic media attention following in its wake contributed to establishing black metal as a musical form and gave rise to countless new bands. The divide between black and death metal became increasingly well-defined.

"We embarked on a European tour after releasing our second album *Indecent and Obscene* in the autumn of 1993. It was immediately apparent to us how the death metal wave was fading," says Dismember vocalist Matti Kärki. "Everywhere we played, black metal was all the rage. Instead of bands being brutal on stage but still keeping a healthy distance to it, black metal brought out a bunch of extremists who took over."

When Mayhem's highly anticipated second album, *De Mysteriis Dom Sathanas*, was released in the spring of 1994, black metal was peaking. To this day, the album is regarded as one of the most important works in the genre. Everything about it was groundbreaking.

The involved parties alone make it legendary. The album features Varg Vikernes on bass and Øystein Aarseth on guitar, with Pelle "Dead" Ohlin writing the lyrics—the music is epic and ice-cold, and above all, the vocals of Attila Csihar from the Hungarian band Tormentor are out of this world.

"The first time hearing the vocals on that album, we all went, 'What the hell is this Attila guy doing? Is it good or is it bad?'" says Peter Stjärnvind, a member of many prominent Swedish metal bands such as Nifelheim, Entombed, and Merciless. "The vocals on the title track sound like a converted monk from *The Name of the Rose* performing a black mass in some cavern. In this context, it is absolute genius—and, above all, impossible to plagiarize."

The murder of Øystein left a void in the black metal scene. IT hoped to keep True Satanist Horde going but soon found himself at odds with Jon Nödtveidt, who had found a different concept he thought suited him better.

"He said he felt more at home in a new Satanic organization called Misanthropic Luciferian Order," IT says. "Jon was one of my closet friends, a true brother in every sense, so it felt like a betrayal. This, along with seeing my creation TSH collapse before my eyes, tore me apart."

Conflict arose between the two groups, and rumor has it that IT was threatened to the extent that he left Sweden for several years. His own version is that he moved abroad after getting fed up both with himself and his personal situation.

Micke "Lord Ahriman" Svanberg, guitar player of Dark Funeral, remembers how the hostility between the leading figures permeated the inner black metal circles for a long time—and how they were in essence challenged to choose sides.

"We refused. Why would we do that? We were all friends and represented more or less the same basic philosophy. It was ridiculous, squabbling about who gets to be leader. Caligula, our vocalist at the time, expressed in a meeting that we had no interest in choosing sides. It was a shame, because we were friends with Jon and IT and the Norwegians. We lost contact with a lot of people after that."

Dark Funeral formed in Stockholm in 1993, and their debut album, *The Secrets of the Black Arts*, was released three years later. By then, the black metal scene was divided. Along with fellow Swedes Marduk and Dissection, Norwegians Dimmu Borgir and Satyricon, and Cradle of Filth from the UK, Dark Funeral brought black metal to a larger audience through diligent and extensive touring. While attracting many new fans, they were also despised by those who felt black metal should be something reserved for the initiated few.

"We went our own way while others spent too much time trying to fit in," says Svanberg. "I see my black soul as the foundation, and that will never change. I've never felt the need to adhere to certain rules and restrictions in order to be labeled true black metal, for 'I am one with darkness.'"

In retrospect, many former members of The Black Circle and True Satanist Horde point out that getting drunk with friends was their main focus, rather than participating in organized, clandestine, transgressive activities. This is irrelevant, however, considering the outcome. These youngsters provided the framework and established ideas that are prevalent within the scene as it exists today.

In the early years of death metal, the concept of being *true* was about loving the music and dedicating your life to it. Playing music out of passion instead of worrying about record sales, knowing every obscure band, and hanging out at all the live shows. Black metal appropriated the term and claimed it as its own.

"People watching from the outside probably find this hard to believe, but there was plenty of self-irony within the black metal scene as well," says Gylve "Fenriz" Nagell of Darkthrone. "A lot of people who just wanted to tag along didn't seem to understand this. And when you lack humor, you become very boring. As much as we wanted to do something wholeheartedly, the fact remains that if you're boring—then you're boring."

Reminded of his own denouncement of former friends Entombed, he claims the critique of Swedish death metal in fanzine interviews was exclusively about the lifeless productions of Sunlight Studio, where Darkthrone themselves recorded their debut.

"This is something I've thought a lot about over the past 20 years. In the '80s, bands went to their local producer to record. What I really liked about that was how each band sounded different. New sounds were created. It was an interesting time. Then suddenly, every album was made in either Morrisound Recording in Florida or Sunlight Studio, resulting in the same clinical soundscapes."

Nagell claims these production styles ruined the scene. Just talking about it upsets him almost to the point of agitated shouting.

"The techniques they used were soon incorporated by *every* single band in existence! And *this* was something that we in Darkthrone eventually had to take a stand against!"

During the latter half of the '90s, the quest for authenticity turned into a competitive sport of sorts. Those deemed not *true* enough got beat up, says Demonia, who asks us not to disclose her real name. She runs the metal blog Demonia and has been involved in Stockholm black metal circles for a long time.

"There was a band called Satan's Penguins poking fun at black metal, and they were tracked down. Everything was dead serious, and joking about black metal wasn't tolerated. Back in those days everyone knew each other, so if some newbie suddenly appeared claiming to be black metal, he was pretty much guaranteed to get beat up. There was a lot of violence."

She says black metal is about taking the heat. To embrace violent things normal people would be repelled by. In short, being as extreme as possible, in as many ways as possible.

"Back in those days, a lot of it was about respect as well—listening to black metal should demand a certain amount respect from people around you. It's really difficult to explain. It is and should be dangerous to listen to black metal."

While one trinity ruled the international black metal scene, another trinity had formed in Stockholm and its surrounding municipalities. The Norrköping band Ofermod, along with Funeral Mist and Malign from Stockholm, remained in the underground while experimenting with more extreme musical approaches.

Thomas Väänänen, former vocalist for Viking metal band Thyrfing, clearly remembers the palpable hostile vibes at mid-'90s black metal gigs in Stockholm. If you didn't wear the right band shirt, you might face having it removed by force.

"I remember Mörk of Malign approaching my friend at a Dark Funeral concert, forcing him to take off his inverted crucifix, on charges of not being *true* enough and thus undeserving of wearing it. That's how it was back in those days. Attending black metal concerts in the mid-'90s was an adventure in itself."

Mörk—who does not want his birth name published—doesn't remember the incident in question but confirms that he and his friends used to confront people they found annoying, questioning them on music and beliefs. Those wearing Mayhem shirts would especially face interrogation. If the answers weren't satisfactory—and if they didn't put up a fight—they'd get beat up.

"We felt that black metal people should be of a certain caliber," Mörk continues. "There was a dignity to uphold. Personally, I don't listen to black metal in the same manner as other music—for me, it's something sacred. Euronymous of Mayhem had an idea of forcing people to fill out questionnaires in order to qualify for buying their records. It would serve as a protective measure against idiots getting hold of their music. I don't go through a deeply spiritual process so people can sit at a party, first listening to us and then Twisted Sister or Tankard. The mere thought of someone having a good time to our music drives me fucking crazy."

Malign formed in the Stockholm suburb of Tensta back in 1994, inspired by Norwegian black metal but also Swedish bands such as Unpure and Unanimated. Mörk says the three members were "young and impressionable," and wanted to be just like Mayhem. The misanthropy combined with the powerful, aggressive feelings the music induced had felt natural, and the band acquired a reputation for violence early on. Vocalist Nord completely stopped showering in order to look as rotten as possible. It ended with "some kind of mold or moss" growing on him, according to Mörk.

Together with Funeral Mist and other Stockholm bands like Werewolf, Svartsyn, and Blackwitch, the Malign members would often hang out in the amphitheater of the Rålambshovs park on summer evenings, causing trouble. Back in those days, wearing black clothes and spikes was uncommon, and people stayed out of their way. What started as intimidation and random fights at concerts soon grew into more serious crimes: robberies and assaults.

"A lot of young men fight in order to prove themselves, but we did it for other reasons," Mörk says. "We came from loving homes but thrived on spreading misery and harming people—I can't quite explain why. There was an urge to tear wounds in the creation of God, and we became completely immersed in the violence. Today, the adult and mature me regards this as completely absurd. Still, the black metal part of me condones it wholeheartedly."

Toward the late '90s, the members of what Mörk calls "the holy trinity"—Malign, Funeral Mist, and Ofermod—start getting organized. Inspired by The Black Circle and other extreme societies, they regard themselves as religious, Satan-worshipping mercenaries at war with God and the Christian message of love.

"Toward the end, we were some kind of career criminals with neither financial interests nor drug dependencies. It was all religious and illegal. Regarding the black metal scene, I feel we had a fair bit of momentum at one point and could have influenced its direction far more—but we lost it. I wish it had led to something further."

He can't articulate what it is he wishes had happened instead.

"The Norwegian black metal bands turned the entire country upside down and left a massive impact. I don't know. Perhaps black metal should only function as a portal into something else—to deeper matters for certain individuals. And that's not entirely reprehensible, I suppose. Yet at times, I feel that if the '60s hippies were able to put an end to a war, we should've been able to start at least one."

By the turn of the millennium, the circle is scattered. Several of the members deepen their religious studies, and Mörk realizes his band has focused too much on violence and not enough on music. In 2001, he puts Malign on hold and is recruited as live bass player for Watain. He stays in the band for five years. In the end, he simply finds it too hard to resist the urge to kick concertgoers in the head—fans who might be doing nothing more harmful than enjoying themselves.

Over the last decade, the black metal scene has been revitalized by bands like Watain, incorporating the genre's aesthetics and sound while upholding a sense of religious solemnity. The genre has also, for the first time, achieved both commercial and mainstream media breakthrough. Today, black metal is often regarded as an art form, more than just a spectacular style of music.

When Watain were awarded a Swedish Grammy in the "best hard rock" category and nominated for several other prestigious awards, black metal took its first step into the halls of the cultural elite. Needless to say, this raging success is also a massive blow to many black metal fans. Mörk is ambivalent.

"It's gratifying in one way, since it gives Watain the opportunity to spread their gospel to a larger audience. Still, it's somewhat disheartening because it means that a lot of people are listening casually to music that should be inducing either nightmares or revelations, depending on the listener."

But Erik Danielsson, vocalist of Watain, has no problem navigating between commercial success and remaining true to the basic philosophy of black metal. The band is very clear about their Satanic conviction and misanthropic views. He's aware of black metal having become something of a trend, and that most new fans in no way qualify as *true*. His position, however, is that as long as Watain are doing precisely what they want and still reap success, it all becomes twice as powerful.

"Both black and death metal is about taking things too far; only then does it fill its proper function. The opposite is what defines poor black metal. There's a source from which everything emanated. As important as being in constant connection with this source is, it's just as essential to constantly allow oneself to be swept forward by its unrestrained power. Otherwise, black metal becomes irrelevant as an art form—at least in the manner in which I want to work with it. What this will come to mean for Watain, I don't want to talk about. People still have to have big balls if they dare to come see our show."

"You have to draw a very clear line between what you do on stage and what you do privately," Bathory's Quorthon stated in a 1987 interview with *Metal Hammer*. Some 20 years later, the exact opposite determines whether you're *true* or not. Of course, the significance of what's regarded as *true* differs between genres and by what one personally regards as fake.

To claim something as authentic is a moral position as well as an aesthetic one.

Today, the question of what's *true* and how to define the derogatory term *poser* might yield responses like "This stuff is only used teasingly, jokingly"—or that it's become outmoded language— perhaps due to the impossibility of proving oneself *true*. However, judging bands or individuals by measuring their authenticity is still very much common practice.

"To claim there's no longer a discussion of what's *true* in black metal is total bullshit. It's as important now as it's ever been. But terms symbolizing something as sensitive as this have to be replaced once they've lost their meaning," says Lars Martinsson, writer for *Close-Up Magazine* and vocalist for metal band Vampire.

"People who paint their faces and have weird opinions are very easy to make fun of. And so, these terms are worn out even faster, precisely due to the conflict between what's assumed to be *true* and what this actually entails. Like the joke of why The Count doesn't drive, 'because walking is hell.' In order to be *true* and genuine in a black metal context, you have to cease being human. Dogmas become silly in the grand scheme of things. Looking at the high-profile bands of today, like Watain and Funeral Mist; they are called 'orthodox black metal' or 'religious black metal.' The content is more or less the same, but with different labels. It's like calling a cleaning lady a 'hygiene technician.' It all revolves around the exact same conflict when Watain pour rotten blood over themselves and display rotten pigs' heads, as when Mayhem used fresh blood and fresh pigs 20 years ago. The severity remains."

Johan Karlsson is not his real name.

IT passed away in February of 2017.

VIII.

Metal and Money

I never thought I was going to sell more than a thousand records. But Dissection quickly sold over 50,000 copies.

— TOMAS NYQVIST, NO FASHION

"**M**y ego will be fulfilled when I've crushed them once and for all."

The melodic, northern accent of Dark Funeral guitarist and band leader Lord Ahriman is barely discernible above the normal sounds of business at the Blå Lotus coffee shop in Stockholm. It is the summer of 2007, and he's here to, among other things, talk about the bitter legal dispute the band is entangled in with Swedish record label MNW.

"My goal is to destroy the entire company. And I'm a stubborn bastard; I'll never give up. You can quote me on that."

Lord Ahriman, less known by his civilian name Micke Svanberg, grew up in the '70s in a residential area of Luleå in the far north of Sweden. He was often bored. Boredom led to mischief and, in his teenage years, alcohol. He got involved in crime, left home, and ended up on the run from the law.

"All of it was dismissed as adolescent pranks since I was so young. We would form gangs, and it was easy to get swept up in the excitement. Everyone tried to outdo each other with crazier and crazier ideas. And you'd just run with it, because something had to happen. At long last, I picked up a guitar. That was my way out, from a lot of things."

He forms the band Satan's Disciples, influenced by much the same music that drives him today: Black Sabbath, King Diamond, and early European thrash metal like Sodom and Destruction. After his compulsory military service, Ahriman moves to Stockholm and forms black metal band Dark Funeral. Their debut is a self-financed EP in 1994. One year later, the band sign a contract with House of Kicks imprint No Fashion. House of Kicks are then bought by MNW Records around the turn of the millennium.

Dark Funeral is one of Sweden's leading black metal acts at the time, and the new ownership is a welcome change at first. The band hopes to see some improvements in areas that have not been to full satisfaction at House of Kicks. Lord Ahriman's inbox is soon full of emails from the new owners. Most of these carry assurances that things are "happening," and "will be greatly improved."

Instead, Dark Funeral's royalties for record sales and licensing fees are frozen, and the band members find themselves in a financial nightmare.

"Everyone in the band was suddenly completely destitute. We're still up to our asses in debt. We can't access the money from our broadcasting and performance rights either. They've shelved our old albums and we're not getting any royalties."

Lord Ahriman sighs. In 2006, the band won an important ruling against MNW in the Stockholm district court. The label has appealed. Ahriman says that he will not rest until he's collected interest on "every fucking minute that has passed."

"If nothing else, I will drive them into bankruptcy. And having the owners slapped with a trading prohibition sounds reasonable."

The odds of a black metal quartet from the far north of Sweden winning a legal battle against a big record label might seem infinitely unfavorable. But for the towering guitarist across the table, there is no other possible outcome, and he points out a character flaw that might work to his advantage in the case.

"I'm a total control freak. I have all the documents, contracts, and so forth—I saved every single thing. There it is, in black and white. MNW on the other hand—so far, they've provided nothing but unverifiable claims."

Ahriman says he's almost impressed that they're trying to take legal matters further, without anything to back their side of the story up.

"It will hit them hard in the end. But it's a classic story: a big label with no respect for the artists. This time, though, they picked the wrong band to mess with."

"Heavy metal has a message to the rest of society," Sebastian Bach, vocalist of American band Skid Row, proclaimed in the VH1 documentary *Heavy: The Story of Metal.* "And that message is 'Fuck you!'"

His reasoning here might help explain the friction between business and subculture mentality in metal. Heavy metal is everything society is not: freedom from responsibility, instead of assuming it. Letting your thoughts wander while doodling a band logo in your school notebook, rather than doing your homework. High volume, ripped jeans, and beer as insulation against life after the weekend. The whole scene consists of outsiders who are there to escape the very things that then slap them in the face as soon as the hobby turns into a career.

But something's happened to the practitioners of the world's most uncompromising music genre. Even corpse-painted devil worshippers archive documents and study the fine print. When your entire existence of blood-splattered escapism is at stake, wildly creative solutions can guard you from financial reality. A heavy emphasis on band merchandise, which is traditionally cash-based commerce, can keep your livelihood out of the eyes of the taxman.

In a time when reality television trailers sport death metal riffs and bands like In Flames and Ghost pack arenas all over the world, there's no denying the extreme metal genre has become highly lucrative. But in a genre where "sell-out" and "rip-off" have been the worst possible insults from day one, how far do you dare take the business side of things?

During the '80s, the video rental business was booming. Calle von Schewen from the suburb of Rotebro had a background in the Stockholm punk scene and worked as a sound technician at Europafilm. One employee benefit was being able to buy used VHS tapes for a few kronor. Meanwhile, punk entrepreneur Johan Hargeby earned extra cash by pirating and selling American and British rock videos.

"That's how I came to know Johan," von Schewen recalls. "He realized he could buy cheap video cassettes through me."

Their idea of starting a record store is born on a ferry ride to England in 1986. Later, one fortuitous day, von Schewen walks by an empty store building in the Stockholm Old Town district. The guys end up leasing it. The House of Kicks record store is opened, initially specializing in punk singles and picture discs.

"Our strategy was to sell cooler stuff than anyone else did, and so we started importing picture discs. We'd occasionally attend record fairs to sell them as well, and all the other merchants wanted to know where we got them from. We replied, 'We're not going to tell you, but we are going to sell them to you.'"

House of Kicks began distributing records to stores in Västerås, Örebro, and Gothenburg, quickly establishing their position as Sweden's premiere importer of heavy music. By the turn of the decade, they'd replaced Heavy Sound as the meeting point for bands and fans within the budding death metal scene.

Von Schewen and Hargeby started considering releasing albums, actually stepping into label territory. The first title is the *Time Shall Tell* EP by Therion in 1990, followed by Desultory the following year.

Despite death metal being all the rage, Swedish bands tended to be signed to foreign labels such as Century Media and Nuclear Blast from Germany or London-based Earache Records. In Gothenburg, the record store/label Dolores releases a few albums, including a Grotesque EP, but apart from that, Swedish labels have yet to catch on.

Ultimately, a young music lover in Strängnäs by the name of Tomas Nyqvist takes matters into his own hands. During a few years in the mid-'90s, his record label No Fashion Records manages to produce several genre-defining albums with acts like Dissection, Marduk, and Katatonia. His knack for spotting talent is phenomenal. Unfortunately, the same can't be said for his business sense. Nyqvist is forced to declare personal bankruptcy when Katatonia attempt to collect the royalties for their debut album *Dance of December Souls*. No Fashion is bought by House of Kicks, who have up until then acted as the label's distributor. With No Fashion comes the back catalog, including all artist contracts.

Dissection's original drummer Ole Öhman recalls the contract between Dissection and Tomas Nyqvist being written in ballpoint pen and just half a page long.

"It was the most hilarious contract ever—and the first one No Fashion ever drafted. It stated that we were entitled to 10% of the record sales. Then House of Kicks took over the label, and suddenly, we were getting 5%. Say what? We never signed any contracts with von Schewen!"

Today, Dissection's first two albums have sold well over 100,000 copies each. Ole Öhman assures us he's seen very little evidence of this make it as far as his bank account.

"House of Kicks probably did well, since they stole the contract from Tomas Nyqvist and then rewrote it without asking for our signatures. We just couldn't be bothered. Katatonia were, however, and that's why Tomas Nyqvist went bankrupt. On the other hand, he spent most of his time lying on his back and spent every penny on pot. He had no furniture, only a naked bulb hanging from the ceiling. It wasn't even lit, since his electricity had been turned off. He was totally broke."

"I lost control of everything," Tomas Nyqvist recalls when we reach him over the phone. He's on his break at the tire company outside Gothenburg where he's been working for years.

As a teenager, Nyqvist was the editor of the *Putrefaction* fanzine, named after a song by Carcass. It was still pre-internet, and he was corresponding with bands and other fanzine editors across the country. *Putrefaction* was soon considered one of the best Swedish fanzines, and Nyqvist decided to also release a few underground bands he would want to hear on record himself.

The ambitious teenage entrepreneur was not quite prepared for his success.

"I never thought I was going to sell more than a thousand records. But Dissection quickly sold more than 50,000 copies. I couldn't sit at home with thousands of records in my living room."

Just as the need to press more albums arises, payment for the first shipment to House of Kicks is delayed. Struggling to stay ahead of the financial tidal wave, Nyqvist accepts an offer from House of Kicks to also handle the production side of things. Without knowing it, the entire label is in all but name taken out of his hands.

"They promised me the moon and the stars, but that's not quite how things turned out. Instead, they took control of my label. They ran straight through me, knowing I was a young guy whose hobby had turned into pretty big business."

Unbound by Merciless was the last album Tomas Nyqvist was involved in. He set up the studio recording and various other practicalities. The record was then released by House of Kicks. Many bands contracted by Nyqvist were annoyed when their music was suddenly released by a label he didn't control.

"They thought I was an idiot for breaking our contractual agreements. But I thought House of Kicks were proper fucking idiots for not keeping their promises to me. On the other hand, I couldn't handle it myself. The constant demand for records meant I needed large sums of money at my disposal, in order to continuously press new ones. I didn't have that, since getting my payments from House of Kicks took so long. This is where they stepped in, with offers of helping me out. And they were real businessmen, through and through."

When House of Kicks took over No Fashion in 1994, it was the first time they exported records from Sweden. The No Fashion releases of Dissection and Katatonia represented a new melodic sound that immediately grew popular.

"It went really well," says Calle von Schewen. "The first Dissection and Katatonia albums are both great albums."

He doesn't quite recognize Nyqvist's version of how things went down. However, with 25 years in the record label business, he knows all too well that there are always different sides to a story. He vehemently denies House of Kicks intentionally moved in on the small label.

"That's the kind of thing people say. But in my opinion, the Dissection and Katatonia albums had never even seen the light of day had it not been for us. Well, they might have, but only in a thousand copies. I think Tomas lost interest after things became too much of a business."

Calle von Schewen gives us a tired smile.

"It's an easy thing to blame everything on being young and ignorant. We never forced anyone to sign anything. We had our offices here in Stockholm; we hung out at the same spots as these bands and met the people we worked with. We had to be able to look them in the eyes."

After Tomas's departure, House of Kicks kept releasing albums with No Fashion as a sublabel. In 1996, the Dark Funeral debut album *The Secrets of the Black Arts* hit the market.

When the Entombed members signed their contracts with Earache in 1990, guitarist Alex Hellid was still a minor and was legally required to provide a parental signature of consent.

Entombed's first international tour was a 10-day romp through Germany, where the band played in front of a thousand attendees every night. It's not until many years later that Uffe Cederlund realizes a minor detail concerning that tour.

"We weren't paid. At all. None of us had the faintest idea that we were even supposed to be. We figured it meant we just weren't very good. We drank that tour away, I believe."

In the early '90s, Entombed became Sweden's first real rock stars within the death metal genre. Nicke Andersson recalls the feelings of success all but disappeared when the first royalty check arrived.

"We only realized later how extraordinarily shitty our contract was. We were actually supposed to release more albums on Earache than we ended up doing. Our manager at the time struggled to find us a way out of that contract, his hair turning gray in the process. That business is still not quite straightened out. I think Earache still owe us somewhere in the range of one or two hundred thousand dollars, at the very least."

As a safety precaution, the band had a lawyer review the contract before signing it.

"But he knew nothing of the music industry, so everything probably appeared to be in order. But it was bullshit. For example, there were publishing rights baked into this. In these types of deals, it's usually a 40/60 split between label and band, respectively. The thing was, in this contract 60% went to the label ... and 40% to us."

In 1991, the band were on their way to the U.S. for their first North American tour. Nicke Andersson worked at the Swedish postal service and applied for a few weeks off. His request was denied, so he was forced to quit his job.

"That trip generated some money at least. And since it didn't occur to me that this income was subject to taxation, things were pretty good for a while. Then I ran out of money and had to live on noodles until more money dropped in. It was pretty okay. Had I only signed a proper deal, it would've been even more okay. I imagine we weren't the only ones who in situations like that."

Unleashed bass player and vocalist Johnny Hedlund works in economics for a living these days. He says the poor negotiating skills of the Swedish bands were related to the fact that death metal was such a new phenomenon.

"It felt as if we were representing a new style of music. Back then, we didn't really think we were in any position to negotiate. Obviously, we're better equipped these days."

Hedlund first says he has no regrets concerning past mistakes, but he changes his mind after a while.

"I would have liked to renegotiate our first record deal. That was a slave contract, seriously. If you sign a contract for seven albums, then you're stuck. You'll be paid as much for the seventh album as for the first. Ten, perhaps 15 years have passed, and you're an entirely different person. Just the inflation during all this time means you lose money."

Entombed and Unleashed are far from the only bands in the Swedish metal underground to sign unfavorable contracts. During the '90s, being ripped off by labels was the rule rather than the exception. Sometimes it was because of exploitive or deceptive contracts, but frequently, it was because the bands simply didn't understand their rights.

"I think the combined roles are difficult to handle for many," says Kristian "Necrolord" Wåhlin, who played in Grotesque and Liers in Wait. "We're talking visionaries here—idealists, in a way. This makes it hard to combine your art with business, because the artistic output is so personal. Somewhere, you're just happy being able to do what you're doing. It's hard to estimate your own monetary value at the same time."

After 17 years as guitarist of Entombed, Uffe Cederlund's views on the music business are mostly cynical. In hindsight, what he laments the most is how no one from the '90s Stockholm death metal scene got involved with the label side of things at an early stage.

"Mayhem should really be credited for dealing with that aspect so early on. None of us did. Instead, the whole thing was exploited by external labels who ruined everything."

Cederlund draws parallels to the American hardcore scene of the '80s.

"You could argue that Euronymous was death and black metal's answer to Black Flag guitarist and label manager Greg Ginn—a somewhat insane and business-oriented chief ideologue. I'm convinced Euronymous knew exactly what those American hardcore guys were up to and realized he could do the same. With us, no one ever really looked into any of that."

During the '90s, House of Kicks established themselves as Sweden's premiere metal label. Calle von Schewen denies stashing anything but experiences and memories, but he adds that he was wealthy on paper for a short while. In 1999, the old Swedish folk rock label MNW bought House of Kicks. One year prior, MNW had been taken over by an investment company with grand ambitions. House of Kicks expected a healthy collaboration, considering that MNW was a larger company with bigger muscles. Crucially, not only the House of Kicks brand but also their distribution deals with foreign labels are included, as well as record deals with all bands tied to No Fashion.

"We thought we'd be able to contribute to MNW. But once we got there, we realized we didn't contribute at all. They were completely uninterested in having us there. We were paid with some money and quite a lot of shares. Perhaps 10 million [kronors'] worth of MNW stock. But then they were no longer worth 10 million."

Around the time of the sale, House of Kicks did not have a contract in place with The Hellacopters. Frontman Nicke Andersson was good friends with von Schewen, and their first releases have been on the label.

"Back then, I thought it was a damn shame," von Schewen recalls. "But today, I'm infinitely grateful it didn't go down that way."

Within a few years, MNW find themselves in financial crisis. In 2003, most employees are let go. The company is bleeding cash, and internal struggles tear the label apart.

"Fortunately, we managed to sell a few shares while they were still worth something. I was able to buy an apartment and a new car. Our deal was valid for three years, and when that time was up, we left and started Sound Pollution."

Sound Pollution is a store in the same Old Town district that House of Kicks once started out in. Also part of the business is distribution, music publishing, and two record labels, home to Nicke Andersson's band Imperial State Electric, among others.

To Hargeby and von Schewen, the MNW disaster was a three-year upfront study of a record label in gradual decline. For Dark Funeral, the damaged caused by the deal would be felt significantly longer than that.

The Dark Funeral court case number is T 13362–04; the file is two inches thick and includes 90 appendices. The lawsuit details unpaid royalties and how band members were pressured into signing new publishing deals in order to be paid for old ones already in effect. It's the story of a band who were unable to sign a new deal at the peak of their popularity, because their current label refused to release them from old obligations.

"I don't think I've ever come across so many incompetent people in one and the same office," says Ahriman.

The coffee cup in front of him is empty. Late afternoon has turned to evening and guests have started leaving the café.

"They've stolen a lot of money from us. And they've stolen our licensing deals, which means copyright infringement. It's worth noting how they don't even bother denying this."

According to Ahriman, this case is something entirely different than the standard "naive rock band signs horrible contract" story.

"It's about them not honoring a legal agreement that actually was in place. They've broken so many of the clauses, it boggles the mind."

Ahriman says they were mocked by the label during a meeting to discuss the problems. In that same meeting, the MNW management freely admitted to owing the band money, assuring them they'll be reimbursed—if they only sign for an additional two albums.

"They said, 'Even though we owe you about a million kronor, we'll only give it to you if you sign the new deal.' I almost went out of my mind and trashed the entire fucking office. There has to be some fucking code of conduct."

One week later, the band spoke to MNW again, who proposed a new meeting.

"That meeting ended with me saying, 'Just so you know, you can go to hell. We'll see you in court,' and the answer I got was 'Yeah, right, go ahead!' They didn't think we'd do it. But we did. And we beat them in the first round."

Like many other bands within the black metal genre, Dark Funeral practice Satanism. One of the foundational concepts is following your ego—an antithesis of sorts to the Christian message of solidarity. What, then, does Ahriman see as the difference between the greed of their label and the Satanic concepts of "might is right?" He considers this for a good while before answering:

"It depends on how you look at it. To them, it's all about money. No soul. And that's something Satanism has—a soul behind it. It's only business in their eyes. Of course, it feels like shit, but we are not defeated, and we do not turn the other cheek. The day will come when we hit back really hard."

In the years of researching the Swedish metal scene in preparation for this book, we've found that longevity is often coupled with an understanding of business.

Therion front man Christofer Johnsson has been a full-time musician for many years. We meet with him at an Italian restaurant in Stockholm. His blond hair is still long, but he's wearing a suit—his fashion sense is only one of the aspects that separate him from most death metal musicians. Another factor is his approach to the practical side of things.

"A band usually has one driving force—the fixer. The person who books shows, finds a rehearsal place, prints the band's first shirts, sets up the demo recording. Bands who lack a driven person like that and just happen to make music good enough to be signed by a label are destined to be ripped off or at least stuck in a multi-album contract."

He says he's always been wary of the contracts he's been asked to sign. For many years, he's been registered as a resident of Ireland, due to favorable tax rules for artists on the Emerald Isle. His band is an established name in large markets like Germany and South America, further contributing to their healthy financial state. Eastern Europe also seem to appreciate Therion's bombastic—and in many ways unique—take on death metal.

In Sweden, however, Therion are mostly unknown to the general population. Only 160 tickets were sold when the band last played Gothenburg. The contrast between the interest at home and abroad is staggering. On their first South American tour, the band needed police to escort them from the airport.

"We sat in the front of the plane, so we were the first to exit as the doors opened. And then we heard the roar. People were standing on the airport roof, waving flags."

The members of Therion first thought they'd shared a flight with the national football team.

"Then we spotted Therion flags in the crowd. We really couldn't understand what was happening."

Few Swedish death and black metal bands can make a full living off their music. Tompa Lindberg is not one them. After the split up of At the Gates in 1996, he's continued to be one of the hardest-working individuals in the scene. Besides vocal duties for metal bands such as Ceremonial Oath, The Great Deceiver, and The Crown, he's also joined forces with classic D-beat punk bands Skitsystem and Disfear. His discography amounts to more than 30 releases. He tried living off the music for two years.

"You have to rely on unemployment benefits, scraping along. It reached a point where it just wasn't possible any longer."

These days, he works as a teacher. Even if Lindberg doesn't live off the music, he represents one of the industry's positive examples in the sense that he receives proper royalty checks every year.

"Since four or five years ago, I get fairly decent regular payouts. Perhaps three months' salary per year. It's mostly for At the Gates, which is pretty good, considering the stuff we did is 15 years old by now. But it did take that long to start getting any money!"

Asked why so many death metal bands signed shitty contracts, he responds:

"Most of us were just happy to release something. Many bands still are."

———

In the spring of 2009, Dark Funeral were set to release the album *Angelus Exuro Pro Eternus* on their new label, Regain Records. In a post on the band's website, Lord Ahriman informed the fans that the battle with former label MNW is over. The announcement contains a sense of relief but also of resignation. It's evident that Ahriman's original plan—driving MNW into bankruptcy—had to be ditched for a different kind of victory.

"Dark Funeral vs MNW/No Fashion Records dispute finally over!

Seven years of pure bullshit has finally come to an end.....un-fuckin'-believable!!!

Without going into any details (which I'm not allowed to either), what's most important here and now is that we finally have obtained the rights to our back catalog, including the publishing rights. That includes: The Secrets of the Black Arts, Vobiscum Satanas, Teach Children To... and Diabolis Interium.

And from now on, NO one but Caligula and I own the rights to above mentioned albums. One may believe I/we would be totally thrilled about this, be running around in pentagrams, throwing bibles in a fire and whatnot, but I honestly, feel pretty empty."

When we meet with Lord Ahriman two years later, all of their old albums have been rereleased on the new label. During our short meeting, his phone is constantly ringing. Dark Funeral will be presenting their new vocalist in a few days, a replacement for Masse "Emperor Magus Caligula" Broberg, who's leaving the band after 14 years. Ahriman types on his iPhone, responds to emails, and sends out press releases. He handles everything concerning the band—updating the website and making sure new merchandise is readily available in the band's online shop. He also made Dark Funeral visible on social media early on, via Facebook and Twitter.

"My reasoning was that, sure, we're the elder generation—old-school and so on. But to survive as a band, you must be represented wherever a new generation of fans accepts you. You won't survive otherwise."

The bass player in a well-known black metal band we talk to notes that, considering how the music business operates today, one should really be grateful for just a studio recording budget or having an album pressed. Don't count your blessings—or royalties. Revenue comes from shows and, above all, merchandise sales. In the last years, the sheer volume of available stuff has skyrocketed while downloads and online streaming have sent record sales plummeting. Shirt designs are endless, and creative innovation runs rampant.

In the spring of 2011, Therion released a board game called "011," created by an Italian game designer. In Flames have their own brand of beer and whiskey. Dark Funeral sold a limited-edition wristwatch with the band logo on it. Ghost pushed the boundaries even further in 2013 when they began selling a dildo shaped like frontman Papa Emeritus II and a metal butt plug, in any size you may desire.

Revenue from popular older records can also keep you afloat. Many bands forfeited these rights by signing bad contracts early in their careers. Lord Ahriman mentions that during his legal ordeal, he received a lot of support from fellow bands who wanted to see a precedent in place.

As for himself, he was forced to learn so much about contract law that he'd like to share the knowledge, and he has already helped several other bands in conflict with their labels. Despite the MNW dispute ending in a settlement, he's pleased with the outcome.

"In the beginning, I was uncompromising in wanting our rights back. We got them, but I can't say much more than that. What I can say is that we had the last word. I managed to pull off a bunch of last-minute maneuvers that drove MNW crazy. Fucking coat-and-tie pansies, sitting in an office with no clue about music. It was a battle of wits, and my strategy was the best! I wish more bands did that."

"So, no one won?" says No Fashion founder Tomas Nyqvist, when news of the settlement between Dark Funeral and MNW reaches him.

"That's a shame, actually. Because it confirms the old, tired cliché that a band can't really touch a big label. The record companies have all the money and power, whereas the bands don't."

Nyqvist tells us that he's now the father of two and that after a few years at the tire company in Gothenburg, he has moved back to Strängnäs. He now works for an automobile retail and wholesale company.

"I suppose I've become some kind of tire pro."

He hasn't entirely let go of his passion for music and occasionally releases records on his new label, Iron Fist Productions. The intent remains the same: to release music he wants more people to hear. A few years back, he put out an album by Tormented. They're from Söderköping and play old-school Swedish death metal.

His records are distributed by Sound Pollution.

Nyqvist is also working with Peter Stjärnvind, who was previously signed to No Fashion with his band Unanimated.

"He released two 7-inches with my side project Damnation," says Stjärnvind. "They sold 1,000 copies each, and he gave me four spanking-new Michelin tires as payment. That says something about his business sense. It was just as Michelin released their X-Ice tire model, which are extremely good and expensive as hell. He's the nicest guy in the world."

IX.

Dissection

*I'm not claiming to be in the service
of mankind; I want to destroy it!
So, don't fucking expect me to do anything
but bring ruin to all!*

— JON NÖDTVEIDT, DISSECTION

THE MOON IS FULL THE NIGHT before Halloween 2004. A long procession of metal fans dressed in black is slowly passing through the doors of the Arenan venue in Stockholm. In contrast to ordinary metal concerts, the mood here tonight feels somewhat muted and apprehensive. There's no drunken shouting, no laughter, only a low murmur of voices. People evaluate each other, inspecting band shirts and discussing how the evening might turn out.

The tour posters covering the exterior walls of the arena read "Fear the Return." For another band, that ominous slogan would simply have been concert promotion. But here, the threat seems very real.

Dissection, one of Sweden's most celebrated black metal bands, are playing their first gig in seven years. Founder and frontman Jon Nödtveidt was released from prison a month ago, after serving a 10-year sentence for accessory to murder.

The demand for tickets has been high. The concert has been moved to larger venues twice, from Klubben to Lilla Arenan and finally Arenan, with a capacity of 2,300. Still, the show has been sold out for quite some time.

The return has been preceded by a swirl of rumors. Two years earlier, Nödtveidt gave an interview to *Slayer Mag*, his first public statement since the sentencing. Soon thereafter, Bård "Faust" Eithun, of Norwegian black metal band Emperor—himself serving time for murdering a gay man in Lillehammer—announced that he was the new drummer of Dissection. This recruitment was made after intense correspondence between the two inmates.

With help from a fan on the outside, Nödtveidt launched a Dissection website while still in prison. From behind bars, he made the call for new band members. Apart from exceptional musical skills, applicants had to fully support the band's Satanic and anti-cosmic concepts. A little over a year later, right after his 2003 release from prison, Bård Eithun left Dissection. In a press release, he mentioned having traveled to Sweden and meeting Jon during a prison furlough. Only then did Bård realize how serious the Satanic focus of the band was. He opted to jump ship.

Inside Arenan, bulky black-clad men in leather vests keep their eyes on the audience. The MLO emblem is visible on a few of these vests: white letters in gothic font and a pentagram with bat wings. MLO is the acronym for Misanthropic Luciferian Order, the Satanic order Nödtveidt has been a member of since 1995.

The vests draw attention. People spot them, discreetly nudge their friends, and exchange knowing glances.

On both sides of the stage, there's a large inverted cross, ending in a trident and with sixes on the three other ends. A large backdrop depicts the grinning skull of the reaper, with the wings of a bat. Under the great scythe the words "Anti-Cosmic Metal of Death" are written—Dissection's own brand of destructive metal.

In the audience, English, Spanish, German, and Dutch accents mix with the predominately Swedish conversation. It is said fans have traveled here all the way from the U.S. and Chile. The merchandise stand is bustling. T-shirts blaring "Rebirth of Dissection" sell quickly, until a man with a German accent and a jovial tone grabs the microphone.

"Would you like to do a party with us? Okay, let's celebrate the rebirth of Dissection!"

The intro for the highly successful album *Storm of the Light's Bane* resounds from the PA. When Jon Nödtveidt walks on stage, carrying his black Gibson Les Paul and fists held high, the audience explodes in a roar. He wears a plain black T-shirt and black army pants. From a chain around his neck hangs a silver pentagram. His head is shaved, and his powerful, wide neck is obviously the result of many long hours in the prison gym. The band lineup was made public only earlier in the day, and they now dive into "Black Horizons."

"Just being here tonight to be with you all is a victory!" he tells the crowd from the stage.

Tattoos cover his arms. Guitarist Set Teitan stands to his right, a slender Italian with a black Flying V guitar and shaved eyebrows. He's moved to Stockholm from Rome to play with Dissection. Bass player Brice Leclercq has come from France. Drummer Thomas Asklund used to play with Dark Funeral.

"Are you feeling good? It's great to be back. I'd like to introduce you to a new song, the coming single 'Maha Kali!'"

The atmosphere in the venue is electric—and difficult to decipher. As the concert progresses, we ask ourselves what we're really doing here. Are we here to listen to one of Sweden's premiere metal musicians or to get a look at the infamous murderer?

The return of Dissection created unrest in the metal scene. Despite black metal being one of the most extreme musical expressions in existence, many (if not most) in the scene—both fans and band members—have never been real bona fide Satanists, or at least aren't misanthropic enough to condone murder. But many have known Jon Nödtveidt since he was a young metal enthusiast who organized gigs in Strömstad, during the late '80s. And they all know him as the frontman of Dissection.

Jon made fanzines, tape-traded, and was one of the primary networkers in the underground scene. Not only was he extraordinarily ambitious; he was known to be exceptionally cordial and charismatic.

Nicke Andersson remembers meeting Jon in Stockholm shortly after his release from prison.

"Boba Fett [of The Hellacopters] and I were DJing when some guy with a shaved head came up and said, 'Hey, Nicke!' It was a bit awkward, I barely remembered what he looked like. Then it hit me: 'Oh, that's right, you murdered someone.' It was very strange."

One of the first to know Jon in metal circles in the '80s was Tompa Lindberg. They hung out socially for many years after Jon moved to Gothenburg and also shared a rehearsal space.

"To me, he was always that friend you'd be joking around with. A funny and easy-going person," says Tompa. "We met at a festival after he was released from jail, and I said something to the effect of 'How are you doing? Still having a rough time?' He replied that 'No, I've left that behind me.' Let's move forward, sort of. He wanted it to be as before between us, that there was no point digging around in that chapter of his life. I suppose it was the only way to move on."

The return of Dissection turns out to be one of the most skillfully executed and well planned the metal scene has ever seen. During the year prior to Jon's release, the band website is continuously updated with new information. Press releases about both the Arenan concert and a European tour are coupled with new pictures of Jon from prison. There are also photos showing Dissection in the studio with a full lineup during furloughs.

A few weeks after his September 2004 release, Jon Nödtveidt gives an interview to Swedish tabloid *Expressen*. Under the headline "I'm Not Proud," he answers questions about his comeback but declines to comment on the murder in Gothenburg. "Out of respect for the victim's family, I don't want to discuss what happened. The only thing I want to say is that I'm not proud of it," he tells the reporter. Asked if the murder is used in promoting the band, he replies, "I'm sorry if it appears that way. Our intentions are quite the opposite. However, it's nothing we're trying to hide. We'd like to move on and leave it behind us."

Since his release from prison, the murder has been given attention in several ways. The motion picture *Keiller's Park*, based on the event and directed by Susanna Edwards, has been shown in cinemas all over the country. The murder was explored in detail in Johan Hilton's *No Tears for Queers*, a book about hate crimes against gay people.

In other music genres, voicing opinions that incite homophobia will result in strong reactions. Concerts with reggae artist Buju Banton are still canceled to this day, due to old lyrics with homophobic content. However, in a music genre that's all about pushing boundaries, tolerance for violence and unpleasant views are more prevalent than anywhere else. No one is protesting Dissection concerts in Sweden. Those who wish to distance themselves from the band do so discreetly. Few dared to comment on Jon Nödtveidt during the interview work for this book.

As Jon begins building up the band again, the metal world watches in fascination.

The band spent most of 2005 recording a new album as well as playing festival gigs in Europe and a few shows in Mexico and Brazil. They were also booked to perform at a festival in Israel, but these plans were foiled by Megadeth vocalist Dave Mustaine. The former Metallica member has converted to Christianity and refuses to play the same festivals as explicitly Satanic bands. "We are Satanists, yes, truly enemies of yours! For we are the antithesis to cowards like you!" Nödtveidt proclaimed on his website.

The two bands were set to perform at another festival in France two weeks later, and Mustaine was so agitated over Nödtveidt's statement that he asked for added security during the concert.

A few weeks later, the band made Swedish headlines as the Swedish Minister for Culture and Education, Leif Pagrotsky, was spotted at an unannounced Dissection concert in Stockholm—billed under the name The Somberlain. Tabloid *Expressen* accuses the minister of enjoying a Satanist concert. The 5'3" politician happily responds that a woman offered to carry him on her shoulders to better watch the show. He also claims he was unaware of Jon Nödtveidt's criminal history.

At a Dissection concert in Kolingsborg in December of the same year, Nödtveidt makes the audience shout, "Kill, kill, kill!" during a song. When he is interviewed by *Sweden Rock Magazine*, the article is given the headline "Murder and Music."

After 11 months in the studio, Walpurgis Night of 2006—a springtime Christian saint's day feast celebrated throughout northern Europe—sees the release of *Reinkaos*.

Reactions are mixed. Fans who expect the third full-length album to follow in the tracks of the hugely successful *Storm of the Light's Bane* are generally disappointed. Instead, *Reinkaos* is a chorus-packed heavy metal album reminiscent of Metallica and Iron Maiden. Jon sings in a clear, more controlled voice than on earlier albums, and his sense of melody is as strong as ever. On various black metal forums, comments suggest that the band has compromised their style to sell more records. Just as many are impressed by Nödtveidt's songwriting talents and his expressed desire to walk his own path.

The cover is emblazoned with a white 11-pointed star. The lyrics are exclusively about the anti-cosmic tradition that MLO promotes and contain Satanic formulas and incantations from *Liber Azerate*, a book written by Frater Nemidial, who is also mentioned as coauthor of both lyrics and music on the album. The booklet includes the address to the MLO website.

In interviews, Jon states that Frater Nemidial is the MLO's Magister Templi—leader of the order.

The album is released by the band themselves, on their own Black Horizons label. Ever since his release, Nödtveidt has been embroiled in a dispute with past label Nuclear Blast over rights to the band's earlier albums. He now rereleases these as lavish Digipak editions.

A few weeks after the album release, Dissection surprises the entire metal community by announcing that the band is splitting up. They will be celebrating the occasion with one last concert at Hovet in Stockholm on Midsummer's Day (another holiday celebrated in northern Europe). The band publishes what is described as the final interview with Jon Nödtveidt on their official website, based on questions from the fans.

Depending somewhat on stage placement, Hovet can accommodate 4,000 to 5,000 people, which are attendance numbers that neither Dissection nor supporting acts Nifelheim and Deathstars can attract in Sweden. And on Midsummer's Day? That holiday is more important to Swedes, metal fans or no, than any other. It is strongly linked to summer, nature, and the countryside, with people escaping the city to celebrate in summer cabins or at the beach.

The band also announce a pre-party on Midsummer's Eve. The two-day event is called Midsummer Massacre.

———

There is a sun shower. The plastic tarps above the outdoor furniture at the Tantogården, on Södermalm in Stockholm, are working double-time. One second, they are sheltering against the downpour, and the next, they're providing shade for today's first guests: four teenage boys in Cannibal Corpse and Carpathian Forest shirts, and at the table next to them, a completely silent group of girls, who seem to be waiting for something—anything—to happen.

A girl in tracksuit pants and a black hoodie with the Dissection reaper logo bids us welcome. Her lip is swollen from a piercing, and she appears to be in her 30s.

"You'll get your stuff from Jon's girlfriend. Come along with me."

On the spacious wooden veranda, a truckload of printed matter, T-shirts, and Dissection albums are being unpacked. Jon's girlfriend, who looks to be in her early 20s, navigates between piles of boxes, poster rolls, and handwritten signs. She's pale, without makeup, and wears black sneakers, cargo pants and a Dissection T-shirt. She gives off a friendly first impression.

She checks us off a list and hurries inside to get our concert tickets and Dissection shirts in size large—"the only size we have, unfortunately"—which are included in the ticket price. She informs us in a German accent that we're also getting a sticker each, as soon as she's located them among all the boxes.

The shirts have the phrase "Rebirth of Dissection European Tour 2004" printed on them, with 36 tour dates in cities such as Leipzig, Osnabrück, and Thessaloniki on the back. The front design appears to depict an eclipse of the sun.

The *The Rebirth of Dissection* DVD, the Arenan comeback concert, plays on a huge screen—barely discernible in the sunlight. The following day's concert is also planned to be released on DVD.

The first of the more prominent guests appear. Mörk of Malign, Erik "Tyrant" Gustafsson, and Pelle "Hellbutcher" Gustafsson of Nifelheim—as well as a cheerful Satanist from Paris who introduces himself as Pierre. He doesn't look the least bit frightening, despite his leather-and-spikes look and a pentagram the size of a toilet seat hanging from his neck. The most eye-catching decoration is found on Pelle's denim vest: a black Nifelheim back patch and inverted crosses surrounded by the biggest studs money can buy. Erik wears a black headscarf and pilot sunglasses.

He's standing in the sun on the veranda, surveying the guests who have gathered on the gravel courtyard. He seems content. Suddenly, he looks as if he's forgotten something important and rushes inside. Shortly afterward, he's leaning over a few screen prints with the text "Nifelheim—Midsummer Massacre 2006" on matte black paper. He methodically numbers them with a silver pen. Erik displays the prints on the wall behind the table and mentions having worked with them in the screen-printing workshop at his place of employment until half past 4 in the morning. We ask how much they will cost.

"Oh, my, a lot! More than you'd want to pay for a piece of paper."

He contemplates for a moment, not quite sure himself.

"Between 5 and 10 dollars."

A young man of the Tantogården staff appears on the veranda, holding a microphone. He watches the drowsy crowd of 30-some black-clad guests with uncertainty, as they gasp in the blistering heat built up under the tarp. He then taps the microphone a few times before carefully speaking.

"Okay, we thought we'd start off with a few signings now. First, you'll be able to get autographs from the band ..."

He pauses mid-sentence, excuses himself, and takes out a handwritten note.

"Nifelheimer!"

He looks around with the glance of someone who's just realized he's out of his depth. Sparse applause mixes with laughter and the odd holler.

Jenny Walroth, Swedish manager for the distinguished metal label Century Media, shows up. She's just spoken to Watain vocalist Erik Danielsson, who'll be standing in on bass for Dissection. He told her that only 950 people have purchased tickets for tomorrow's concert at Hovet.

"I don't think Erik cares. He's super-pleased to play with Dissection either way. And the stage props are apparently completely insane; he'll have his own ramp to walk up and down."

On the veranda, Jon's girlfriend has located the pile of black glossy Dissection stickers. She calls out to us timidly as we walk by. She seems to manage keeping perfect tabs on which guests have yet to receive theirs.

The three tables in front of her are now filled with stacks of albums, posters, neck-laces, hats, cigarette lighters, flags, even thongs—all with the Dissection logo. Duct-taped cardboard signs show prices in both kronor and euro. T-shirt in girlie sizes go for 190 kronor or 20 dollars. Thongs with the reaper logo are at 100 kronor or 11 dollars. If you're just on the lookout for a cheap souvenir from tomorrow's concert, key rings can be had for as little as 2 dollars.

The planning and production of all this must have taken forever. The selection is absurdly huge in relation to the attendance at Tantogården—well below 100 people.

The traditional Swedish red-and-white facade of the main building seem to glow in the afternoon sun. Blasting from the speakers is the intro to "Black Horizons" from Dissection's 1993 debut album *The Somberlain*. It sounds as if the band is playing their way through a storm in a dark forest.

Over the searing bed of music, an 18-year-old Jon Nödtveidt sings:

I am the almighty, the one with wisdom wide
I am the great shadow and from daylight in my tower I hide
I have seen the abyss and all that lies within
I am the great shadow and I was born in sin

The song races full-speed ahead. The album is not regarded as the band's top effort, but the voice and the guitar melodies still glow with an intensity few bands could match during the early '90s, when the Swedish metal scene was dominated by death metal with heavy guitars and low-pitched vocals. Dissection's debut has aged well. It's also a clear reminder of how little the death metal genre has evolved musically over the last decade.

Ole Öhman, who was part of the first Dissection lineup and played drums on the album in question, looks pained when we bring up the debut.

"Yuck! There's no groove on it at all! I hated recording it, and I hate listening to it," he says, shaking his head, bringing the three sixes behind his ear into view. It's the same tattoo the devil's son Damien has in the horror movie *The Omen*.

"Ole hates everything," Deathstars vocalist Andreas "Whiplasher" Bergh confirms later that evening.

The Nifelheim signing session is interrupted by a sudden rainfall. The pattering against the roof tiles mixes with tunes from a forthcoming split EP, on which Nifelheim share vinyl with Brazilian veterans Volcano. It will be the first Nifelheim release in six years.

Shortly after 8 p.m., three familiar figures move through the thin crowd in the elon-gated main building. Drummer Thomas Asklund is dressed plainly in black jeans and a T-shirt, wearing his reddish blond hair in a ponytail. Set Teitan wears a bomber jacket decorated with Dissection's spiky inverted cross and as per usual appears to have only one facial expression in his repertoire—the glare. Someone mentions that he wrapped up the previous night with what's seemingly becoming his social trademark: getting into a nasty bar fight.

Jon Nödtveidt wears a black sweatshirt with a drawing of something like the red devil from the Iron Maiden album *The Number of the Beast*, coupled with the decidedly non-Iron Maiden-esque message "Fuck the world!" Neither of Dissection's three members would distinguish themselves or even be noticeable in a crowd of average Sweden Rock Festival visitors. At least that's our first impression, before noticing Jon's new facial tattoo: a tribal-influenced design along the left side of his face, and behind it—just over the left ear—a pentagram with the upper point broken off. According to the Satanic philosophy to which Nödtveidt subscribes, the standard pentagram encapsulates inner power. The broken pentagram unleashes this power, creating chaos.

People quickly arrange themselves in a long line, leading to a table set up on the indoor stage—bottles of sparkling water and Coke have been placed next to silver and gold markers. As soon as the band settles in, a repetitive ritual spanning two hours begins. Fans hand over records and posters, say thanks and shake hands. They shuffle one by one behind the three musicians, with friends standing below the stage with cameras at the ready. Thomas and Jon give the horns and pose with solemn faces as the cameras flash.

A young man has brought his electric guitar. Jon exchanges a few words with him and then signs it with a gold pen. One guest sits in a wheelchair. Jon approaches him for a quick hello. After an hour, guitarist Set Teitan's restless gaze shows increasing signs of irritation. It's obvious that he's had enough and would rather be kicking back with his friends over at the bar.

Jon's patience appears endless, however. With unrelenting enthusiasm, he poses with a young man wearing glasses, then shakes the hand of his friend waiting by the stage. He seems oblivious to everything except giving the small crowd what they came here for.

We say hello, shake hands, and remind him of our interview request. He gives a composed and alert impression and seems completely unaffected by the fact that the sum of his life's work most likely will receive a less-than-triumphant finale.

Jon quietly looks at us for a brief moment. He then gives a vague reply about having already done his last interview but adds that it depends a bit on what we want to ask him. His manner of speaking is soft and friendly, bordering on hypnotic. When we leave him, we're still not entirely sure whether he'll grant us a proper interview or not.

———

The stage construction inside Hovet is impressive. Two long ramps run up the sides, flanking a huge drum riser decorated with the broken pentagram motif. An enormous steel hendecagram—an 11-pointed star—hangs above the stage. Four massive black-and-white tapestries hang from the roof. Camera equipment is rigged all across the stage with a long crane positioned in front of the mixing desk. No expense has been spared in regard to documentation and concert experience.

Few will get to experience it properly. The meager ticket sales become painfully obvious in the big venue, despite the stage having been placed in the middle of the floor, thus halving the capacity of the arena.

The audience fills a fraction of the floor. The ones who've made it here are fervent above and beyond the average concertgoer, however, and they're treated to a magnificent show. Jon Nödtveidt is radiant as he takes the stage. It looks and sounds like the concluding performance it's been announced to be. The closing song "Maha Kali" ends with Nödtveidt smashing his white Gibson Flying V against the stage floor, throwing it into the audience.

With the spotlights turned on and the venue lit up, he jumps into the audience. For over an hour, he stands on Hovet's carpeted floor posing for pictures, giving the odd hug, chatting, and hanging out with fans. A young boy who appears to be no more than eight years old has managed to catch the broken guitar. He approaches and asks to have it signed. The two pose together as the boy's father takes pictures. When Jon finally leaves the floor, heading to the afterparty inside the steamy changing rooms backstage, there's barely anyone left in the big hall.

———

One week after Midsummer Massacre, Jon calls us. He's considered our request and has decided to give us an interview after all—under the condition that we sign a contract, granting him full approval of the text.

We set up a meeting at Vetebullen, an old blue-collar café on Hornsgatan in Stockholm. Jon wears a Dissection shirt, black army pants, and sneakers. A pair of generic black sunglasses lie next to his coffee cup on the green plastic table. He produces a bag of gifts: luxurious vinyl versions of both *The Somberlain* and *Storm of the Light's Bane*, a girlie shirt, two stickers, two flags, and the key ring from Midsummer Massacre.

"Looking back on the almost two years since I was released, it feels unreal," enthuses Jon. "It's been really exciting and fun and, for me personally, completely fucking unbeatable. Needless to say, I had my hopes and expectations and was looking forward to being getting out, but you can't really comprehend what it means. When you've been on the inside for seven years, it's simply not possible to grasp it properly," he says with a wide smile.

"Take the Rebirth concert at Arenan. Never before in the history of the band had there been so many people at a headlining gig. And after so many years!" he muses.

Jon was born in Katrineholm to a Norwegian father and Swedish mother in 1975, but the family soon moved to Strömstad, close to the Norwegian border. There, he grew up with his younger brother, Emil, and baby sister, Sara.

The Beatles' "She Loves You" is the first song he remembers listening to. But like so many others, he soon gravitated towards heavier tunes. Both of his parents were teachers, and the 7-year-old Jon sometimes came along to class, where he was introduced by older students to AC/DC, Mötorhead, Accept, and Iron Maiden.

"It's hard to pinpoint, but there was something about metal I found instantly appealing. Sometimes, I'd hear a song playing on the radio—AC/DC's 'TNT,' for example—and I immediately went, 'Oh, what the hell is this?' You know, how you'd immediately put a cassette in and start recording? It became my biggest interest. Accept was probably the band I felt strongest for. *Restless and Wild* is a really fucking good album. It was probably my favorite record. It was something special—a little harder than everything else and a little rawer. It was so fucking good."

Iron Maiden and Metallica soon became other favorites. His father, Anders, was interested in music, and there was always something playing in the house, from rock to classical. In the fall of '83, Anders drove 8-year-old Jon and his friend Mattias "Mäbe" Johansson to Stockholm to see Def Leppard play at Draken. Both parents wholeheartedly supported the musical interest of their sons, until the day their mother Katarina found records with W.A.S.P. and Dead Kennedys in Jon's bedroom.

"She went completely crazy and tore down my posters from the walls. I had covered them with W.A.S.P. and other bands. When you're eight or nine years old, you don't find it silly when bands pose with raw meat and blood. Look at those pictures today and you won't be able to take them seriously. My mother didn't appreciate it at all, though. But I had a very kind grandmother in the same town, who I could visit after school sometimes. I had my own room there and was allowed to put up whichever posters I wanted to."

Around this time, the mid-'80s, hard rock and metal were still controversial genres in Sweden. Distorted guitars and a rough attitude were sufficient grounds for a band to get accused of devil worship—which, of course, led to even more kids being attracted to the genre in turn. Jon tells the story of his mother saying he could put up whatever posters he wanted, once he was old enough to understand what the bands were singing about.

"So, I started asking my father about everything. 'What does "balls to the wall" mean, Dad?' 'To kick a ball against the wall,' he replied—haha."

The young Jon finds out the true meaning of "fuck like a beast" from someone else.

At nine years of age, Jon starts to play his father's acoustic guitar. He learns basic chords and teaches himself to play his favorite songs. He takes music lessons for a while but doesn't particularly enjoy playing ballads, so he soon quits. Together with his close friend Peter Palmdahl and younger brother Emil, he begins playing in various band formations.

Peter Palmdahl remembers a joke band they once had, which they called Kill.

"Jon had an old guitar amp, and we'd scream straight into the stereo. We sang Metallica and Anthrax lyrics, just using random cool words, since we didn't know much English. It was nothing worth calling an actual band. Anders and Katarina just saw it as good fun. My parents thought so as well but probably kept a somewhat more watchful eye on us from then on."

Peter describes the Nödtveidt family as "extremely musical." Jon and Peter were the primary school's only metalheads, with long hair, denim jackets, and studded wristbands. During recess, they'd draw monsters and zombies.

"Jon was artistic but completely hopeless at sports. He was accepted into the soccer team, mostly because he had status within the group, since he was a metalhead and hung out with cooler kids. He gave that up once we entered our teens, when everything came to be about music."

Together, they began listening to increasingly harder music. Peter Palmdahl was a big Slayer fan, and bands like Venom and Metallica shared shelf space with Accept, Iron Maiden, and other hard rock acts. During summer breaks, Jon created his own magazines for fun. One of them was called *Varning* (Warning) and consisted of cut-out pictures from *Kerrang!* and *OKEJ*.

Jon also began writing his own songs, with simple riffs and lyrical phrases, forming the band Thunder with Emil and some classmates. They rehearsed at the local music school in the evenings, playing mostly covers but also writing original songs together as a band.

In the fall of 1987, when Jon was 12 years old, they entered Rock of Bohuslän, a talent show for demo bands organized by the 14 municipalities in the province. Thunder placed third in the finals. Jon wanted to start playing heavier music but found little support from his bandmates. So, he scrapped Thunder and formed thrash metal band Siren's Yell with Peter Palmdahl, Mäbe Johansson, and Ole Öhman.

"Jon played the guitar, Mäbe bass, and since I was the only one to have gone through puberty, I had to sing. Jon would sometimes sing along to the choruses, and it sounded squeaky as hell—absolutely hilarious. I have a video of it somewhere," says Peter Palmdahl.

In the final years of the '80s, the underground metal scene in Sweden was seething. The two friends discovered *Slayer Mag* and went on pilgrimages to the record store Dolores in Gothenburg, hunting for albums like Morbid Angel's *Altars of Madness* and others by Sepultura, Kreator, and Carcass. Jon started working on his *Mega Mag* fanzine and got in touch with other zine editors such as Tompa Lindberg in Gothenburg. Jon was the most active tape-trader in the area.

With an impressive sense of initiative, Jon also began organizing metal gigs at a youth center in Strömstad when he was 15 years old. The first of these is with Tompa's band, Grotesque, as well as Therion from Stockholm and local band Nosferatu. Jon performs with the thrash band Rabbit's Carrot.

"A huge crowd turned out for that concert," Jon recalls. "An entire train packed with beer-drinking Gothenburg metalheads—'Onkel' and that lot. And then, of course, lots of clueless disco people who only turned up to check out what was going on. They stood there in complete astonishment when Grotesque took the stage with spikes and inverted crosses. Afterward, there were rumors of a Satanic mass being held out in the youth center."

Shortly thereafter, Jon, Ole, and Peter formed a new constellation with harder musical aspirations and much darker lyrical content. The new band is called Dissection.

Ever since the days of Black Sabbath, hard rock and metal have been associated with Satanism and a fascination with spiritual darkness. With more extreme iterations of rock music came more explicitly Satanic themes, even if the bands seldom harbored genuine occult beliefs. Like most other metal fans, Jon Nödtveidt had filled numerous notepads and school books with neatly drawn skulls, bloody monsters, and inverted crosses.

"The reason I was drawn to metal in the first place was the presence of something dark in the music—meaning in the actual music. Not just in the image. I'd say it was probably Slayer who acted as gateway into Satanism for me personally. They had lyrics that could be interpreted as Satanic on *Reign in Blood*. It was cool and ballsy, and you didn't really think about it much deeper than that."

Within the death metal scene, quite a few bands utilized Satanic symbols and occult themes in lyrics and cover artwork.

"There were bands who claimed to be Satanists. I remember Tompa, for example, telling me how he was a Satanist. I was 14 years old at the time. Coming into contact with people claiming to be Satanists made me contemplate the issue on a deeper level. What does Satanism mean, more than pentagrams and inverted crosses? I began researching and gained some insight into what lies beyond these symbols—something dark and interesting," Jon explains.

In the late '80s, long before all the literature in the world became available through the internet, coming across esoteric books could prove difficult. Especially in a small town like Strömstad, where just finding the British magazine *Metal Forces* would be unusual enough.

When Jon traveled to Gothenburg to buy records, he also visited bookshops to order everything from Simon's *Necronomicon* to Anton LaVey's *The Satanic Bible*—books mentioned in album liner notes and in interviews with other bands at the time. He borrowed books about Sumerian mythology at the library, studied encyclopedias, and read everything related that he could get his hands on. Peter Palmdahl remembers how most people in the extreme metal underground called themselves Satanists. Even those who didn't subscribe to the belief system were carving inverted crosses into their arms at parties, wore pentagrams around their necks, and kept black pillar candles on their bedside tables. It came with the territory.

"I'm trying to remember when I built my first inverted cross," Peter Palmdahl says. "I think I was 15 years old. All the people you'd meet were dressed in black, and the music was so fucking black. It gave you the guts to say, 'I'm a Satanist; I hate Jesus and Christianity'—but you didn't really question things more than that."

Just like everything else he was interested in, Jon Nödtveidt took Satanism to an entirely different level than the rest of the group.

"We never questioned each other, not in Dissection. Never. We rarely had any ideological discussions at all. We took each other for granted; we were a unit who were all heavily into it," says Palmdahl.

While networking and making friends in the scene, Jon kept writing music and lyrics for Dissection. He was the given frontman—the inspired one, the force of initiative and charisma. He recalls how the band quickly became a vessel for his spiritual quest.

"I'd explore my innermost thoughts in the lyrics, concepts like death and darkness, everything transcending this life. The deeper I got, the stronger I felt that something was calling. The interest in itself grew so vast that I started identifying myself as a Satanist. After a while, I found others who shared my interests."

Through his industrious correspondence, Jon befriended Morgan Håkansson from black metal band Marduk. Morgan started helping out with *Mega Mag*. They met in person at Bergslagsrocken in 1990 and conducted interviews with a few bands, including Morbid Angel. Jon's father Anders Nödtveidt had driven Jon and Peter Palmdahl there by car and came along to the festival. Around the same time, Jon befriended Tony "IT" Särkkä of Abruptum, an older guy from Finspång. He also called himself a Satanist, and the two immediately bonded.

In the early '90s, death metal had made quite a commercial breakthrough, and bands like Entombed and Dismember suddenly garnered attention outside of metal circles. There was an immediate division: Either you join the other death metal bands on their mainstream path or you delve deeper into evil and the dark side. The competition really kicked into high gear when Pelle "Dead" Ohlin, took his life in 1991.

Just a few days after the suicide, Dissection performed in Falkenberg as supporting act to Entombed and played the Mayhem song "Freezing Moon" in commemoration of Dead.

In Strömstad, Jon kept organizing gigs and a festival he calls Böldfest—a play on words in reference to the Swedish term for the bubonic plague, *böldpest*. Several bands formed in the area, and news of an emerging scene in Strömstad spread outside the town borders. Metalheads from both Norway and other parts of Sweden started coming to the shows. Jon got to know Øystein Aarseth and Varg Vikernes. At parties, they got drunk and discussed Satanism.

When IT formed True Satanist Horde, Jon Nödtveidt hoped to carry out serious Satanic discourse.

"Everyone was so fucking young, but this was still meant to be something serious," says Jon. "And then, of course, you felt compelled to act on things to assert your standpoint."

"Jon soon ended up in TSH, of course, along with Ole Öhman and a few others," says Peter Palmdahl. "The whole thing felt as if it was some kind of sanctuary for IT. He stayed at Jon's place all summer, drinking beer and hanging out. IT was a cool guy but looked far worse than anyone else. He was of mixed descent—Native American heritage, among others—so his appearance was quite unique. He was three years older, had a beard and black hair, and wore double bullet belts. And he'd cut himself underneath his eyes. He showed us how to cut yourself at some party, and we were very impressed."

Dissection recorded their debut album *The Somberlain* with producer Dan Swanö at Unisound Studio in Finspång. By then, the band had spread across Sweden. Jon was attending high school in Eskilstuna, after dropping out of school in Strömstad. Ole Öhman lived in Karlstad, John Zwetsloot in Gothenburg, and Peter Palmdahl still in Strömstad. *The Somberlain* was released on No Fashion Records in 1993 and quickly sold 50,000 copies.

In Eskilstuna, Jon joined black metal band The Black and started a Swedish mail order division of Øystein's record shop, Helvete. He was in an arts program in school and worked as a photographer's assistant on the side. Simultaneously, it's a turbulent time with a lot of mischief and partying—especially with members of True Satanist Horde. He ends up being expelled from school after voicing support for Satanism in local newspaper *Eskilstuna-Kuriren*.

"A lot of it was about expressing myself in a strong, concrete, and rebellious manner," says Jon. "We hated Christianity and so we burned churches, for example. We were ready to kill and die for what we represented. Very simple and primitive, but also, for some of us, these were acts of utmost honesty."

Dissection soon made a name for themselves and headed out on a European tour with British act Cradle of Filth. Back home in Sweden, the group of friends kept pushing boundaries, both within themselves and others. Ole Öhman remembers how he and Jon were once apprehended by cops at a disco in Hunnebo.

"We were drunk and disorderly. The pigs came and drove us several fucking miles into the countryside and dumped us by the road. 'Now you walk on home and sober up!' That was the wrong method. We picked up sticks and threatened motorists the entire way back. First thing that happens when we arrive back in town is we get arrested again. But the cops couldn't be bothered to drive us out there again, so they let us go. Two idiot metalheads, right on the Hunnebo town square, where everyone was queuing up for their late-night hot dog. The entire square went completely silent. There was a lot of stuff like that going on. Jon was perhaps the funniest person in the world when he was in that mood."

Dissection recorded *Storm of the Light's Bane*, returning once again to Unisound in Finspång and releasing it in the end of 1995. It immediately got glowing reviews and is today regarded as one of the major Swedish metal albums, with an estimated 200,000 copies sold. The band headed over to the U.S. for a 6-week tour with At the Gates and American death metal gods Morbid Angel.

"I lived in Los Angeles in those days, so I joined the tour for a few dates in California," Orvar Säfström remembers. "Tompa was a really old friend of mine, but even though we had met before, this was the first time Jon and I really hung out. We had a great time. Jon got in a very heated argument with the Morbid Angel tour manager after the show in Corona. Dissection were the opening act but refused to go on stage until they were goddamn ready. The guy cut their set short and screamed at Jon afterward, but Jon just told him to go fuck himself. He was completely uncompromising."

As Dissection are celebrated all over the world, Jon was growing increasingly frustrated over people in the black metal scene. He felt that no one took Satanism seriously, only adopting it as a cool image to suit their needs. This was especially evident in situations when the police got involved; people got scared and shied away.

"In 1995, I was completely disillusioned by the so-called Satanists of the metal scene, far more interested in worshipping their record collections—*Bathory* with the yellow goat and Mayhem's *Deathcrush* with pink cover—than in picking up a book. It was so fucking silly, and people were cowards. I myself preferred the company of people who were genuinely interested in something and who had the guts to stand up for it," says Jon.

He was also disappointed with True Satanist Horde, thinking they were all talk and no action.

By then all Dissection members lived in Gothenburg, and Jon encountered a Satanist who showed up to local black metal gigs. He was well versed in the occult, Satanism, and black magic, and they became close friends. Together with two others, the organization MLO—Misanthropic Luciferian Order—was established. Jon saw the opportunity for serious occult work. The two become inseparable.

His friends noticed Jon becoming more and more immersed in his new interests, disappearing from the gang. He was seen around town with his new friend, picking fights and making enemies out of old friends. They begin to worry about him.

IT and the other members of True Satanist Horde were aggravated by Jon's defection to MLO, and a deep feud was ignited. Jon Nödtveidt scoffs.

"I was a member of True Satanist Horde and, of course, told them about MLO. 'Look, now here's MLO—if you're willing, there's the chance of participating in serious stuff.' But no one was interested. That's when the split occurred. We were given an ultimatum by TSH—that we had to leave MLO. It was a threat toward their false pedestal. They realized that no one would respect them once there were people involved in true Satanism. It's real easy to act tough if there's no resistance, no one standing up to you. Now suddenly, people were. And then things stopped being all fun and games."

One night in July of 1997, Jon and his new friend had been out partying with the Nifelheim twins. They'd been to the restaurant Kompaniet and dropped by the strip club Chat Noir close to the Gothenburg central station. Passing through Kungsparken, they come across Josef ben Meddour, a 36-year-old gay man from Algeria.

A few hours later, he was murdered with two gunshots—one in the back and one to the head—by the water tower on top of the Ramberget mountain on Hisingen island.

Jon Nödtveidt was arrested in December of 1997 and held in custody for 11 months before being sentenced to 10 years in prison by the Court of Appeals for accessory to murder and illegal possession of a weapon. His accomplice was sentenced to 10 years for murder.

THE FINAL INTERVIEW WITH JON NÖDTVEIDT
CAFÉ VETEBULLEN, July 6 and 12, 2006

Why is this the last interview you'll be giving?
"So much time has passed now that we no longer want any part of the metal scene. We have nothing to do with it, more than being a band with fans who are into metal. We don't represent the same things other bands do. In our eyes, there is no Satanic scene within metal to be part of. And at the same time, the metal scene has distanced itself from us."

In what way?
"Because Dissection are too controversial. Many are blinded by external aspects—my prison sentence, for example. That I have returned and resurrected Dissection. You're not allowed to do that. People think I should hide in shame for the rest of my life. I'm not ashamed of who I am, nor am I ashamed of my actions. I stand behind what I've done and accept the consequences."

Can you understand why people react the way they do?
"From their perspective, I can understand it. This is, of course, because they, either instinctively or consciously, realize that we're nothing like them. We are something entirely different; we have nothing in common any longer. I've had a set of benchmarks and a framework when writing *Reinkaos*. Certain principles. I'm not going to make any fucking black metal–sounding album. Black metal is fake to me. Black metal is pretentious. They scream about Satan but don't mean it at all. They wear theatrical makeup, spit blood and fire, and roll around like idiots on stage—but they don't mean a word. That's been my basic benchmark: Dissection is no fucking black metal band."

Has it ever been?

"We are a Satanic metal band, and then people can make what they want of that. Black metal has been synonymous with posers to me for a long time."

Dissection don't even sound like death metal any longer.

"Dissection play Satanic metal. Period. People come up to me and say, 'What the hell, you don't have any blast beats on the album?' No, because that was my primary rule—to absolutely not have any blast beats on the record! That really was rule number one. No. Fucking. Blast beats. On this album. I have more respect for bands like AC/DC and Motörhead. They sing 'Highway to Hell' and things like that but never claimed to be Satanists. Rappers are more Satanic than virtually any metal band; they shoot and kill more people. How many within the metal scene come from a background in which they've been forced to resort to violence?"

Extremely few, and that's one of the most interesting aspects of the genre.

"Let me put it like this: Out of all subcultures in existence, metal is the wimpiest. It's almost only middle-class kids who always had everything served to them and never had to fight for anything. Even punks are more extreme; at least they fight with the police and throw Molotov cocktails. I have more respect for them. Within metal, people would never dream of turning the things they sing about into real action. When doing exactly that, it becomes evident how much of an outsider you really are."

What are you going to do now that the band has split up?

"Much has been about going all the way with Dissection, which means seeing it through to the end. All lyrics on all albums have been about death—the great dissolution, Armageddon. And with *Reinkaos*, we've reached the point where it's time to kill the band. It's no longer possible to continue on the physical plane. It's got entirely to do with the things we sing about, the concepts we touch on in our lyrics and music. They're not fairy tales. Behind all the mythological, symbolic forms we depict, there is a spiritual reality we're part of and wish to become one with."

What does that reality look like?

"Spiritual freedom is a concept permeating all religions; it just means different things. A person worshipping the creator of this world might have as his goal to become one with the creator, but he doesn't want to live like a physical person. As a Satanist, I want to wipe out this creation entirely—restoring the original chaos and becoming one with it. Of course, there are religions that speak of similar things, where this world is considered a lower form of existence and the one who created it is evil. I could mention Gnosticism, with strong parallels to the Satanism I represent. It stands for 'insight through enlightenment,' and my goal as a Satanist is chaos-gnosis—insight into chaos."

And what does that really mean?

"Gnosticism is based on the understanding that this world is wrong—that there's a driving force within you wanting to break free. In traditional Gnosticism, this is called the divine spark. In Satanism, we call it the black flame. Gnostics believe one must seek the god within—all other gods are false, oppressive, or enslaving. The Satanism I speak of is an aggressive satanic Gnosticism, for we identify as enemies of this world. We are ready to do whatever it takes to free ourselves and the chaos trapped in here. That's why everything that's happened during this journey has been but different phases of the end. Personally, I've always felt ready to go all the way, and that's what's going to happen."

In what way did you feel it was time?

"It's actually felt like that for quite some time."

Even as you were writing music in prison?

"The band's concept is so much bigger than the band itself, so it's not only about its existence. It's about religious and spiritual concepts beyond us as people and as an active group. It's more about wandering the Left-Hand Path, and the band's music has been an expression and a way to channel that pursuit. The longing for the end, the longing for death, the longing for the dark—to become one with chaos and put an end to life."

Even physical life?

"Yes, to end this cosmic prison. That longing has been with me the entire time. It might have been just a seed that has been allowed to flourish during my journey. Go back and read the old lyrics, and you'll see the same driving force there. That was no joke; everything was absolutely honest. I identify with the darkness, with chaos. That's why my ultimate goal is to transcend beyond this physical condition."

By dying?

"It's not possible to permanently travel beyond the physical condition unless you die. So of course, death is the aim. That's what we've said from the start. This is also the concept of Dissection—Anti-Cosmic Metal of Death. And why do we call it the metal of death? Because it's about death, genuinely."

Are you planning on taking your own life?

"If I'm not killed by someone else, then I will, of course, commit suicide. I have no plans of going on living until I expire of old age—it's such an alien notion that the very thought was never there. Ever since I was 15 or 16 years old, I've planned to take my own life."

Why haven't you already?

"There have been things keeping me alive. And of course, I've wanted to accomplish certain goals. It's not as simple as saying, 'I hate life, so now I'll commit suicide,' and then everything falls into place. I don't believe in that concept. If you do something like that, it has to be for a reason. The cosmic prison is a reality. I'm no atheist who believes that this is everything—I believe in the spirit, a spiritual driving force that lies beyond this world. And that's the essence I identify with, that I intend to set free."

What is death to you?
"I became incredibly fascinated with death early on. To me, it's always been apparent death isn't the end, just the end of life here now. But it's not the end of me or what lies beyond. Death is a beginning, a new opening. It is the gate one must pass. To me, it's been evident that you can't become one with chaos, you can't become one with darkness, before crossing the threshold of death. Until then, you can, of course, awaken the flame within—you can rouse the power and identify with it. But as long as you live in a human body, you'll be a purely physical organism walking a physical planet. For me, it's always been the goal to get out of here to become who I really am. I must find the answer to the riddle of why I'm here and why I search for something else."

Have you always been searching?
"You can, of course, go back and analyze my childhood in different ways. The fact that I upset my grandmother when I was six because I made figures of clay that she thought looked like the devil. This driving force must have been lying dormant and then flared up at different stages. It's really about exploring it and finding oneself more and more."

When did you first become aware of this flame?
"I can't answer that. What I do remember is an emotional arousal from certain tales, stories of dark monsters and creatures. There were things that evoked my emotions, but I was too young to understand what it was really about."

The punishment you received for what you did, was it worth it for you?
"Certainly. Punishment, I don't know—no punishment can be worse than being born into this world. This is why I refuse to let myself be governed by laws and morals built on lies. Hence, no human can judge or punish me. The damage has already been done."

You were born here though, so whether you want to or not, you've inherited human reactions and emotions.
"As a human, you consist of a brain programmed with human inhibitions; as an organism, you're adapted to being human. It's not a peaceful breakup, tearing free from the cycle or from that role. This can only be accomplished through violence. Spiritual but also physical violence. I'm not trying to be evil or tough. I'm not trying to convince anyone about anything; I'm just trying to be myself. It just so happens that this world stands in my way."

But this means that there is good cause to fear you.

"That's just the way it is. I didn't ask to be born encapsulated in physical form, but at the same time, I'm not running around attacking people up or committing acts of cruelty just for the sake of it. It's not your fault, and it's not my neighbor's fault—it's a fundamental flaw in the whole cosmos."

I think that's what people believe. That you are completely unpredictable. People really thought that something was going to happen at Midsummer Massacre.
"Did they really?"

That the whole place was going to blow up.
"Why would I be that predictable? Of course, there's an underlying discomfort people feel when it comes to Dissection. Most dislike this feeling. Then, of course, some are drawn to it. Being a Satanist is not about committing a bunch of pointless atrocities. That would be retarded, going around carrying out acts of violence all the time."

During the True Satanist Horde period, an elderly man was stabbed on the street by someone who wanted to be part of your crowd. How did you react then?
"That was completely unnecessary. There was no reason for it."

Did you ever consider the power you had—that people would do things like that to impress you?
"If someone chooses to do a thing like that, then he'll have to take responsibility himself. What am I supposed to do? It's so fucking ridiculous to even talk about."

I don't think it's ridiculous to talk about it, because this is what's so difficult to understand.
"If you're 16 and see someone get stabbed, what do you think? I played in a band singing about killing mankind. Today, I would probably have a stronger reaction, since it's so meaningless. When it happened back in those days, it just happened."

How, then, do you react to big events such as the Estonia ferry tragedy or 9/11? Is it a good thing, when as many as possible die?
"People die every day. People get upset with each other and make war. Objectively, what am I supposed to react to? Estonia didn't affect me in the slightest; 9/11, however, I thought was more interesting from a symbolical perspective. To me, it represents an attack on the enemy, even if I don't stand for the same things as the Taliban do. Of course, I enjoy watching harm done to the world order. But then, I was, of course, hoping for another world war to break out."

Would you like to see World War III?
"At the time, it didn't feel that far-fetched, and it would have been interesting from an ideological perspective. Why then do I think it's a good thing? Because I enjoy seeing

someone standing up to oppression, bringing more chaos into the world. Stabbing an elderly person in the street does nothing of the sort."

When did you become known to the police as a Satanist?
"When I was 16. Occultus, the Mayhem vocalist at the time, was visiting Strömstad. He'd been waving a knife around in a pub, and they called the police. We'd already left by then, but the cops came to bring him in. It ended with me being apprehended for resisting arrest and attempted aiding and abetting. I was charged, which brought up a lot about Satanism that had nothing to do with it."

Where did that come from?
"We had pentagrams and looked a certain way—especially back in those days, when there was more of an explicit black metal look, with long black hair and inverted crosses. At the trial, the prosecutor spent most of his time defining Satanism. He brought up a bunch of books and explained how Satanists sacrifice children and all kinds of things. It was a parody. That was my first encounter with law enforcement, and our relation has not been a particularly rewarding one ever since."

Can incidents like that have contributed to you further embracing the black flame? Did it corroborate your conclusion that you were surrounded by idiots?
"Of course, I saw it as a blatant provocation by the police. Needless to say, this generated headlines in the local papers. '16-year-old arrested for attempted aiding and abetting.' How they needed three police cruisers to get the angry teenager under control. Afterward, there was talk all over town about the SATANISTS! Certainly, I'm a Satanist today but can't claim to have known much about it when I was 16."

Did the police keep an eye on you in connection with church burnings in the '90s?
"I was arrested together with The Count and Bård in Norway in the spring of 1993. We were accused of robbery and had to spend the night in isolation cells in Oslo. We were grabbed at a gas station in the center of town. Suddenly, we were surrounded by police, who handcuffed us and took us in. We had to spend the night there being interrogated about a robbery, and of course, there was no evidence whatsoever."

Did you do it?
"We were 100% innocent. They released us the day after; it was just harassment. They probably recognized The Count, who'd been in the papers and was under suspicion for the church burnings."

What contact did you have with the outside world while in prison? With family and friends?
"I was in steady contact with my family during the entire sentence. Then there were several friends I kept in touch with through letters, but for the most part, I lived my life

on the inside. It would've been too much having my thoughts on the outside all the time, while being physically imprisoned. I always had the attitude that you just have to do the time and make the best of it."

You were pretty bulky at the first gig.
"I'd just been released and had a bull neck after heavy deadlifts on a regular basis. Huge portions of oatmeal for breakfast. The advantage with prison is that time is on your side; you only need to see the upside to it. If there are things you wish to immerse yourself in, like writing songs, then you can. I found my routine."

Do you value things more these days?
"I try to. Of course, I wish I had more time to do certain things. But I definitely believe that I'm consciously trying to cherish what I'm experiencing right now. It's not only that I've played really cool shows; just the feeling of no longer being incarcerated is amazing. The sensation from getting out of prison didn't really subside in the first six months. First waking up every day in my own apartment, and then we went on tour directly afterward. The last two years have been the happiest of my life. I'm, of course, not saying that it's only been fun. It goes without saying that there have been rough patches to get through."

What do you mean?
"Fighting for and enforcing things you believe in is not always easy. Just releasing your own album isn't as simple as people seem to think. If they only knew how much work goes into it. It's a big fucking difference compared to just leaving it to somebody else. And an entirely different responsibility, especially with such an emotional attachment. This is important. On occasion, I have felt that I've taken on too much responsibility for my own good."

Do you have control issues?
"Sure, I'm a real control freak. It's just something I need to accept. I wasn't always, but then everything went to hell because I didn't make sure things were going the way they were supposed to. That's why I've become insanely meticulous with everything. 'Nooo, we refuse to do this because we want it a little bit more thaaat way.' It feels absolutely fantastic that we managed to release the album, how we've rereleased the back catalogue and broken free from a slave contract. We have given the finger to this entire world, except our fans, and done everything the way we wanted to. And we've played fucking Hovet as well! Imagine the feeling of being hurled straight into this from seven years in a vacuum. It's been an extreme reversal."

Would you risk going back to prison?
"Obviously, you have to accept that it just isn't possible to adhere to the laws of society if you wish to live as a Satanist."

How did you change as a person during your time on the inside?

"I was 22 years old when I went in, and I've spent almost a third of my life in prison, so of course, I'm not the same person today. Perspectives change when you're imprisoned and you come to evaluate your life. The constant supervision and control is always there. You get used to it, even if you don't accept it. You always want to get out of there. I felt I could benefit from getting through the experience."

Did you use your faith to get through the sentence?

"No, but I used the time to immerse myself in matters I didn't have time for on the outside, to the extent that it was possible. After a few years, I was allowed to have my electric guitar in there. I would play and write music. Some kind of activity is compulsory. You either have to work or study. I took part in inmate work activities for a while—carrying out braindead tasks like winding cords, assembling different electrical boxes, and things like that. At times, I've also studied subjects that were made available."

What did you study?

"Mathematics, philosophy, Swedish, English. High-school subjects."

Where were you imprisoned?

"First, I was placed in the national prison intake at Kumla. If you are sentenced to more than four years, you'll be sent there for an evaluation of where to carry out the term, and if certain restrictions are warranted. Back in those days, you were called a 7:3 if you were thought to be especially dangerous. That means no furloughs, nothing. You're not told anything about your circumstances in the judicial system besides that you'll be placed in a high-risk prison under maximum security until you're reevaluated. I served for five and a half years before the duration of my sentence was determined. With seven months left, I was moved to a low-security prison."

Can you describe the difference?

"It's like a normal prison, but without any walls. Oftentimes, you'll be able to go out and work in a factory. The sensation of coming to an open institution after six years behind walls was of course absolutely amazing. Not that I was out of prison, but I was no longer locked up deep inside the heart of the judicial system. That's how I felt for the majority of my sentence."

Did you ever contemplate escape?

"You have to be quite insane to be imprisoned and not contemplate escape. Of course, I thought through all possibilities, but it's not easy escaping from a Swedish maximum-security prison. You'd have to take a hostage or have someone aid your escape during transportation or a supervised furlough. You can't just climb over the wall. You can't even walk up to it. Construction-wise, it's not possible to dig your way out. I would've had nothing to gain, trying something like that. My goal was always to get out and keep doing certain things. My goal was never to disappear and hide in the jungles of Brazil."

You must have been serving with some of the hardest criminals in Sweden.
"During most of my incarceration, I had the toughest conditions you can have unless serving a life sentence. I've done time in harsh prisons with people who are in for a long time. I had 10 years. The first one I was sent to after the prison intake was the class 1 section of Tidaholm. The average sentence on my block was 10 to 12 years. The guy with the shortest had six years, and he was regarded a short-termer—everyone thought he had a really short sentence."

Are you allowed any contact with women in prison?
"There are female guards, but you're not allowed to have any relations with them—not a good thing if discovered. Then, of course, there are women who are drawn to men in prison."

Did you have any prison groupies?
"I had a girlfriend when I was caught. We stayed together a year and a half into my sentence. We wrote lots of letters while I was in custody. Then, when I'd been placed, it was possible to meet for a few hours in a gray and boring visiting room at Tidaholm. She traveled from Gothenburg to Falköping by train, then took the bus and so on. We split up after a few months. Still, I'm surprised it lasted that long. I then got in touch with a girl I started corresponding with, and who I then pursued a relationship with, during my time in prison."

Did you ever meet?
"She came and visited."

Is this the girlfriend you have now?
"No. I was actually single when I got out."

Why did you place Midsummer Massacre on Midsummer's Day?
"It was convenient, from a planning perspective. Perhaps we could have waited another month. To us, it was a suitable date."

When did you start realizing that Hovet was perhaps not going to sell out?
"Our ambition was to play a really fucking good concert, record a DVD, and put on that stage show for those who wanted to come see us. We're as pleased as can be. It couldn't have gone better."

You don't think that perhaps the audience could have been larger?
"The audience can always be larger."

When it was announced you were doing this, people thought you were insane. After all, it's the Midsummer weekend in Sweden.

"We wanted to once and for all present Dissection the way we see the band. It was absolutely killer. Sure, we could've done a long club tour and earn significantly more money from it. Instead, we chose to invest in an elaborate show and a DVD, which is so much more rewarding. Closing the Dissection chapter in a worthy fashion—in a manner of our choosing, which those who were present clearly appreciated a lot."

How could you even afford this? I've heard it costs over 20,000 dollars to rent Hovet.

"20,000 is the deposit. Regardless if there is a single attendee, that's their guaranteed take. I mean, I can assure you that the calculator was put to good use. Even if you end up earning or losing money on such an event, the added value is being able to put on a gig like that. Also, not everything is about what ends up in your wallet right away. You can do things like this if you're the one in charge, when the band has no middlemen. If we want to use money we've made from album and merchandise sales for this evening, then sure. It's worth it."

There are two DVDs on the way, your old albums have been rereleased on CD and vinyl, and you have lots of merchandise. Is there any risk you might be overestimating the interest in Dissection?

"I don't know what would be overestimated in that case."

Is there a demand for all of this?

"Yes, of course."

Why did you get that facial tattoo?

"It felt good. That's how calculated that was. I've always wanted a facial tattoo. The feeling I had afterward was of being something other than human. The tattoo made me reconnect to underlying instincts. A manifestation of the beast in some way."

When did you get your first tattoo?

"It was fairly late, not until 1995. The MLO tattoo was my first—the Ushumgal pentagram. It's one of our symbols. I've had a lot of work done in prison too. You don't sit there exactly following all of the rules. There are some creative people in there."

Was that using ballpoint ink?

"Someone's girlfriend smuggled in tattoo needles and ink, then we built a tattoo machine from an electric razor. I once made a tattoo machine from a Walkman."

So, you learned something from building those electrical boxes?

"I once made a tattoo needle from a guitar string. It was difficult as hell; I had to use a thick string and then sharpen it at the end. I don't think it turned out that good. All of my flames are made in prison. The guy who made them was a tattoo artist, but it was with a prison machine. He made shading needles and round liner needles and all kinds of things from pipe cleaners. I made that seal in prison; it's a seal that stands for the *geburim*—those who carry the black flame."

Can you detect people who carry the black flame by only looking at them?
"You have to get to know people. The chaos burns in a select few. The rest are completely uninteresting. The only way I'm a racist is that I oppose the human race; all people are equally worthless. No skin colors are better or worse than others. People are so trapped in their own prejudices and thoughts. They would never understand. There is no point in discussing with an insect."

Is that what it's like for you, talking with people who do not carry the black flame?
"Well, you won't sit down and try explaining something to an earthworm lying on the road."

No, but do you feel like you're talking to an earthworm when explaining things to us?
"I can't make you understand chaos if you do not carry chaos yourself. If you have the chaos within, you can search inside and try to grasp it, but I can't make you understand. That's my point: People essentially misunderstand the entire point and see only their own prejudices."

People see that a person was murdered.
"People die every day. We will all die one day."

True, but not all of us by someone else's hand.
"I'm not claiming to be in the service of mankind; I want to destroy it! So, don't fucking expect me to do anything but bring ruin to all! People shouldn't misread the situation and expect a Satanist to follow laws created by humans. They can do whatever they want—kill me or put me in prison—but they'll never quench the flame I carry. I'm willing to accept that. I have accepted this. Some have tried to kill me, and others put me in prison."

Have many people tried to kill you?
"No, but I've been in situations where attempts have been made. And I'm still alive today."

How has your family reacted to all this? Do they understand you?
"I can't say that they understand me, but they do understand that I'm being myself. What else can I do? I'm not asking of anyone to understand more than that. If someone treats me as a human being, they obviously have themselves to blame. If so, they've misunderstood everything despite all the signs. Just open your eyes. I'm here, and one day I will manage to escape. That's all I want."

At the end of the summer of 2006, Jon calls and says he'd like to rewrite the contract regarding his approval of the text. He wants Dissection guitarist Set Teitan to read and review the chapter, since he's going away.

We meet at Vetebullen again. Jon is dragging two black suitcases behind him. He says he's already told us everything he wants to say. We ask where he's going.

"To Transylvania," he says smiling.

We agree to draft a power of attorney, and we all sign it. The contract needs duplicates, and we decide to meet at Stureplan, in the city center, later in the afternoon. Something feels wrong.

When Pelle "Dead" Ohlin took his own life, he wore a shirt with the print "I ♥ Transylvania," and in some parts of the black metal scene, it has been a morbid joke referring to committing suicide. We consider his words. Is he going to commit another crime and then disappear? Perhaps he's really going to Transylvania, to leave his old life behind?

A few hours later, Jon waits for us at Stureplan and gives us the copy of the new contract. He's harried and looks a bit on edge but remains cordial as always.

"Thanks for everything," he says while giving us a sturdy handshake.

"We really hope to see you again," we answer.

He looks at us and chuckles. Then he quickly turns around and crosses the street at Kungsgatan.

———

On August 15, 2006, police break into Jon Nödtveidt's apartment in Hässelby, a suburb west of Stockholm.

Neither his father nor brother Emil has been able to reach him for several days. And alarmingly, there's been a postcard with a list of people he wants his father to thank for him. When his girlfriend calls from Germany to tell them of a farewell letter she's received, the family contacts the police.

They find Nödtveidt dead on the living room floor, in a circle of candles. He's shot himself in the head with a revolver. In front of him lies a Satanic grimoire, an instructional book for magic.

Jon Nödtveidt was 31 years old.

———

Four years later, we meet Set Teitan at Mariatorget in Stockholm. He comes straight from the gym and wears a hoodie with Watain logos, the band he's played live with since Dissection split up.

Jon's departure left a vast hole in Swedish black metal circles. The excitement ignited in the wake of his prison release subsided. MLO have changed their name to Temple of the Black Light.

Set Teitan came to Sweden to play with Dissection and says he has no plans of moving back to Italy. Today, he handles everything related to Dissection and does what he can to keep Jon Nödtveidt's legacy alive—from overseeing the Midsummer Massacre DVD production to reviewing this very text.

He describes his friendship and collaboration with Jon as one of the most important events of his life.

"I've never experienced such a strong connection with another person. He was like a brother to me, and he's still highly present. Everyone has their own path to wander in life. But of course, I miss him."

Jon Nödtveidt's father, Anders, has declined to be interviewed for this book. He writes in an email, "Sorry, I want no part of the book. I've tried supporting Jon as best I could, but enough is enough." Jon's brother, Emil, also declined our interview request.

The Midsummer Massacre show has yet to be released on DVD.

Photo: Anders Tengner

Heavy Load, 1981. Eddy Malm, Ragne Wahlquist, Styrbjörn Wahlquist, Torbjörn Ragnesjö.

Photo: Jon Jefferson Klingberg

Ragne Wahlquist, Heavy Load,
Solna subway station, 2006.

Photo: Combat

Ice Age, 1987. Victoria Larsson, Sabrina Kihlstrand,
Pia Nyström, Tina Strömberg.

Agony, 1988.

Candlemass, 1987. Jan Lindh, Leif Edling, Messiah Marcolin, Mats Björkman, Lars Johansson.

Øystein "Euronymous" Aarseth, Mayhem, early '90s.

Ace "Quorthon" Forsberg, Bathory, 1984. Promo photos for the debut album *Bathory*.

Quorthon at the Berlin Wall, 1988.

Quorthon and Boss in the Elektra studio, 1985.

Mayhem. Jan-Axel "Hellhammer" Blomberg, Pelle "Dead" Ohlin,
Øystein "Euronymous" Aarseth, Jørn "Necrobutcher" Stubberud.

Anders and Pelle Ohlin at the breakfast table in Västerhaninge, 1983.

Pelle Ohlin and Jens Näsström.

Pelle Ohlin in Jordbro, late '80s.

Necrobutcher and Dead.

Leif Cuzner, Nicke Andersson, and Daniel Strachal at summer camp, Dalarna, mid-'80s.

Grotesque, photo session for *Incantation*, 1990. Alf Svensson, Tompa Lindberg, Kristian Wåhlin.

Photo: Chelsea Krook

Unleashed, 1989. Fredrik Lindgren, Robert Sennebäck, Anders Schultz, Johnny Hedlund.

Photo: Chelsea Krook

Nihilist, 1989. L-G Petrov, Johnny Hedlund, Leif Cuzner, Alex Hellid, Nicke Andersson.

Photo: Orvar Säfström

Tomas Skogsberg and Nicke Andersson, Sunlight Studio, 1990.

Drawing by Kristian Wåhlin, late '80s.

Photo: ©Nuclear Blast

Photo from the Dismember album *Like An Everflowing Stream*, 1991. Matti Kärki, Fred Estby, Richard Cabeza, David Blomqvist, Robert Sennebäck.

At The Gates, Valvet, 1990.

Siren's Yell, 1988. Jon Nödtveidt, Mäbe Johansson,
Ole Öhman, Peter Palmdahl.

Poster for thrash gala in Strömstad, organised by
Jon Nödtveidt, 1989. Carbonized never played,
and was replaced by Therion.

José Afonso of Portuguese black metal band Decayed,
Crille Nilsson, Susanna Berglund, and Metalion,
Stockholm, 2003.

Lord Ahriman, Dark Funeral, 1997.

IT, Finspång, 1993.

Peter Stjärnvind, 1991.

Photo: Peter Palmdahl

Photo: Vejde Gustafsson

Pelle and Erik Gustafsson, Hisingen, 1998.

Caskets backstage, Uddevalla, 2006.

Photo: Sanna Johannesson

Nifelheim at Getaway Rock Festival, Gävle, 2011.

Photo: ©Jon Kristiansen

Photo: Jon Jefferson Klingberg

Erik "Tyrant" Gustafsson, Kolingsborg, Stockholm, 2005.

Jon Nödtveidt, Hovet, Stockholm, 2006.

Photo: Jon Jefferson Klingberg

Jon Nödtveidt on the arena floor after Dissection's final concert, Hovet, Stockholm, 2006.

Victor Brandt and L-G Petrov, Örebro, 2009.

Alex Hellid, Örebro, 2009.

Maria "Black Virgin" Ström, Ullared, 2009.

Photo: Andreas Carlsson/Rockfoto.nu

Hammerfall, Getaway Rock Festival, Gävle, 2011.

Photo: Magnus Norman

Demonia, 2011.

Photo: Jon Jefferson Klingberg

Matti Kärki, the Sweden Rock Cruise, 2006.

Photo: Jon Jefferson Klingberg

Nicke Andersson, Hultsfred, 2011.

Photo: Jon Jefferson Klingberg

Tompa Lindberg at the Grotesque reunion gig, Stockholm, 2007.

Muskelrock, Blädinge, 2011.
Clockwise: Headbangers by the big stage. Kongo
Magnéli in front of the Bullet bus. John Miki Thor.
Bullet guitars. Staffan Hamrin. Hampus Klang.

Niklas Kvarforth taking in the beach, Halmstad, 2006.

Kim Carlsson at a Shining gig, Stockholm, 2005.

Photo: Jon Jefferson Klingberg

Niklas Kvarforth as "Ghoul", Halmstad, 2007.

Niklas Kvarforth modelling for the
fashion company H&M, late '80s.

Photo: Jon Jefferson Klingberg

In Johan Hallander's apartment, Halmstad, 2006.

Photo: Ika Johannesson

Erik Danielsson, Stockholm, 2009.

Photo: Ika Johannesson

The decayed raven, Sundsvall, 2010.

Photo: Watain Archives

Erik Danielsson, New Orleans, USA, 2008.

Photo: MODUA

Watain on tour, 2011. Erik Danielsson, Håkan Jonson, Set Teitan, Johan Frölund, Pelle Forsberg, Tore Stjerna, Alvaro Lillo.

X.

By Men, For Men

*Girls weren't supposed to be involved
in anything significant.
If an album had a woman on it,
it was immediately considered
less brutal.*

—ALEXANDRA BALOGH

HARD ROCK AND METAL have been predominantly male domains since the beginning. When death metal and the second wave of black metal emerged in the late '80s, not only were they the most aggressive forms of metal yet known, it was also the first time that women weren't used as sex objects.

"Black metal is about violence, brutality, and evil. It's not so much about gender and sex," says Alexandra Balogh.

"Putting a naked chick on an album cover would be considered wrong and stupid," she continues. "That's an aspect of the genre that I found appealing. As a black metal girl, everything was unisex; you didn't dress any differently than the guys did. Sometimes, if I wasn't wearing makeup or earrings, people thought I was a dude. I found that somewhat of a relief. In school, people would be poking me, wondering what I was."

Balogh grew up in Finspång, and she's one of only a few women to have appeared on a Swedish extreme metal album. She wrote and performed the piano piece "No Dreams Breed in Breathless Sleep" on Dissection's second album, *Storm of the Light's Bane*, and has contributed to albums by Vondur, Ophthalamia, and Darkified. She's also a composer of orchestral music.

Having always been philosophically and religiously inclined, the satanic and occult lyrical topics drew her to black metal. As the girlfriend of IT, Abruptum's vocalist and the founder of True Satanist Horde, she found herself in the center of the mid-'90s black metal scene. But unlike Mara, who was also part of the group, she was never truly welcomed inside the circle.

"I imagine Mara was more useful—she took action. They probably considered me too delicate and vulnerable. I was first and foremost seen as female, rather than one of the pack. It's not as if I was left out, but I suspect that it was because I was someone's girlfriend."

When she tried acting tough, the guys would tell her to knock it off.

"I was more the person making coffee. But I lived there as well, so while they were planning things, I'd be drawing under the table. I was part of the scenery, you could say. But in a positive sense. I'd dye their hair sometimes."

Her interest in Satanism was often questioned but never her musical proficiency and passion. Balogh had studied classical piano since she was four years old and was very good at it. When Dissection asked her to compose something depressing, she did—but at the same time, she was fully aware that women didn't hold a high status as musicians within the scene.

"Girls weren't supposed to be involved in anything significant. If an album had a woman on it, it was immediately considered less brutal. But not everyone was of that opinion—Dissection for instance—but that might have been because I wasn't invading their turf. I imagine it would've been very different if I'd started growling."

One woman who's made a name for herself by doing just that is German-born Angela Gossow of Swedish band Arch Enemy.

Arch Enemy formed in Halmstad in 1996, after Mike Amott returned to Sweden after a few years with legendary British death metal band Carcass. Arch Enemy released a few celebrated albums but stayed out of the spotlight. Only after recruiting Angela as vocalist in 2001 did they see a commercial breakthrough with the album *Wages of Sin*. Today, they are one of Sweden's major acts in the genre.

Angela sings with a deep, throaty growl—she snarls and screams. Judging only from her vocals, few can tell she's a woman.

"When I began singing in bands in the early '90s, I'd get plenty of comments. 'That's not going to work; you're a girl.' I had to listen to stuff like that for many years. But then I noticed how many were drawn to the band because I was a woman. Today, it's entirely different—we get a lot of respect."

In the early days of metal, only a handful of women managed to make a career out of it. Ex-Runaways guitarist Lita Ford was one of them. Other examples include the German Doro Pesch, Canadian Lee Aaron, American Wendy O. Williams, and the members of the British band Girlschool.

As the genre took on new forms, even fewer bands featured women. In thrash metal, there was Sabina Classen of Holy Moses from Germany, Witches from France, and Ice Age from Gothenburg, Sweden. The early American death metal scene had vocalist Lori Bravo of Nuclear Death as well as the all-female band Derketa. Bolt Thrower from the UK featured female bass player Jo Bench. That was more or less it.

As the Swedish death metal scene sprang to life in the late '80s, only a few girls were present—even in the audience.

———

Maria "Black Virgin" Ström lives in a yellow wooden cottage in the woods in Ullared, about an hour and a half southeast of Gothenburg. The lawn is wet from rain earlier in the day, and in the cluttered yard sits an old toilet, a rusty grill, and quite a few empty beer cans. Maria's silver Volvo 240 is parked in the driveway, one of many Volvos she's had through the years. Above all, she's preferred Amazons.

A black Volvo Amazon was the vehicle that transported her and neighbor Maria Staaf, two years her junior, to gigs all over the west coast in the late '80s. First, it was catching local punk bands in nearby Halmstad and Falkenberg, then up to Gothenburg,

Fagersta, and Sarpsborg in Norway to see the new death metal acts. At this point, the scene was very small. Everyone knew Staafen and Strömmen, as they were nicknamed. They worked in Ullared during the week, Strömmen in a plastics factory and Staafen at a mechanical workshop. On weekends, they'd always be out and about.

While women remain a minority in today's Swedish death and black metal circles, back then, they were incredibly scarce. Maria Ström can count the girls on one hand.

"You had Chelsea and Nina in Stockholm, then Lena and Therese in Örebro. Perhaps a few others scattered around the country, but they were usually someone's girlfriend."

She was given her alias "Black Virgin" by Tompa Lindberg of Grotesque, when she was up for the drummer position in one of the early incarnations of the band.

"I was a virgin, quite simply," she says, laughing. Her cat, Bigfoot, hides under a blanket on the bed that doubles as a couch.

The alias has followed her to this day. At 46, she still uses Black Virgin as her email address.

She brings out a bunch of photo albums from parties and concerts of the era. The entire Swedish death metal elite show up, with round cheeks and wispy beards, in blurry snapshots from gigs in Strömstad, at the rock club Valvet in Gothenburg, and at the home of Uffe Cederlund in Stockholm.

Sure enough, very few of these photos have women in them, except for Strömmen and Staafen themselves.

Back in those days, the scene was so tiny that simply being into the music was enough to garner respect. She never felt her music interest was in question.

"Since we'd show up at every gig, it wasn't really an issue. It was completely obvious that we lived for this music."

Maria "Staafen" Staaf has lived in Stockholm for many years. She remembers how good it felt when the two of them would leave Ullared and spend the weekends together, far from the boring little town.

"I always saw myself as different from the chicks who just tag along with some guy, I want to do things myself. At every place I worked, there were only guys. First, I worked with assembling furniture and then at a mechanical workshop. I've always been heavily into cars and motorcycles. I've probably had pretty unusual interests for a girl; maybe it's got to do with my mother working and my father always being at home with us when we were kids. He ran his business from home, and it was always me and him. I never saw my mom around."

Staafen says she was never especially girly. Rather, the social circles were so asexual that she became one of the boys. She notes how the guys rarely brought their girlfriends along to concerts and parties, and when women actually did show up, they'd be uninterested in the music.

"That's pretty much always been the case. The extreme guys often have totally normal girlfriends, which I cannot understand. It's something I've thought about a lot. They live the hard lifestyle, but still want to have the Madonna. If you want respect in traditionally male circles, then you almost have to become like a man—and then many of the guys get turned off. It's tragic."

The word "girlfriend" often comes up when discussing gender roles with both men and women in extreme metal. Being a girlfriend and discovering the music through your boyfriend is not ranked high on the stringent *true* scale.

Chelsea Krook hung out in Stockholm's early death metal crowd—and she remembers how she and the other girls in the gang would treat new girlfriends differently.

"It was really difficult for the girls who came after us; they weren't accepted at all. At the time, I felt that they'd break the status quo—girls always cause trouble. We were in denial about even being girls; we were like the guys. Those who were strong and dared to embrace their femininity were rejected because they did not fit in with our image of what the circle should look like."

Chelsea moved to Sollentuna from the United States when she was 13 years old and got to know Nils "Nisse" Gullbrandsson and Rikard "Rille" Synstad—friends of Pelle "Dead" Ohlin—on the bus back home to the suburbs. She started hanging out with the Stockholm bands before they were even bands and was immediately recruited to come up with macabre words for lyrics, then proofread them. She sees nothing strange in the fact that both death metal and then the second wave of black metal have so little to do with feelings and sex.

"We were kids, there were no feelings, and everyone was pretty asexual. We pretended to be Satanists and watched horror movies. I don't think anyone would've appreciated songs about emotions, it just wasn't very interesting. Few of these guys had girlfriends. People had just come out of puberty."

The website of black metal band Pest from Stockholm states: "PEST plays pure black metal in the old vein; no females or keyboards involved." Even though that specific statement might be a bit tongue-in-cheek, it's still a pretty good example of what people used to think—and still do to a certain extent—about women in black metal.

"The attitude toward women isn't that great," confirms Demonia, who runs a metal blog by the same name. "The general assumption is that girls can't do it. Girls aren't extreme. I personally don't think women belong on a black metal stage. As fans, sure, but not as musicians. I think it looks silly."

She points out that she likes metal artists such as Doro and Lita Ford. It's primarily in black metal that she'd rather not see women on stage. Demonia is convinced a female black metal band would never garner respect in metal circles. Women should quite simply stay out of the genre, unless they're prepared for a hostile and extremely challenging climate.

"It's a genre by men, for men—with exceptions, of course. You must have followed it for a long time to understand and made the journey from hard rock to death to black metal. Those who jump straight into black metal often think it's just noise. I've been through a lot. A lot of trouble and a lot of fights, animal sacrifice, destruction, and people who've hurt themselves and others pretty badly."

Demonia started listening to metal when she was four years old, when her stepfather would use VHS tapes of live concerts with Twisted Sister and Black Sabbath as a proxy baby sitter. In the car, he would blast metal at maximum volume, and objections would only make him mad. A few years later, Demonia inherited his turntable, amplifier, speakers, and all of his records—and began developing her own interest in increasingly heavier music.

At 16, she joined a few older friends from Umeå on a trip to Stockholm to see Morbid Angel play at the Melody. They spent the night at the home of Johnny Hedlund of Unleashed and went to House of Kicks to stock up on demo cassettes, albums, and fanzines. Back home, she started exchanging letters with bands and people all over the world, and her tape collection grew steadily. Through tape-trading, she got to know the small Swedish metal scene of the time and has been faithful to it ever since.

Today, on Demonia, she posts photos and writes about concerts and parties in Stockholm's extreme metal scene, along with the odd post about MMA.

While in school, she'd mostly hang out with guys. She drove a moped and played video games. Other girls found her strange.

At 20, she moved to Stockholm. She was already there every month for concerts anyway and had started dating a local guy.

"He wasn't playing in any bands when I first met him. Something I've always, always had to put up with are questions like 'Are you seeing him because he plays in a band?' or 'Do you know L-G because he plays with Entombed?' Almost everyone who listens to metal plays in a band! I only know a few people who don't! Everyone who's been into it for a long time knows each other; the scene isn't that big."

Demonia mentions how she seldom meets women whose level of music interest matches her own. There are only a few in each country.

"Most got into metal through their boyfriend and then developed that interest through someone else. I built my own interest, and I'm as passionate about it to this day. My records will be passed on; all demos will be preserved. I don't know many who are as extreme as I am—just because they didn't choose metal themselves."

Demonia is used to being the only woman in most metal situations. We ask how she's been affected by constantly being in a gender minority, and she says it's made her "fucking strong."

"I had no choice, I can't show up as some brittle little girl that people can step on. I don't want anyone to slap a gender on me; I see myself as one of the gang and often know more than the guys when it comes to music. I realized early on that I had to learn a lot about the music, otherwise I'd never be accepted. If you're a girl, everyone assumes that you know nothing—being female is something negative in this context. You're like a subhuman. As soon as I met a guy I didn't know, there'd be a full interrogation with a hundred questions to test me."

All of the women we speak to note how their knowledge is constantly challenged. But being completely ignored is worse.

At the end of the '00s, Susanna Berglund ran the metal store Black Hole on Södermalm in Stockholm, selling secondhand records and merchandise. She's listened to harder music since she was 12 years old and discovered grunge after an upbringing filled with opera. Grunge led her to metal, and since her teens, she's been going to gigs and hanging out with people who would later play in bands like Tribulation, In Solitude, and Watain.

"A typical example is when Erik from Nifelheim and I went to a gig in Örebro to see Inquisition from Colombia. One of the band members came up and said hello to Erik and another male friend who was with us. He shook both their hands, but completely ignored me. And that's not the first time this has happened."

Like in many other teenage subcultures, identification and connection within the genre is often accomplished by specific clothing, haircuts, and other attributes. You listen to a specific type of music and read certain books.

Norwegian Runhild Gammelsaeter spent her teenage years in Seattle, where her father worked. Together with Stephen O'Malley and Greg Anderson, who would later form Sunn O))), she founded death metal band Thorr's Hammer in 1996 and wrote for *Descent*—the first American fanzine to pay attention to the growing Norwegian black metal scene. Today, she makes her own music and released the doom-inspired solo album *Amplicon* in 2008.

"When it comes to the male role, I think black metal people regard themselves as very masculine—and that's correct to a certain extent. They are tough and hold distinct and strong opinions. They carry a lot of aggression that's expressed through the music. At the same time, they probably think more about their appearance than other men. There's a sense of vanity in the long hair and the use of makeup. They are rarely muscular and don't necessarily fit the image of the traditional prehistoric man, the ultimate symbol of testosterone. Individuality is highly important in the genre; they are confident and upright. My impression is that many of them are more masculine in their ideology and mentality than the purely physical."

When we ask Alexandra Balogh what she thinks characterizes the male norm in black metal, she starts laughing.

"It was really important not to have split ends! The hair should always be properly groomed. Greasy was okay, but not frayed. Some had toiletry bags full of hair-care products. We'd talk a lot about each other's hair: 'He's got hair this long, and there are no split ends at all!' One guy in Norrköping had an amazing mane, and it turned out he didn't even use shampoo. That was a real eye-opener there—okay, perhaps all these products are the wrong way to go? He told us that the secret was to only rinse the hair, without shampoo, because it doesn't damage it as much. It was a huge revelation."

———

Like in many other male-dominated circles, there's a deeply ingrained homophobia within metal. It's difficult to determine how seriously the fleeting homophobic comments are meant to be taken, but it's clear that many have difficulty handling same-sex feelings. It's worthy of note that to this day, despite metal being a massively popular genre, only a handful of musicians have come out of the closet. Judas Priest vocalist Rob Halford is the most famous example; he revealed he was gay in a 1998 MTV interview. Dan Martinez, the vocalist and guitar player for American grindcore band Cretin, transitioned into a woman in 2008, and is now living as Marissa Martinez. It is possible there simply are no other bi, gay, or trans men within the top echelon of the metal world, but it hardly needs to be said that statistics render this highly unlikely.

Kristian "Gaahl" Espedal—the vocalist for Norwegian black metal band Gorgoroth who's known as a violent hermit who's spent time in prison for torture—came out in a 2008 interview with the German magazine *Rock Hard*. The reactions were immediate. One faction dismissed him as a wimp who never made good music anyway—typical that he should happen to be gay as well. The other bloc proclaimed him even cooler than before, since fucking guys in the ass must be the most ultimately Satanic act one could perform.

Rob Halford never felt he had hidden his sexuality. The leather and studs he wore in Judas Priest, the foundation of classic metal fashion worldwide, was something he borrowed directly from gay clubs in Soho, London.

For Gaahl, the development has been entirely different.

Born in a small village on the Norwegian west coast in 1975, he joined the black metal band Gorgoroth in 1998. Known for both voicing controversial opinions and committing violent acts, he's been sentenced to prison twice. In 2002, he was found guilty of assault, and in 2004, he received 14 months of jail time for aggravated assault and torture after holding a man captive in his home and collecting his blood in a cup. Gaahl himself claims he was acting in self-defense after being attacked by a hitman, due to a grudge with connections to the earlier prison sentence.

Gorgoroth soon established themselves as one of the most extreme bands in the Norwegian scene. In 2005, Gaahl became a household name in the international metal world through the American documentary *Metal: A Headbanger's Journey*. In the interview, Gaahl sits in a dark basement, sipping a glass of red wine. When asked what inspires Gorgoroth, time seems to come to a halt as he ponders in complete silence while giving reporter Sam Dunn a blank stare. Then he simply answers, "Satan," and takes another sip of wine.

The short clip can be seen on YouTube and is a great example of the potentially hilarious clash between dead-serious black metal and unsuspecting curiosity.

In 2007, American magazine *VICE* sent a film team to Gaahl's cabin in Espedal, a tiny mountain village owned by Gaahl's family that bears their surname. The rumors of his crazy and erratic behavior were quickly affirmed. The documentary shows conversation to be very forced, and the crew members are clearly frightened of him. The scene gradually worsens as Gaahl takes the lightly dressed Americans on a hike to his grandparents' hunting cabin on a nearby mountaintop. The weather takes a bad turn, heavy snow is falling, and visibility is minimal. Gaahl marches on up the mountain, in boots and a leather coat, while the crew begin worrying about getting out of there alive.

So, when this immensely dark and frightening black metal icon suddenly came out as gay, a shock wave went through the metal community.

Gaahl meets us in central Bergen on a summer day in 2010. He leads the way to Stenersens samling, a museum for contemporary art, and we take a seat in the café. He's a regular.

"I suppose I broke all stereotypes of what a homosexual man ought to be like," he says.

The barista serves him an Americano.

"I can't understand this need to divide people into stereotypes like that. The homo milieu is just as rigid—many are afraid to be themselves. They fear breaking the norm."

Shortly after the *Rock Hard* interview, it became known that Gaahl spent a lot of time in the company of a young clothing designer named Dan DeVero. Norwegian magazines immediately began printing articles about how Gaahl was about to leave music for a career designing clothes with Dan.

This commotion surrounding Gaahl's sexual orientation was crowned by news of him being cast in the leading role of the black metal musical *Svartediket* (The Black Ditch) in the esteemed National Theatre in Bergen. These days, he's dating 20-year-old Robin, who's currently on a holiday in the mountains with his family.

When we ask why black metal appears to be such an asexual music style, he doesn't understand the question.

"What do you mean? I'm not a sexual person; I don't think in terms like that."

But surely, you have sex?

"No, actually, I don't. I can't comprehend that urge at all, because I don't understand sex. I call myself a homophile, but I'm not homosexual. To me, it's an aesthetic attraction. I think people are too obsessed with sex."

We finish our coffee and go out on the town. Gaahl is a quiet man, but he's polite and attentive. People stare at him in the streets. At the National Theatre, a young man in a white shirt and heavily waxed hair asks if it's really Gaahl. "Yes," Gaahl answers, and he is then asked to pose for a picture. "That's all right," he agrees, and the two are photographed by the young man's eager friend. As we resume walking, the two are still giggling with excitement

"That happens all the time. I've become something of a celebrity, and I'm not quite sure how to relate to it," Gaahl says with a wry smile.

It's not every day that a man with several convictions for violent crime becomes a popular household name.

One likely explanation is the exciting mixture of condoning church burnings—which Gaahl did shortly after accepting his role in *Svartediket*, with outraged debates as a consequence—and on the other hand entirely breaking all preconceptions about gay men.

Gaahl claims all of his sentencings clearly state that he acted in self-defense, albeit with a disproportionate amount of force. He says black metal is about being a warrior and about waging war against oneself.

"There's no room for soldiers in black metal, because soldiers follow orders—a warrior fights with his heart. There's a huge difference between the two."

He points out that there are, of course, female warriors—though not as many, since women are rarely brought up to fight for themselves.

"There's a lot of romanticism in black metal—not between people, but toward things like nature. And perhaps the love for the ego."

Gaahl mentions how he fell in love for the first time in his life at 31 years old. He says he's attracted by aesthetics rather than sexuality and explains it as being drawn to his boyfriend Robin's essence as a whole.

But you're dating a 20-year-old—doesn't he want to have sex all the time?

"Yes. If there's an absolute emergency, I suppose I'll have to rise to the occasion," Gaahl laughs.

Gaahl brings us to a wine bar he often frequents. He's a huge wine enthusiast and primarily drinks natural wines, without additives. As we enter the combined bar and restaurant, we're welcomed by the American owner, Joseph, who happily greets Gaahl. A somewhat tipsy lady in the bar gives Gaahl a big hug and a playful tug on his beard. As we sit down to order, he says he's still not quite used to physical contact.

"A few years ago, I certainly wouldn't have let anyone pull my beard, if you know what I mean."

Dining with Gaahl is an experience. He orders hake with cauliflower puree, clarified butter, radishes, and pickled red onion. Joseph pairs the food with Arcese, a white wine from the Piedmont region. Gaahl sticks his nose in the glass to check the bouquet, first looking somewhat skeptical. He ultimately decides to try a glass of the cloudy wine.

The sensation is so overwhelming, he's rendered speechless. After a moment of silence, he looks up with misty eyes.

"Really, this is ... it's so perfect."

When Joseph comes by to ask how it tasted, Gaahl is bubbling with praise.

"At first, I thought something was missing, but with the onion now in my mouth, it's absolutely perfect. I cannot praise this food enough."

Joseph gives a nod of satisfaction.

"I thought so."

At the Bergen Gay Galla in January 2010, Gaahl was named Homosexual of the Year for his contributions in broadening the image of what a gay man can be. He says the award made him happy.

"The main reason I accepted the homo prize is that I can see how a lot of people are struggling with coming out. I've been contacted by many individuals, both in metal and outside, who haven't found the courage to open up yet. No fellow musicians, though—only fans."

The American internet forum Infra-Iridian was launched in 2007 and was active for a few years. It served as a meeting place for gay and bisexual metal fans who were having difficulties finding their place within the scene and who received little understanding from gay circles, where metal fandom is rare.

The forum moderator calls himself Vyldr. He believes there's definitely far fewer gay people within the metal world than in other subcultures.

"People generally discover their sexuality before immersing themselves in a subculture, and the extremes of the metal world doesn't seem to appeal to most LGBT people. Either that, or there are loads of metalheads who remain in the closet—but we don't think that's the case."

Vyldr makes reference to a quote he's read from Gaahl.

"Metal musicians don't come out since artists want to be known for their talent and creativity, rather than private life and sexual orientation."

———

A common denominator for essentially all the women we spoke to while working on this chapter is that they describe themselves as tomboys. They say they have a desire to cultivate their inner aggressions and don't feel trapped by the female stereotypes of society.

"I've been really lucky in the sense that I was always able to do what I wanted," says Chelsea Krook.

During a brief period in the '90s, Chelsea played bass for the Stockholm band Expulsion, but says she wasn't good enough. She tried starting a few other bands but couldn't quite find the motivation, despite having the urge.

Today, there are plenty of women playing metal, compared to the '80s. Gothic metal often combines male growling with female opera singers. Most significantly the Danish black metal artist Amalie Bruun and her solo project Myrkur has garnered much praise. But of course, also a lot of resentment. In an interview with *Kerrang!*, Myrkur talked about the reactions:

"I get everything from death threats to hate videos. There are long think pieces about how I'm ruining black metal and I'm the worst thing to happen to anything."

She concludes that it is mostly the fans that complain, not other male musicians, and that she could not care less.

Above all, an increasing number of women have started listening to extreme metal. Sometimes, half the crowd at black metal gigs are female. Despite this, there's still not many women playing in death and black metal bands.

Runhild Gammelsaeter believes very few women feel compelled to create such aggressive music.

"There's not many women who can play guitar that fast or hit the drums that hard or scream as loud as black metal requires. These guys have been playing guitar since they were kids—been nerdy and practiced a lot. They've had a special interest for the occult and been in opposition—rebelled against society and religion. From my experience, it's rare for women to go through this process as strongly. I also believe there are very few women interested in wearing corpse paint and singing songs about Satan. They simply aren't interested in expressing themselves in such brutal ways. We might find it interesting to watch men doing it, but engaging in it ourselves is an entirely different matter."

Angela Gossow of Arch Enemy has a lot of contact with young women who are interested in metal, and she's seen a clear trend during her 20 years as an active death metal musician. She says her generation, born in the '70s, live in two worlds. They were brought up by mothers who, on the one hand, witnessed the advances of the women's movement in the '60s but who still allowed themselves to be governed by old traditions and values.

"The generation emerging now has changed—that much is evident. The teenage girls who are 14 and 15 today are completely different; they're a lot stronger. Should they feel disrespected, they'll say so. It's more accepted for women to be loud, compared to when I grew up.

Angela has also noticed how there are more women attending concerts, especially in Scandinavia. Meanwhile, she still receives a lot of emails from girls who have trouble finding bands to play with.

"It's also an age thing. You're generally insecure and sensitive in your teens, and that's when hierarchies are established. But I still believe things have changed—the metal scene evolves, as does the rest of society."

Angela Gossow left Arch Enemy in 2014 and was replaced by Alissa White-Gluz. She currently works as manager for the band.

Demonia's blog is no longer active.

XI.

Entombed

It really sucks coming home from a tour
only to find you've actually lost money.

— ALEX HELLID, ENTOMBED

"THERE ARE STILL UNRESOLVED ISSUES because of the split," says Entombed guitarist Alex Hellid.

It is the summer of 2017, and he is talking about the band he's been a part of the past 28 years. The group that embodied the Swedish death metal phenomenon in the early '90s has in recent years made headlines, due to a legal battle over the band name. It's a battle between two factions: One set of musicians is fronted by original singer L-G Petrov, who since 2014 have been officially calling themselves Entombed A.D. The other is a project led by Hellid, joined by two other original members.

Since 2014, Entombed A.D. have released two full-length albums and have toured frequently. From the Hellid camp, no new music has been heard. There have, however, been collaborations with two symphony orchestras and (as is increasingly common) a signature microbrew beer.

In conjunction with the releases of *Back to the Front* (2014) and *Dead Dawn* (2017), the members of Entombed A.D. have repeatedly given their side of the story, the split with Alex Hellid, and the bitter name dispute. We've heard stories of a band leader preoccupied with way too many things—how Hellid held the others back, stood in the way of musical creativity, and refused to share the control of the band.

We've heard significantly less from Hellid himself. In an interview with *Sweden Rock Magazine* after the split in 2013 he said very little but admitted that his "tongue is itching."

"They tried to make me say things," he states when we reach him on the phone in the early summer of 2017. "But I believe that I'll be better off the less I say."

Eight years earlier...

It is early afternoon in the small town of Örebro, two and a half hours west of Stockholm. L-G Petrov has already been out for a drink or two to cure his hangover. He's standing near the coffee service in the concert hall, a big square room where the Amon Amarth crew are busy building the main act's stage decor.

L-G is wearing a faded black hoodie and a knitted black cap. In just a few minutes, he will pull it over his eyes and stretch out in the backstage couch upstairs. At the moment, he's sipping coffee while blearily watching some roadies roll out a backdrop depicting the Aesir god Thor locked in combat with a dragon. One of the guys says this is the best stage so far on the tour.

Entombed have no roadies, a hired bass player struggling to learn the band's classic material, a guitar player who's having difficulties with his new pedal board—and a hungover frontman.

Drummer Nicke Andersson and guitarist Uffe Cederlund, the two musical engines of Entombed, haven't been involved with the band for twelve and four years respectively. A few days ago, the tour was struck by an unexpected tragedy. The bass player of UK supporting band Evile suddenly and unexpectedly died, forcing them to cancel.

"Blood clot," Petrov explains. "It traveled up his leg."

The singer gestures along his own leg. When asked if it felt strange to go on stage and sing about death after that, he answers briefly.

"No, it happened so fast."

L-G Petrov is a man of few words. He uses short sentences, consisting of one to three words. Sometimes even fewer. A substantial part of the communication with his touring buddies seems to be by way of glances, nods, a crooked smile, or the occasional handshake.

Entombed are roughly one week into this tour supporting Amon Amarth, another Stockholm band with roots in the late '80s underground scene. The fact that Petrov is still active 20 years later is in itself remarkable. When establishing a new metal genre together with a handful of other teenage death metal pioneers back in the day, few of them probably saw their style of play as something that would later resonate with middle-aged folks, and it was even less imaginable that the musical form would ever be considered "retro."

Many of the Swedish death metal bands of the early years are still alive and kicking, even if their financial realities differ vastly. Bands like Merciless, Grave, and Necrophobic still release albums and tour but don't live solely off the music. Other acts, like Therion and Dark Tranquillity, have become professional musicians, thanks to relatively stable careers.

Many of the more successful bands with roots in the scene had their breakthroughs years after the death metal explosion in the early '90s and have carved their own niches within the genre. Some examples are Amon Amarth, Opeth, Meshuggah, and even In Flames.

After the turn of the millennium, Entombed refined their punkish death metal, often referred to as death 'n' roll. Every new album cemented their position as a reliable band that delivered the goods.

In 2002, they surprised the metal world by working with the Royal Swedish Opera in the ballet *Unreal Estate* by performance artists Carina Reich and Bogdan Szyber. In these shows, Entombed played live in the orchestra pit. *Serpent Saints* from 2007, Entombed's ninth studio album, entered the Swedish album chart at number three.

"Time for another cigarette!" L-G proclaims. Amon Amarth guitar player Johan Söderberg is standing on the loading dock. He shares Petrov's passion for playing cards, an interest that has kept them up late nights on the bus.

"You're on again tonight," the blond guitarist says.

"Same time," Petrov answers.

"Same place," Johan replies.

A while later, Amon Amarth's English drum technician Chris is done suspending a plastic drape with a Viking motif from the drum riser.

"Check it out, Fredrik, we've put up the drum riser banner now—the one we used on the Slayer tour!" he shouts to Amon Amarth drummer Fredrik Andersson, who just entered the hall.

Andersson's kit is surrounded by simple but effective décor: lighted stairs on both sides of the stage and two platforms with built-in blue spotlights at the edge of the stage. Above it all towers a giant backdrop featuring Thor and the dragon.

"So, what do you think? Is the right side up?" Chris asks, pointing at the plastic drape decorated in Old Norse fashion strapped to the front of the riser.

"If it looks good to you, it's fine by me," the drummer responds.

"But I don't know what's up or down," the tech counters.

"I'm not wearing my glasses," Fredrik says. "Is it runes or ornaments on that one?"

"I'm not sure."

"If they're ornaments, then it doesn't really matter," the drummer explains.

"I'd say ornaments. But they could be runes, for all I know," Chris says.

The shared dressing room is housed in a large conference hall on the second floor of the building. Amon Amarth's guitarists are at their laptops on opposite sides of the room. Neither of them say a word, and it's as quiet as a church. When a cell phone in a plastic bag begins to ring, the only discernible movement is Johan Söderberg slowly tilting his head somewhat and then returning his attention to the computer screen. Instead of yoga classes and herbal therapy, maybe people with burnout syndrome should be sent to this setting: a spot on a tour with two of Sweden's hardest-working death metal bands.

There's a table in the corner with bread, fruit, water, wine, beer, and liquor. Next to it is a sofa in black imitation leather. The members of Entombed will spend a significant part of the day in it. Alex Hellid shows up, says hi, and shakes hands.

The athletic guitarist handles everything concerning the band, from running their own label, Threeman Recordings, to acting as tour manager. He's always on the move and quickly passes through the room on his way to the stage.

L-G is on the couch with the cap pulled over his eyes. He's looking worryingly still, but when the other members talk to him, he responds. He will remain in this vegetative state for most of the afternoon. In the chairs next to him are Olle Dahlstedt, Entombed's drummer for the past three years, and sound technician Olle Sandqvist.

Dahlstedt just opened a paperback crime novel by Jo Nesbø, while Sandqvist's literature of choice is *The Darkest Room* by Johan Theorin. He tells us he's always reading on the road and has been able to combine the touring life with online classes in history.

Right below the stage, Alex Hellid has lined up his stomp boxes. His pedal board, made out of an old car mat, has seen better days. He explains that the simple design is a result of increasingly strict airline security following 9/11. Circling him on the floor are close to a dozen effect pedals in varying stages of wear. After careful consideration, he places them one by one on the new board.

"This is really an experiment," he says, explaining how he's combining effects and amplifiers in hopes of creating the effect of two guitarists on each side of the stage.

"But in reality, I'm not too sure of the settings. With some of these, all I know is they make a different sound when I step on them."

Amon Amarth's guitar tech, Steve, shows up, with his long hair and moustache. He also gets involved in Hellid's project. He heads off toward the stage, returning with a long strip of black Velcro that he cuts into smaller pieces with a Swiss army knife. He then helps Alex secure the pedals in their new positions.

Hellid tells the story of when Page Hamilton, of the American alternative rock band Helmet, showed him his pedal board.

"It had three separate levels. It was the most insane thing I've ever seen."

"Then you should see Dan Spitz of Anthrax," Steve remarks. "Three racks, tons of loops, and three different wah-wahs. And then he's had blue LED lights installed in every piece of gear. So unnecessary!"

Hellid points out it's mostly about what you can afford. Steve says we're talking about a fortune here.

"Besides, you can only hear his solos in the PA. And they suck!"

When finished, Alex Hellid places four Marshall amps on top of each other on the left side of the stage. The towering construction is swaying toward the ceiling, and he tightens an orange strap around the stacks, to keep everything in place. He hangs a black Flying V around his neck and begins to adjust the equipment meticulously.

The bands share most of the backline on this tour, including the gigantic drum kit. Olle Dahlstedt is currently warming it up with the groove from "Here Comes Pippi Longstocking."

When Hellid finally gets his things properly set up, a crushing wall of sound akin to a jet engine blasts through the hall. His tone is coarse, massive and heavy as bedrock.

The sound check kicks off with the Motörhead-ish title track from *Serpent Saints*. The song begins with a spooky recorded guitar intro, played by Dahlstedt from an MP3 player. Then the band fires off the opening riff, built around the same devil's tritone interval that Tony Iommi used in the song "Black Sabbath." Petrov emerges on the stage just in time for the vocals. Cell phone in hand, he actually manages to sing the entire song without once taking his eyes off the display.

"Texting Mayhem," he says when the song is finished. "Reminding Attila to come when we're playing Oslo," he clarifies.

Jonas Björler, bass player of The Haunted, shows up by the stage. He lives nearby and has come to hang out with his old friends. He says the engineer is asking what they think of the sound.

"Quite promising actually—what do you think?" Olle Dahlstedt asks behind the drums.

"We'll see," the seasoned Jonas replies. "Something always goes wrong."

In the conference room upstairs, two-year-old Tyr is running around between bags, instrument cases, and YouTube-engrossed death metal musicians. Tyr's father is the somewhat less demonically named Ted Lundström. In just a few moments, his B.C. Rich bass will thunder through the venue's sound system.

Amon Amarth is the most jovial—and popular—Viking metal band in Sweden. The music is grandiose and melodic death metal. The Viking theme has become more pronounced over the years, in lyrics as well as the band's image. The band formed as Scum, named after a Napalm Death song, in the late '80s. The UK outfit came out of the grindcore punk scene, a leftish band with lyrics tackling social topics. The Amon Amarth of today seems light years away from those punkish roots, even if the vocal style of frontman Johan Hegg is not too far removed from the one Napalm Death once shocked the world with.

The fact that Amon Amarth is playing in front of roughly 500 ecstatic fans this Wednesday night is actually kind of a twist of fate. For many years, they remained one of the more obscure acts of the Swedish scene. The catchy melodies in their songs could be one of the reasons for their popularity. Their penchant for Viking elements could be another, especially among the metal fans.

Afternoon has passed into evening, and concert promoter Andreas is about to drive Entombed to the aptly named Virus Bar for dinner. It's turned dark outside by the time we squeeze into the car. In the front seat, Hellid notes that a car just ahead has 666 in the license plate, but no one in the group has the energy to come up with a suitable witticism.

Virus Bar hasn't opened for the night yet. Both the band and the booking agency, Aska, are friends with Kenta, the owner. He welcomes them, quite literally, with open arms. Kenta is a loud giant of a man with a clean-shaven head and a long beard in hair ties. He's a musician himself, sharing the spotlight with former Entombed bassist Jörgen Sandström in The Project Hate MCMXCIX. He greets every person he doesn't know with the same phrase.

"Hey, man. Who the fuck are you, and how many people have you fucked?"

The classic Swedish dish *pyttipanna*, a form of skillet with meat, potatoes, and onion, is on the menu. Everyone gets a handful of drink tickets for the after party. Once back in the dressing room, drummer Olle Dahlstedt says it's time to take out the gig shoes: a pair of trainers reinforced with black duct tape. He assures us that everything you wear on stage gets absolutely drenched in sweat. He says stage sweat differs from all other kinds of perspiration in one specific regard.

"You can run or play soccer as much as you like, but you will never smell as bad."

"It's a different compound," sound engineer Olle adds.

"There's less alcohol in jogging sweat," Hellid says, and remarks that even urine smells good in comparison.

"Here, try this!" Dahlstedt says, holding up his shirt. "And if you think that's bad, you should check out L-G's clothes."

The vocalist hasn't put his phone down since the sound check, and his mind seems to be elsewhere.

"Listen to this," he says, reading from the small display. "'About what time do you go on stage?' asks Jenny from Eskilstuna/Not blonde anymore!'"

Victor Brandt lets out his hair and puts on an Evile shirt and a pair of very tight black jeans. During his 2-year stint as bass player for Norwegian black metal band Satyricon, he got used to wearing much more elaborate stage outfits. In a soft northern dialect, he tells us he doesn't miss it.

"Corpse paint is mostly a hassle. You walk around all night getting things smeared. But in a way, it felt good to put on your war paint before walking on stage."

Entombed gather by the stairs to the stage. The audience is here, but it's hard to determine how many have actually showed up. The background music in the PA goes silent, and an anticipatory roar rises from the crowd. Then the sound of an old country waltz from 1960 begins playing, and the soothing voices of The Louvin Brothers proclaim that "Satan Is Real."

> Satan is real, working in spirit
> You can see him and hear him in this world every day
> Satan is real, working with power
> He can tempt you and lead you astray

The quartet stand in a circle, shoulder to shoulder and heads close together. They clasp each other in a football-style hug, scream in unison, and then enter the stage. They open with "Serpent Saints," close enough to Motörhead's "Iron Fist" in certain passages to make you wonder if it's an exploration of the borderland between tribute and cover. In this case, it is quite possibly a musical quotation so appealing, it wouldn't really be classified as plagiarism. Motörhead revitalized hard rock in the late '70s and early '80s by fusing blues-based rock with punk, thereby creating a form of prototype to what then became thrash metal. Entombed did something similar when their brand of death metal turned musical preconceptions upside down.

On the far side of the stage, Hellid's diligent footwork makes his Flying V sound like half an orchestra. In breaks, he switches off two of the four amps with an A/B pedal, only to then hit them full force again.

"ARE THERE ANY DEATH METALHEADS HERE TONIGHT? Petrov shouts to the crowd.

"This is 'SUPPOSED TO ROT'!"

The band plays the nearly 20-year-old track, and all the headbanging you could ask for on a Wednesday night in the town of Örebro erupts. L-G Petrov's stage presence is not dominated by macho rock poses. Instead, it's based on demonic frowns, monstrously twisted fingers, and chaotic body language.

By the end of "Left Hand Path," Hellid loops the slow minor melody from the horror movie *Phantasm* and then adds a concrete slab of doomsday chords on top of it. As the monotonous and heavy riff creates a hypnotic effect, L-G leaves the stage. Once he is out of sight, he slumps down and coughs. As soon as the encore begins he reenters and finishes the concert with head held high. Once Hellid has hammered out the final chord, and the band has left the stage, the frontman sums up his performance with a smile.

"I was a little tired today."

Upstairs in the makeshift dressing room, Amon Amarth guitarist Olavi Mikkonen is setting up his instrument, a blue Gibson with custom inlays of runes in gold.

"We have these guys who help us with woodworking. I wanted a real Viking axe," Olavi says while proudly showing off the details. His own name is in runes underneath, a dragon motif is on the front side, and a stylized A graces the pickguard.

"That's the only thing I'm not that happy about. It would have been cooler with an additional dragon's talon there."

Amon Amarth's tall and bearded vocalist, Johan Hegg, appears just before the show. He is joined by his girlfriend, Maria, and her parents, Per and Maja. They live nearby—a friendly couple in their 6os. Per says he's never met his daughter's boyfriend in a concert setting before. They had dinner a little earlier, and he could tell something was different.

"You could tell he was focused."

Per hasn't heard the band's music before but seems to have an idea what to expect.

"I won't be able to tell if they're good or bad," he laughs.

Hegg wanders over to the bar and kindly asks us if we'd like something. Per wonders if he is nervous. Hegg says no, adding that his mind just feels a little divided.

Once backstage he straps on his broad leather bracers and ties a string to his belt, where he fastens a large drinking horn.

The dressing room is almost empty. Alex Hellid is constantly on the move. Despite following him and the band for eight hours, we still haven't been able to pin down a proper interview.

L-G Petrov is not done for the night. First, he has to go on stage for the song "Guardians of Asgaard," where he shares vocal duties with Hegg, just like on the album *Twilight of the Thunder Gods* from 2008.

"It's not quite time yet, right, L-G?" Olle Dahlstedt remarks without checking his watch. After seven shows, he seems to know the schedule in his head. Downstairs, the stage is filled with smoke, and Amon Amarth opens their concert with "Valkyries Ride." To a drum beat as heavy as artillery fire, Johan Hegg marches onstage and greets the people of Örebro with a victorious gesture. Not only has the Viking theme evolved over time—Hegg has also turned into a grand entertainer. When he's not screaming lyrics about Valhalla, battles, rainbow bridges, and Norse gods, he is spurring the audience on and toasting them with his drinking horn.

A few songs later, L-G is ready by the stage. Steve gives him a friendly nod from his small working space. He holds up a bag of cinnamon rolls, but Petrov shakes his head, and Steve makes a gesture that somehow communicates: "Oh, that's right, you're about to sing."

"This next song is about two brothers united through everything," Hegg says into the mic, signaling L-G to walk on stage. As the band begins, Hegg fills the horn from a can of Guinness by the drum riser and then grabs the microphone.

Standing firm against all odds
Guarding the most sacred home
We protect the realm of gods
Our destiny is carved in stone

Then Petrov's even more piercing voice takes over.

Three evil giants of the south are constantly on the attack
With lies of fire from their mouths
But we always send them back

In the chorus, both vocalists go all in.

'Cause we are guardians
Guardians of Asgaard

While most of the audience are only watching the spectacle on stage, a group of skinheads have stripped their shirts and now start up a violent mosh pit. They move in circles, occasionally slamming into each other. A long-haired guy next to them is shoved to the side. He pushes back and gets a headbutt in his chest. A fight seems inevitable. The thick fog coming from the stage makes it even harder to make out what's going on.

Halfway through the show, smoke has seeped into the adjacent conference rooms, setting off the fire alarm. Per and Maja leave through a back door, and we run into them in the elevator. They look happy, and Per comments that Johan has "both the vocal chords and physique for this."

A few hours later, the smoke has cleared and the stage lights have been shut off. Johan Hegg is relaxing backstage with his Maria. The bearded frontman unstraps the drinking horn and peels off his tight, sweat-drenched jeans. He puts on striped underwear and a black T-shirt with Marvel superhero Thor on it. He sits down on an office chair next to his girlfriend and tells us the whole band used to wear drinking horns on stage but had them confiscated by New Zealand customs.

"And I'll soon need a new one—mine has a crack and has started leaking."

Outside the venue stage gear is being loaded into a white truck. By the time every last item has been loaded, it is way past midnight. Alex Hellid is making sure his Marshall amplifiers are in the right spot in the trunk. His day is not over until every last piece of equipment is off the sidewalk.

We've just spent 12 hours with the band, and Hellid has worked constantly.

Entombed used to have a crew helping with humping and setting up equipment.

"But it really sucks to come home from a tour only to find you've actually lost money," he says while throwing a final glance in the truck.

He says he's able to live completely off the music now, but that it requires a lot of work with the business side of the band.

The face of his wife is tattooed on one of his underarms. On the other are the names and birthdates of his children. If you know your metal history, you can imagine the difficulties in supporting your family by playing death metal. As the house DJ fittingly plays "Never Surrender" by Saxon, Hellid tells us he's seldom tempted to get a normal job.

"I don't think anybody is offering the kind of money I'd need to do that."

His vocalist is nowhere to be seen. The booker, Andreas, says he saw L-G a while back, heading for the afterparty.

"I don't think I've ever seen anyone look that thirsty."

A little later, the entire touring group is at the Virus Bar. The DJ is playing Ozzy Osbourne's "Bark at the Moon" and "High in Highschool" by Madame X, and the bar manager serves Entombed two pizzas, which the four members share equally down to last slice. Alex Hellid sits by a bar table with a beer. He looks content. When we ask him if touring takes its toll, he answers that this is like a vacation compared to family life.

While L-G is outside smoking, shooting the shit with a group of local characters, Alex tells us a story few have heard.

"L-G was actually very close to landing the leading role in the movie *My Life as a Dog* in 1985. He got through all the auditions until there were only two guys left."

One can only speculate as to what would have become of Petrov's death metal career had he starred in an Academy Award–nominated feature film. Or how the Swedish death metal movement would have been affected by the absence of Petrov's signature voice, in the scene's most celebrated band.

Alex feels that L-G, even today, has a special relation to cameras.

"He's completely natural in front of them. Myself, I get all uncomfortable when somebody's filming me."

Since the departure of Uffe Cederlund in 2005, Hellid has been the only guitarist of Entombed, despite the fact that two guitars would be ideal to recreate the band's classic sound. The task of finding a replacement for Cederlund has dragged out indefinitely.

"You want someone special but without a ton of attitude. That's the problem. Everyone special has attitude!"

Most of all, Hellid wanted to bring in Leif Cuzner, his former bandmate who once created the signature sound of Swedish death metal when they were in Nihilist. But he committed suicide in Canada in 2006 before Hellid had time to ask. For this tour, Entombed are honoring him with the words "Leif Cuzner – R.I.P." on their backdrop. This night, however, Amon Amarth's lighting technician has not allowed them to use it.

Hellid says that in the early days of the band, he saw himself, Uffe Cederlund, and Nicke Andersson as a trinity.

"As soon as one disappeared, the others needed to balance that out."

Today, he can see a crucial difference between the two and himself.

"They were incredibly talented. But that also meant they got bored easily, and then they started ruining things for themselves and made everything difficult."

He says Petrov and himself are musicians of a different breed.

"We're more like 'Hey, can you believe this works? Amazing that we can still do this!"

———

In April of 2013, a trademark is filed with the Patent and Registration Office of Sweden for the name Entombed. The applicant is L-G Petrov. Three weeks later, Alex Hellid files a similar claim. The metal world watches in astonishment as two versions of Entombed emerge. It soon becomes evident that a protracted dispute is behind this legal circus.

In October of 2012, Alex Hellid became severely ill. He was very close to having an aortic rupture and underwent surgery. Simultaneously, Petrov and the other members were looking for a studio to make their first full-length album in five years. In the spring of 2013, the recordings began. Alex Hellid did not participate. On August 10 of the same year, Hellid and Petrov shared a stage for the last time.

You could argue that the story of Entombed began in fact with a name dispute. The group, then known as Nihilist, received a letter from an Atlanta band with the same name. Nicke Andersson remembers the Americans asserting they had a legitimate record contract and rights to the name.

"We didn't feel like arguing. But maybe we should have. I think Nihilist is a better band name than Entombed. There's something really wicked when you have '-ist' at the end."

In 1997, some 10 years after forming the band, Andersson left. He remembers feeling they had come as far musically as they could. The band was at an airport, flying between two festivals, when he broke the news.

"I felt I needed everyone to be there when I told them. Then Jörgen went to the bathroom and I just felt, 'Oh, fuck.' Then when he got back, everyone was gonna go grab a sandwich. I just thought, 'Can't they all fucking sit down now? This really sucks!' Finally, everyone was there, and I told them I was leaving. But the run-up to it was the worst."

Nicke believes it didn't come as much of surprise, seeing as the band hadn't enjoyed playing in quite some time.

"I think many bands just keep going. There's some money coming in and it pays the rent. And you never question why you're still gigging. But I did one more tour after that. Our manager forced us to keep a tight lid on my departure."

Nicke Andersson was replaced by Peter Stjärnvind, and then several other member shifts followed. In 2005, original guitarist Uffe Cederlund left, mostly due to a conflict between him and Hellid.

"It turned sour," Uffe remembers. "I just wanted to rock as much as possible. He felt I was becoming a problem, as he couldn't say yes to all the shows I wanted him to book."

In February 2014, Alex Hellid and Uffe Cederlund performed their classic album *Clandestine* together with the Gävle Symphony Orchestra and a choir. A newspaper journalist interviewed Hellid, who said there was no split, that Entombed formed a long time ago, and that everyone was free to start another band. He assured the journalist that great things will come from the turmoil and that no one needs to worry about Entombed coming to a halt or making less interesting music.

"If there is to be any point in making a tenth album, then we need to raise the bar and do it properly. That's how it must be."

Six months later, L-G Petrov and the other current members release *Back to the Front* as Entombed A.D. In interviews, Entombed A.D. relate their version of the split. They say Hellid has wanted to create a landmark album to put Entombed back on the map but that the ambitious project has been more time-consuming than the other members found acceptable. Instead, they choose to release a new album, the first in seven years, and to get on the road as soon as possible.

In December of 2014, the Patent and Registration Office awards all rights related to the Entombed brand to L-G Petrov.

In October 2016, Hellid, Andersson, and Cederlund take part in another orchestral production of *Clandestine*, this time with the Malmö Symphony Orchestra. They also perform the full album on a metal boat cruise arranged by *Close-Up Magazine*. From a legal standpoint, these two concerts are done without proper rights to the band name.

In February 2017, Alex Hellid launches a beer called Entombed Sweden. In the comment section of the metal community website Blabbermouth, the news is largely met with disapproval. Someone ironically states that at least the guys focus on what's important. Another writes that he doesn't feel much like drinking a beer that tastes like a corpse.

In May 2017, a new verdict arrives. All four original members—Nicke Andersson, Alex Hellid, Uffe Cederlund, and L-G Petrov—share the rights to the name Entombed. A press release is issued, together with a photo within which Anderson, Hellid, and Cederlund are clearly looking pleased. The trio say they are content with the verdict and that this will allow them to focus on forming the best possible Entombed.

Alex Hellid answers our phone call for the first time in years.

In a short conversation, we agree to get back to him with suggested dates for an interview. This is followed by a daily routine. We call several times a day, we leave messages, email and text him with possible dates. We get no response whatsoever. This goes on for nine weeks.

It's a beautiful day in late May of 2017. L-G Petrov shows up precisely on time, at the outdoor seating of a restaurant in Stockholm. He seems more energetic than when we met eight years ago, and it turns out he's just come from an outdoor gym close by. He's chosen our meeting spot because it's right by his morning walk, on days when he's not out touring. He tells us a typical day starts with breakfast at home in Skärmarbrink followed by a brisk walk by the Årsta bay. There are several outdoor training facilities along the way, and sometimes he'll be out several hours. Currently, he's got a week off and spends his days staying in shape and studying lyrics.

"I didn't use to think about things like that, but it's amazing how much you can accomplish if you plan your time well. We've done two albums and toured our asses off. Done what a band does—or should be doing, I'd say."

He tells us there's a consensus in the band now, regarding birthdays, for instance, that they're not a valid reason to reject an offer to play. This can get quite emotional for members with family and children, something L-G doesn't have.

"'Cause I'm a still a kid myself, ha!"

L-G explains how live offerings for bands like Entombed A.D. seem to have increased in recent years and that they're exploiting this fact to the greatest extent they can.

"We did 160 shows last year! One year, we counted 128 metal festivals in Germany alone! If you want to play, you can just do it."

On his phone, L-G has photos of himself with a host of metal celebrities, like King Diamond, Sebastian Bach, and King ov Hell—of Abbath and Gorgoroth fame—in full corpse paint. He also shows us a video of the gigantic mosh pit in front of Entombed A.D. at a festival in Jakarta, Indonesia, attended by 20,000 people.

He describes the last years with Alex Hellid in the band as increasingly frustrating.

"We could have done so much more in those years. He kept holding us back. He wanted to take his time, Mr. Hellid. If you communicate, then things happen. When we get an offer to play now, an email goes out to all members right away and everyone answers within the hour. And nobody says, 'Sorry, I can't make it,' three weeks later."

L-G says the whole band was at a meeting with the record company and decided to record a new album. They started rehearsing new songs, and everyone but Alex was there.

"We would receive text messages where he asked us what we were doing. We'd answer, 'But you were at the meeting—we're writing new songs.' So we stuck to the plan, and followed it through. Then the album came out, simple as that."

It became evident the guitarist wasn't interested. L-G says it felt liberating to enter the studio without Hellid.

"All of a sudden, things went smoothly. That sensation was channeled through the music in a good way. You know 'Aaahhh—let's go!' More power, more freedom. We—as in me, Nico, Viktor, and Olle—have been in this band longer than anyone else in Entombed. So, for us, this is the natural state of things. Everyone quit in one way or another. It's a little late to come back and cry about it now."

At the same time, the split with his childhood friends clearly pains him. He describes it as "an unnecessary evil that's been confined to its own dimension." He calls it "the bubble," and he'd rather not step into it.

"Fortunately, we've been able to disconnect from that and just focus on playing. And we've had a shitload of fun. Sometimes you're reminded of it, but the thing is it has nothing to do with the music. It's just a tiny bubble."

It's not exactly clear how the final verdict will affect Entombed A.D., but L-G has no plans to change things, least of all the band name. He also tells us that Entombed A.D. have created a beer together with the Danish brewery Mikkeller. The name Entombed is not on the bottle, however.

"We just didn't feel the need to market it as an Entombed A.D. beer. It sold great anyway. Victor is a real beer fanatic, so he's the one who made it happen. We took care of it while we were on tour. You don't need to halt everything else for two years just to brew a beer, hahaha! We call it the Freeman beer."

Why "Freeman?" That's very close to Threeman, the record label run by Alex Hellid.

"We just picked a name. But sure, it was partly a … you know."

A middle finger?

"Yeah, but it's not important, really. It got 96 out of 100 on ratebeer.com. In a bar, a full 75cl bottle is expensive as hell."

A week later, we meet Ulf Cederlund. He approaches, pushing a bicycle. A red bike helmet with a Repulsion sticker is hanging from the handles. He says he's really trying to get out and bike more often. He asks us who else we've talked to for this text and confirms that Alex Hellid can be very hard to reach.

"Nicke is the same. He won't even answer when I call! Getting a reply to a simple text message can take a week and a half. I'm not sure if they've crashed into the wall, so to speak. If Nicke has too much on his hands, and if Alex can't really cope with everything after nearly dying."

He gives it some thought.

"It could be stress-related. I'm trying to think it's some sort of illness, so that I won't get pissed off. Maybe mostly to not get disappointed when there's so much talk and so little action."

After quitting Entombed in 2005, Uffe has played in several constellations and bands, the D-beat group Disfear probably being the most well-known among them. He toured with them frequently for four years, until the bass player Henrik Frykman became ill and later died. Following that, Uffe has taken classes to complete his high-school diploma, had a son, and moved to a communal apartment building in a suburb of Stockholm.

When Entombed played the *Close-Up* boat show in late 2016, it was first time in 20 years that Nicke, Alex, and Uffe shared a stage. Also present with Entombed that night were Edvin Aftonfalk and Nicke's brother, Robert Andersson, from the group Morbus Chron, on vocals and bass respectively. Orvar Säfström joined the band on stage for the song, "Crawl." Shortly after, the same lineup performed *Clandestine* in Malmö. First the full album in an orchestral performance with the Malmö Symphony and Orvar Säfström handling vocal duties, then again the same night as a straight death metal concert. Uffe describes it as fun but very difficult.

"Nicke was insane when he wrote that album. You can play those riffs, but the changes are so fucking fast. It's really hard keeping up. I love everyone I've played with, but when I play with Nicke, something comes right back at me. I have to constantly push myself to the limit, because he challenges me. I think everyone who's ever played with him feels that way. You feel as if you're growing as musician," says Uffe.

Uffe confides that he and Nicke have talked about doing more shows, and even a new album, but that Entombed is not really a proper band at the moment. There are no plans for a tour. But he doesn't feel they cling on to the name.

"What's fair is fair. I think it's terrible when Entombed A.D. play a show in Stockholm, and then *our* band history is printed in the program. It says Entombed was an important part of the death metal scene. But the other members of Entombed A.D. were never a part of that. That's false advertisement," Uffe laments. "It's not about hogging the Entombed name, because we absolutely want to play using that name. It's about L-G registering the name for himself. That was just wrong, since Nicke, Alex, and I formed the band. Or the four of us together, if you'd like. Nicke more than anyone."

According to Uffe, Nicke Andersson's importance to the history of Entombed is so great, he was present in spirit even after his departure.

"Maybe you can't hear it on *Same Difference*, but I've always had him in mind. To play in Nicke's band, you must respect him in a way that I don't know if Nico or Olle does."

He emphasizes the legacy of Entombed being an integral part of the name dispute. Someone needs to be responsible for keeping the band catalog available. Parallel to doing so, he tries to come to terms with the fact that Entombed A.D. have the word Entombed in their name, and that he doesn't think it's OK. He would have preferred L-G to just market the band as his new project. The fact that Hellid has high ambitions, taking his time, is not cause for hijacking the band name.

"He just had an extremely close call with death. And they decided to record an album behind his back. If he says, 'No, we're not making an album,' then they just have to accept that. But I don't want to put L-G down either, and I think he is obviously a big part of Entombed. He's been the frontman and vocalist of the band for so many years, even if he's done things I don't agree with."

Uffe says things might have taken a very different turn had L-G just come to him, Nicke, and Alex, and suggested they all collectively register the band name.

"Then maybe we could have agreed on him playing under the Entombed name. That would have been completely different. But for a period there, the new guys in Entombed A.D. owned the name Entombed. What were they thinking? These are friends of mine. If I see them in the street, I take a detour. I don't feel like saying hi to them."

Before we part, Uffe asks us how his childhood friend L-G is doing. He seems relieved when we tell him L-G seems to be doing fine.

"L-G loves touring, just traveling around playing and meeting people. And head-banging. That's his whole world, since he never built a regular life back home. I'm sure he felt all that being threatened when Alex got sick, and I think the prospect of not being able to tour with Entombed really bothered him. It's not surprising if he's taken that anxiety and placed it in a bubble that he then hid away."

For three months, we've tried to reach Alex Hellid for an interview. With just two weeks until the book goes to print, we send him a text message offering for him to fact-check the text and read our questions for him. He answers immediately that he'd very much like that. We send him the questions and suggest two new dates for the interview. He informs us that he unfortunately won't be able to see us on any of those days either.

Rock bands existing in two or more parallel versions is not as unusual as one might expect. The Beach Boys and Thin Lizzy are well-known examples. Another is the progressive rock act Yes, who have decided not to seek legal action against three former members using the band name "Yes featuring Jon Anderson, Trevor Rabin, Rick Wakeman." L.A. Guns guitar player Tracii Guns disbanded his version of the band in 2012, concluding that "with two different versions of the band running around, neither band does the other one any good, and I think it's disappointing for the fans, ultimately."

In 1994, former Saxon members Graham Oliver and Steve Dawson joined forces under the moniker Son of a Bitch. Since 2000, however, they've called the band Oliver/Dawson Saxon. From then on, years of conflict with the other existing version of Saxon have followed. Geoff Tate, vocalist of the American band Queensrÿche, was fired from the band in 2014, and then formed another band with the same name. After legal negotiations, he rechristened his band Operation: Mindcrime, after the popular Queensrÿche concept album.

What these cases all have in common is that they deal with bands that have been around for a long while. Several lineups using the same band name is in many ways an indication that a genre has reached its middle age. That the Entombed dispute concerns a death metal band is perhaps a sign of the times.

XII.

Well, Sieg Heil Then?

*No one is going to tell me
what Thor's Hammer stands for.
I will tell them what it
stands for.*

—JOHNNY HEDLUND,
UNLEASHED

"THE TIME HAS COME for war and retaliation against vandals and other pests!" Månegarm vocalist Erik Grawsiö shouts as he gazes out over the audience.

It's just past 8 p.m. at Nordic Rage 2009 in Boden, in the northernmost county of Sweden, just a few miles from the Arctic circle. Dark Funeral and Wolf are the main attractions at the festival. It seems like the majority of festivalgoers have not yet arrived. Nevertheless, Månegarm has attracted a dedicated crowd of fans. As Janne Liljekvist checks the sound on his electric violin, he is greeted by a loud cheer. Some have traveled all the way from Stockholm to catch their set. The intro to the song "Vedergällningens tid" (Time for Retribution) kicks off: The tempo is majestic, and the folkish themes emanating from Liljekvist's violin soar, melancholy over heavy guitar riffs.

Månegarm began as the straightforward black metal band Antikrist in 1995. They soon changed their name and began to draw new inspiration from Old Norse mythology and folk music, which is not uncommon in a genre that is as extreme as it is thematically limited.

The impact of sing-along-friendly guitar riffs combined with folk music melodies is unmistakable at Månegarm's concert. Parallels between this music style, called pagan metal or folk metal, and elements of the white power scene are also quite evident. Månegarm's stage appearance only serves to reinforce this conclusion.

The band's two guitar players have buzz cuts, and all members wear combat boots, black military pants, and black shirts with shoulder cuffs displaying the band's symbol—a combination of the Viking runes Madr and Gifu. Liljekvist sticks out the most. With his round glasses and straggly hair, he looks like a folk rocker making his way to woodworking class.

On each side of the stage, the band is flanked by simple decor consisting of two rectangular banners with rune motifs. Erik Grawsiö sings with a clean and clear voice, sometimes transitioning into a primal black metal growl.

Victory to those of the lore, for the root of Yggdrasil
Victory to the children of Midgaard against the hate of vandals
The hammer falls with a boom, horns blow a song
Blood eagle is carved for evil deed, the time of retaliation!

The final song tonight is called "Sigrblot." The promotional clip on YouTube is a low-budget affair where band members traipse through the woods, blow birch trumpets, drink from mead horns, and tap shamanic drums while spirits dressed in white dance on the moors.

Judging from the reaction of this crowd of diehards in northern Sweden, "Sigrblot" has become the signature song of the band. In a quiet section toward the end, Erik Grawsiö recites what sounds like a prayer to the Æsir—the Norse war gods.

> Odin, Allfather, wielder of Gugner, lord of ravens
> Grant us victory, we who have gathered

A little later the same evening, we find ourselves by an open fire, in a big teepee that has been raised on the courtyard behind the stage. We discuss cultural heritage, politics, and the band's relation to both the leftist-oriented metal media and the neo-Nazi movement. Musicians in Swedish white power circles often refer to their genre as *freedom rock*. When asked if they play freedom metal, the members of Månegarm refuse to take the bait. Instead, Janne Liljekvist is visibly irritated.

"Freedom metal? What the hell is that? And why do you even ask us that question?"

Metal with elements of Old Norse mythology is a vital subgenre within the scene today. The Viking heritage and its symbols are used by an increasing number of bands, categorized under the Viking metal label. This development has come about alongside the rise of Swedish nationalism. Since the 2010 elections, Sverigedemokraterna ("Sweden Democrats"), a nationalist political party, has had seats in Swedish parliament.

Death and black metal has always been about pushing boundaries—both in regard to increasingly raw and brutal music and to provocative lyrical content. Especially within black metal, bands rarely shy away from proclamations of hatred against humanity and the desire to see it wiped out. But despite widespread—and in many cases extreme—misanthropy, exceedingly few bands within the metal scene want to be associated with political issues, much less right-wing extremism. Our attempt to understand why resulted in a chapter that no one has any real desire to be featured in.

Unlike punk rock, metal has often had an ambiguous relationship to politics. This might stem from the fact that fantasy and escapism have always been underlying themes. Metal has long been, above all, a form of entertainment.

Yet while demons and swords always had their place, metal bands have also touched on current issues from time to time. Black Sabbath's "War Pigs" and "Children of the Grave" deal with war and nuclear weapons. The treatment of these subjects wasn't all that different from left-wing and dystopian art of the same time period. Other examples include Megadeth questioning the norms of society in "Peace Sells," Anthrax honoring Native Americans in "Indians," and Sepultura subjecting us to political riots in "Refuse/Resist."

However, hard rock and metal bands have always flirted with Third Reich aesthetics. Lemmy Kilmister of Motörhead was a longtime collector of Nazi regalia and often wore an iron cross around his neck. Several of Lemmy's bass guitars were decorated with iron crosses, and he groaned publicly when told the symbol is not permitted on stage in Germany. On the other hand, Lemmy often spoke out against racism of all sorts. Personally, he called himself more of an anarchist than anything else.

"I only collect the stuff. I didn't collect the ideas," he told the *Idaho Statesman* in an interview in 2010.

When Kiss had their breakthrough in the '70s, they were accused in Europe of using the SS logo on their records. The fact that both frontmen are Jewish is immaterial. On German editions of Kiss albums, the band's name is spelled with reversed Z's to this day.

When thrash metal hit the streets in the mid-'80s, the music skewed aggressive, while lyrics quite often turned to social topics. Even if some thrash acts sang about chainsaw massacres and violence, themes like the threat of nuclear conflict and the general horrors of war began to appear on lyric sheets. An increasing number of bands wrote songs about environmental issues. Cover artwork depicted mushroom clouds, figures in gas masks, and other symbols of societal collapse. While some bands simply reveled in symbols of destruction, others professed an environmental concern worthy of Greenpeace. The cover of Nuclear Assault's third album shows a picture of the earth with a "HANDLE WITH CARE" stamp.

Close-Up Magazine's founder Robban Becirovic believes the underground culture of thrash and death metal in the '80s bordered on socialism.

"Everyone would help each other out. A demo tape would set you back two bucks. The cover charge for a gig could be two or three dollars. Bands in different cities set up concerts for one another. There was such a great unity, and never any fighting."

He also points out that plenty of lyrics back then were critical of society.

"There was an interest in environmental protection. Death metal was eco-friendly before the term even existed. And Therion's first album was practically all about McDonald's being evil assholes."

Far from everyone regarded metal as a suitable platform for progressive or constructive messages, however. A significant segment of the genre instead focused on horror movie violence and an almost reverent use of death symbols. For years to come, this would manifest exclusively in violent lyrics, gross-out imagery, and a form of entertainment that—even if far beyond the framework of political correctness—was never anything but sheer entertainment.

When the second wave of black metal hit Norway and Sweden in the early '90s, this fascination with violence would diverge from metal aesthetics into real-world actions. While the audience for death metal were horror enthusiasts with non- (or anti-) intellectual interests, many black metal fans were kids trapped in a social netherworld between philosophy and crime. According to Robban, the black metal wave of the '90s quenched much of the collectivist spirit.

"All of a sudden, everyone was supposed to think only of themselves and act really fucking tough. And I usually say that it was our fault all this shit happened," he says. *Close-Up Magazine* published several interviews that contributed to the '90s black metal wave in Scandinavia.

These interviews were all done in writing, which Robban says was no coincidence.

"This is often the case with these black metal geeks. They want to sit at home and come up with answers that will make them seem a lot smarter than they really are. Just try it yourself—tell someone to their face crap like 'the Berlin wall shall be rebuilt.' It's just ridiculous."

In the early '90s, Robban would sometimes cross paths with Euronymous, Varg Vikernes, and others associated with the loose congregation known as The Black Circle. Robban's impression of the people who would go on to make headlines was that they were a bunch of insecure individuals at best.

"They were misguided brats, really. When I said hi to The Count, his handshake was flaccid, as weak as a child's. I met Euronymous at a pizzeria once. The only thing I remember was him saying something about Albania, which got him excited enough to wave his table knife around. We spoke of doing an interview, but he didn't want to do it on location."

Around the same time, the political climate in Sweden at the time was marred (as it is today) by strong polarization on immigration. New Democracy, a short-lived right-wing populist party, were voted into parliament, while Ultima Thule reached the second slot on the Swedish album sales chart, between Nirvana and 4 Non Blondes, with their colloquial combination of raucous punk rock and nationalistic lyrics.

House of Kicks went so far as to post a sign on the cash register stating they did not sell Ultima Thule material. At the same time, House of Kicks' distribution network sold albums by convicted murderers and church arsonists. Tolerance for violence has always been high in metal, but far less so is its patience for right-wing extremism.

If you really wanted to listen to aggressive music with an openly right-wing populist message in the late '80s, you had to turn to skinhead punk rock. With the second wave of black metal, however, bands with clear Nazi connotations began popping up. Varg Vikernes's Nazi sympathies are often mentioned as a springboard for the direction—despite him never promoting such ideas through Burzum. The phenomenon was soon termed National Socialist black metal and included bands such as Infernum from Poland,

Grand Belial's Key from the U.S., and Germany's Absurd. The founding members of the latter murdered a classmate while still teenagers.

In the mid-'90s, Robban Becirovic noticed how racist elements in the scene were on the rise. As editor-in-chief, he'd sometimes handle unacceptable ideological positions by confronting them directly. In other situations, he would simply exclude certain bands. One act left out in the cold was Unleashed.

In 1995, the second issue of the neo-Nazi publication *Nordland* featured an article about Unleashed. Despite the Swedish death metal band having shifted to Viking-themed lyrics on their third album, *Across the Open Sea*, the optics of their band name displayed alongside straight-up Nazi acts, such as Pluton Svea and Midgårds Söner, were naturally disturbing to many in the Swedish scene.

Suddenly, wearing a Thor's hammer and doing a Nazi salute were considered two sides of the same coin. While *Nordland* magazine was discontinued just four years later, the inclusion of Unleashed in a Nazi context would have lasting consequences for them.

With his leather jacket and long hair, Johnny Hedlund looks as though he's been frozen in time since the Swedish death metal wave of the '90s. When we meet him in 2007, it's been 18 years since he formed Unleashed after the breakup of scene forerunners Nihilist. He thinks the future looks bright for Unleashed after years of tour fatigue and other stressors.

The Nazi stigma brought about by the 1995 *Nordland* article has remained. Johnny firmly denies that the band has a racist or Nazi message. So, why did they even agree to speak to *Nordland*?

"We had made a decision to speak with all magazines that wanted to feature us. We don't choose the media; the media chooses us—that's how we looked at it in the '90s. Granting every request obviously has consequences. You could also go through the trouble of investigating everyone who asks for an interview. 'What's this organization? Why do they want to interview us?' We didn't bother about that, but I suppose we probably should have."

Johnny says the Nazi rumors never would have even begun if people had actually read the interview.

"They would have realized I clearly didn't share the political sentiments of *Nordland* magazine. Because I told them we had fans of all colors coming to our gigs and that I don't give a shit about their politics. Unfortunately, people just saw our name on the cover and drew their own conclusions."

Johnny finds nothing strange in the fact that bands like Unleashed are of interest to the extreme right, since they do use Viking symbolism.

"Also, we no doubt sold a lot more records than any of their shitty bands ever did. We used to joke about White Aryan Regurgitation. They'd be all enthusiasm and no skill whatsoever. Of course, they wanted to find a bigger act to put on their front cover. And they did—in us."

Nevertheless, in a 1993 article in the widely read Swedish tabloid *Aftonbladet*, an Unleashed member stated that "Sweden is accepting too many immigrants." The quote was displayed out of context and without a source reference. The article was an interview with Johnny Hedlund and guitarist Tomas Måsgard, together with two members of the Christian metal band Veni Domine.

So, are the xenophobic rumors surrounding the band completely unfounded?

"I think we actually said about 10 percent of the things in that article," Johnny estimates.

He says the journalist either came up with stuff himself or that the statement was part of a longer train of thought that was edited out.

"My mother called me in tears when it was published. I didn't understand anything because I hadn't read it. But needless to say, none of it was accurate."

Several times during the conversation, Johnny mentions his mother having been upset about rumors surrounding the band. In 2003, this reputation had an unexpected consequence.

In the early '00s, Dave Grohl of the Foo Fighters started a side project called Probot where he invited in guest vocalists from different corners of the metal scene. Among the participants were Lemmy, Tom G. Warrior of Celtic Frost, and Venom's Cronos. Grohl had initially wanted Johnny to contribute as well. But in a later interview with *Close-Up Magazine*, Grohl mentioned having heard that Hedlund is a Nazi and thus decided not to contact him.

Johnny believes immigration policies should be founded on humanitarian grounds. He says the 1989 job market crash had an unfortunate timing that was exploited by forces such as the Swedish faction of White Aryan Resistance, New Democracy, and white power bands like Ultima Thule. Johnny adds that these players wanted to attach themselves to Unleashed, to turn them into political tools.

For Johnny, the extreme right's appropriation of Norse symbols makes it even more important to hang on to them.

"My stance is that no one is going to tell me what Thor's hammer stands for. I will tell them what it stands for. They shouldn't be allowed to put their spin on it. Had we had refused to do the interview, they would've written about us anyway. And what would the article have said then?"

Johnny says that he and Unleashed drummer Anders Schultz have worn the Thor's hammer since they were kids. It started in school when they were taught about the religions of other cultures but nothing of their own roots. Hence, Old Norse mythology became extra appealing and has been a consistent theme on Unleashed albums since 1993.

Another reason was that so many bands were already writing about Satanism. To Johnny, the Thor's hammer represents a lot of things.

"The values found in the Hávamál verses of the Poetic Edda, which I'm happy to promote, deal with friendship, loyalty, hospitality, humility, wisdom, courage, and power. The list goes on."

With the Viking as symbol, Johnny claims he wants to depict the struggle of life—even for modern humans with roofs over their heads and food on the table.

"I'll gladly describe a Viking standing in a field with sword and shield and then try linking this to the present. We have a roof over our heads. We have heat. Fine. Despite this, many in our society live pretty challenging lives. I try to give them—and myself—some self-confidence. Everything comes down to interpretation. You can read the Bible or the Quran whichever way you want and say, 'This is what these guys stand for—they're all out of their fucking heads.' This is unfortunately something we tend to do in Sweden."

In the early summer of 2004, *Close-Up's* editorial team received an unexpected tip. Christofer Johnsson, founding member of Swedish symphonic death metal band Therion, was a member of the Sweden Democrats. The party has roots in the neo-Nazi movement but have gained mainstream popularity in recent years after adopting a more slick, media-friendly image. Shortly thereafter, *Close-Up* brought up the subject in an interview with Johnsson. The conversation led to a 5-page article, in which Johnsson claimed to have joined the party only to access literature and be able to form his own opinion about their views. He mentioned how he was also a member of the even more extreme National Democrats, for the same reason. When the issue hit stores, reactions were swift.

Close-Up's online forum was flooded by condemnations of both the Sweden Democrats and Christofer Johnsson himself. Others felt the magazine had labelled Johnsson a racist without proper grounds. Eventually, the contested band leader himself joined the debate. Christofer had previously been the treasurer of occult order Dragon Rouge. He pointed out that at best, the Sweden Democrats had received enough money from him to cover a cup of coffee.

When we speak to Christofer Johnsson, four years have passed since the article. We meet him in the parking lot behind the Royal Swedish Opera in Stockholm. Johnsson wears black trousers and a suit jacket, and his long blond hair is tied in a ponytail.

"Have you been to the Gothenburg Opera?" he asks as we walk to a nearby restaurant. "The acoustics are garbage there. How utterly typical of Swedish left-wing potheads to invest money in stuff that doesn't work."

This is one of the first things he says to us. When we ask about the 2004 *Close-Up* interview, he sighs and says it was difficult discussing his SD membership, since it's tied into so many of his other interests. And the whole affair is related to his lack of trust in mainstream media. He's learned to seek information from alternate sources.

"So, I told the reporter, 'Don't print any of this!' Because regardless of what I say, a bunch of left-wing extremists will go, 'They're Nazis!' And then bring up the German Nazi party of the '30s."

People drawing such conclusions are the very same folks who call police fascists, Johnson says.

"And claim all conservatives are fascists. That interview was more of a discussion in which I tried explaining myself, which I was hoping he wouldn't publish. Then I called their editor-in-chief and pleaded with him, 'Please don't print this, because it will cause a lot of problems for me.'"

Christofer says that while the magazine allowed him to rephrase certain replies and approve the final draft, the rumor about him as a potential Nazi reached far beyond the Swedish border.

When we contact Christofer again in the summer of 2011, he's at his home in Ireland but mentions that he plans to move back to Sweden again, permanently. To this day, he remembers the *Close-Up* interview as an unpleasant intrusion into his private life.

"At first, I was completely blindsided and shocked when the question came up but at the same time felt both violated and apprehensive about what the magazine would print. And I was actually not in any way engaged in SD when my membership was exposed. On the contrary—I was a passive member, mostly due to my great interest in politics and the history of ideas. I tried explaining this, but it ended up a bit unfocused. Some people thought that I just didn't want to admit to liking SD."

He says that besides engaging in animal rights and environmental issues, for a long time, he was primarily interested in the theoretical aspects of politics and society. He then moved to the Stockholm suburb of Botkyrka, a low-income neighborhood with a high-density immigrant population.

"Something happened there. A 16-year-old girl was raped on the lawn outside my apartment, while I was inside partying and listening to music with a friend. The harsh reality of a 16-year-old schoolgirl became part of my reality, and I felt really bad about it."

He remembers how his girlfriend at the time didn't feel safe walking down to the subway station alone. He says he didn't understand why until the day he was called a faggot by a gang of 13-year-old immigrant boys, because of his long hair. By the time he'd decided to move from Botkyrka, people were setting cars on fire in the parking lots.

"This is my story, but I'd like to think I'm not entirely unique. If well-situated inner-city metalheads were forced to live in a problematic area for a year as they're expecting children, I think most people with a brain would react in some way. With that said, obviously, not all of them would choose the Sweden Democrats just because I did."

Christofer Johnsson mentions having become a father a few years back, which was yet another reason to get involved for the sake of someone else. He increased his volunteer work, personally handing out 25,000 copies of the Sweden Democrat party newspaper leading up to the 2010 election. For a few years, he was acting chairman of the party's local chapter.

———

Marduk of Norrköping have released 14 albums since forming in 1990. For the band's musical driving force, guitarist and composer Morgan Håkansson, all aspects of the band must work as a unit. Marduk's music has always been very extreme, and their lyrics combine traditional black metal Satanism with tanks and historical battles. Fittingly, their stage attire consists of army pants, combat boots, and corpse paint.

When Sveriges Television aired an interview with Håkansson in 2006, they also played part of the song "The Hangman of Prague," detailing the exploits of SS officer Reinhard Heydrich. The segment was reported to the Swedish Broadcasting Commission. Christian newspaper *Dagen* published an op-ed piece in which Marduk was called "the new face of neo-Nazism" and accused Sveriges Television of ignoring their policy of not broadcasting white power music.

The commission later cleared the program of wrongdoing, as the song couldn't be determined to be exclusively propagandistic. It was also concluded that neither the lyrics nor the interview with Morgan Håkansson had instigated or inspired any criminal activity.

Marduk have been accused of being Nazis ever since their 1999 album *Panzer Division Marduk*, but Håkansson never bothers denying anything.

"I could just as well deny being a socialist or subscribing to any other ideology that I've never said a word about."

His historical interests can be partly ascribed to the fact that his maternal grandfather fought for Germany during the Second World War. Sometimes, he adds the family name Steinmeyer to his own. He points out that no one would even consider accusing someone of being a Nazi because they made a movie about World War II.

"And if you say, 'I want to murder all Christians,' no one reacts. But write a song about the Second World War and people lose their shit."

When asked if he's a Nazi, he says he'd never answer such a question publicly, but that for him Nazism is primarily a political idea that died in the spring of 1945. An idea with powerful symbols that still inspire him.

"There was a reason they worked as well as they did."

Regardless of Morgan Håkansson's political sympathies, Marduk can hardly be placed in the National Socialist black metal category. Rather, the band is part of a long, if controversial, tradition of metal with historical lyrics.

The increased use of Nazi symbols in black metal can often be attributed to the genre's long-standing ambitions to offend and shock by any possible means. Sometimes, the individuals adopting these symbols are wholly unprepared for the results of such a move.

At a 2007 gig in Essen, Germany, Taake vocalist Hoest performed with a huge swastika painted on his chest. This stunt set off a wave of negative reactions and resulted in several canceled performances. On the band's website, Hoest stressed how Taake wasn't a political band. He also admitted that using the swastika on a German stage was a mistake:

"On the other hand I strongly feel that Black Metal bands should allow themselves to use ANY kind of destructive/negative symbolism, as the basis of this expression is above all: EVIL(!) Black Metal is still not, and should never become, harmless like all other styles of housebroke metal. Frankly, I find it prepostrous [sic] that we get away with lyrics about murder, torture, rape, necrophilia and suicide, but get boycotted for wearing a symbol on ONE single occasion. A part of our mission is to invoke negative feelings, so I found it quite appropriate to remind our German audience of their biggest shame. (--) We will now censor certain symbols for the rest of the tour, and we truly apologize to all of our collaborators who might get problems because of the Essen swastika scandal (except for the Untermensch owner of that club; you can go suck a Muslim)!"

This incident is but one of many examples of how black metal bands tend to get caught between their will to provoke and the consequences they face when actually succeeding. It also illustrates why metal bands with sights set on an income-generating career are better off steering clear of anything associated with right-wing extremism.

"Well, sieg heil then?"

A long-haired young man in a Watain shirt calls out to a guy leaving the crowded restroom of a 2006 Watain show in Linköping. The two men happened to stand a little too close to each other at the urinal. What almost escalated into a fistfight instead turned into camaraderie and a Nazi salute. The gesture is not returned.

Watain vocalist Erik Danielsson often claims that black metal should not be politicized. At the same time, his band has often been accused of right-wing extremism. Nazi salutes are not uncommon at black metal concerts, and Watain shows are no exception.

After their 2006 performance at the Party San Metal Open Air festival in Germany, one of Watain's band members wore a T-shirt with the logo of German National Socialist black metal band Absurd. A journalist reported this to the festival management and had the band thrown out for the evening. Rumor spread fast in the metal world, and since then, Watain have received both threats and warnings from the antifascist network Antifa. Several concerts in Europe have been canceled when Antifa contacted the event organizers and informed them of the band's purported right-wing links.

Erik Danielsson shows little understanding for such activity.

"They work with politics; we work with religion. We have nothing to do with each other. Why should some communist idiot be allowed to restrict our religious crusade by claiming we're skinheads? It pisses me off."

He says the band did find the whole thing quite entertaining but that Watain have bigger problems with the animal parts in their stage décor upsetting militant vegans and animal rights activists. He believes people are trying to figure out what truly represents the devil in Watain. Using regular Motörhead aesthetics in a black metal context evokes completely different reactions.

"The black metal framework enhances the effect. That combined with extreme statements about entirely different things—people are prone to equate the two. It remains truly dangerous. It's the only thing you're not allowed to praise."

When we ask him why it's so important not to be associated with right-wing extremism, he laughs.

"But we love Nazism. What metalhead doesn't? In the same way we're fascinated by the sinister atmosphere and aesthetics in dictatorships like North Korea or the Soviet Union, there's an equally strong appeal in the visual expressions of Nazism. It's simplistic, violent, radical, fascist, uncompromising, extravagant, and stylish. And highly controversial, which is an attraction in itself. What's not to like?" says Erik, and then deadpans:

"Apart from the fact that the end goal of Nazism is to save the world, and for everyone to live in nice, white-picket-fence Aryan societies."

He stresses how he does not share that goal. Instead, he sees Watain as an expression for a lawless and chaotic darkness. He's well aware of the Nazi black metal bands that exist but doesn't care for them.

"They're just skinheads in black metal uniform. There's nothing dignified about that at all."

Morals aside, another more pragmatic reason to avoid the Nazi label is that it complicates business. After the Party San incident, Watain could barely play in Germany for a while. He's also aware that there's no way back for a band that's acquired a reputation as Nazis.

"That really makes you a Nazi band. And for us, that would feel so lame, cheap, and fucking unclean. It's almost like the Aghori sect in India, who are only given attention for eating human flesh while no one contemplates the wide-spanning philosophy behind it."

He adds that there's often a reason why certain bands get a right-wing reputation. In the case of Watain, they've done the odd Nazi salutation, just to piss people off.

"But who the hell hasn't?"

Nevertheless, as early as on their first demo, *Go Fuck Your Jewish God*, the band positioned themselves against Judaism. Erik points out that the title was more of a teenage provocation than an anti-Semitic stance, but he says that there's still something in there that makes sense to him. He emphasizes that his disdain for Judaism is restricted to specific aspects of the religion's dogma and distaste for religion in general.

"The Jews are the only serious practitioners of white magic left in the world. No Christians today sweat in front of their altars, trying to rouse the spiritual currents of the world. Within Judaism, there's still a strong magical branch. But from a purely racial aspect, I could not care less."

In certain regards, the black metal scene's use of Third Reich symbolism can be seen as an extension of the early punk movement, where bands such as The Stooges, Sex Pistols, and Dead Boys made use of Nazi regalia and swastikas. Examining the common denominators between Satanism and Nazism, the two come off as quite disparate expressions, sharing a number of elements. They are both ideologies based on violence, superhuman ideals, and antihumanism.

The former website of the Satanic organization Misanthropic Luciferian Order contained a number of Satanic aphorisms colored by fascist ideology. Democracy is denounced, whereas the "superman" is celebrated. "The elite can never degrade itself and sink to the level of the unworthy scum; democracy must therefore always be fought by all and any means necessary." Another passage states that "Only through terror can the elite minority make itself heard, through the wailing of the subhuman majority."

Misanthropic Luciferian Order was a religious order, not a political organization. Despite this, many elements of the MLO agenda were almost indistinguishable from hardline right-wing ideology. The exception is perhaps MLO's explicit ultimate goal: to lead creation back into a formless, primordial darkness. That agenda is not applicable to a political left-and-right scale. However, it does contain an obvious appeal to people with an extremist disposition.

———

"We are no longer Nazis."

Månegarm violinist Janne Liljekvist answers the question of what separates today's version from the black metal band formed in Norrtälje more than 20 years ago. There's a moment of awkward silence. His bandmates give him stern looks, indicating he's said something deeply inappropriate.

"I tried to make a joke," he adds quickly. "We've never been Nazis, even if some people probably thought we were."

The band's towering bass player, Pierre Wilhelmsson, confirms how the Nazi reputation has followed them from the very beginning.

"But if someone interprets us that way, it says more about them than us."

Janne says the situation was further complicated after a few players in the utmost right-wing circles used their music, without permission, in connection with the Salem march—an annual extreme right-wing manifestation outside Stockholm.

"It feels terrible. Had they asked us, of course, we would have denied the request. And if we could hit delete and erase our music from this context, we would."

Guitarist Jonas Almqvist joins the conversation, pinpointing in one sentence why it remains problematic to pose brazen questions about political convictions to metal musicians.

"Political convictions are private. It has nothing to do with the band or the music."

Månegarm themselves would possibly accept the label pagan metal, a movement that, according to Pierre, is more exciting now than ever. Metal bands around the world, it's fair to say, are inspired by their local musical heritage.

"Arkona from Russia, for instance. In earlier days, you'd see a Spanish band with a Nordic image. I like it a lot more now, when bands are doing their own thing."

Could you say that it's more acceptable to have leftist sympathies than right-wing leanings in metal?

"Not only in metal circles," Janne responds immediately. "That goes for all of culture."

Set Teitan was caught on film doing a Nazi salute on stage at Watain's 20th anniversary show in Stockholm in January 2018. In a post on Facebook, the band explained that the "arm movement" was not meant as derogatory and underlined that they approve of diversity. The post was taken down a few hours later, after massive criticism from fans, accusing the band of "bending for the politically correct elite." Nonetheless, Watain chose to temporarily part ways with their live guitarist.

A U.S. tour with Taake was canceled in the spring of 2018 due to the swastika incident in 2007.

A few weeks later, an antifascist activist group revealed that two members of Marduk had ordered propaganda material from the right-wing terrorist group Nordic Resistance Movement. This lead to them being banned from a Stockholm festival. Marduk vehemently denies the allegations.

XIII.

A Lesson in Suicide

Honestly, if I didn't have any enemies,
I would say I have failed.

— Niklas Kvarforth, Shining

LESS THAN A HUNDRED PEOPLE have shown up at Club 666 near Mariatorget—a basement bar in one of the most affluent parts of Stockholm. The turnout this cold October night in 2005 is meager, but then again, promotion for the show has been limited to black-and-white flyers posted throughout the neighborhood. They would be easy to miss among all the other posters and bills, even though the wording, printed in thin, spiky lettering, has promised something out of the ordinary:

TOTAL DESTRUCTION
LORD DEMON PRESENTS:
SUICIDE / BLACK METAL NIGHT
The first, and probably last, concert ever in Stockholm.
On stage: SHINING
Supporting act: Ondskapt

An illustration at the bottom of the flyer depicts a razor directed at the wrist of a child. Arrows point along the veins leading up to the elbow. The phrase "Remember kids … it's down the road, not across the street. Make it count!" encircles the informative drawing. The image is quite blurry on the Xeroxed flyer. You would need a few seconds to take in the message: This is a suicide manual.

It's hard to guess exactly what the audience is expecting from the show tonight. There's something intriguing in the words "first," "last," and "ever" on the poster of a band promoting suicide. No doubt, many have come to experience something extreme.

"How many of you are here for Shining?"

The advertised supporting act, Ondskapt, have canceled for unknown reasons. The replacement is the black metal band Valkyrja. The vocalist is guzzling a bottle of beer while staring out from under his bangs. Like the rest of the band, he barely looks old enough to be allowed into the club.

Most of the audience ignores his question. Only a hardy-looking man dressed in black takes the bait and waves his arm, shouting, "Yeah!"

The Valkyrja vocalist takes a deep breath, then screams:

"DIIEEE!"

There is a moment of awkward silence, before Valkyrja manages to begin their final song.

In the bar, Erik "Tyrant" Gustafsson mingles with Set Teitan. Most people just hang out in the different nooks and crannies of the basement, waiting for the main attraction.

The girl in the merchandise stand is named Kat. She's from the south of Sweden and speaks with a heavy accent, hampered even further by a monotonous, drugged-out cadence. While her arms show no signs of self-harm, they boast an impressive collection of tattoos. She is overly enthusiastic about all things concerning Shining.

"Buy the album, listen to the music, and read the lyrics. You'll love it! This one is very inspired by [Swedish writer and poet] Stig Dagerman," she says and shows us a CD of *Shining II – Livets ändhållplats* (The Last Stop of Life), featuring song titles like "Att med kniv göra sig illa" (To Harm Yourself with Knives) and "Ännu ett steg närmare total utfrysning" (Yet Another Step Closer to Complete Isolation).

The fourth track is quite simply called "Död" (Death). At first glance, the cover artwork seems to be completely black, but closer inspection reveals a desolate coastal landscape under a bleak sky with a fragment of light at the horizon. The only text in the entire booklet is the same sentence, written 22 times: *"Du är värdelös och jag vill att du DÖR"* (You are worthless and I want you to DIE).

Kat says that Shining have only played six concerts in total, despite the band's history going as far back as 1996.

"But there'll be a lot more now."

The conversation comes to a sudden stop as the band walks onstage and drummer Ludwig Witt, who is also a member of the stoner band Spiritual Beggars, counts off.

A wave of distorted minor-key harmonics floods the venue. The heavy, sludgy riff is really just two chords repeated over and over. The effect is hypnotic. Then the tempo doubles, and the crowd erupts in ferocious headbanging.

Vocalist Niklas Kvarforth looks out over the roiling sea of hair. His bare torso is thin as a rake, and he wears a black bandana. Blood runs from both his arms, which are sliced up with two long cuts from the shoulders down to the forearms. His eyes are wide open, his gaze radiating mad triumph. Like a Moses figure, he raises his bleeding arms over the audience and starts singing in a voice coming more from his throat than his vocal chords:

Fanatisk hängivelse / Karvad i hud
Född att dö / Förankrad vid livet
(Fanatical devotion / Carved in skin
Born to die / Anchored to life)

He crouches at the drum kit, pulls out a utility knife, and cuts a few more gashes into his arm. A collection of huge scars form an occult symbol across his back. The drums dive into a blast beat, with the same two chords still hammering the crowd. Kvarforth discards the knife, chugs some of his beer, and picks up the microphone again.

Skrääämmande ärooo dööödens enerverande skuggaaa!
(Terrifying iiiiis deeeaath's maddening shaaadow!)

With little regard for the tempo of the song, he draws the words out endlessly. In between lines, he flicks his tongue at the audience, sometimes breaking into maniacal laughter.

The rest of the band is a motley crew. At far right is guitarist John Doe, also the driving force of the Gothenburg-based black metal outfit Craft, who recently released their *Fuck the Universe* album. He's wearing dark sunglasses and looks a bit older than the rest. At center stage, bass player Johan Hallander weaves intricate melodies underneath the monotonous buzzing wall of guitars. His instrument is coated in coagulated blood, and his arms are covered with thick, reddened scars. The other guitarist, Casado, wears a bright-colored sports shirt, and his Epiphone SG hangs high up on his chest. Looking like some kind of mix between a Salvation Army soldier and a pop star, he appears to be in a splendid mood. Aside from the ambiguously motivated suicide message, the biggest mystery of this band is just why the hell this guy is in it.

By now blood is also flowing from several audience members. A young man in his 20s with a black hoodie and a shirt with the words *Förintelse och libido* ("Annihilation and libido") makes five deep cuts in his left forearm with a razor he's brought along. The red gashes grow as the song "Ett liv utan mening" (A Life without Meaning) builds to a crescendo.

A girl with long burgundy hair and a shirt reading, "Make a change—kill yourself!" crawls onto the stage and says something to Kvarforth. He shakes his head and pushes her off. Another girl stands on her knees halfway up on stage, singing along to every word with tears running down her face. Kvarforth seems to cherish every moment. Again, he raises his arms above the audience, as if to bless them. On his left ring finger is an engagement ring.

After the show, the young man in the *Förintelse och libido* shirt stands in the bar by himself. He's rolled the sleeve of his shirt all the way up to the shoulder. His left arm is a bloody mess. His right hand is holding a glass of beer. We ask if we can take his picture. He says yes but disappears before we have time to ask his name.

Half an hour later, Niklas Kvarforth is standing outside the venue. He wears a thin green army jacket and looks cold in the harsh fall night. Occasionally, fans walk past him saying, "Great show!" Someone offers him a cigarette. We explain how we're working on a book and that we'd like to speak with him. He mumbles, "You can write whatever you want," and then responds with monosyllabic answers, eyes peering defensively into the night.

Why do you cut yourself on stage?
"To enter an aggressive, extroverted state so I can convey the lyrics properly."

What did the girl in the audience want?
"To drink my blood."

What did you tell her?
"That she wasn't worthy. Why should I grant her that privilege? Just another sick and broken soul allowing herself to be soiled by another—what's the point? No one's worth it. Every person is a cancer and should be exterminated."

Even you?
"Have I not been clear enough? I thought I was clear enough! I hate myself, I hate you, and every living human soul."

Have you ever seriously contemplated suicide?
"I've been institutionalized a few times, but now I'm trying to thwart my suicidal tendencies. Because if I die, then who's left to preach?"

What's your goal with Shining?
"Shining is about staring straight into the eye of negativity. Full speed ahead into ruin. Our goal is for as many as possible to die. We can't do it by executing people at our concerts, even if that would be wonderful!"

What would be wonderful?
"If we could execute people at our shows. But that would only work for one show; then the entire band would go to prison. Instead, we want to urge others to commit suicide. And I presume you noticed the effect we had on the audience—half of them were cutting themselves!"

What is it about humanity that you don't like?
"Look at yourself in the mirror."

Niklas speaks in a muted voice through clenched jaws, as a cold wind sweeps along Hornsgatan. He says that his general hatred toward humans is one of the reasons why he recently left Stockholm for the smaller coastal city of Halmstad.

Online articles about Shining paint the picture of a band in turmoil, with a frontman open to influences far beyond the boundaries of metal. We learn that Niklas Kvarforth recommends heroin, loves the melancholy Swedish rock group Kent and singer Dido, but hates life "in all its perverted forms." Bass player Johan Hallander once played in the experimental self-harming band Tortura.

The story of Shining began in 1996 as a solo project of then-13-year-old Kvarforth. Two years later, a temporary lineup recorded the *Submit to Self-Destruction* single, released on Niklas's own label, Selbstmord Services. Their first full-length album, *Within Deep, Dark Chambers*, was released in 2000. The bleak and barren music heavily resembled Burzum. Lyrics were written in complicated English and recited in a harsh, aggressive voice. The booklet contains a seemingly authentic photo of a guy in classic thrash metal outfit. He's wearing a leather jacket, jeans, and sneakers—and is dangling from a noose in the ceiling.

The text in the album insert is a detailed account of a tumultuous recording session where the band faced all kinds of complications. Drummer Wedebrand had to leave temporarily due to an injury, and much of the music was recorded with a click track. Upon his return, Wedebrand then had difficulties staying in tempo. A more severe problem arose from the fact that Wedebrand wanted to murder the album's guest singer Andreas Classen, the vocalist from the German band Bethlehem. In the text, Kvarforth also explains how he and the drummer reasoned when recruiting bass player Tusk:

"... After all, me and Wedebrand knew that if such a person as Tusk, whom I hated beyond comprehension, would start playing with us, that would cause a more negative atmosphere within the band, certainly strengthening the vision we had and still have."

Hardly to anyone's surprise, Tusk was out of the picture just a year later.

In the spring of 2004, Kvarforth became heavily depressed and was institutionalized. The subsequent recording of the band's fourth album took a heavy toll. According to a September 2005 interview in *Odium Magazine*, the hard work combined with "lack of medication, family problems, and back-stabbing" caused band members to leave due to the "tremendous negativity." Selbstmord Services went bankrupt.

When half of the recordings were erased due to a technical mishap, Kvarforth could no longer handle the situation. In early August of 2004, he announced that Shining had split up.

Yet guitarist John Doe made several attempts at persuading Niklas to reform the band, and in February 2005, the new lineup was complete. A new record deal was also signed with French label Osmose Productions.

On a promotional photo on the Shining website, John Doe shows off two badly scarred underarms. Underneath, the words "Let the Self-Destruction Blossom" is written in bold.

———

Rock music about harming others is hardly anything new. Bands encouraging their own fans to end their lives, however, wasn't common even in the creative chaos of the Norwegian black metal wave in the '90s.

The first known piece of music connected to suicide is not a metal song. In 1932, Hungarian pianist Rezső Seress composed the song "Vége a világnak" (The World Is Ending). The following year, poet László Jávor wrote new lyrics for the piece, calling it "Szomorú vasárnap" (Sad Sunday).

The text contains phrases such as "My heart and I have decided to end it all," and the song was immediately accused of causing an outbreak of suicides.

In 1936, the song was translated into English as "Gloomy Sunday," but it was with the 1941 recording by Billie Holiday that it became a real hit. Since then, it's been recorded by artists as diverse as Sinéad O'Connor, Elvis Costello, and Diamanda Galás. The urban legend of the song's suicide-inducing qualities was rekindled when Seress himself committed suicide in 1968. He first jumped out of his apartment window, and after surviving the fall, he strangled himself in the hospital. The day of his death was a Sunday.

In the early days of heavy metal, lyrics quite often touched on life-affirming themes like freedom, comradery, love, partying, and giving an oppressive world a collective middle finger. When Ronnie James Dio repeated the phrase "die young" in the dreamy midsection of his song of the same name, he gave death a more romantic sheen than perhaps anyone had before him in a metal song. Still, it was Ozzy Osbourne, not Dio, who was first accused of inspiring a suicide through metal lyrics.

In 1984, 19-year-old California resident John McCollum killed himself while listening to the Ozzy album *Blizzard of Ozz*. He still had his headphones on, and the first side of the album was cued on the turntable, with the track "Suicide Solution." McCollum's parents sued the singer, claiming he directly influenced their son's suicide. In 1988, the case was dismissed by the court. Several artists, among them Judas Priest and Marilyn Manson, have been since been accused of either triggering suicides or of promoting murder.

American punk legend GG Allin is often considered a forerunner in the use of the artist's own body as a means of shocking the audience. His live shows in the mid-'80s became notorious: He would smear himself with feces and urine and hurl himself onto broken glass. The shock element appeared to be an end in itself, and Allin went all in.

In a 1988 interview for American punk magazine *Maximum Rock'n'roll*, GG Allin announced his intention of carrying out an on-stage suicide on Halloween the following year. The act was prevented by a prison term, however. History would come to repeat itself, as Allin was imprisoned every Halloween thereafter until he died from a heroin overdose in a New York apartment in June of 1993.

When Scandinavian death and black metal bands in the early '90s refined the heritage of Venom and Slayer, violent tendencies were not only aimed at others. Self-harm became a marker for subcultural affiliation. Suddenly, having an inverted cross carved into your arm was as much a part of the metal uniform as wearing a bullet belt, a leather jacket, and a band shirt. At parties, people would listen to records, drink beer, and then challenge each other to see who could cut themselves the most—and the deepest.

At the same time, the glorification of death and suicide grew even more prevalent in the scene.

Andreas "Whiplasher" Bergh recalls a rumor capturing the spirit of the era perfectly.

"People were always saying Mayhem planned to blow their own heads off, with explosives tied around their necks. But that never happened."

Jan Axel "Hellhammer" Blomberg remembers another idea discussed back in the day to actually hand out razor blades to members of the audience. Today he clearly distances himself from suicidal messages aimed at young people, but this didn't stop him from playing drums in Shining for several years. He describes the other members as "special, but really cool."

"It was entertaining. The last time I traveled to Sweden to play with them, one of them stuck a fork in his arm just for fun."

———

In the summer of 2006, Shining celebrated their tenth anniversary with a show in Oslo. As part of the performance, the band brought up a fan on stage, allowing him to cut himself. As the young man bent forward, Kvarforth began slicing his back with a scalpel. Several audience members started crying, and a general sense of panic spread through the venue. The local promoter climbed onto the stage to halt the spectacle, and the young man was lifted down. He was a familiar face to us: It was the same person we'd taken a photo of a few months ago, after he cut his arm at the Shining concert in Stockholm. It turns out his name is Kim Carlsson, and he's from Jönköping.

Over the course of several months, we keep trying to reach Kvarforth to ask follow-up questions to our brief conversation on Hornsgatan, but our emails get no response.

The following winter, the Swedish National Board of Health and Welfare publishes a report stating that the number of young women receiving medical attention for self-harm injuries has risen 40 percent in less than 10 years. In Swedish newspaper *Svenska Dagbladet*, psychotherapist Therese Sterner comments on the report. She says the increase is largely due to self-harm being discussed more openly among young people, especially on the internet. She points out a high risk of contagion and mentions as an example that, if a young woman starts cutting herself at a psychiatric ward, the behavior can spread quickly among other patients.

Self-harm and the subgenre called depressive metal appear to be gaining ground parallel to each other. At Repulsive Records, a Stockholm record shop that has since closed, shopkeeper Peter tells us most customers simply refer to the style as "suicide." Usually, he would recommend something by Australian one-man band Abyssic Hate or by Forgotten Tomb from Italy.

Peter mentions how more and more people have been asking for a Swedish band called Lifelover. As it turns out, the vocalist of Lifelover is none other than the elusive Kim Carlsson.

Most of the self-harming people we speak to while working on this chapter are in their 20s. Is the age factor somehow indicative of their mental status and a worldview focused on youthful searching? A passing phase leading to a future as stable individuals with humanistic values? Perhaps the answer can be found where it all began.

Finspång is a small mill town located between Lake Vättern and the coastal town of Norrköping. It was here, in a basement studio a stone's throw from the city center, that producer Dan Swanö recorded the fabled sessions with self-torturing black metal duo Abruptum in the early '90s—perhaps the first band in the world to literally make self-harm an integral part of their sound.

First appearing in the late '80s, the duo took their name from the Italian word for abyss.

In an interview with *Close-Up Magazine* in June 1992, Øystein "Euronymous" Aarseth spoke with pride about the coming Abruptum album *Obscuritatem Advoco Amplèctere Me* on his label, Deathlike Silence Productions. "This album is the most fucked-up thing that's ever been recorded. It's not ordinary music, but 50 minutes of evil. They subjected each other to brutal torture in the studio, and you can really hear them suffering."

The exploits of the self-torturing duo would soon become an urban legend of sorts in metal circles. One of the two members, Morgan "Evil" Håkansson, would become one of the staunchest forces within the Swedish black metal scene as leader of Marduk. The second member, IT, rumored to be too evil to have a human name, would remain a peripheral character outside the inner black metal circles. Details concerning Abruptum's studio recordings were shrouded in obscurity. This only contributed to their reputation as the evilest duo in the world. The few band photos in circulation showed two somber characters in primitive corpse paint and homemade studded bracelets, staring back at the beholder from bleak surroundings.

Today, Dan Swanö remembers the recordings as a hybrid of a black mass and drunken revelry in the dark.

"I still don't know exactly what went on in the studio. The lights were always all switched off; the only thing illuminating the room was the sheen emanating from my recording equipment. I remember IT cutting his arms with a dull utility knife, and there was blood absolutely everywhere on our nice, new, wall-to-wall carpet."

For one of the Abruptum recordings, Swanö simply rigged up the microphones, set the reverb sends up to max, hit record, and went home for a cup of coffee.

"When I returned 40 minutes later, the album was finished. I know nothing about what transpired during that session—they might have been sacrificing animals in there for all I know."

Swanö also recalls how on one occasion, they trapped IT underneath a couch, in order to induce his claustrophobia.

"Anything to invoke genuine pain, genuine anguish, and so on. I never took it fully seriously; I was more of the studio guy. But I was fascinated by the impact of what we did down there."

The notoriety of the recordings became clear to him only later, when other bands he worked with were fascinated by the fact that IT was living in the same town. Swanö was at this point a member of the death metal band Edge of Sanity, and a young producer on the rise. He was also the one who introduced the two Abruptum members to each other.

Morgan Håkansson remembers how he clicked immediately with IT.

"We had a lot of ideas about how to push music beyond new thresholds. We tried to achieve audio effects no one had heard before, like the sound of cutting yourself."

He doesn't want to talk about what happened during those recording sessions.

"There's really not much to say. It's not something to bring into the public spotlight."

Besides the diabolical atmosphere, Abruptum's music had more in common with noise and other experimental genres than with metal. Most of the songs lacked traditional structures and consisted primarily of muffled walls of sound, tortured shrieks, and abysmal sound effects.

The band's third album, *Evil Genius*, actually came with a razor blade along with the tagline: "Includes Razorblade—kill yourself!" The album was released by Hellspawn Records, the label run by former Dark Funeral guitar player David "Blackmoon" Parland.

We catch up with Parland backstage at Hovet, after Dissection's 2006 Midsummer Massacre concert. He gives a somewhat confused impression but lights up when reminded of old times.

While speaking excitedly of the "razor album," the cigarette in his hand burns all the way down to the filter.

"IT was a totally fucking evil guy. I remember us going to a hardware store in Stockhom to buy 2,500 razor blades. They asked what we were going to do with them. I said we were going to use them for a video recording. It cost us 4,000 Swedish kronor, and we spent an entire day putting them in the CD cases."

But he doubts anyone who bought the album actually heeded the call.

"Not to my knowledge, at least. We mostly did it because I felt we needed a special marketing strategy. And we sold 2,700 copies of the album, which wouldn't have been possible today. Two years later, the entire label went to hell."

In an email, IT wants to know why we only want to speak to him about Abruptum. He points out that he's also been active in bands such as Ophthalamia, Vondur, War, and most recently 8th Sin.

When we reach IT over the phone, he speaks with surprising candor for a person with a near-mythical history. However, he doesn't want us to reveal his birth name. He has some difficulty in remembering details concerning the Abruptum studio sessions, as he says he entered a trance state during the recordings.

"My memories are only small, fragmented images or sensations of chaos, hatred, darkness, and blood."

IT was born in 1972 and grew up with a hard-working mother, who had four children, three jobs, and an alcoholic, physically abusive husband. He never met his own father. He mentions how early experiences of domestic violence left him with deep emotional scars and how he always felt like an observer. How he would behold the world from outside, without participating in it.

"I think a lot comes down to me being so young when my mother was abused, how I couldn't help her and felt powerless because of it."

As the years went by, he came to regard himself as increasingly different. He had difficulty finding someone who could relate to him, and he gradually felt less and less human. He adopted the name IT, which he's stuck to since.

He first harmed himself at about 12 years old. He remembers being excited by the experience.

"I've always been a very self-destructive individual, so of course, I've harmed myself even outside of Abruptum. I still cut myself on occasion. I can't really say why."

Since childhood, he's had depression lurking beneath the surface. Above all, it manifests itself in suicidal thoughts. He's been on disability support his whole adult life, after being diagnosed with panic disorder. Still, he says he's feeling better these days.

"I feel in control over who I am and what I want. Instead of taking antidepressants and going in and out of the mental hospital, as I used to, I practice meditation, shamanism, and martial arts."

But his views on humanity and the world haven't changed to any great extent since his youth.

"I guess I feel like I always have—that mankind is a fucking virus. A cancerous cyst spreading from one place to another. Once we've killed everything in one location, we move on to the next and bring ruin there too. At the same time, we are the antivirus ourselves, since we'll ultimately bring about our own destruction."

IT mentions his Native American heritage. His biological father was Apache and came to Sweden in the early '70s after spending some time in Morocco. His mother met him one day at Stockholm Central Station. She was eating a hot dog in between her two jobs.

"He walked up to her, threw the hot dog in a wastebasket, and took her out to a proper dinner."

He has no idea what happened to his father.

"I've heard he was run over by the subway and died. But since he was an illegal immigrant in Sweden, there was no proper investigation as to whether it was actually him, or if it was just an accident, or if he ended up there some other way. At the time, my mother was married to one of several men who beat her. I think my father was a glimmer of light to her, somewhat of a guardian angel."

An angel it didn't end well for.

"No, but that's usually the case. Just look at Lucifer."

One of the texts in the New Testament speaks of a meeting between Jesus and a man living among the graves, who was harming his body by cutting himself with sharp stones.

In contemporary studies of the phenomenon, the typical self-harmer has been female. Some experts have gone so far as to connect the behavior to the female sex. The Swedish book *Hål i huden—kvinnor som skär sig* (Holes in the Skin—Women Who Cut Themselves) by psychotherapist Per Wallroth describes a depressed woman suffering from amenorrhea, a complete loss of menstruation, who slices her arms in an attempt to recreate her menstrual bleeding.

In 2009, a survey of 1,000 young people in southern Sweden caught the attention of the media. The study showed one out of four people around 15 years of age had harmed themselves at least once. And for the first time, self-harm behavior among young boys was also proven more common than previously believed.

At a Watain concert in Linköping, we meet Emelie Zorsha, a woman in her 30s who turns out to be part of a circle within the Swedish black metal scene where ritual bloodletting is an everyday reality. Also, she belongs to a sexual minority engaged in what is called bloodplay: cutting one another as part of sexual foreplay. She claims this is a pretty big thing in the black metal scene.

"Both Christianity and many nature religions regard blood as something sacred," Emelie explains. "We still celebrate it through Communion to this day. To me, that's what bloodplay is about: a man prepared to bleed for me, to allow his life and the sacred liquid to come pouring out. It's not difficult making someone else bleed—but if you choose to bleed yourself, then you've given the most intimate of gifts."

She was 16 when she made a man bleed in a sexual situation for the first time. Her fascination with sharp objects developed, and she started collecting knives. For a while, she had a romantic relationship with Shining bass player Johan Hallander. She remembers it as a "fun time."

"It was like 'Shall we break in the new knife tonight?'"

Zorsha says she was one of the first ravers in Sweden and that the rave culture continues to be a big influence in her life. What she likes most about it is the escape from reality.

"Most of the things that amuse me are as far from reality as possible. I don't read any newspapers or watch the news, and I only read books dealing with horror, science fiction, fantasy, and fairy tales. I find reality too painful to want to be a part of it."

She tells us she's a member of several charity organizations, but their publications always go straight into her recycling bin, unread.

"I absolutely do not want to find out anything more about what's going to hell in the world. Because I would shoot myself the next day. It feels so hopeless when you've worked in a grocery store, and you know that what you recycle in a month is what they throw away in an hour. Still, you have to do it. You can't just stop giving a fuck about everything."

Emelie suggests that psychiatric disorders aside, there are many different reasons why people cut themselves. Most of these can be found within the black metal scene.

"Perhaps it's about time that guys become a bit destructive and turn their negativity toward themselves, instead of the surrounding world. Cutting yourself used to be more of a girl thing."

Zorsha has known Niklas Kvarforth for many years and describes him as very special.

"He's actually one of the most enigmatic people I've ever met. He likes to shock. And sure, I know a lot of what he does is for effect. On the other hand, he's cut himself alone at home so many times too. He's absolutely covered in scars."

She points out that she is not the cause of the thick, worm-like scars on Johan Hallander's forearms.

"They're slicing him up on stage now. When I cut him, I'd take care of the scars, tape up the wounds, and make sure they only ended up as thin lines. The band doesn't care, not when they're out drinking afterwards. On the last tour, he had to go get stitched up twice."

Kim Carlsson of Lifelover wears knee-high black boots, stretch jeans, and just a faded black hoodie, despite the temperature being below freezing. He says he likes to shiver.

It's been two weeks since the Shining gig in Oslo, where he cut himself on stage and then allowed Niklas Kvarforth to go at him with a scalpel. The plan was for Kvarforth to cut the word "Shining" on Kim's back, in commemoration of the band's tenth anniversary. He's pleased with his efforts, despite having been dragged off stage by the promoter. After all, he made people uncomfortable.

"Crying girls warm my heart. It's so miserable, beautiful, and innocent. You reach inside and touch them; it's a nice feeling."

Kim talks about cutting himself as part of becoming whole, but he doesn't want to analyze it too much. He says that everyone he knows has cut themselves at least once. He started six years ago, to see what it looked like underneath his skin. He was surprised by how good the pain felt. And then he couldn't stop.

"There are so many ways to harm yourself—so many different items to hurt yourself with. It's like I can't help myself from trying everything out. I can choose to suffer, and I like it. This is something that's developed over the years. It started when I was younger, and I've always been quite antisocial."

Kim began listening to black metal when he was 11. The music gave him a feeling of mental cold and resignation toward everything in existence. He wanted to get away from other people, from their breathing, their bodies, and their whole existence. The best way of listening to black metal, he says, is alone in the forest on a cold winter night, with only the landscape and darkness as company.

"Excluded from everything and left alone in an empty space. I love it. Striving for everything that is out of the ordinary. Beyond society, beyond mankind."

He makes music under the moniker Hypothermia and runs a record label called Insikt (insight). He releases albums with the Umeå band Woods of Infinity, among others.

Kim's coworkers sometimes talk about young women who cut themselves. None of them have seen his arms, since he's always wearing long sleeves.

"So, I'm sitting there next to them, all sliced up, listening to them talk about women cutting themselves as an act of rebellion against parents and society, showing how they can take control over their lives. It's true to a certain extent but has nothing to do with me."

During the Shining gig in Stockholm, Kim shared his bloody razor blades. He says others cut themselves with them and smeared themselves in his blood. It wasn't until afterward that they asked him if he had any diseases. But he says he doesn't.

"Not besides the psychiatric ones."

His mental status has been subject to evaluation for a long time. But he has yet to receive a diagnosis.

"They're dragging the assessment out and keep finding new things all the time. 'This guy has most of them' was the first thing they said. But surely, you can't have everything."

Four years ago, he got a female friend to start listening to Shining. Since then, she's tried taking her own life several times. Kim says she was influenced by the band's message in at least one of her suicide attempts. He has no problems with that. Instead, he supports her choice.

"I don't particularly care if people live or die. Everyone deserves to die to some extent; everyone is contributing to someone else's misery in some way."

We point out how everyone also contributes to someone else's happiness.

"Of course, that's the beautiful contradiction."

Professor Jan Beskow is a specialist in psychiatry and social medicine and has worked with suicide studies and prevention since the late '60s. He's the author of several books on the subject, including *Suicidalitetens språk* (The Language of Suicide) from 2005, which is now course literature at several universities and colleges. Beskow believes that the terminology of suicide needs to be developed in order to further prevent it. He says people in general have merely three words to use: suicide, suicide attempt, and suicidal thoughts.

"Most are afraid to speak about it at all. Since suicide is so individual, such a limited vocabulary is insufficient. Those who sink into depression have no language to handle emotions about wanting to kill themselves. If we had a richer and more nuanced language with which to speak about suicide, we could achieve so much more."

According to Beskow, most people engaged in self-harm seek to counter their anxiety.

"When sufficiently frightened, people often enter a form of dissociative state in which they don't feel alive. They turn completely stiff. And when cutting themselves, they discover how it doesn't seem to hurt. And so, they cut deeper and deeper. The closer they get to the veins, the thought is raised: 'Why, look, I can die.' They reestablish contact with their selves and can come back emotionally."

The feeling can even be perceived as a means of survival. But Beskow points out that self-harm behavior, just like alcohol and drugs, soon becomes a habit and thus increasingly risky. Suddenly, the feeling isn't as strong, and so you have to cut deeper. Visible self-harm often attracts the long-awaited attention and sympathies from the surrounding world, which is also dangerous.

"They are suddenly taken care of by people and given attention, which spreads the behavior. It's important to be careful when committing such patients to the psych ward, because they contaminate others and cause a lot of additional problems."

On the other hand, Beskow says that for many, the thought of suicide can be comforting.

"It's a way out. 'The thought of suicide is a great consolation: By means of it, one gets through many a dark night,' a philosopher once said."

Beskow is well acquainted with the prevalent glorification of suicide in some subcultural currents. He even has a term for it.

"It could be regarded as a placeholder for death. A lot of people have suicidal thoughts but can't bring themselves to follow through. And then there's a general psychological law, saying it feels good when others carry out what you would like to do yourself."

He mentions several websites where visitors are incited to commit suicide, and he claims they have contributed to speeding up the suicidal process. What could take years now might happen in a week or a few days.

"It's a risk factor for troubled youths with psychiatric disorders. You could almost see it a form of unlawful incitement. People are encouraged to commit severely destructive acts."

When it comes to the methods of different metal bands—using music, lyrics, and imagery to induce suicidal urges in the listener—Beskow's research implies they can be efficient. He speaks of an English study where suicidal tendencies were induced in a laboratory.

"They used sad music. You could also show sad movies or talk about tragic things. When this has been done in a clinical setting, even healthy people have become dismal. Luckily, it passes quickly for them, but people with a history of depression and suicidal thoughts, on the other hand, get these urges back. Music can be used to promote all kinds of things. Suicide as well, of course."

———

When we travel to Halmstad to meet Niklas Kvarforth again, it's a warm day in June 2006. The gangly man waiting for us on the couch of the Scandic Hallandia hotel lobby looks almost ridiculously young, despite being 23 years old. He wears red Puma sneakers, jeans ripped at the knees, and a white long-sleeved shirt with a Shining design. At closer inspection, his mousy buzz cut appears to be an emerging mohawk. The reception staff glance at his arms, zebra-striped with scars and red gashes.

Niklas shakes our hands and asks if the journey from Stockholm went well. The hostile character we spoke to in Stockholm seven months earlier is long gone.

It's been a little over a week since he called to ask about the story we were working on. He claims the reason why he didn't contact us before is that he rarely checks his email.

Niklas has invited us to spend a full day with him and the band in Halmstad. He says people have "strong fucking tendencies" to misinterpret the element of suicide in the lyrics and imagery of the band.

"Suicide is a theme we used in two songs on the first album and one on the second. Really, which band hasn't done that, regardless of genre?"

When our conversation touches upon the suicide song "Gloomy Sunday," Niklas's eyes light up.

"You could say it was the equivalent of Nine Inch Nails' song 'Hurt' of its time. Listening to it cuts through your body, like a bullied ninth-grader hearing [Swedish pop band] Kent for the first time."

His west coast accent shines through as he mentions that things haven't been going too well with his partner, Angela, and their relationship. He moved out six months ago. He tells us he's been unable to put the relationship behind him emotionally and that he's been "highly receptive" to things lately. We're also told that bass player Johan Hallander was released from the psych ward a few days ago. The band's new guitarist, Peter Huss, also manages an Airsoft battle simulation field called Unreal Steel, where prospective bodyguards come to shoot at each other with plastic projectiles via replica weapons.

"He's obsessed with all things military and is a pretty strange person. Probably the most disturbed out of all of us."

Niklas asks if we're hungry and says there's food available in the hotel lobby. We get pasta salads and ask if he wants something.

"No, thanks, I'm on a diet," he says patting his almost concave belly with an ironic smirk. A while later, he mentions having to go collect money, as he hasn't had any for several weeks. He's still in financial ruin since Selbstmord Services, his record label, went bankrupt.

Niklas starts going through the agenda of the day. He says he'd like to barbecue later, how the scent of cooking meat is one of the few things that brings him satisfaction.

"I thought we'd head out to the beach, to get some sense of accomplishment this summer. After all, you're in the city of three hearts. The most beautiful city in the world!"

Soon, we walk northward along the main street. Niklas says his goal is for Halmstad to be associated with local hero Per Gessle, Roxette guitarist and vocalist, in the daytime, and with Niklas Kvarforth at night. He borrows 100 kronor from us to buy cigarettes in a store. We're on our way to Johan Hallander, who has moved into Niklas's old apartment.

"Or Johanna, as I call him. He's not worthy of being called anything else. What's interesting about him is that he wants to be miserable. He's like a tiny marionette."

The day before yesterday, the two of them went to Niklas's former brother-in-law Pierre's house. The plan was to celebrate the emotionally volatile bass player's birthday. It all got out of hand when Pierre suddenly attacked Johan with his fists and Johan's stitched-up self-inflicted injuries tore open.

"Five minutes later, there was blood all over the living room floor," Niklas says, while pointing out he doesn't have such violent relationships with all of his bandmates.

"I have a wonderful bond with our drummer Ludde. He calms me down."

Preferably, he'd like to keep the drummer out of interviews so as to not cause any problems.

"He has kids, and his ex-girlfriend is very worried. I fully understand that. There's nothing especially controversial about his other band, Spiritual Beggars. They're a much better band than Shining, though. Really annoying, but that's how it is. The ironic thing is that many of the lyrics on their first album are about my ex-girlfriend, since she used to date their vocalist. 'Angel of Betrayal' is one of them."

He then tells us of a conversation he once had with Jan Axel "Hellhammer" Blomberg while he was in the band.

"I said, 'After what you've been through in Mayhem, one singer shooting himself and a bass player murdering the guitarist, it must be pretty relaxing for you to play with Shining.' He said Shining was much worse."

Niklas grins and turns onto a back street leading away from the city center.

"I believe that if you get involved in Shining, you destroy a big part of your life. Johan Hallander, who we'll be meeting soon, is a perfect example of this."

Johan lives in a beige apartment building, a 5-minute walk from the main street. Niklas looks up at a window on the second floor and shouts the bass player's name. He says there's a door code, but the landlord refuses to share it with them, citing an increased risk of burglaries.

The door opens, and Johan Hallander lets us in. He's wearing flared jeans and a black T-shirt. His long brown hair is all over the place, and he looks like he just got out of bed. Niklas asks how he's doing. The bass player mumbles an incomprehensible reply.

The floor of the studio apartment is full of empty beer cans and scattered album covers. A couch is standing against one wall. Johan immediately sits down and lights up a cigarette. Along the opposite wall, there's a stereo setup with two gigantic speakers. Niklas is fidgeting with a pair of nunchaku he's found on the windowsill.

Johan's arms are badly bruised by cuts in various stages of healing. Just below his right shoulder, there's a fresh scar so big, it looks like someone's taken an axe to him.

In an alcove, someone has written the word "*tomhet*" (emptiness) in blood with large letters on the wall, a remnant of yet another party that went sideways. In the bookshelf, there's a book called *Häxkonst* (Witchcraft). There's a period of unnerving quiet— Hallander is clearly not well, and we find it hard coming up with something appropriate to say. We flip absently through the witch book. Page 16 contains a recipe for the "soup of hell." "Fucking killer band name," Kvarforth comments. The library card pocket says it belongs to a high-school library in the Stockholm suburb of Farsta and was due back in October 1998.

Hallander seems genuinely surprised when we ask how he's doing.

"How I'm doing? Not too good at the moment. I've been committed for a while and was only released the day before yesterday. I've been institutionalized from time to time. For depression and so on."

Niklas giggles by the window, saying something about how wonderful it is that you're shaped by your own actions. Hallander sighs.

"I went there and had myself committed by my own accord. Just look at my arms. It's quite easy to get admitted when they look like this."

He says his condition this time around was better than when he's ended up in the mental hospital before. Back then, he had actually tried to kill himself.

"But I don't do that any longer. Really, the only thing I do now is ..."

"Living the life," the vocalist at the window interjects.

"Yes, exactly, living the life. But sometimes that gets taken a bit too far. And then you might need a little help getting back on track. There's hell, and there's purgatory. Hell is when it's really rough. Purgatory is right now, when we sit here."

Hallander says there are many sides to his self-harm behavior. When he lost his virginity, the girl he was with accidentally broke his nose. He realized he found sexual pleasure in bleeding. Shining, on the other hand, gives him spiritual pleasure.

"Shining's music meant a lot to me even before I started playing in the band. I bought the first single when it was released. The music speaks to me in a way that most other music doesn't. It creates a certain mind frame of hatred, sorrow, and depression."

In the stairwell on the way out, the two talk about when they tried to create a pillow room from empty bag-in-box wine containers. And about that night when the word "emptiness" was written in blood on the wall. A member of the black metal band Malign was visiting. According to Niklas, he cut himself, ate his own flesh, and drank three glasses of his own blood. We point out that this sounds a bit hard to believe.

"Yes, but he started acting really strange afterward too."

On the way to our car, Niklas insists on stopping for ice cream. The sun is shining and there's a line to the counter.

"Can you smell that? The scent of the most wonderful city in the world," says Niklas.

We argue that he's really a form of an antithesis to everything the quaint coastal town of Halmstad stands for.

"But it's the contrast that makes it so good. It's magical. That's what makes me stay on track, because I don't see all that much shit here as opposed to when I lived in Stockholm. If I had stayed there, I probably would have wrecked myself with heroin."

Niklas asks if we've read Stig Dagerman and proceeds to praise the author, who, according to him, also hated Stockholm. He's very fond of Nobel Prize laureate Pär Lagerkvist, especially his novel *The Dwarf* from 1944.

"It should really have been called 'He who wants to push the button to wipe the world out in two seconds.' I don't think you could find a more concise explanation of the concept of misanthropy than that book."

Niklas says most people who call themselves misanthropes haven't understood the meaning of the word.

"Misanthropy isn't exclusively about humans but a sheer hatred for life in all forms. How can you claim to be a hater of life and humans and at the same time love nature? Nature is the primary whore, the original harlot," he says between mouthfuls of ice cream.

On the way to Niklas's apartment to meet the rest of the guys, we make a stop at a post office where Niklas needs to pick up an envelope. He talks nonstop in the car and has an almost pathological tendency to churn out spectacular metal gossip. At the moment, he's talking about people in the '90s black metal scene in Stockholm. Niklas started hanging out in those circles when he was only 13.

"There was this girl called Maria who later killed herself. Maria hated just about everything. She was in the middle of a phone call with a friend when saying, 'Nope, this is no fun any longer.' Then she hung up and shot herself. She was completely fucked in the head after having dated Holocausto, the vocalist of Beherit from Finland. He was a real fucking pervert. Do you know what he did? He sharpened his teeth and ate the flesh of his own arm while he was recording vocals!"

We leave the car in a shaded parking lot outside a small shopping mall. Niklas is off to do his errand. Johan Hallander sits in the backseat by himself. He says his first album was *Wings of Tomorrow* by Europe. He bought it at a flea market when he was five years old.

His first really heavy album was Merciless' *The Awakening*.

"My father was a metalhead. He played all the Whitesnake classics—to this day the best band in the world, in my opinion."

He says he's made three suicide attempts. The first time was three years ago. The second one was just before he moved from Stockholm to Halmstad. The third was during a recent tour, when he walked out into a heavily trafficked street in Milan.

"I was exhausted, that's all," he says about the latest incident.

"The other times it was for reasons too personal to discuss. I sincerely doubt I'd do it again."

He says his suicide attempts have nothing to do with Shining.

"The only band to have ever made me hurt myself was Abruptum."

At 12, he listened to one of the band's albums in his room. He smashed his head into the wall for the entire duration of the record. Still to this day, he has no idea why. His parents weren't home. Two years later, he cut himself for the first time. He adds how he's always liked putting out cigarettes on his body and has about 200 burn scars on his arms and chest. Johan shows a scar from Hungary, when Niklas punctured one of his veins. He says it was "like a fountain of blood."

"As I mentioned before, part of my sexuality is that I like blood. That's why I think it can be an appropriate aspect of the aesthetics. For the spectator. I'd do anything for art. I'd be willing to die on stage."

So, what do his parents think about the fact that he cuts himself and plays in a band with antihuman sentiments?

His father supports him, he says, but his mother doesn't like it at all. He grew up with both his parents, but whether that was a good thing is up for discussion. When we ask what he thinks of Kvarforth hurting fans during shows, his voice grows harder.

"I support this fully. I think humanity is repulsive. I despise egoism above all, how people turn away instead of seeing what the world looks like. Say you're standing outside Pub Anchor in Stockholm. You pass by the park next to McDonald's, where people deal drugs. Fifty feet away, some guy is beating his girlfriend. At the bus station, there's a gang of immigrants assaulting an old lady because she won't give them her handbag. You refuse to see this. Or you see it but keep walking, thinking it's none of your business. You think, 'Everything is great. I'm strolling around here, enjoying life,' instead of opening your eyes and embracing what's going on around you."

Johan Hallander doesn't think it's relevant that the members of Shining engage in the same kind of behavior he's just described: assaulting the audience, doing drugs, and glorifying violence, both privately and at concerts.

"I'm just saying that you have to realize that a great many things are wrong with this world. I think a lot of people live in a bubble. I don't see any light whatsoever."

Kvarforth's place turns out to be a three-bedroom apartment in one of Halmstad's less prosperous suburbs. On a shelf in the hallway, his passport lies next to a nylon stocking given to him by a female bartender in Holland.

Guitarist Peter Huss has joined us. Peter is heavyset with shoulder-length dark brown hair and is wearing a shirt featuring fellow Halmstad residents Vile Scar. Niklas immediately offers a flurry of ironic comments.

"You have to support the local scene! Stay in the good books of your tough Satanist pals. Keep it within the brotherhood, so to speak."

He invites us to sit down by the low glass table in front of the small television in the living room. Niklas wants to show us a few video clips. The TV is currently showing a dark-haired young woman massaging his shoulders after a gig in Hamburg.

"I talked her into it. Her boyfriend wasn't too happy about it. And the Norwegians we were touring with, Urgehal, were really jealous."

Niklas fast-forwards. The TV shows Johan Hallander backstage somewhere in the Netherlands. He's cut his forehead and is cleaning the blood from his bass. In a different clip, Hallander's arms are covered with fresh cuts so big, they look like gaping mouths.

The DVD begins to skip. Niklas calls the DVD player a whore and says he hates it.

"In that case, I'd be happy to take it home again," Hallander says.

"In that case, I'd be happy to knock your teeth out," Niklas answers.

We try to interview Peter Huss in the bedroom, but Niklas is now playing the new Celtic Frost album at deafening volume. We ask him to turn it down.

Peter tells us he's currently unemployed and that he's not really running Unreal Steel.

"But I'm a bit involved, you could say."

Does he recognize Niklas Kvarforth's description of the band as "the stronghold of destructivity?" He says he hasn't quite gotten into it yet and that he didn't know anything about the band when he joined.

"The only thing I knew was that Ludde played with them."

Peter describes himself as an "average guy." He has no direct opinions about Shining's message.

"Not really. If the rest of the band want to do it, it's fine by me. It's not my concern what they get up to. I do my thing, and they do theirs."

What's his stance then on the possibility of Niklas's intentions being successful: getting young, healthy human beings to harm themselves?

"The question is if they're really all that healthy to begin with."

Huss goes quiet, and the only sounds are minor chords from an acoustic guitar Niklas is playing on the other side the bedroom door. He says he finds the band's fans to be strange and extreme. How some of them appear to be "completely fucking obsessed"— he can't hang with people like that.

Niklas comes in and sits on the bed. A wasp buzzes past the open ventilation window. The vocalist looks pale and says something about being petrified of wasps and all kinds of bugs.

We present him with Professor Jan Beskow's conclusion, how the most important tool in the fight against suicide is to break the silence around the topic. What's Niklas's take on the possibility of his suicide-oriented lyrics actually doing more good than harm? He sounds like a politician when he delivers his answer.

"It's a shame, but nothing I can do much about, unfortunately. Had it been possible, then I would have. For instance, I can always hope Johan will one day do the right thing and slice his wrists up."

Niklas claims fans of Shining have killed themselves as a result of their message and that he is happy about it.

"Of course. That means we've accomplished something that theoretically shouldn't be possible for an individual just sitting down to write some music. I believe it's the result of me putting my very soul into it, and this has in turn soiled the music. And people have absorbed this on a personal level. That's why it's gone as far as it has."

You can joke about the paradox in wishing the life out of your fans, we tell him. After all, if they're gone, there will be no one left to buy the albums.

"Yeah, yeah. But everything is a paradox. For example, sitting here talking about how good it is that people harm themselves to our music. When in reality, it's shit."

Kvarforth shifts perspective and starts speaking about himself in the third person.

"Perhaps Niklas doesn't really want this. Because it hurts him just as much. He might not die from it, but it soils his soul. Hurting yourself and hurting others is the exact same thing."

Niklas looks at us intently. We ask him what diagnosis he's been given. He says that he's been found chronically manic depressive with aggressive tendencies.

"They also claim I'm a schizophrenic, but I don't agree with that at all. I don't take any medication whatsoever. They bring my thought protocols to a halt and ruin every-thing for me. The medicine doesn't help; it only alleviates the symptoms. And those who prescribe it usually have no idea what they're doing, mental disorders being so individual."

Niklas says he found himself in free-fall shortly after the move from Stockholm. The darkness around him had become too much. Then he met Angela. In the relationship with her, he found temporary salvation. He says he owes her a lot today.

"When they came into my life, I was dying. Without Angela and her daughter, I would never have survived—I guarantee it. I would have gone all in on the heroin or blown my head off. I had no future prospects at all. But then I met a woman who could punch me in the face and throw bicycles at me. I was schooled in a way. I'm still young; I have a lot to learn.

The doomsday themes from the living room stereo mix with the buzzing of the wasp, which has now made its way inside. Niklas gives the window a concerned look and says he's not feeling too well. He hasn't eaten anything today. It's time for that barbecue.

At the grocery store, Niklas grabs a rack of ribs and a packet of white napkins with red hearts on them.

"Huss!" he shouts when it's time to pay at the register. The guitarist pulls out his wallet. Ludwig Witt waits behind the wheel of a red Mazda in the parking lot outside. Niklas sits in the passenger seat. He rolls down the window, gnaws the meat off one rib, and then throws it out. We drive down to Östra Stranden beach, where Witt fires up the disposable grill.

"When do you put the hot dogs on?" Huss asks.

"We are suicide black metal—we do whatever the fuck we want," Kvarforth replies.

Five minutes later, he curses his burnt, black hot dog. He says he's so hungry, he could kill someone.

Two months later, the Gates of Metal festival in Hultsfred has reached its final, trembling hours. On stage, HammerFall finish their set with the song "Hearts on Fire," with the national female curling team as backup singers. The track was the official song of the team for the 2006 Winter Olympics. Erik "Tyrant" Gustafsson is in the beer tent, shouting that he is a Bolshevik. Jan Axel Blomberg gives a toast to some of the nine-man-strong crew traveling with Mayhem. Most of them had the task of decorating the stage with slaughterhouse waste. Two hours earlier, Mayhem had finished their set. Hungarian vocalist Attila Csihar wore a mask made from a sliced-off pig's face, and his singular vocal performance puts most of the competition to shame.

Jan Axel is worried, though. A few days ago, he received a phone call from Niklas.

"He sounded really down and said he feared for his life. He was supposed to meet us here at the festival and come with us to Norway, but I'm still waiting for him to return my call. I fear for the worst."

He says it has to do with Niklas's former partner. That her bodybuilding brothers are out to get him.

It doesn't take long for the internet rumor mill to start churning. Could it really be that the band's frontman has finally suffered the utmost consequence of his message? On the Swedish alternative online community Helgon.net, the discussion thread on the subject is soon shut down. Most of the posts are frustrated. Someone with the handle "Selbstmord" (Suicide) from Stockholm writes, "Stop starting these discussion threads," and refers to the band's manager, while "Hängsnara" (Noose) from Solna writes: "I really don't understand what you want to achieve with these constant referrals to the band's mouthpiece. Is it difficult to answer yes or no to the question if he's alive or not?"

After four weeks, the band's manager, Conny Jarlestål, publishes the following message on the band's website:

> *A couple of days ago, we received a letter from a person very close to Kvarforth telling us that Kvarforth has decided to leave this world behind, and has, as a kind of last act, introduced a new singer to replace him for future events of Shining. All that we know for 200% is that Kvarforth has been missing for the past 4 weeks and might be dead we don't really know… for us, the band, this comes as no surprise as he has been suffering from extreme anxiety and depressions the past 6 months, and some truly extreme things, considering his own personal life, occurred dramatically right before he disappeared. However, we wish to send our deepest regrets to our friend and sadistic leader Kvarforth wherever he might be!*

On Helgon.net, the final digital traces of Kvarforth remain online. The sentence "I was born alone, I lived alone, and I died alone" was put on his personal page the week he disappeared. On the discussion forum, speculation runs rampant about what's really happened. Some think that he's retired to an island in the South Pacific, in order to play volleyball with girls in bikinis. Others claim to have seen his dead body. Within the inner circles of the scene, most people are skeptical regarding the claim that he has taken his own life.

We reach Conny Jarlestål over the phone when Niklas Kvarforth has been gone for two months. He describes the time around the disappearance as nightmarish.

"Fans from all over the world had gotten hold of my phone number and called at all hours of the day. I received around 300 emails per day."

People from Germany, Hungary, Bolivia, and China got in touch, wanting to know what happened to the vocalist.

"At the same time, I was hounded by both the band and label, as they were wondering what was going on, since I was the last person who saw him."

Conny Jarlestål says that he constantly receives reports of Kvarforth's body having turned up, everywhere from Romania to northern Africa, and he suggests fans should get a life instead of calling him.

After the disappearance, it's been left to him to deal with everything regarding the release of the new album, entitled *Halmstad*.

He says the album is being prefaced by a concert at Diezel in Halmstad. It will be the first gig with the band's new vocalist, Ghoul. He doesn't want to reveal who's behind the pseudonym but emphasizes that it's not Kvarforth. The new vocalist is from Hungary.

We ask if we should pass anything on to Niklas, should we run into him.

"I don't know. Punch him in the face!"

On February 3, 2007, we return to Halmstad. The taxi driver dropping us off outside, Diezel says that we're lucky. It's the prettiest day so far, in a winter with dismal weather.

The sign above the entrance is just as gaudily colorful as one would expect from an alcohol-free rock club operated by the city's department of culture. It's hard to imagine a more ironic theatre for this evening's attraction. Shining, despite its band leader gone missing, have managed to finalize a new album and are celebrating with a concert meant as an introduction of the new vocalist, Ghoul.

Conny Jarlestål is a short guy with a dark prison buzz cut. The sleeves of his black sweatshirt are rolled up, displaying the tattoos on his forearms. He speaks with a virulent intensity despite being visibly exhausted.

"This is definitely the last time I ever organize a concert," he says.

Asked if the preparations have gone well, he answers with a decided "No."

"One of the supporting acts were two hours late. The other band's bus broke down in Gothenburg. And when they finally made it to Halmstad, they got lost. As a result, one of the supports have to play after Shining, since drummer Ludwig Witt has two gigs booked for the evening. Immediately following this show, he has to drive to Gislaved and play with Mathias Holmgren from the dance band Barbados."

When speaking of attendance numbers, he sounds significantly more enthusiastic.

"We have people coming from Switzerland, Germany, and Denmark. And from Norway, since I'm organizing the concert with someone who's from there. We have marketed it in our respective countries."

A few hours later, February darkness covers Halmstad. The first signs of what's about to go down this evening appear. A cluster of ghostly figures hang around the fast-food grill. They all wear black clothes, drink cheap beer, and slowly drift down the street. Outside Diezel, the queue is already growing long, and it's not even 7 p.m. yet. Some people have read online that doors were supposed to open at 6. Everyone is growing restless as the harsh cold finds its way through thin sneakers and denim jackets with Bathory back patches.

"I've heard of people being trampled in queues but never of anyone freezing to death," says a young man who's come all the way from Östersund in the north of Sweden.

Speculation about Ghoul's identity has been running rife up until now. Even in the queue to Diezel, many hope for Halmstad's most unlikely rock hero to return.

Ingela and Natalia, both 16, are convinced that Ghoul is actually Niklas Kvarforth.

"It even said so in the local newspaper *Hallandsposten*," says Ingela. "My sister partied with Attila Csihar and Nattefrost at their hotel last night, and they also said that Kvarforth is Ghoul."

"Niklas is funny," she continues. "He used to have a record store here in Halmstad. I remember going there once when I was 13 or 14. 'Do you want to hear real black metal?' he said. 'Yes,' I replied. Then he played Kent at full volume."

The girls are both in ninth grade and say one of their teachers recommended the Shining gig to the class.

"She said, 'I hope you're going to Shining tonight!'" Ingela says, laughing.

She adds that the teacher might not fully understand what the band stands for. Natalie has her own term for depressive metal with suicidal themes.

"To me, it's cuddly toy music. Listening to it when feeling sad is like hugging something warm and soft."

On stage, final preparations for Norwegian supporting act Dødheimsgard are underway. Two roadies fold out a black sheet with three sixes in an angular font and hang it on the wall behind the drum kit. The Dødheimsgard members enter the stage. One of the guitarists has painted his entire upper body white and is completely bald except for some strands of hair on his neck. The vocalist is short with a buzz cut and has painted his entire upper body red.

"He looks like the head of a dick!" a Halmstad resident in bullet belt and denim jacket comments.

Dødheimsgard grab their instruments and put on a showcase of black metal, focusing more on melody than aggression. In the third song, the sheet with the three sixes falls off the wall.

If the average Dødheimsgard's Norwegian supporter seems to be around 26, local Shining fans appear to be at least 10 years younger. The event is an all-ages show, and lethargic teenagers sit in worn-out sofas with multicolored patterns in the cafeteria. The youth center atmosphere would have been perfectly completed with milk and cookies, but the only thing sold in the bar is Shining albums.

Up front, Natalie and Ingela have disappeared among leather jackets and long manes. A bit further back in the audience, we spot Emelie Zorsha getting her digital camera ready. Along the side of the stage, friends of the main attraction have lined up. Among the recognizable faces, we notice Jørn "Necrobutcher" Stubberud.

To a mournful sound of a muted trumpet, Fredric Gråby, Peter Huss, Ludwig Witt, and Johan Hallander make their way on stage. The audience welcomes them with a roar worthy of a national team having won a championship. The door to Diezel's backstage room is ajar, and a cold light is seeping through the gap. This is the suicide metal's equivalent of Christmas. Time has come to see what's under the tree.

Ludwig Witt makes a quick lead-in, and the band unites in a drawling riff. At that very instant, Mayhem vocalist Attila Csihar rises from a crouched position behind Peter Huss' guitar amp. He wears black makeup around his eyes and his nose and skeleton teeth painted on his lips. His brown hair is in disarray, and he wears a sackcloth bag with only a hole for his hand gripping the microphone. In his simple yet effective stage attire, he looks like a hybrid of a voodoo priest and a character from *The Wizard of Oz*. He stumbles about the stage in spastic movements. He falls to his knees in front of the drums. His vocals are wordless and shift from sobbing to increasingly frenzied shrieks.

A dark shape emerges from the shadows next to the stage, standing by the drum kit with his back turned to the audience. The tall individual is wearing a silk coat with a hood covering the face. Attila kneels and allows himself to be swept into the coat, only to throw himself to the floor in the next second, remaining motionless. The cloaked creature turns to the audience, throwing off the ankle-length costume. The revealed figure has taken the concept of corpse paint to an entirely new level. The skin is deathly pale, flaky, and covered in black spots. The arms look half-rotted. There are small patches of hair on the white head. The black eyes stare out into the audience with a gaze so intensely dark, it's hard to meet it without shuddering.

The figure grabs a microphone, throws his right arm out in a Nazi salute, and says in a calm voice.

"Ein volk, ein reich."

Niklas Kvarforth is back.

Immediately following the gig, bass player Johan Hallander quits the band. Reports of blood and drunkenness on stage result in scandalous tabloid headlines. *Sweden Rock Magazine* asks Niklas if his disappearance wasn't just a cheap marketing ploy.

"Who cares what homo sapiens think?" he answers.

During the late fall of 2008, the band prepares for the release of their new album *Klagopsalmer* (Psalms of Lamentation). *Close-Up Magazine* sends a reporter to the Sahlgrenska University Hospital in Gothenburg. Kvarforth has been treated for manic depression and paranoid schizophrenia there for the past two months. He poses for the camera, sitting in his hospital bed in a small, bleak room with the collected works of Stig Dagerman resting in the windowsill. His new beard is thin and unkempt, and he wears a T-shirt stating, "Born and raised in Knutby." Knutby is a small Swedish community strongly associated with a murder in 2004, where the pastor of a Christian sect brainwashed his young mistress into murdering his wife. Niklas speaks enthusiastically about his new medications. Zyprexa for the hallucinations. Effexor for anxiety. Lithium for his mood swings. Theralen to sleep.

He speaks of a chaotic exile in Norway and about his struggles with amphetamines and heroin. Now he's left both Oslo and his destructive life behind and met the love of his life in his new girlfriend, Helena.

He's accepted the diagnoses he's been given. This in turn has granted him a new, healthier outlook on life as well as a new goal. He wants to start a family. He adds that he still hopes to ruin people's lives, but from a distance and through his music.

Over the years we've worked on this book, misanthropy and suicidal messages have become standard features in the black metal scene. Even Ghost stated in a 2010 interview with *Sweden Rock Magazine* that they work for the annihilation of mankind. This is a testament to the shift in core values that has taken place in the metal genre in recent years.

At the same time, the purely depressive genre has shown impressive vitality. Among all the acts with melancholy and madness as themes, there's Lifelover and Ondskapt from Stockholm and Bloodline from Sundsvall. Internationally, they're joined by names such as the French band Nocturnal Depression and Trist from Czech Republic.

When we visit Niklas Kvarforth again, he resides in a one-room Eskilstuna apartment that he's shared with his partner, Helena, for two years. We arrive around lunchtime on a warm Sunday in May of 2011 and find that the Shining front man has gained weight and suffers from the shakes as a side effect of his psychiatric medication. There's a razor blade on the coffee table in the tidy apartment, but Niklas assures us it's only used to cut up drugs. He shows off his whiskey collection and treats us to a glass of 19-year-old Laphroaig.

Despite giving a significantly calmer and seemingly more harmonic impression, Niklas comes off as frail. After half a bottle of wine and a line of amphetamine, he seems to feel better. He stresses how he's no junkie.

"I only use it in a professional context."

We are told that his disappearance from Halmstad had nothing to do with his ex-girlfriend's bodybuilding brothers.

"I had gotten tangled up with other, significantly more dangerous elements."

About his time in Oslo, he says it went very well to begin with. He found work as a bartender and did such a good job, he was promoted to manager, tasked with everything from booking DJs to organizing work schedules. But then he started doing too many drugs and had to quit.

In order to support his mounting heroin addiction, he says began selling sex to men, something he claims he did for the first time in Stockholm when he was 13.

"How do you think I could afford to start Selbstmord?"

Niklas Kvarforth was born in 1983 and grew up mainly on Södermalm in Stockholm. His parents divorced early, after a stormy relationship ending in domestic abuse. His father is a criminal and has spent time in prison for several violent and drug-related crimes.

"He was in jail with Jon Nödtveidt for a while," says Niklas, and asks Helena to pour him another glass of red wine. His own hands are shaking too much.

His mother had a long career in the entertainment industry, working as a tour manager among other things. In her last years, she had an executive position at Sveriges Television. When Niklas was a child, she dated famed music producer Lasse Lindbom, who gave him a nylon-stringed acoustic guitar. That was Niklas' first instrument.

As if to prove to us that it's true, Niklas calls Lindbom from his cellphone to ask what brand the guitar was. "Yamaha," Lasse answers, somewhat confused over the phone.

Niklas is aware people often think he's lying. He freely admits he has a tendency to exaggerate. However, many of the bizarre things he's told us over the years check out. For example, the rumor that he was a model as a child. He digs around in a box and pulls out the old shots from Swedish modelling agency Stockholmsgruppen. And there he is: eight years old, with a boyish look of mischief.

"Cute, huh?" He says with a smile. "I just wish they gave me more money; my mother spent it all playing bingo. Then again, I got to come along with her and drink hot chocolate."

Only a few years later, as a 12-year-old, he tried amphetamines for the first time. He says he's always had a noise in his head and that he got in trouble in school early. Always looking for new experiences, he got into contact with older men who paid him to watch them masturbate. The practice was first introduced by a 60-year-old moonshine dealer named Kenta. Niklas was 13 years old.

"He wanted to play strip poker and liked being peed in the mouth. He got to watch me masturbate and gave me blowjobs."

Niklas says his self-destructive tendencies made him do it. He knew he was heterosexual but still wanted to force himself to have sex with men, even if, he points out, he never actually fucked them. Through Kenta, Niklas got in touch with other men. He says what transpired left him "perverted" and made him nauseated, but he kept doing it for the money.

"It turned into a form of addiction to the self-destruction."

In the same period, he started hanging out in the black metal crowd, where he soon earned a reputation for having no boundaries.

"I think that's what made them fascinated by me. I cut my back up so deep, I could see my own spine. I took everything to extremes in a way no one else really did."

When we ask him how these early experiences have affected him, he says they turned him into "a mean fucker."

"I think my passion for darkness is the result of all this, even if the choices were mine to make."

Kvarforth refuses to blame his mental state on his childhood. He thinks that's a coward's cop-out. Instead, he goes into a long exposition on the benefits of being subjected to traumatic and terrible things when you grow up. He says that all the shit will leave you better equipped to face the cruelty of the world.

"That's one of the worst things I know of: people blaming their problems on poor upbringings. Of course, my background has contributed to my mental problems. But to say 'I'm this way because of what happened to me' is a cheap way out. I know why I am the way I am."

He says his love for Satan is the real source of his persona. But he won't elaborate on how he's come to that conclusion.

"Satanism is something I won't discuss in the context of Shining at all. It's too personal."

But it's evident that his troubled relationship with his mother has dominated his life. He's often spoken about her in interviews and said they had a very intense and challenging relationship. One moment, he'll describe her as a mother who desperately tried to help her son, moving down to Halmstad to support him. In the next, he says she was mentally unstable and that she hired some bikers to break his kneecaps.

"But we were actually becoming closer again, after all the years of shit. And then she died," he says, looking tired.

There are several pictures of his mother in the apartment, and he's had her name and date of death tattooed on his arm. He mentions being let into the hospital to see her body. She died a few days after Christmas Eve of 2009 from a blood clot in the brain.

"I snapped a picture with my cell phone camera and sent it to Erik in Watain. I thought it might be inspirational to him."

Both Niklas and his partner, Helena, are bipolar. Dating someone with problems similar to his own has forced Niklas to stay focused. He even goes as far as referring to himself as good-hearted lately. He's decided to live with the woman he loves and their two cats. He implies that he'd probably be dead by now if it not for Helena.

"Then I would have pushed everything as far as I could already a year ago, following through on my final plan."

He doesn't want to reveal the details of that plan.

"If I let people know, they'd do everything to stop me."

In the afternoon, we prepare to hit the town. Niklas puts a bottle of Valium and a butterfly knife in Helena's purse and then we're off. He explains that for most of his life, he's lived as a criminal. Someone in his situation always needs to be prepared to defend himself.

"When you represent the things I do, you have to be prepared to make enemies. Honestly, if I didn't have any enemies, I would say I have failed."

We sit down in an outdoor bar along the main street. Niklas is in a good mood and says Shining has recently been presented with an opportunity that few bands could even hope for: a favorable contract with a major record label, with plans to promote the band on a much higher level. Instead of touring with obscure black metal bands, they could now be supporting big mainstream acts. Niklas won't mention any names, as negotiations are still going on. He also tells us the band has a new manager, who's talked him into signing a contract where he promises not to use razors on stage.

"But sometimes, I'll break a bottle and cut myself with that instead. Simply because I look for the kick it gives me."

Niklas hums along to the classic Swedish pop song "Sommartider" (Summertime) and downs a shot of Jägermeister. He has several reasons to be cheerful. The band's latest album, *Född förlorare* (Born Loser), entered the Finnish album charts a few days ago. It has reached the second slot, beaten only by Lady Gaga. The music video of the song "Förtvivlan—min arvedel" (Despair—My Heirloom) has reached 50,000 views on YouTube in a week.

Niklas is well aware that no other band has managed to sell misanthropic metal to the masses.

"But give us six months on a big label, and you'll see."

When we ask him if the depressive black metal phenomenon isn't a peculiar conclusion of a music genre that was initially about happiness and kinship, he agrees.

"But that was in 1980. It is 2011 now."

Shining released the albums Redefining Darkness in 2012, IX – Everyone, Everything, Everywhere, Ends in 2015, and X – Varg utan Flock (Wolf Without A Pack) in 2018.

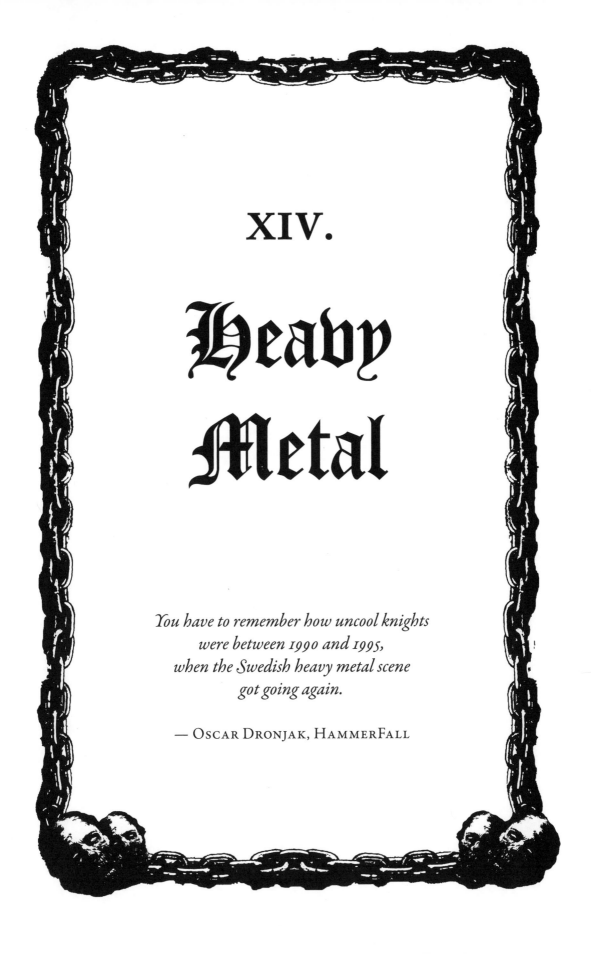

XIV.

Heavy Metal

You have to remember how uncool knights were between 1990 and 1995, when the Swedish heavy metal scene got going again.

— OSCAR DRONJAK, HAMMERFALL

ou would be hard-pressed to label heavy metal as a function of youth culture anymore. From its emergence as a teen movement, the genre has steadily grown more and more popular with music lovers of all ages. Early fans tend to cling to their metal roots as the years progress, while new generations keep discovering the genre in its old-school form and further filling the ranks.

Nowhere is this more abundantly clear than at the Muskelrock (Muscle Rock) festival in the small Swedish village of Blädinge.

The colorful old paintings on the walls of Tyrolen Park's stage look like something out of a children's book. They were created by the artist Sven Truedsson some 50 years ago, when local interest in the venue was at its peak. Families used to watch lighthearted theater here, and on weekend nights, young couples might have danced to the slinky rhythms of a touring jazz orchestra. Tonight, the cheerful images form a surreal frame for Czech heavy metal band Drakar, four men in their 60s who mix croaking growl-vocals with rusty blast beats in a chaotic performance.

The grass fields surrounding the park are filled with tents and trailers. It's a Friday afternoon in mid-June of 2011 and the festival has just kicked into high gear. In a narrow space behind the outdoor stage, Bullet's guitarist, Hampus Klang, is deep in conversation with the band's helper, Staffan Hamrin.

Bullet formed in 2001 in the city of Växjö and have since established themselves as Sweden's reigning champions of '80s-style heavy metal. Since the first Muskelrock in 2009, they've been the resident band of the festival. Tonight, they're determined to outdo themselves and have brought along an alarmingly overpowered pyrotechnic arsenal, considering the low ceiling of the old wooden structure. In front of Hampus and Staffan are two large boards lined with fireworks.

On the other side of the stage wall, Drakar vocalist Ivan Sekyra is shouting in English so shaky, the only decipherable sentence is "We want to tell everybody 'thank you!'" Standing next to the stage is festival manager Jacob Hector, a tall, dark-haired man in his mid-20s. He smiles and tells us that this particular concert is part of a collaboration with the I Hate Records label, having recently rereleased Drakar's old albums.

"We feel this is a fun booking, since it's without a doubt their only chance of ever playing Sweden."

The concert is over and Prague's number one gray-haired draconian quartet are packing up equipment. Bror Alfredo Marcolin, better known in the metal community as Messiah, walks up the narrow path leading to the stage. He's doing a guest appearance later the same night. In the late '80s, he established himself as the monk-attired, doom-dancing vocalist of the Swedish band Candlemass. Nowadays, he works in a gigantic computer server hall outside of Stockholm, while writing material for a solo album.

He wants to show his appreciation and share some supportive words with the members of Drakar. When frontman Ivan walks by with his gig bag, a comically one-sided conversation ensues.

"Hi, I am Messiah! I used to sing with Candlemass. I just want to thank you for a good show!"

The Swede's friendly greeting is met with only a hesitant nod before the Czech continues walking toward the parking lot. When the next band member shows up, Messiah makes a second attempt, once again to be met by a puzzled look. But the large singer won't give up so easily, and soon, he has repeated the same phrase to every member of the band without so much as a reply. Not only are Drakar clearly lacking basic English skills—they seem to suffer from severe hearing loss as well.

A stroll among the tents and RVs outside the park proves that the metal aesthetics of the '70s and '80s are kept alive by older fans, and that they've also been adopted by an entirely new generation.

On the provisionary campgrounds, kids in ruffled shirts and spandex have set up their tents next to middle-aged caravan couples in identical Pentagram shirts. On the two festival stages, '80s acts like Thor from Canada, Finnish veterans Oz, and British four-piece Girlschool play next to significantly younger Swedish heavy metal acts such as Wolf from Örebro, Gothenburg ensemble Helvetets Port, and Portrait from Kristianstad, who successfully try to emulate early Mercyful Fate.

The festival is living proof of the most evident trend in metal over the last decade—the renaissance of classic heavy metal. Genre titans Iron Maiden and Judas Priest once again fill stadiums, and a growing contingent of young fans celebrate the roots of the genre with bands like Black Sabbath, Uriah Heep, Deep Purple—or Pentagram from Arlington, Virginia. Fronted by haggard singer Bobby Liebling, these legends will take the brightly colored stage as main attractions on Friday night.

Not that long ago, studded bracelets and lyrics about dragons were controversial elements in metal, as well as sing-along choruses, extravagant stage clothes, and just about everything else that made kids go crazy about the music in the '80s. This has had major consequences for some of those who are paving the way for the return of heavy metal.

The term "heavy metal" was first used in a musical context in the late '60s. In 1968, American band Steppenwolf sang about "heavy metal thunder" in the song "Born to be Wild," and music critic Barry Gifford of *Rolling Stone* called the music of fellow countrymen Electric Flag a "synthesis of white blues and heavy metal rock." Heavy metal soon became associated with the aggressive hybrid of jazz and blues rock performed by bands such as Black Sabbath, Deep Purple, and Led Zeppelin. Which bands should or should not be categorized as heavy metal has been the subject of constant debate ever since.

In Sweden, the more common expression *hårdrock* (hard rock) was widely used, giving way to the term "heavy metal" with the emergence of The New Wave of British Heavy Metal in the early '80s. The movement inspired countless young kids to pick up instruments and dream of spandex. One of them was Joacim Cans, born in 1970 and growing up in a time when the Swedish magazine *OKEJ* heavily favored visually exciting bands.

At 11, he first heard the British band Saxon's album *Strong Arm of the Law*, and from then on, all of his savings were invested in records from the local radio store in Mora. He would finance his purchases by selling lottery tickets on the city's main street. In the mid-'80s, Cans moved to Gothenburg with his mother and sister. He was first recruited as vocalist and guitar player for Eternity, a speed metal trio inspired by the *Walls of Jericho* album by German band Helloween.

To further develop his voice, he attended the renowned Musician's Institute in Los Angeles—a metal-oriented institution associated with skilled instrumentalists, hair extensions, and exorbitant fees.

The emergence of an alternative music movement, with its epicenter in Seattle, completely redrew the musical world map. Grunge, spearheaded by bands like Nirvana and Soundgarden, lured an entire generation away from metal.

When Cans returned from his musical studies in the U.S. with crushing student loans, he was taken aback.

"There were no metal bands left. People told me, 'Give that up. Grunge is what people want to hear now.' But I wasn't interested in playing music I didn't like."

Former heavy metal giants saw themselves playing smaller venues, as were German bands such as Gamma Ray and Running Wild—proponents of an even more decimated metal scene.

"Iron Maiden came to Gothenburg in 1995 and played Kåren, in front of perhaps 800 people. It might have been sold out, but heavy metal was not in great shape. And no one really thought things would turn around," says Cans.

He decided to drop his musical aspirations. When guitarist Jesper Strömblad called to tell him about a band called HammerFall, Cans hesitantly agreed to play one show. HammerFall had reached the semifinals in a local rock talent show and needed a replacement for their vocalist Mikael Stanne, who was on tour with his other band, Dark Tranquillity.

As Cans opened the door to the rehearsal room, he was greeted by tunes he immediately recognized. Still to this day, he remembers his first verbal exchange with guitar player Oscar Dronjak:

"Stormwitch!"

"You know of them?!"

"Of course, I have all of their albums."

"What? You have *Eye of the Storm*?"

"I most certainly do."

"Hey! Even I don't own that one!"

In the rock band competition, HammerFall were beaten by rap metal group LOK, but Joacim and Oscar had found each other musically.

HammerFall's debut album, *Glory to the Brave*, was released in 1997. As a metal band with clear melodies, in a music scene dominated by black metal and the hip hop-influenced nu metal, the group clearly bucked current trends.

HammerFall played power metal—an offshoot of heavy metal with catchy melodies, high-pitched vocals, and a bombardment of sixteenth notes. The band's image was heavily inspired by knights and fantasy aesthetics, something Dio or Yngwie Malmsteen might have toyed with 10 years earlier but that was hopelessly antiquated by the '90s. This, of course, made the band stick out even more. Oscar Dronjak, who wore the most adventurous stage attire, recalls how some of the audience would laugh as they walked on the stage.

"You have to remember how uncool knights were between 1990 and 1995, when the Swedish heavy metal scene got going again. But we thought it was cool."

The band sang about crusaders, which Dronjak believes to be especially appropriate, since their music has always expressed sentiments of pride.

"And we really were crusaders—for heavy metal! But unlike crusades in history, ours is only positive. We're not forcing our beliefs upon anyone. Our message is: 'If you like it, come hang out with us!'"

The response to *Glory to the Brave* was strong, especially in German metal magazines *Rock Hard* and *Heavy Oder Was?* (Heavy or What?). The band's second album, *Legacy of Kings*, was released one year later and went straight to the German album charts. As people began to realize that HammerFall was a band that was passionate about old heavy metal, Cans noticed how many different types of metal fans voiced their support for them.

"However you choose to look at it—all of the influences in thrash, death, and black metal stem from heavy metal and the '80s. A lot of people thought it was great to see a band make this kind of music work in the late '90s."

When their third release, *Renegade*, reached the top of the Swedish album chart and quickly sold 45,000 copies, the immense success of the band began to annoy metalheads who were anxious for the genre to remain exclusive. Some even thought HammerFall was a joke band.

It soon became popular to denounce HammerFall within the Swedish metal scene. T-shirts with a crossed-over HammerFall logo were circulated.

"Apparently, that shirt sold really well," Cans says, amused.

The band tried not to be bothered, but the depths of this new hatred soon became evident. When Joacim Cans and his girlfriend visited a rock bar during the Gothenburg city festival in 2002, a group of strangers tried picking a fight with him. One of them was man with a southern dialect, accompanied by a woman. He said HammerFall should be executed, that he felt sick just seeing them. Joacim refused to be provoked, so the man instead started spitting at him, and suddenly, the woman attacked Joacim's girlfriend. When Joacim tried to intervene, the man smashed a beer glass in his face. Joacim was taken to the hospital, where he received 25 stitches. The incident left deep emotional scars as well.

"I became very reserved. The guy who did it had long hair and looked like every other fan, so I began feeling threatened every time I was surrounded by guys with long hair. I no longer knew who was who."

At the same time, the attack partly defused the anti-HammerFall trend that had become quite prevalent in the local scene.

"Afterward, I met a lot of people who thought it'd gone too far," says Cans. "Even if they didn't particularly care for the music, they felt that enough was enough. When we released *Crimson Thunder* in the late fall of 2002, it felt as if many fans had started finding their way back to us."

Since their formation in the mid-'90s, HammerFall have released 11 albums and two compilations. Through the years, they've established themselves as perhaps the most popular Swedish heavy metal band. After participating in the Swedish version of *Clash of the Choirs*, a reality talent competition, Joacim Cans is also one of the metal scene's most recognizable faces.

HammerFall's positioning as one of Sweden's biggest metal acts paved the way for a heavy metal renaissance in the country.

"Even if HammerFall didn't mean very much to us musically, they played an active role in giving melodic metal a second chance," says vocalist Joakim Brodén of Sabaton.

Sabaton play power metal with lyrics almost exclusively dealing with historical battles. The band's commercial breakthrough came with their 2005 sophomore album *Primo Victoria*. However, back when they started out in 1999 they were primarily focused on Dimmu Borgir-style black metal.

"What we really wanted to play back then was melodic metal, but the problem was no one could sing melodically back then," says Brodén. At the time, he played keyboards in the band.

Sabaton choosing to play black metal despite being into classic heavy metal is a typical example of how much bigger the extreme factions within the scene were compared to the melodic back then. The success of HammerFall re-opened that door.

These days, Sabaton plays over 100 shows per year and own both a tour bus and their own recording studio. The band has played with both Judas Priest and Iron Maiden.

Despite the power metal wave, the early '00s was a difficult time for heavy metal in general. Örebro band Wolf refused to give up despite a bumpy road. When we ask the band's guitarist, Johannes "Axeman" Losbäck, to explain the difference between heavy metal and power metal, his answer is short: "You can wear power metal, but you can't take off heavy metal."

His bandmate, vocalist and guitarist Niklas "Viper" Stålvind, approaches the same question in a somewhat more educational manner.

"Heavy metal sounds like [the] British working class, whereas power metal—as our drummer once stated—sounds like yodeling with double bass drums."

Wolf released their first album in 2000. At early shows, the band would play both their own material and covers. Stålvind observed how, after a few beers, the audience would sing along to Accept and W.A.S.P. songs, convincing him that a new dawn for classic heavy metal was on the horizon. He was wrong.

"Instead, HammerFall and German metal came along. We just looked at each other and said, 'Okay—so this is what it's going to be?'"

Seven albums in, Wolf are no longer hermits of their musical direction. They've been joined by Bullet, Enforcer, and Ram and are sometimes referred to as The New Wave of Traditional Heavy Metal.

"We're in our own world. 'What's the flavor of the week—is it Helloween from 1987 or Iron Maiden from 1995?' We don't care. Everything is just metal to us!"

In Wolf's case, this means falsetto vocals, V-shaped guitars with bloodstain artwork, and lyrics about historical tragedies like wars and witch hunts.

"We'll never write lyrics about red wine and eternal sunlight. That's not metal to us," says Losbäck.

Instead, he feels that the metal tradition is to write about things below the surface— what scares you.

"That's why we began listening to metal, because it was cool and awesome. And we still think so."

Stålvind stresses how metal makes you happy, despite dark musical expressions and lyrics. He won't elaborate further, but his guitarist colleague continues.

"If you pour in blood on one end, beer comes out the other. What happens in between, I can't really explain. It's just a process."

Gylve "Fenriz" Nagell constitutes one half of the Norwegian duo Darkthrone. They have released 16 albums since their 1991 debut, making them the most productive band in the black metal genre. In a segment on Norwegian television show *Lydverket* from 2007, Nagell played Uriah Heep's 1973 album *Sweet Freedom* as one of the records that had most influenced him. In the grim, dogma-laden '90s, a musician from such an extreme band would never have praised a blues rock album with lyrics permeated by '60s free love concepts.

Nagell says it's only natural that not much attention was given to the originators of the genre during the peak of death and black metal, as that was a period of musical development.

"Back in the '80s, the '70s felt quite boring, to be honest. A contributing factor was how buying anything besides Deep Purple albums required traveling to London."

Aside from his Darkthrone duties, Nagell also operates the music blog Band of the Week, where he shares his musical findings in all branches of metal. Among many others, he's praised Swedish metal bands such as In Solitude, Ghost, and Enforcer. It's only natural for him to highlight classic metal. That's where you can trace the roots of both the scene at large and his own musical endeavors.

"Also, anyone can get hold of just about anything these days. I'll offer suggestions on my blog, which people then recommend to their friends—and so the good stuff spreads. This is why I find it especially surprising how some people still have such terrible taste in music," the Norwegian says, laughing.

There are many examples of how the origins of metal have recently come to be valued more highly. When Swedish veterans November reunited to play on a ferry cruise to Finland in 2007, the audience contained both members from Nifelheim and Watain.

Instead of a one-off show, November's gig became the start of a new active period for the band. When bass player and vocalist Christer Stålbrandt compares the scene of today with the early '70s, he's amazed by the age discrepancies in contemporary fans.

"Today, people who like hard rock range from 15 to 50. It's a very wide span, and this was never the case in 1970. It was an entirely new time, and we broke fresh ground. You didn't have to be older than I was to be totally into Dixieland."

───

An athletic young man with an electric guitar occupies the center of Tyrolen Park's stage. He is dressed only in a black and red headscarf and a pair of—to put it mildly—revealing black spandex pants. The band is from Gothenburg and they're called Helvetets Port (Gate of Hell). They are currently performing a song about a Japanese swordsman, a theme hardly in style a few years back. Then again, the same could be argued for the shaky falsetto vocals delivered by frontman Tomas "Witchfinder" Ericsson in the intense afternoon sun.

"He swore an oath under the moon that he'd become …" sings the young man in spandex, with a little help from his bandmates.

"…shogun! The warrior of the rising sun! Shogun," the quartet chants over guitar harmonies. Next to the pumped frontman is guitarist Kongo "K. Lightning" Magnéli, dressed in meticulously retro attire: white sneakers, sports socks over black spandex, sweat bands, a black-and-blue tank top, a moustache in need of trimming, and a blond haircut straight from the heyday of '80s metal.

Helvetets Port not only play classic metal but also succeed, with eerie precision, in looking like bands who were in their prime before some of the members of Helvetets Port were even born.

"Here's a new song. Note that 'new' in this context certainly doesn't imply *modern*," Witchfinder says and receives roaring approval from the crowd.

The guitarist of Portrait is in front of the stage with his fist in the air. Next to him is Robin, a guy in his 20s. Shortly after saying hello, he encourages us to give the band's bass player a Nazi salutation.

"He likes it, because he has a really sick sense of humor."

Robin came to the festival with his friends Joakim and Anna. They're all in their 20s, are from southern Sweden, and appear to be in full agreement about why the metal bands of the '80s were the best.

"They had really big dicks," says Joakim.

All three are friends of Helvetets Port and store their alcohol in the band's caravan parked just outside the park. It turns out to be something of an antique, painted black and decorated with a red flag with the band's initials, specifically for this festival. No one else is around when we get there. While Joakim is picking the lock to the beer storage, Anna notes how she finds Witchfinder attractive and that she would definitely fuck him.

Outside the entrance to the festival backstage area, Kongo Magnéli has taken off his shirt and is carrying a Marshall amp. He has a mild Gothenburg accent, was born in 1982, and is currently studying to become a professional driver.

"I'm just about to qualify for semitrailers now, and then I'll be a bona fide trucker with a saggy old man's ass."

What he likes most of all about Muskelrock is the sense of community. In comparison, he finds Sweden Rock Festival too commercialized. When he started attending SRF, the ticket price was 600 Swedish kronor. Today, a full pass will set you back more than 2,000. Apart from the financial aspect, Muskelrock also allows him to both experience and meet artists who never had a commercial breakthrough.

"Especially Thor, an old hero of mine who I've spoken to a lot today. He's in there now," says the guitarist and nods toward a circus wagon on the other side of the fence.

Magnéli mentions having served with UN troops in Afghanistan when a roadside bomb injured his back and neck in October of 2010. One of his best friends, squad leader

Kenneth Wallin, died in the blast. He was 22 years old. Magnéli was more fortunate and was able to return home two months later.

"Thor says I'm his hero. And he's mine, so that feels great."

The gangly guitarist notes how most people probably don't think of him as the military type.

"But I'm actually a paratrooper."

He chuckles, excuses himself, and then carries his guitar amp toward the parking lot.

On the smaller of the two festival stages, Nicke Andersson is playing with his current band Imperial State Electric. Between two songs, he expresses his gratitude for the opportunity to play the festival and adds how his band might not be the heaviest of the evening.

"But we're giving it all that we've got!"

After the concert, we find him standing in the bar. He's drinking beer and tells us that his band played the more pop-oriented Siesta! festival in Hässleholm the previous day.

"We were one of the hardest bands there, but here, it's the other way around."

Behind the big stage, preparations for Bullet's performance are in full swing. Flamethrowers and smoke bombs have been placed at the edge of the stage. Marshall amps, Gibson guitars, and drums are being lugged along the tiny path. A heavily built middle-aged man wearing an ill-fitting blond wig, a ski cap, and a yellow sports jersey sits in the grass just outside one of the two circus wagons serving as dressing rooms. He speaks with an American accent and greets us with the sturdiest grip of the festival. John Miki Thor—frontman in the Canadian band that also carries his surname—would, if it wasn't for the bizarre attire, easily blend in with the bouncer crew of a small-town nightclub.

He formed the group's first incarnation way back in 1976, then called Thor and the Imps. Thor, whose résumé also includes numerous bodybuilding titles, made himself known in the '80s for combining heavy metal with a muscular warrior image.

These days, Thor promotes his sports clothing brand and plays around 50 shows per year with his band. He expresses great appreciation for this festival and says he is so happy to meet the friends he has here.

When asked who these friends are, he responds, "This guy, for instance," hugging a passing festival worker wearing braces.

A little later, the space in front of the stage fills up with people as Thor enters the stage to introduce 83-year-old fakir El Salama. His real name is John Blixt, and his career as an entertainer spans over five decades. Before an increasingly restless horde of Bullet fans, his performance is as astounding as it is confusing. It ends with him swallowing a rusty hedge clipper, and after having failed to put out a torch with his mouth, it's time to turn the stage over to newer kings of popular entertainment.

Bullet vocalist Dag "Hell" Hofer wears wide studded armbands and a T-shirt with an image of Thor and the phrase "Only the strong came to Muskelrock." Everyone but

Hofer and drummer Gustav Hjortsjö wears black leather jackets. Despite constant references to heavy metal, most of Bullet's songs are more akin to AC/DC's brand of rock. The passionate rock heritage is clearly visible in everything from coordinated poses to the pyrotechnical effects, with sparks pouring down dangerously close to the photographers between the riot fence and the stage.

Much to the delight of the crowd, the song "Bite the Bullet" features guest vocals by Thor himself. The occasional missed phrase is compensated for by the heartwarming and very unlikely situation: an over-the-hill heavy metal legend from the other side of the Atlantic, finding a new audience in the Swedish countryside.

Next to the stage, Staffan Hamrin is prepared to carry out his mission as acting pyrotechnician, carefully pushing buttons on various gadgets and remote controls. When the final chord draws near, the special detonator for the explosives on top of the roof is brought out, with a certain degree of reverence and trepidation. Immediately after pushing the button, Staffan runs a few steps to steer clear from to the blast.

But nothing happens. He sighs and returns to his spot.

After the gig, he discusses with Gustav Hjortsjö what might have gone wrong there.

"Unfortunately, you can't really set off a bomb to check that it works," Staffan notes.

"But we should be able to check the electricity by connecting a light bulb or something," says the drummer.

Back in the '60s, Tyrolen was a hotspot for entertainment. The reason the premises were built way out in Blädinge was partly due to difficulties in obtaining an alcohol license in more populated areas, but also due to the growing number of cars. Being located in the crossroads of four larger cities meant that Växjö, Alvesta, Olofström, and Karlshamn were all within 30 miles. This gave Tyrolen a potential audience in excess of 100,000 people.

Business grew increasingly worse in the '70s, alongside reoccurring problems with drunken brawls and disturbances. Since then, several attempts have been made to reopen the place.

Bullet guitarist Hampus Klang and his friend Jacob Hector bought the park from the son of Olle Olofsson, the founder. Hampus mentions how they host a variety of events such as motorcycle and veteran car meets, cafés, and flea markets.

"Every Wednesday, there's a performance by an artist or stage magician. We once had someone bring along a real tank engine, which he put on display. It was very popular, even though not much happened besides the hellish sound the engine made when he started it."

Hampus explains that life as a multifaceted heavy metal cowboy isn't particularly lucrative, which is why he and three others in the band live in old circus wagons. Exactly where they're parked is a well-kept secret.

"I found mine for free on an online auction. And afterward, I've been told my trailer actually stood here at Tyrolen for many years. That feels great."

Night has fallen and Staffan says perhaps he should put something on besides the gray sweatpants and the short fringed leather vest with studs that he's worn all day. He found it in a garbage room.

"Can you believe what people throw away these days?"

When he heads off to the Bullet tour bus for a change of clothes, he offers to show it to us. The black, dented vehicle is a 1964 Volvo that the band bought for 10,000 Swedish kronor after a major storm wrecked their first bus in 2005. Staffan says this one was essentially scrap too from the beginning, but it's been refurbished by Bullet members with some help from their neighbors.

"Everyone in the Hector family is a car mechanic."

Most of the inside has been arranged as one big room, with long couches along the sides. It's a mess of clothes, CD covers, stereo parts, and trash. The vehicle has taken the band everywhere, from the north of Sweden to German festivals. Staffan mentions how it's used for a very un-Swedish way of marketing—as the bus drives onto the festival campgrounds, the band members stand on the roof setting off fireworks.

"Imagine the effect! People crowd all around. That's how you get fans."

Heading out on longer German tours, Bullet usually leave their bus at home.

"Should we be subjected to vehicular inspection, the bus would stay in Germany permanently."

According to Staffan, they rarely have trouble with the police in Sweden.

"Most of them understand that the guys traveling in this bus aren't troublemakers. They just want to drink beer and play metal."

In the dark birch grove outside the dressing room, members of Thor and Bullet hang out with friends and festival workers. The atmosphere is friendly, and a bearded man in his 50s offers us whiskey. He introduces himself as Sven Klang, and he turns out to be Hampus's father. He says he loves this life and that he loves his son, adding that, of course, that goes for all his children.

When Girlschool, four middle-aged women from south London who've played together since 1978, show up with their instruments, everyone in the small backstage area unite in a spontaneous applause.

In the outdoor bar in front of the big stage, youngsters with fully tattooed backs are served by a bartender in a T-shirt proclaiming, "Thor is strong." The counter is covered by old posters for Swedish dance bands with names like Curt Haagers, Kellys, and Bert Bennys. Portrait can be heard from the smaller stage some distance away, covering Mercyful Fate's "Black Funeral," with Messiah Marcolin on guest vocals.

It's hard to envision a more fitting conclusion, if not for the evening then at least this chapter. Long before the '60s, when Tyrolen was built, this place was an outdoor dance floor where people met to dance to the tunes of folk music violins. Tonight, heavy metal appears to be as close as we'll get to a contemporary equivalent. Just like folk music was said to be the devil's music, luring young couples to their fate in the 18th century, metal has always been aligned with sinister forces. And like the dance bands on the faded posters, metal has always been abhorred by intellectuals and the cultural establishment.

At the park entrance, a grim-faced man in his late 60s makes sure everyone is wearing a festival wristband. He introduces himself as Sven and mentions having watched drunken people pass this gate for more than 40 years. His experience is that there are two categories of individuals.

"There are regular folks, and then there's the Muskelrock audience."

He feels that the attendees here are good people.

"They might make a mistake or two, but they never cause any real trouble. And they never get too drunk, even though they drink all day."

A little later, festival general Jacob Hector happily notes how 1,200 people have bought tickets for the festival—900 was the break-even number.

When we tell him we spoke with the old man at the entrance, he smiles and says that he's called Sven på Netten ("Sven on the Netten"), after his place of residence.

"He comes here and works for free, because he really enjoys it. However, he once asked me something he couldn't quite understand about our audience. 'Why do they bring their tape recorders to the festival, when there's live music?'"

The young festival promoter laughs heartily, even though he's probably told the same story countless times before.

Sven på Netten passed away just a few days after Muskelrock 2017. He was 67 years old.

The festival celebrated its tenth anniversary in 2018. Thor was of course invited back.

XV.

Watain

I've never been able to relate to black metal in a lighthearted way. To me, it's always been close to something sacred.

— Erik Danielsson, Watain

"**WE WANT PEOPLE TO STARE** into a burning temple. Attending a Watain concert should be like stepping into the most fanatical church imaginable, with mass in full swing. It's a place with no rules whatsoever."

Erik Danielsson speaks calmly. Occasionally, his voice is drowned out by the screeching of subway trains passing above. The sounds give an increasingly claustrophobic dimension to the atmosphere in the Wolf's Lair, the bunker Watain rents from Stockholm Public Transport.

Boxes with old sheep's heads and animal bones are stacked along the walls, and a sickly sweet scent permeates the air. In the small pantry area, there are plastic bottles filled with blood in various stages of putrefaction. Other bands used to rehearse here as well, but after Watain moved in, they've dropped off one by one.

"I want to give insight into a reality people pretend isn't there, that most of them shrug off or avert their eyes from, should they accidentally come across it. Since both society and the world we live in is built on order, this is what's considered good. On the flipside, what we're doing will be perceived as evil. That's the world we want to show people."

Outside the bunker, the band's matte black van and a rented trailer are being loaded for a mini tour through Västerås, Sundsvall, and Luleå. The tour is a warm-up for the three-month long campaign through Europe, the U.S., and South America later in the fall.

It's the end of the summer of 2010. Watain recently released their fourth album, *Lawless Darkness*, establishing their position as one of the world's most extreme black metal bands. Erik Danielsson wears a Watain tank top, black spandex pants, and worn cowboy boots with rusty buckles. From his neck hangs a silver pentagram, and around his waist is a bullet belt. He gives us a tour of the sizable lair.

On the wall of the small room inside the steel door to the street outside, someone has smeared "Hungry are the damned" in blood.

"That was Dave Lepard," says Erik.

The former vocalist for sleaze rockers Crashdïet went to school with Erik in Uppsala. Dave committed suicide in 2006. Erik mentions how he always was a bit peculiar and did things like showing up to school wearing only leopard underwear.

In the rehearsal room, Watain members are packing their instruments. There's a small altar in the corner with candles and a skull. A filthy denim jacket hangs on the wall, so encrusted with blood that it's completely stiff.

The adjacent room has two huge steel crucifixes resting against the wall. Next to them there are large plastic IKEA bags with custom-built iron torches. Along one wall, there's a workbench equipped with both solder pens and welding equipment. This is where the band and their friends construct all their stage props.

"This is of utmost importance," says Erik. "All our things are made with an incredible passion, and you can feel that when you're on stage with them."

A few screen-printing frames lie on a bench. Together with Erik in Nifelheim, Erik Danielsson reprints rare shirts with old metal bands. They recently made shirts with the legendary Italian band Bulldozer.

In the bunker's far end, they've built their Wolf's Lair bar. Here, Watain can party without being bothered. They tend to get into fights when going out drinking together. The largest wall is covered with a gigantic painting of the goat on the cover of Bathory's self-titled debut. All the Watain members bear tattoos featuring the same design.

The ceiling is covered with a camouflage net and hanging from the walls are framed photos from the band's history. These collages were produced for the band's tenth anniversary, which was celebrated with a concert in Uppsala in the winter of 2008. One of the montages contains flyers and clippings from early underground press. Three of them feature photos taken during tours, behind the stage, or in their rehearsal space. There's one of Erik holding a carving knife and smiling happily while slicing up a suspended pig's head. The band members, plump-cheeked and just out of childhood and puberty. The same band members five years later, touring Europe with Dissection. A smeared pool of blood on a filthy floor. A sheep's head with its tongue hanging out and two nails in the forehead. Erik next to his idol, Tom G. Warrior of Celtic Frost, from a tour the bands did together a few years earlier.

Over the last five years, Watain has grown from an obscure but respected black metal band to having their latest album recommended on Sweden's leading television morning show. While Watain signify a generational shift within the scene, they maintain a strong sense of black metal tradition, which shines through in everything they do. The same goes for the band's fanatical approach to their Satanic convictions and image.

In interviews, Erik Danielsson has proved to be witty, intelligent, and more or less impossible to throw off balance. Countless articles about them have painted a picture of Sweden's—and perhaps even the world's—most extreme band. We read about live shows that were so over the top that audience members vomited, and about a band who every night put on stage clothes so putrefied there are maggots living in them.

"A lot of people appreciate the same thing about Watain as they enjoy when watching horror movies, it's something brutal and frightening but from a convenient distance," Erik explains. "But they need to understand this is not a horror movie. Remember that— this not a fucking joke!"

The Satanism propagated by Watain is based on the idea of a primordial chaos behind the framework of humanity's perception of reality. The goal is absolute liberation from the laws and structures of our cosmos and to merge with the chaotic darkness that lies beyond. It's a daily struggle manifested in different ways. One example is how the members of Watain strive to live outside society to the greatest extent possible. To be off the grid, never receive any mail, or have to deal with the state in any way.

Erik says he constantly challenges his fears, trying to reach deeper into the dark and explore what's there.

"Seeking the darkness is an inherent call within me. To always search that which is unexplored and prohibited. I was also introduced to this music at a very young age. Black metal really encourages you to explore actively. If you want to get something out of it, you have to participate. Perhaps it's the longing for something more exclusive," he says while pulling on his beat-up leather jacket.

"I'm convinced there's a much larger reality than the one presented to us on television, in newspapers or around the living room table. And without a doubt, a huge part of that reality still lies in the darkness."

On the street outside, guitarist Pelle Forsberg and Watain's head of security, Marcus Tena, already sit on their Harleys. They're racing each other to Västerås. When the traffic lights turn red, the roar from the exhaust pipes echoes throughout the affluent Enskede neighborhood.

Erik Danielsson also owns a custom-built bike, but due to Watain's hectic tour schedule, it's been deregistered. He doesn't have his driver's license yet either, but says that shouldn't be a problem, as long as he takes it easy on the road.

"Everything could always go to hell, right?"

Around 3 p.m., the Watain van rolls into in the parking lot outside this evening's venue in the Västerås harbor. The building is an old factory converted into a bar and rock club.

The band unloads their equipment from the trailer under the watchful eye of Johan Frölund, who's in charge of everything stage-related. Amplifiers, instruments, filthy boxes with bone parts and animal skulls, bottles of blood, and boxes of merchandise are carried into the venue.

All Watain members wear identical leather vests decorated with various symbols representing the band—a wolf's face with open jaws, a trident, and the word *Watain* in a gothic font. Aesthetics are clearly borrowed from the biker world.

The band's core has always been the trio of vocalist Erik Danielsson, guitarist Pelle Forsberg, and drummer Håkan Jonsson. Since 2007, bass player Alvaro Lillo from Chile and Italian guitar player Set Teitan have joined them on all concerts and tours.

Watain and their inner circle are a close-knit brotherhood. The concert promoters smile awkwardly and seem a bit nervous to approach the band. Their generous offers of help carrying equipment are met with silent stares—but eventually a nod.

To avoid dealing with unwanted contact with people, Watain have brought along their friend Marcus Tena. His job is simply to stay close.

"When we're on tour, everyone in the band is on edge, and there's often trouble," Erik says. "Trouble that quite often escalates into something serious, which is why we bring along Tena. It's great insurance to have him around."

Nifelheim drummer Peter Stjärnvind is at the mixing desk, wearing very tight blue jeans and a Bathory shirt.

"This is my first job after studying to be a sound engineer," he says while putting on a CD of Saxon's *Strong Arm of the Law* from 1980. He cranks the volume, and the British heavy metal riffs fill the venue.

"This is the sound I had in mind for tonight!" he calls out to the band, getting only grunts in response.

The supporting acts arrive in vans and start hauling in their equipment. Coming along for two gigs this weekend are heavy metal band Ram from Gothenburg and Linköping death metal band Repugnant. They've brought girlfriends and a bunch of pals and have already begun partying. The supporting acts have been carefully selected by Watain. They avoid touring with other black metal bands, since they don't find any of them up to scratch, with the exception of their friends in Nifelheim.

Watain stands around their van in the parking lot. Most of the equipment has been loaded in, and Set has begun sound-checking his guitar. Wearing a leather vest, army pants, and a Watain shirt, he plays a solo on his black Flying V. He runs through fast metal scales to annoy Peter, who stares in the direction of the stage. When Peter's had enough, he shuts off Set's wireless and all goes silent.

Set looks into the venue.

"What are all these people doing here?" he asks sullenly.

"It's the support bands," says Pelle, and everybody laughs.

Being constantly surrounded by other human beings is a cruel fate that you have accept as a misanthrope. The members of Watain deal with this in different ways. Erik is the most sociable. Pelle gives a silent and intimidating impression. Håkan seems quite shy.

In a small room by the bar, Hampus Eriksson is assembling Watain's well-stocked merchandise table. Erik Danielsson has studied graphic design and is one of the contemporary metal world's most distinct artists, heavily inspired by the genre's history. He's made hundreds of shirt designs, and the demand for new prints is huge.

Hampus was born in 1990 and plays in death metal bands Degial and Invidious from Uppsala. He remembers when he first heard of Watain.

"There was a rumor about them beating up people who wore Watain shirts. People would be talking about them, but I never saw them around. I was really scared of running into them."

His childhood friend, Emil Svensson, who is drummer of both Repugnant and Degial, agrees.

"They were very mysterious, and the only thing you knew about them was that they were dangerous."

Then Hampus became friends with Pelle and has been working with the band's merchandise for a year. Hampus says hi to Matthias Müller, drummer of American black metal band Negative Plane, who Watain have toured the U.S. with. He's shown up in Västerås with his girlfriend. They're on holiday in Sweden and have mainly stayed in Stockholm.

"It's just insane how many metalheads there are here!" he says, impressed. "Wherever I go, I see people with band shirts. Really good, obscure bands at that."

Matthias grew up in a small town outside Munich, Germany, but moved to the U.S. as a teenager. Today, he lives in Long Island, New York. He says he always felt like he was the only one listening to black metal. As we share a cab to a local record store for a Watain signing session, he looks through the car window and points in fascination to all the young people wearing metal shirts.

When we arrive at the closed store, there's about 30 fans in black outside, waiting in silence. Matthias is in awe.

"This is amazing. Do you have any idea how good you've got it here in Sweden?"

Inside the store, Erik, Pelle, and Håkan are preparing a black backdrop with the Watain logo, ornaments in white and red, and a cloth over the table. They ask the manager to kill the lights. They light candles and fill a silver chalice with blood.

Lawless Darkness is playing as the doors open, and there's quickly a line with silent, solemn fans. Most of them are guys in their 20s with albums and posters. Pelle, Erik, and Håkan sign the merchandise with a silver pen and then sprinkle blood over it. There is very little talking. The only words uttered are "thanks" and the odd fan daring to ask a question. The reverence and respect are palpable. Once the signing is over and the band's gathered their stuff, it's as if the air becomes easier to breathe.

The fans smile happily and make sure to keep their records horizontal, to keep the blood from dripping off before coagulating.

Erik's girlfriend, Marie, has arrived to the store along with Set's girlfriend, Sara. Pelle is engaged in a vivid recollection of a video he saw on the internet the other day in which a man tied up his testicles for months, cutting off all blood flow.

"They were completely rotten. It was so fucked up. He could just pull them off, without effort!"

He recommends a Swedish website with images of corpses and bodily experiments.

"Really, some of the stuff on there is fucking disgusting. Even I feel a bit sick watching it."

And that's saying something. Within the black metal world, Pelle Forsberg is known as a man who is extremely resilient to pain, who won't hesitate to take a butcher's saw to his arm just to see what happens.

"I cut off my nipple once when I was bored. The weird thing was that it grew out again, looking exactly the same," he says with a certain degree of satisfaction.

Back at the venue, the audience is gathering. Many have travelled from Stockholm to see Watain, who have only played the capital a handful of times.

In the dressing room, wild tour anecdotes are spouted at the same pace as the backstage beers are emptied. How Alvaro smashed a bottle inside the bus on the last U.S. tour and glass fragments got lodged in his eye so badly, he almost went blind. Once at the hospital, he refused to submit a blood sample and was then smuggled out by Johan in order to make the flight back to Sweden.

Alvaro grins broadly. He was born in 1971 and is by far the oldest in the band. Ten years ago, he moved from Chile to Germany with his death metal band, Undercroft.

"Then I started coming to Sweden to hang out with bands. I met a girl and had a daughter. You know how these things happen," he says smiling.

A story that keeps coming up recounts Watain's three-day break in Florida during their 2007 U.S. tour, and how the band turned this opportunity to rest into a party of epic proportions. One morning, Erik woke up on the floor in the hotel room and saw a huge bloodstain on the wall. He didn't understand anything. Suddenly, Håkan woke up and projectile vomited blood, salt water, and sand. Then he fainted. It turned out that the band had spent the preceding day on the beach with the intention of "digging the biggest fucking hole ever."

They managed to drag the ailing drummer onto the flight, but once they arrived in Mexico City for the next gig, he was in such poor shape he had to be rushed to the hospital. All the sand and water he'd swallowed had infected his lungs and he was diagnosed with severe pneumonia.

With only one hour to go before the concert, it was evident he wasn't going to be able to play.

Outside, hordes of restless fans were waiting.

"Not the sort of crowd who'd accept a cancelation, so to speak," Erik notes dryly.

The band quickly concluded Erik was the only possible replacement for Håkan, having been a drummer initially. But he couldn't sing while playing. Set, who at the time had only played with Watain for a few months, had to take over vocal duties. A video clip from the concert shows Erik approaching the altar as usual, greeting the audience with raised arms, but instead of going to the microphone, he turns around and takes a seat at the drum kit. The audience goes silent in confusion but resume roaring once Set begins singing. Despite everything going well, Set was so stressed out, he got a fever after the show.

Johan had to give Håkan antibiotic injections, and after a few days, he was well enough to handle the drums again.

"Someone always ends up in the hospital," Johan says tartly. "On the last European tour, Pelle injured his elbow after throwing himself down a staircase. Then Alvaro had to get something looked at—I can't fucking remember what it was."

As the concert approaches, the atmosphere grows tense in the dressing room. Erik is tapping his feet so intensely that his boot buckles rattle. He wears a grim face and seemingly wants everyone to get out. Peter Stjärnvind, on the other hand, is talking nonstop, delivering a steady stream of gossip about metal colleagues.

"Do you know what L-G once did in a Swedish grammar exam? For the word *skriva*, he answered: 'skriva, skrevde, skraft!'"

While impossible to translate into English, everyone present laughs. L-G Petrov, vocalist of Entombed, is often the subject of ridicule. Another name mentioned several times during the evening is Harry, bass player of Håkan's old thrash band, Die Hard. Håkan recently left the band, since after the birth of his son he only has time for Watain. Someone asks how old the baby is.

"Three months and two days," Håkan answers with a quick smile.

Harry seems to be known for being a real nuisance when drinking, and the word backstage is that he's extremely drunk tonight. Just a few minutes later, he stumbles into the room. Erik immediately tells him to leave. Harry laughs, fidgeting with his beer bottle while trying to stand up straight.

"I'm serious, Harry. Fuck off!" Erik hisses and stares at him.

Suddenly, the whole backstage area goes silent.

Harry grins and leans backward onto a table, but the top is loose, so he crashes to the floor along with several beer bottles. Erik's eyes light up and he jumps him. He punches him in the face several times, despite being a lot shorter, and Harry is too drunk to offer much resistance. A few of the Repugnant members drag him out of the room. After the door has been shut, Erik sits down and stares straight ahead. Suddenly there's a muted ambience in the room, with the occasional giggle. Erik's girlfriend, Marie, watches him in silence.

Peter is still cackling happily.

"Skraft! Do you get it?"

Before their gig, Watain evacuate everyone from the dressing room. Preparations are important, and the band isolate themselves for at least half an hour to get into the right mood. They put on their stage clothes, apply black-and-white theatrical makeup, and smear themselves in pig's blood. No one is allowed anywhere near them.

At midnight, the venue lights go off, and an intro with ominous church organs blasts from the PA. When the band enter, the stage is illuminated only by candlelight. An altar with 13 burning black wax candles, a ram's skull, and a brass chalice full of blood stands in front of the drums. The stage is decorated with skulls, two big inverted crosses, four metal columns, and skeleton parts attached to thick chains. Hanging on both sides are red banners with the Watain howling wolf head in black and white.

The five musicians stand with their backs to the crowd, arms stretched toward the ceiling, fingers forming the horns. Pelle and Set weave together melancholic and sinister guitar leads as the band unites in "Malfeitor," a song from *Lawless Darkness*. In addition to the corpse paint, Erik has an intricate pattern drawn over half his face. He bangs his head like a madman between his lines. Pelle sings along to every word.

Between songs, Erik takes the chalice from the altar and pours its content over his face and chest. Blood splatters the audience, and an acrid smell spreads through the venue.

"This song is dedicated to the brothers and sisters who are no longer with us," he says as the band heads into "Legions of the Black Light" from their third album, *Sworn to the Dark*.

After the gig, the venue empties slowly. The black-and-white checkered floor in front of the stage is sticky with spilled beer, glass shards, vomit, and a big pool of blood.

An American girl with a Watain tank top and big orange hair enters the backstage room. She stands in a corner, looking at the band while they carry their equipment to the van. She calls herself Vega Natas and follows Watain on their tours around the world. So far, she's seen 28 concerts in 10 different countries. She's very satisfied with this evening's show.

"A Watain gig ravages your every sense so completely that you become immersed in it. The smell of rotting flesh is so intense, I can taste it—the heat from the fire, the pain from the agitated audience, and of course, the purely musical attack. In that condition, when senses are so overloaded they go entirely numb, I can find a place within myself that is entirely pure. To me, traveling to a Watain show is like a pilgrimage. It's a highly rewarding spiritual experience."

Vega Natas lives in Las Vegas and works as a tattoo artist. Håkan takes the time to speak with her briefly.

"I don't understand where she gets the money to travel as much as she does," he says and continues carrying his equipment to the van.

Erik finds it difficult to handle the most dedicated fans. While he, of course, appreciates how Watain reaches and affects people deeply, he doesn't like their submissive attitudes. He hurries back into the dressing room and only briefly says hello to Vega Natas.

Harry staggers into the small dressing room. Erik gives him a cheerful hello and takes a beer from the fridge. The fight appears to have been forgotten.

At the sound desk, Peter Stjärnvind collects his equipment.

"I'm so fucking satisfied, but right after the gig, some guy in an In Flames shirt came up to me and said it was the worst sound he'd ever heard!"

He laughs.

"But it's impossible to take that shit seriously, coming from some guy in a sports jacket who likes drum triggers and overproduced Gothenburg bands."

In the parking lot, there's a long discussion about whether the band should spend the night in a hotel in Västerås or drive through the night straight to Sundsvall for the next gig. It's 3 a.m. and everyone is exhausted.

They finally decide to pass on the hotel and squeeze into the van with what remains of the backstage booze.

The first black metal album that Erik Danielsson ever heard was *Under a Funeral Moon* by Darkthrone. His best friend's older sister was a metalhead, and she made sure the young boys got to hear all the latest albums. Erik was 11 years old and recalls "almost shitting himself" the first time he listened to it.

"I didn't think it was fun in any way; Darkthrone were absolutely macabre. I listened to maybe 10 seconds at a time and kept asking myself what the hell this was. I immediately realized music couldn't be more powerful than this."

He describes his upbringing in Nåntuna, a suburb of Uppsala, as safe and good. His parents were permissive and supported their son, regardless of what he wanted to do. The most important thing to them was that he followed his heart.

So, Erik immersed himself in all the black metal he could find. Simultaneously, churches were burning in both Sweden and Norway, and then Øystein "Euronymous" Aarseth was murdered. Erik's first concert was Dark Funeral in Västerås. He was 14 years old.

"It was a really exciting time, when black metal felt genuinely dangerous. You could open any random metal zine and discover loads of new bands. It made a huge impression on me."

The religious aspect of black metal soon became important. Erik studied lyrics and was drawn to the philosophical dimensions of the music. His grandmother was "extremely Christian," and he wonders what impact that might have had on him. As a child, Erik and his siblings would often go with her to church on religious holidays. But he stopped going once he discovered black metal.

"Immediately after meeting the devil in different shapes at age 12 to 14, I began questioning the church. It was such an obvious adversary to everything beautiful I'd discovered, all that was unrestrained. At the same time, I was fascinated by the church experiences I had, seeing people kneeling in front of an altar. The idea of religion was always appealing in a way. Not the things that were worshipped, but the act of worship in itself."

Erik started going into Uppsala on weekends when he was in his teens and soon met Pelle Forsberg and Håkan Jonsson, two friends from the district of Årsta who were also into black metal. They were easily recognized, being the only other people Erik had seen in Uppsala with leather jackets and bullet belts. They exchanged phone numbers on the first night they met, and from there, everything happened pretty fast.

Watain formed in 1998, when all three were 16 years old. The name was borrowed from a song by the American band Von. No one knows exactly what the word *watain* means, but the Von members claim it came to them as they were writing the song in a drug-induced haze, after experimenting with black magic.

The day after Watain's first rehearsal, the newly formed band printed shirts at Pelle's and Håkan's school and began producing flyers.

"We immediately became uniform. One thing we all agreed on was that a black metal band isn't something you just have—you do it for real. It's hard to trace exactly where this ruthlessness came from. We spurred each other on. We did nothing besides rehearsing and never spoke about anything else when we met. Then we'd head out to fight and drink like maniacs."

The trio organized death and black metal gigs in Uppsala and traveled to Stockholm to watch bands in the Vasa Park. Their urge to pursue extremes made Watain notorious at an early stage. *Go Fuck Your Jewish God*, the first demo of the band, earned them a record deal, and soon, the trio was touring Europe with prominent black metal acts like Dark Funeral and Rotting Christ from Greece. The second album, 2003's *Casus Luciferi*, established Watain as a force to be reckoned with.

Journalist Elin Unnes, previously editor-in-chief at *VICE Sweden* magazine—which featured Watain early on—credits one of the reasons for the band's success to them always being consistent.

"The first time I met Erik, he told me about how the band does everything themselves. How he'd boiled horse hooves to make glue for his fanzine. That's when I started thinking that perhaps they were going to make it big. Erik is also extremely skilled at conveying the image they want us to see; he's highly aware of how he comes across."

It wasn't until spring of 2006 that Watain played their first Swedish headlining gig. The concert at The Rock in Linköping has become the stuff of legend, since the band had built special blood cannons that short-circuited and sprayed rotten pig's blood on the audience before Watain had even entered the stage. The stench filling the basement venue was so overwhelming that many vomited immediately, and people fled out into the street.

The plan was for the audience to be drenched in blood as the gig finale, and there was supposed to be a lot more of it. Electrical mishaps aside, the gig spread the name "Watain" far outside black metal circles.

Elin Unnes was on location in Linköping and remembers it as one of the best concerts she's ever seen.

"I regard black metal as an art form, a performance art that sometimes spills over into real life. You never know where it ends and where reality begins. With Watain, boundaries between the religious, artistic, and musical are very blurred. But art must be allowed to challenge; you have to see how far it can be taken. As individuals, the band members are extreme and can do really disturbing things, which is why you believe what they're singing about."

These days, Watain are usually content with only using the blood on themselves on stage. It's an important part of the transformative process taking place as the band gets ready. Above all, the transformation is about eradicating all distance from what they're about to do on stage.

"I've never been able to relate to black metal in a lighthearted way. To me, it's always been something almost sacred. I've neither been able to, nor had the urge to joke about it. To me, as with the other members, it's always been deadly serious. The importance of the music disappears as soon as you distance yourself from it."

He says the stench can be difficult to endure if he's not in the right state of mind, but the blood acts as a catalyst when it's time to go on stage.

"Regardless of what mental state you've been in, it all slips away when you put on those clothes. Once you pour that blood all over yourself, you just can't joke around anymore. You are no longer in charge. And that's something immensely powerful."

The dead animals and rotten blood symbolize transformation from life into the unknown, he says.

"Most black metal accessories can be tied to ancient ceremonial traditions. Both scents and facial paint are used in shamanistic magic and also in older Norse mysticism. Besides looking cool, there's a reason why all of these things have lived on since Venom brought them back. And that's because they work. We want to present an experience for all senses. By incorporating smell, we slam yet another door in the faces of people who want to pretend they're watching a regular rock concert."

Erik Danielsson says it often feels as if it's not him standing on stage.

"But the guy standing there, in my body, is filled with fire. And a force powerful enough to move mountains."

One day he hopes to return home from a tour with no memories from the concerts.

———

The van arrives in Sundsvall shortly after 9 a.m. on Saturday morning. A drowsy Pelle stumbles out. He still has black makeup around his bloodshot eyes. Leaving Västerås the night before, the van was pulled over at a gas station by the cops. The officers looked suspiciously through the passenger windows, shining a flashlight. After a quick inspection of Johan Frölunds driver's license, they were allowed to continue.

"Things like that happen all the fucking time," a seasoned Pelle notes.

He turns around and retches up some gastric acid on the asphalt. Crille Nilsson from black metal band Unpure, who's helping Johan with the stage show, gives him a puzzled look. Pelle pats his belly.

"I have a diaphragmatic hernia. It started about a year ago. It started hurting like hell, and since then, I can't eat without drinking a lot of fluid or the food will get stuck in the cardia, which is fucking painful. What's extremely annoying is how I'll throw up at any time."

He hasn't consulted a doctor yet but thinks perhaps he should.

The rest of the band stagger out of the van and stretch their limbs. Håkan has barely slept at all. Alvaro's eyes are so red, they seem fluorescent. As usual, he's in a splendid mood and smiles happily at the fact that they're permitted an early check-in to the hotel. The other guests stare unashamedly at him as he drags his worn bag through the lobby.

This evening's concert in Sundsvall is part of the festival Nordfest. The venue is located in what's usually the Scandic Hotel's bar and conference area. The ceiling is low, and the decor seems to be stolen from an '80s cruise ship.

Johan Frölund and Crille Nilsson unload Watain's equipment and stage decor on the rust-red wall-to-wall carpet. Despite only having slept for an hour after driving all night, Johan is unable to relax until everything has been set up. A local Watain fan just dropped by and left a plastic bag with two dead ravens. Johan's plan is to impale them on stage.

"They're so rotten, maggots are pouring out. It's going to look great."

Johan Frölund has worked with Watain since 2001. He and Crille were at a concert with the Japanese black metal band Sigh in Västerås and met the Watain members who were there to sell their fanzine. They soon discovered that they had similar ideas about how black metal should be presented on stage. Since then, Johan has been like a fourth member of the band.

One of his first creations were the approximately meter-high inverted crosses, acting as candelabras and kerosene lantern holders. Since then, he's crafted everything from chain barriers to blood-vomiting goat skulls. He dedicates a lot of time into planning and coming up with new solutions for different stage designs.

New this year are four digital flamethrowers ordered from Norway. One of them has just been returned from service, and he can't quite get it to work. Together with Crille, he's pushing different configuration buttons on the display until its nozzle finally starts gushing fire.

"They cost close to $7,000 USD. But the bastards didn't lie on the shipment note when they sent them to me from Norway, so we had pay full custom duties. An additional $900 USD!"

He tries out different height settings for the flames spewing from the machines. The heat is ferocious.

"It's a fine line. I want fire and fucking lots of it. We maximize everything as much as possible, in relation to what's feasible."

At Watain's 10-year anniversary concert in Uppsala, precisely what can never happen happened. Halfway through, the fire alarm went off, and the entire venue had to be evacuated. At Norwegian festival Hole in the Sky the week before, it got so dangerously hot in the venue, the wall paint started melting.

"We had fire bowls, flamethrowers, and the tridents with lanterns. It looked fantastic—people were crouching because it was so hot."

Johan says the stage temperature can reach up to 160 degrees. Watain are considering buying a cooling system for Håkan, who is most exposed to heat, since his drum kit is usually placed in between fire sources.

Watain bring their own skulls and blood when playing in Sweden. On tour in Europe and especially the United States, they make sure to enlist local suppliers. Fans often bring different types of dead animals to be used on stage. Even though they bring these cadavers from show to show, Watain rarely have any problems in customs.

"It works surprisingly well. We've driven over borders with human body parts, but the customs officials were only interested in Alvaro's bullet belt," says Johan, smiling.

He declines to mention which body parts.

Johan works as a welder on Norwegian oil platforms in the North Sea. He toils day and night for two weeks and is then off work for a month. He looks like the typical roadie with his long hair in a ponytail with several ties. Broad black suspenders hold up his blue jeans and, just like the band members, he's wearing a Watain shirt.

Pelle is now awake after a few hours of sleep. He sits at a table with a marbled plastic surface, sipping a cup of coffee while changing guitar strings on his white Flying V. It's encrusted with old blood and filth. He's been on extended leave from his job as a printer for the local newspaper for close to two years. In most cases, you'd lose your job after that long, but he says they appreciate him so much, they go to extra lengths to keep him. He rents out his Uppsala apartment and has been living in Wolf's Lair for the last year.

"But the air has become so fucking bad in there. We had a fan to get some circulation, but during the heat wave last summer, it was so fucking hot that it broke down. One day, I discovered green mold growing on the bedclothes, and that's when I packed up and moved into my girlfriend's place."

He believes the air and mold made his stomach troubles worse.

We ask him what his parents think of his lifestyle and Satanic beliefs.

"They wondered in the beginning. But now they see the attention we get and how we're making money, so everything's fine. And my dad helps me out when I get in trouble with the law."

Pelle Forsberg's father is chief district prosecutor at the international public prosecution office in Uppsala. Pelle says he's been involved in cases concerning resisting arrest, among other things, but so far, he's not been convicted of anything.

Erik stands on the venue floor with a cup of coffee, observing the construction taking shape. On stage, Johan is assembling flamethrowers, and he checks how close to the black concrete ceiling the flames reach.

"Johan and I have the same kind of pirate mentality when it comes to solving problems," says Erik. "He is completely essential to Watain."

Last year, Johan and Crille visited North Korea. They took the Trans-Siberian Railway to Pyongyang and then traveled around North Korea for a week with a guided group. Erik sent a few cassettes with Watain songs with them, which Johan smuggled in and planted when given the chance. He left one in the subway system and another at a daycare center. Erik credits metal tapes spread behind the Iron Curtain in the '80s for giving rise to bands such as Korrozia Metalla.

"It would be a dream come true to achieve the same effect on someone in North Korea."

Once the stage construction is completed, the band members head off to drink beer in the hotel's basement sauna. Set goes to the gym for a workout.

Before the tour, Erik warned us that no one in the band wanted us there. If we attempted to speak to the other band members, they're likely to refuse, he said, so we should stick to him. He's very keen on having the band documented.

But we find the situation mostly reversed. Erik is the one who seems to find us annoying and in his way. He asks us to leave the backstage on several occasions and gives disinterested and indifferent answers to our questions. When we ask to take a photo of his back patch during a calm moment before sound check, he snarls that this could've been done at any time.

He hasn't put us on the guest list for the gigs, so we're forced to sneak into the Scandic by pretending to be friends of Alvaro's.

During the evening, the band and their girlfriends primarily stay backstage. Nordfest has a mixed lineup, and it's fairly evident that most attendees are not here for orthodox black metal. Erik and Set sit quietly in the hotel's breakfast room, which now serves as catering area.

Suddenly, members of the hardcore band Raised Fist enter, trying to get fired up before their gig. They wear blue jeans and tight-fitting white tank tops over their wide, muscular chests.

"Come on, guys, for fuck's sake!"

They're so pumped up, they bounce up and down. Erik slowly turns around and gives them a cold stare.

"Let's jam like the DEVIL!" they shout.

Erik puts his hands on his hips, looking as if he wants to kill them. But the members pat each other on the back and head out to play their hardcore to the exhilarated audience.

"They should really watch what they say," Johan's girlfriend, Malin, hisses.

Erik slowly shakes his head.

Approximately halfway through the show, the music suddenly stops and the venue goes black. Vocalist Alexander Hagman collapses on the stage floor. It turns out, a cable has been jammed under the riot fence and has killed the power. As Hagman grabbed the fence while holding the microphone, it short-circuited, and he got an electric shock powerful enough to knock him out.

The Watain camp is overcome with malice, but that quickly passes as they realize the short circuit knocked out both the mixing desk and the computerized lighting console, which means all sound and light presets are gone. The audience is forced out of the venue, and Watain have to sound-check all over again.

As they finally go on stage, delayed by several hours, a big portion of the audience has already left. The stench emanating from the rotten ravens on two inverted metal crucifixes is so strong, many turn back at the door.

It's a strange gig. The band is focused and full of energy, but the audience includes people who don't seem to understand what kind of band Watain is and keep dancing into people. A man hassles several women in the audience, and Watain look increasingly annoyed on stage.

Afterward, many of the band's friends are confused over the strange mood in the audience. We suggest that people weren't prepared for the potent aroma.

"Why on earth would someone go to see Watain but not want the smell? It makes no sense to me whatsoever. Those people have no right to be here," says Gottfrid Åhman of Repugnant.

The Sunday morning breakfast buffet atmosphere is somewhat subdued. The after-party in the rooms and corridors went on until 5 a.m. In order to make it to the Luleå sound check in time, Watain left early this morning, straight from the festivities.

Johan Frölund is taking the train home to Stockholm, only to then travel to Norway and be flown with a helicopter to the oil rig where he's about to start another 2-week shift.

He's been talking a lot about his travels in North Korea over the weekend. The primary reason he and Crille went there was to personally experience a real dictatorship. They also wanted to see the Mass Games, enormous performance art gymnastics held every few years.

"You never know when they're going to be put on, but as soon as I read about it, we booked the trip immediately. It's the ultimate stage production."

Mass Games is a huge exhibition in synchronized gymnastics. Tens of thousands of children and teenagers are drilled over the course of several years to wield papers in different colors, creating huge patterns, while an equal number of gymnasts perform complex choreography.

Johan says he was as giddy as a schoolchild when entering the huge stadium.

"All of my expectations were fulfilled. It was insane: 20,000 people, and that's just the backdrop!"

His eyes light up as he scoops more scrambled eggs onto his plate.

"It blew away everything I've ever seen on stage before, and that was just the intro!"

———

A few weeks after the Swedish dates, Watain set off on a month-long European tour that was immediately followed by intense touring through the U.S. and South America.

After the first gig in Chile, Erik Danielsson collapsed.

"We played at a Hells Angels club with a low ceiling, using burning tridents. Everyone in the audience had eyes big as saucers. It was total intensity and over 100 degrees."

Once he got off stage, he found himself unable to move. Touring with Watain is a taxing affair, and Erik is used to being extremely fatigued after shows. But now, he was suddenly unable to move his body at all.

He can still feel the effects of the breakdown and chooses coffee rather than beer when we meet him at a restaurant in Stockholm on a spring evening in April of 2011.

The promoters brought him back to the hotel that night, but despite being exhausted, he couldn't sleep and instead spent all night awake with severe anxiety. The following day, the band went to Santiago. Before the gig, Erik was shaking backstage. A doctor was called, and he was diagnosed with both dehydration and low blood sugar. By eating some candy, he made it through three songs before collapsing and having to be helped off of the stage. As he was lying in the backstage area, he heard security shouting.

"Afterward, we were told there was a fight in the audience after I left the stage. Someone pulled a knife and stabbed eight people. As the crowd started leaving the gig, there was a riot and someone threw a tear gas grenade," he says while sipping his coffee.

"I was given sporadic reports about this at the same time that I felt, 'I'm dying. I'm dying.' It was pretty intense."

The day after, Watain flew to São Paulo and Erik was brought straight to the hospital. He was put in a wheelchair and given an IV. The doctors performed various tests and his brain was X-rayed. Waiting for the test results, he worried.

"The first thing we did after the Hells Angels club was get tattooed. I was sure I'd been infected with something from the needle. HIV, hepatitis A, B, C, Z—whatever."

But the doctors couldn't find anything, and Erik was instead diagnosed with burnout syndrome. He left the hospital with strict orders to stay in bed for a week and to not lift a finger. He immediately felt better finally knowing what was wrong with him.

"It was really interesting to see how there's no space whatsoever between the mental and the physical."

Erik mentions another example. Touring the U.S., Johan Frölund developed a massive infection. Every night for several weeks, he'd been impaling rotten pig's heads on stage with an open wound on his finger. One day, he was unable to get out of bed and had to be taken to the hospital by ambulance. If he'd gotten there a few hours later, the doctors would have had to amputate. Erik says Johan was floored for several days afterward.

"The day after I was released from the hospital in São Paulo, I felt pretty good. Then Johan told me he'd gotten sick again; it was like being punched in the face. I could immediately feel it in my body. I almost collapsed."

After getting back from the tour, Erik has started working out in an effort to prepare his body for the efforts required from long tours. Above all, he needs to be in better physical condition for the mental transformation he surrenders to on the stage every night.

"I don't think it matters how easy I take it during the day. Regardless of how you choose to interpret what really happens to me on stage, mentally or physically, it's something extremely powerful. It's a radical change to who I usually am. I perceive it as positive, something beneficial to me that makes me feel good, but I suppose this was an indication that no matter how much I like being on stage, my body doesn't agree entirely. At least not for three months straight," he says with a grin.

The time since *Lawless Darkness* was released in the summer of 2010 has been one big triumphant procession for Watain. The trio were the first black metal band to win a Swedish Grammy in the best hard rock category. When the winners were revealed on the stage of the Stockholm Royal Opera, it felt completely natural to Erik.

In his acceptance speech, Erik compared recent natural disasters, like the floods in South America, drought in Australia, and mysterious mass bird deaths, with Watain receiving a Grammy. The audience laughed and whistled. When he went on to thank their brothers and sisters, alive and dead, and the band finished off with a "Hail Satan!" the audience didn't seem to quite know how to react, and many started giggling.

At the afterparty, Håkan and Pelle got so drunk on free booze that security asked them to leave the premises. Erik stayed behind, curiously mingling with the Swedish artist elite. Among others, he posed with Christian pop star Carola for a picture, in which she smiles with delight as he makes the devil horns.

In the case of Watain, there's no longer any talk of sellout. The band receiving a Grammy feels more like a natural step in their meteoric rise. Erik has been interviewed in both Swedish television and big tabloids and appears baffled over the media exposure they're getting.

"It's a strange situation being interviewed by a major newspaper—strange in the sense that I don't understand how they can open the gates for us, how little they've understood of what we represent."

Today, every Swedish hipster interested in pop culture knows about Watain. Erik says he's forced to work all the harder in preventing the attention from getting to him. Instead, he focuses on how to best utilize it in realizing his visions for Watain, like performing at an internationally renowned outdoor opera stage a few hours from Stockholm.

"I'd like to play in the huge quarry at Dalhalla, and that should be easier to accomplish if you've won a Grammy. And I'd like to do a music video with Jonas Åkerlund."

At the same time, it's a constant struggle, getting people to understand how Watain really take their lyrics and Satanism seriously. And this becomes increasingly difficult as more people get into the band.

"I desperately wish people would speak of Watain in terms of 'Ah, yes, those fucking bastards,' rather than 'Hell yeah, they're so cool—I have the latest T-shirt!' We have broken bones and fought for Watain, and we will wear our tattoos and vests to the grave. To us, this is life or death, and I want people to know that."

Watain released the albums The Wild Hunt in 2013 and Trident Wolf Eclipse in 2018.

Glossary of Metal Genres

Metal fans tend to have their own, often strong opinions on how to best describe the subgenres of heavy metal. Many bands tread the very thin line between different styles and thus become subjects of heated debate. The genres also develop over time and have to be continously redefined. Here is a basic description of the subgenres that we mention in this book.

Hard Rock
A general term used to describe the heavy, distortion-based musical style that emerged in the late '60s and early '70s, with roots in deep blues and jazz.
SEMINAL BANDS: Led Zeppelin, Deep Purple, Black Sabbath.

Heavy Metal
An earlier synonym for hard rock. Today, it is used to describe the style of music that, during the latter half of the '70s and early '80s, represented the darkest, toughest pole of the hard rock spectrum.
SEMINAL BANDS: Iron Maiden, Judas Priest, Accept.

Hardcore Punk
A faster and rawer style of punk rock. Developed in the mid to late '70s, it's often referred to as simply hardcore.
SEMINAL BANDS: Black Flag, Misfits, Dead Kennedys.

Oi!-Punk
A slower subgenre of punk rock. Also developed in the late '70s, it's often associated with hooliganism and soccer. The style is characterized by gang vocal choruses and a thick British accent.
SEMINAL BANDS: Sham 69, Screwdriver, The 4-Skins.

Thrash Metal
An aggressive mash-up of traditional heavy metal and the high tempo of hardcore punk. Debuting in the early '80s, it is characterized by lightning-fast "sawing" guitar riffs and shouting/screaming vocals.
SEMINAL BANDS: Metallica, Exodus, Slayer.

Speed Metal

Another high speed iteration of heavy metal, developed in the mid-'80s. This style is more melodic and less informed by punk rock than thrash metal.

SEMINAL BANDS: Agent Steel, Helloween, Annihilator.

Doom Metal

Extremely slow and heavy metal that developed in the beginning of the '80s. It expands on the heritage of Black Sabbath, mainly, with downtuned guitars and sludgy riffs.

SEMINAL BANDS: Candlemass, Saint Vitus, Trouble.

Crossover

A musical movement during the late '80s that combined the energy of thrash metal with the raw DIY aesthetics of hardcore punk.

SEMINAL BANDS: D.R.I., Corrosion of Conformity, Suicidal Tendencies.

Grindcore

Ultrafast metal with roots in both hardcore punk and death metal, which developed during the '80s.

SEMINAL BANDS: Napalm Death, Repulsion, Terrorizer.

Death Metal

Brutal subgenre that debuted in the transition between the '80s and '90s. Characterized by a high tempo, constant double kick-drum patterns, complicated song structures, downtuned guitars, and atonal, so-called growl vocals, its lyrics often feature dark themes such as splatter and death.

SEMINAL BANDS: Morbid Angel, Entombed, At the Gates.

Black Metal

An even more extreme form of metal, featuring satanism and death as main themes. Developed in the early '80s, it earned itself worldwide attention a decade later due to connections with church burnings and murder.

SEMINAL BANDS: Bathory, Venom, Mayhem.

Power Metal

Characterized by catchy melodies and strong, high-pitched vocals and complemented by energetic, precise 16th-note guitar-chugging. War and fantasy themes dominate the lyrics. This style experienced a rapid rise in popularity at the end of the '90s.

SEMINAL BANDS: HammerFall, Stratovarius, Sabaton.

Author Biographies

IKA JOHANNESSON has been one of Sweden's major music journalists for the last 20 years. She has worked mainly as a writer for different publications and as editor-in-chief of *Sex*, an interview magazine about alternative popular culture, but also within radio and television. She is currently the anchor of *Kulturnyheterna* (Culture News) on Sveriges Television. Ika is from Gothenburg but lives in Stockholm.

JON JEFFERSON KLINGBERG combines his writing with his music career. He plays the guitar for veteran Swedish band Docenterna and used to wield the axe in internationally known rock group Whale as well as several local death metal bands at the end of the '80s. His first novel was published in 2008. He has but one tattoo: the Manowar eagle on his lower arm. Jon is from the small town of Stugun in the rural province of Jämtland but lives in Stockholm.

Acknowledgments

Ika Johannesson wishes to thank:
My family: Johan, Franka, and Cora. Orvar "Rain Man" Säfström for the translation. Bengt Johannesson, Ann-Che Minneskjöld, Sanna Johannesson, Vejde Gustafsson, Åse Berglund, Roger Gustafsson, Annika Fagerlind, Ingela and Tobbe (for the food!), Christoffer Röstlund Jonsson, and Kajsa Boglind. Extra special thank-yous to Emil Arvidson for good advice and Nathan Larson for making the American version of the book shine—you are both incredible people.

Jon Jefferson Klingberg wishes to thank:
Karin Porshage, Charlotte Enström, Vejde Gustafsson, Sofia Hultman, Anders "Rune" Johansson, Essy, Jakob, and Margareta Klingberg, Erik Koskinen, Arvid Lind, Bo Anders Persson, Joar Tiberg, Po Tidholm, and Martin Widholm.

Without you, there would be no book:
Lord Ahriman, Jonas Almqvist, Nicke Andersson, Orvar Anklew, Alexandra Balogh, Robban Becirovic, Johan "Apocalyptic Desolator" Bergebäck, Andreas Bergh, Jan Axel "Hellhammer" Blomberg, Susanna Berglund, Jan Beskow, Linus Björklund, Anders Björler, Jonas Björler, Victor Brandt, Joacim Cans, Kim Carlsson, Martin Carlsson, Uffe Cederlund, Olle Dahlstedt, Erik Danielsson, Demonia, Mia Dracena, Oscar Dronjak, Leif Edling, Johan Edlund, Peter Ekberg, Daniel Ekeroth, Nico Elgstrand, Hampus Eriksson, Chrille Eskilsson, Kristian "Gaahl" Espedal, Börje "Boss" Forsberg, Pelle Forsberg, Anders Fridén, Johan Frölund, Gylve "Fenriz" Nagell, Christopher Friman, Runhild Gammelsaeter, Rex Gisslen, Jan Gradvall, Erik Grawsiö, Angela Gossow, Jonas Granvik, Erik "Tyrant" Gustavsson, Pelle "Hellbutcher" Gustafsson, Gädda 5, John Hagström, Johan Hallander, Staffan Hamrin, Hans Hatvig, Jacob Hector, Johnny Hedlund, Johan Hegg, Alex Hellid, Marcos Hellberg, Vanja Hermele, Hempo Hildén, Roger Holegård, Jörgen Holmstedt, Peter Huss, Morgan Håkansson, IT, Anders Iwers, Anders Jakobson, Conny Jarlestål, Mäbe Johansson, Nick Johansson, Christofer Johnsson, Håkan Jonson, Sabrina Kihlstrand, Hampus Klang, Sven Klang, Björn af Kleen, Eero Koivisto, Jon "Metalion" Kristiansen, Chelsea Krook, Niklas Kvarforth, Matti Kärki, Tompa Lindberg, Mattias Lindeblad, Janne Liljekvist, Alvaro Lillo, Marcus Linnér, Johannes "Axeman" Losbäck, Kongo "K. Lightning" Magnéli, Eddy Malm, Mara, Messiah Marcolin, Lars Martinsson, Frederick Melander, Olavi Mikkonen, Micke "Mimo" Moberg, Matthias Müller, Mörk, Vega Natas, Jon Necromancer, Tomas Nyqvist,

Jens Näsström, Emil Nödtveidt, Jon Nödtveidt, Anders Ohlin, Daniel Ohlin, Peter Palmdahl, Gunnar Palmgren, David Parland, L-G Petrov, Mattias "Indy" Pettersson, Sebastian "Vengeance From Beyond" Ramstedt, Calle von Schewen, Johan van der Schoot, Olle Sandqvist, Maria Staaf, Mikael Stanne, Peter "Insulter of Jesus Christ!" Stjärnvind, Henrik Stockare, Maria Ström, Pelle Ström, Jørn "Necrobutcher" Stubberud, Christer Stålbrandt, Niklas "Viper" Stålvind, Niclas Sundin, Dan Swanö, Sven på Netten, Emil Svensson, Jacob Swedberg, Set Teitan, Marcus Tena, Anders Tengner, John Miki Thor, Trish, Peter Tägtgren, Elin Unnes, Thomas Väänänen, Ragne Wahlquist, Styrbjörn Wahlquist, Erik Wallin, Jenny Walroth, Martin Wegeland, Olof Wikström, Ludwig Witt, Pierre Wilhelmsson, Patrik Wirén, Kristian Wåhlin, Emelie Zorsha, Jonas Åkerlund, and Ole Öhman.

Feral House
1240 W Sims Way #124
Port Townsend WA 98368
www.feralhouse.com

Blood Fire Death
The Swedish Metal Story

Original Swedish 2011 edition, Alfabeta Bokförlag
9789150113341
Copyright © Ika Johannesson and Jon Jefferson Klingberg

Copyright 2018
US ISBN: 9781627310673
© Ika Johannesson and Jon Jefferson Klingberg

Translated to English by Orvar Säfström

Page 2 photograph by Vejde Gustafsson

Designed by John Hubbard / emks.fi
following the original Swedish edition

10 9 8 7 6 5 4 3 2